1975

book may be kept

FOURTEEN DAYS

PRINTED IN U.S.A.

The Community:
Approaches and Applications

The Community: Approaches and Applications

Edited by MARCIA PELLY EFFRAT

THE FREE PRESS
A Division of Macmillan Publishing Co., Inc.
New York

Collier Macmillan Publishers
London

The Free Press
A Division of Macmillan Publishing Co., Inc.
866 Third Avenue, New York, New York 10022

Collier–Macmillan Canada Ltd.

Library of Congress Catalog Card Number: 73–16604

Printed in the United States of America

printing number
1 2 3 4 5 6 7 8 9 10

Contents

Contents

Approaches to Community: Conflicts and Complementarities*

MARCIA PELLY EFFRAT

York University, Toronto

Two main controversies—over territorial grounding and over the range of functions—have divided theoretical research on community into four main research traditions. Each of these is discussed in terms of its development, contributions, and inadequacies. Other controversies—over participatory democracy, over local autonomy, and over the role of physical design—are examined in relation to efforts to construct communities.

Trying to study community is like trying to scoop up jello with your fingers. You can get hold of some, but there's always more slipping away from you. When we talk about community research, we can—and often do—refer to material on community organizing, action, and planning as well as more traditional research on interaction patterns, institutions, norms, and roles within phenomena characterized as communities.

Not only is the range of subject matter broad but it is also divided into differing camps, whose debates with one another continue heatedly and underlie much of the research being done. But the jello analogy holds in this sense too, because in the process of debate the controversial issues have become mixed together in a gelatinous mess of hypotheses, research, and value judgments. It is difficult, then, to differentiate these issues, and to see what positive and negative implications do in fact derive from em-

*I especially want to thank Andrew Effrat for his valuable substantive and stylistic criticisms of earlier drafts of this paper as well as for his most substantial assistance in the editing of this collection. I also want to thank William Michelson, Barry Wellman, Gail Regan, Ray Pahl, Joe Feagin, and Chuck Tilly for their useful critical comments on earlier drafts.

phasis on one or another point of view. In this paper, however, I shall try to do just that.

I have divided this paper into three main parts. The first part deals with the two main theoretical issues of contention, and the four major research traditions based on different positions vis-à-vis these issues. Towards the end of this section, I suggest a way of pulling these positions together conceptually. The second section explains how the organization of the book is based on this way of integrating these different approaches. I also indicate how the perspectives of the authors in this book relate to the major controversies. The third section moves from a focus on theoretical research to a consideration of the literature on efforts to plan for and build community. The controversies in this literature are of a somewhat different sort (though no less heated), and I have attempted to present the main arguments on each side.

Conceptions of Community

The term "community" is frequently invoked in tones of profundity by ideologues (social scientists as well as "laypersons") from the far left to the far right. Like motherhood and apple pie, it is considered synonymous with virtue and desirability. Indeed, much of the problem in identifying the various definitions lies in separating the content of the conception from the value-laden imagery of warmth and camaraderie attached to it in many cases.

However, there do seem to be at least three main conceptions among North Americans and Britons which, though similar in some ways, can in fact be distinguished from one another. Briefly, these conceptions can be categorized as follows: (1) community as solidarity institutions, (2) community as "primary" interaction, and (3) community as institutionally distinct groups. Each of these conceptions has been used as the basis for more than one theoretical approach. Let me elaborate briefly on them.

(1) Community as Solidarity institutions. In this usage, community refers to those spheres or institutions of society whose function is to produce solidarity. Institutions in this sense comprise specific spheres of behavior characterized by particular norms and roles. Communal institutions would be those in which the legitimate forms of behavior tend to engender warm feelings of closeness and belonging. The family, ethnic groupings, voluntary organizations of various kinds, and residential groups are all examples of such institutions.

This conception involves a focus on the normative. In other words, scholars attempt to characterize the rules and roles common to all communal institutions, rather than—as in (3)—looking at the institutional and social structure of a grouping of people called a community. Communal institutions are seen as the potential integrators of today's society (see, e.g., Parsons 1966:10), whether the integration is based on affirmation of the status quo (see, e.g., Effrat 1970) or revolutionary activity. For example, Selma James (1972: 6-7) sees these institutions as the ones where women can gain revolutionary consciousness and where their actions can have revolutionary impact, because their roles in these institutions are given greater priority than are their roles in the economic or political structure.

(2) *Community as Primary Interaction.* In this conception, it is not the institutional context and the complex of processes associated with it that define community but rather the nature of the interaction among people, and the existence of close relationships among them. Thus, community here refers to interpersonal interaction characterized by informal, primary relationships. Both the relationships and their content are relevant objects of study. Bell and Newby (1971: 24), for instance, point out that while Toennies's original explanation of Gemeinschaft[1] "included the *local* community, [it] also went beyond it . . . it referred to social bonds . . . characterized by emotional cohesion, depth, continuity and fullness."

In a similar vein, Minar and Greer (1969: 331) suggest that

> Community is then an aspect of the way men relate to one another, the away beyond the coerced and the necessary, the "functional requisites." primary dimension of human interaction, that aspect which goes far and

Wellman (1968) looks at the nature of people's primary ties and their supportiveness as influencing the manner in which they cope with emotional stress.

(3) *Community as Institutionally Distinct Groups.* In this conception, a community is a group of people who share a range of institutions (economic, political, social) on the basis of their belonging to some familiar social category (e.g., as defined by ethnicity, occupation, life style, or residential location). Thus the focus here is partly on institutions, but not simply communal institutions. Rather, community refers to *a segment of the population* who tend to interact with one another in overlapping friendship networks, to share similar interests and outlook, and to participate in common institutions. For example, we hear reference made to the "freak community," the "Jet Set," the "community of scholars," the "Chinese community." This use of the term "community" is particularly common in the study of racial and ethnic relations and of social deviance, and implies research on the social organization, "consciousness of kind," etc., of such groupings of persons. For example, Kramer and Leventman (1961) have examined the Jews of a midwestern city in terms of their values, styles of life, voluntary organizations and interaction patterns.

One frequently used basis for membership in such a group is residential location. People who live in the same neighborhood, area, or city are considered to be part of the same community. The relevant territorial area is itself often referred to as "the community." This use of the word community causes considerable confusion, but it is also perhaps the one usually intended in the term "community studies." This conception (and the resultant confusion) has emerged largely from urban and rural sociology and social anthropology. Thus, for example, of the ninety-four definitions from the literature of these fields examined by Hillery (1955), seventy-three included area as one of the major defining characteristics of a community.

These, then, are the three main ways of conceptualizing community. All of the definitions share an emphasis on the informality and solidarity engendered by relationships and/or social organization. This is in agreement with Hillery's finding (1955: 118) that, after area, the two most commonly included components in definitions of community were common ties and social interaction.

Focusing on these three conceptions, however, does represent a somewhat North American and sociological bias. Some British social anthropologists, for example, have conceived of community in terms of concern with processes of social exchange, social control and reciprocity.

The Foci of Theoretical Debate and Major Research Traditions

Two issues emerge which, more than any others, have consumed a great deal of the intellectual energy expended in theoretical debate over the problem. These issues are (1) whether community involves many different functions, or only a few; and (2) whether community must be grounded in a particular, delimited place, or whether it can exist among people who are territorially dispersed.

At first sight, these issues might not seem a sufficient basis for serious, ongoing debate. Each, however, has important and different implications about when and whether people can be considered alienated or isolated from personalized support, what kinds of behavior people can expect from fellow community members, the relation between shared facilities and interaction, etc. Below I shall get into these and other implications more deeply.

The two focal issues in the study of community yield a fourfold division of approaches to community based on the possibility of two positions with respect to each issue. These four major research traditions are represented in Table 1. The methodologies and theories falling within any one box of the table may differ, but those within a box do tend to work in the same general direction, to support the same main points, and to find similar empirical phenomena worth investigating. Let us, then, examine each of these research traditions in terms of its assumptions, historical development, contributions, and inadequacies.

Table 1 Community: The Four Major Research Traditions

| | Number of Functions Provided by the Community | |
	Many	Few
	I. The Compleat Territorial Community a. Holistic examination of villages, small towns, even ˙ cities b. Research on municipal power structures	II. The Community of Limited Liability a. Studies of small-scale neighborhood and the process of neighboring b. Holistic studies of larger-scale urban subareas c. Social area analysis
Necessary		
Territorial Grounding		
Not Necessary	III. Community as Society a. Research on minority groups (ethnic, deviant, sexual) b. Research on common-interest groups (occupational, professional, life style)	IV. Personal Community a. Research on communal institutions b. Studies of voluntary organization membership and participation c. Social network analysis

A word of caution, however, at the outset: none of these positions is the "right" one. The differences among them are differences in the basic definition of the problem for research. Thus, some of the controversies among them are empirically unresolvable. On the other hand, some of the conflicts concerning research problems generated by these approaches can be investigated empirically. A good example is the question, "Do communities decline in importance with urbanization?"

(I) The Compleat Territorial Community

The main assumption of most of the research of this type is that small towns, villages, etc., constitute communities that can be considered "mini" social systems. In these places, everyone knows everyone else at least by sight, and social relations are informal. In other words, it is assumed that the residents comprise a community that is a relatively self-contained social environment supplying its members with a wide range of services.

A number of theoretical approaches to be discussed below—the community as microcosm, human ecology, the rural-urban continuum, "mass society" theory, community power analysis, and the "communal organizations" perspective—are comprehended within this research tradition. All such studies have proceeded more or less on this assumption that "true" communities are relatively autonomous social systems.

(a) Community as microcosm. This approach originally grew out of field work in social anthropology. Anthropologists would spend a year or so in a preindustrial village gathering information on all aspects of life. In this type of research, the tribe, the village, and the society were usually considered coterminous with one another, with solidary relationships existing among all members. The whole complex was classified as a tribal community.

In the late 1920s, researchers in the United States began applying these techniques to towns, villages, and small cities in their industrialized society. One of the earliest and best examples of this kind of research was the Lynds' (1929) study of Muncie Indiana. In Britain the first research of this kind was undertaken by Americans in rural Ireland in 1932. The project was begun by W. Lloyd Warner, and completed by Arensberg and Kimball (Arensberg, 1939; Arensberg and Kimball, 1940). Also under the general direction of Warner, other "landmark" American studies were undertaken of Newburyport, Mass. (Warner and Lunt, 1941, 1942), Natchez, Miss. (Davis, Gardner, and Gardner, 1944), and other, smaller towns. After Arensberg and Kimball's study, there was no major study of a British community until just before, and then after, World War II, when research was conducted in Wales (Rees, 1950).

Research of this kind is still being done, although more frequently by British than by American sociologists.[2] Such research, like the studies of "primitive" communities, tends to be holistic, examining social, political, and economic organization. Often, there is the claim (whether or not it is explicit) that the community under study represents a microcosm of the total society or some important segment of the society.

A good example of this kind of research is Frankenberg's study in the mid-1950s of Llansaintffraid Glynceiriog on the border of Wales. According to Frankenberg (1966: 86), the village

> looks compact and isolated, a self-contained community in the elbow of a steep-sided valley. There are hills of slate refuse giving the impression that it is a quarrying village. Two disused and partly ruined mills show that once quarrying was not its only industry.

A variety of factors contribute to the segregation of the roles of the sexes in the village, so that Frankenberg was led (1966: 92)

> to suggest, with some exaggeration, but much truth, that [here quoting Frankenberg 1957] "except for a brief period of courtship and early marriage, there seem to be two villages, one of men and one of women which rarely mingle." . . . Although the sexes do not mingle in public, they do meet, and the occasions of their meetings give rise to conflict

which adds to the interest, and paradoxically to the unity, of village life. Women in fact form a corporate group in Glynceiriog which determines the pattern of much of social life. Unlike the men, they share common work problems and spend nearly all their time actually in the village. They meet each other in the shops and constantly visit each other informally for cups of tea. They discuss village affairs while sewing and preparing equipment for social functions. When in the few mixed committees, there is a conflict of interest, the committee often splits into groups of the two sexes.

Frankenberg deals with a conflict which arose between men's and women's groups over the disposal of funds of a carnival committee. The decisions involved split the committee and, temporarily, the village, and illustrate the way sex-role separation influenced the social organization of much of village life. Resolution of the conflict by means of blaming outsiders suggests one of the means by which villagers maintain unity.

(b) Human Ecology and the "Natural Community." Human ecology was developed in the 1920s and 30s by sociologists at the University of Chicago. They argued that plant and animal ecology could provide a model for the study of human social and territorial organization. Just as biological phenomena coexist in a habitat by finding a suitable ecological niche, so, they argued, do different social and ethnic groups coexist in a city by sorting themselves into different "natural communities" located in particular districts. They applied this argument to the city of Chicago, where they located various areas inhabited by different types of people and proceeded to study these "natural communities."

In line with their theoretical framework, they said that they were trying to examine how these groups of people fit into their territorial areas. In other words, they wanted to look at the "fit" between the social and the physical, similar to the way, for example, in which cacti "fit" desert conditions. However, although they did describe the physical appearance of the areas defined as natural communities, they did not really relate physical to social organization (cf. Michelson 1970, ch. 1). What they did was use aggregate social characteristics (such as the crime rate or mental illness rate) and characteristics of social organization (such as the life styles and behavior patterns of residents) as descriptive of specific parts of the city.

Zorbaugh's study, The Gold Coast and the Slum (1929), and Wirth's (1929) study of the Jewish ghetto are examples of this kind of work. For example, Zorbaugh (1929: 46–47, 62, 63) notes that

in Chicago all that is aloof and exclusive, all that bears the mark of l'haute société, is crowded along the strip of "drive" between the Drake Hotel and Lincoln Park, or along the quiet, aristocratic streets immediately behind it. Here is the greatest concentration of wealth in Chicago. Here live a large number of those who have achieved distinction in industry, science and the arts. Here are Chicago's most fashionable hotels and clubs. Here live two thousand of the six thousand persons whose names are in the social register of Chicago and its suburbs, and these two thousand include in their number those who are recognized as leaders of "society."

There is a concentration of real leadership on the Gold Coast. Not only is there a concentration of wealth, but there is a concentration of contributors to civic and social organizations. . . . There is a concentration of specialized ability and achievement. . . . And a study of the boards of directors and trustees of civic and social organizations of the city revealed the fact that there is, as well, along the Gold Coast, a concentration of active leadership.

. . . the exigencies of the social game demand that "society" live in certain neighborhoods, attend certain finishing schools or universities, belong to certain clubs, patronize certain of the arts, serve on the boards of trustees of certain social and civic organizations, hold certain political prejudices, and, above all, conform to a common ritual.

(c) Community and the Rural-Urban Continuum.   The rural-urban (or folk-urban) continuum is essentially a more modern version of Toennies's Gemeinschaft-Gesellschaft dichotomy. Redfield introduced this continuum with his work on the Yucatan Peninsula in Mexico, begun in the late 1920s. With the publication of his book *The Folk Culture of Yucatan* in 1941, Redfield's typology gained popularity through the late 1940s and early 50s. In his book, he examined four different sized communities and argued that each represented a different stage in the process of urbanization. The particular stage of urbanization in a community was reflected by the orientations of its inhabitants, its social and economic structure, and its relative autonomy. In other words, he characterized the communities as representative of different points on a "folk-urban" continuum, in which "folk" and "urban" society were "ideal types."

Yucatan, considered as one moves from Merida southeastward into the forest hinterland, presents a sort of social gradient in which the Spanish, modern, and urban gives way to the Maya, archaic, and primitive. This volume results from a study of four communities chosen to represent points, not too unevenly distributed, along this gradient. These four are: Merida, the only large city; Dzitas, a town situated on the railroad; Chan Kom, a peasant village; and Tusik, a tribal village of semi-independent Maya in Quintana Roo. . . . Dzitas, Chan Kom and Tusik are in that order increasingly distant from Merida, where social change, for Yucatan, originates and from which social and political influence emanates.

In the tribal village maize is not a money crop, and its value does not respond to prices established in outside markets; in the peasant village the reverse is true. Yet it is notable that in the latter community maize has both a religious and a commercial aspect: The role of wealth in determining status increases as one goes from the remote village toward the city. Compared in the same order, the four communities show increasing degrees [sic] of individual freedom with reference to the control of wealth and the undertaking of commercial ventures. It is in the villages that family estates are to the greatest degree preserved. Individual ownership of land, while known everywhere, becomes usual as one approaches the city. Associated with these progressive differences in commercialization are progressive differences among the communities with respect to the division of labor: (1) it becomes more complex; (2) as between the sexes it becomes somewhat less rigidly defined; (3) collective effort becomes rarer and individual effort commoner; and (4) the discharge of special function, from being predominantly sacred, becomes secular.

The general conclusion is that the same relative order, corresponding to their spatial order, serves to range the four communities as to the progressively increasing or decreasing extent to which several general social or cultural characters are present. The less isolated and more heterogeneous societies are the more secular and individualistic and are the more characterized by disorganization of culture. [Redfield 1941: 13–14, xvii–xviii, xx]

The use of ideal types as a theoretical technique for dealing with concrete empirical phenomena is always tricky. The ideal types and the actuality tend to become confused and identified with one another not only by readers but even by the scholars doing the research. The phenomena investigated then tend to be seen as fixed, unchanging entities, forever possessed only of the characteristics assigned to them in the typology.

This was the case with Redfield's work, and became the basis for subsequent criticism. According to Bell and Newby (1971: 44), "This typology ... focuses attention on the city as a source of social change and obscures the wide range of values and ways of life of individuals at the folk end of the continuum (and, for that matter, the urban end). . . . Redfield, indeed, so framed his basic questions that folk societies would necessarily appear more organized than cities. His typology overlooks the stability and success of city life. . . ."

Reexamination of some of the same rural villages by Lewis (1951) and Avila (1969) has indicated diverse ways of life and active responses to new conditions rather than the homogeneous traditionalism and resistance to change postulated by Redfield of folk society. Lewis points out that Redfield's bias toward folk communities as a desirable way of life leads him to omit various phenomena from consideration.

The impression given by Redfield's study of Tepoztlàn is that of a relatively homogeneous, isolated, smoothly functioning, and well-integrated society made up of a contented and well-adjusted people. His picture of the village has a Rousseauan quality which glosses lightly over evidence of violence, disruption, cruelty, disease, suffering, and maladjustment. We are told little of poverty, economic problems, or political schisms. Throughout his study we find an emphasis upon the cooperative and unifying factors in Tepoztlàn society. Our findings, on the other hand, would emphasize the underlying individualism of Tepoztlàn institutions and character, the lack of cooperation, the tensions between villages within the municipio, the schisms within the village, and the pervading quality of fear, envy and distrust in interpersonal relations. [Lewis 1951: 428–49]

These criticisms, and those of others, have led to considerable reworking of Redfield's underlying theory that urbanization destroys the folk community. Frankenberg's more recent, and more sophisticated, analysis (Frankenberg 1966) looks at differences in roles, role sets, and attachment to roles, economy and division of labor, and patterns of integration and conflict, but he points out that urban areas still contain many "rural" components, while many rural forms, such as the neighborhood, persist in cities. He explains (1966: 286), "For convenience, I call my models 'rural' and 'urban,' aware that this begs many questions about the nature of towns and cities. "Urban' might more accurately be called 'less rural.'" Despite this awareness of the rural aspects of urban life, however, there is much less consideration in Frankenberg's framework of the urban aspects of rural life.

(d) "Mass Society" and the Decline of Community. "Mass society" theory, popular in the mid-1950s and early 1960s, deals with the same problem; i.e., what is the nature of a "community" in urban-industrial society. Although the perspective and approach of mass society theorists were different from Redfield's, their main hypothesis was identical: that advanced urbanization leads to the "eclipse of community" (cf. Stein 1960). According to Kornhauser (1968: 58–59):

> "Mass society" is best understood as a term denoting a model of certain kinds of relationships that may come to dominate a society or part of a society. . . . a "mass society" is one in which many or most of the major institutions are organized to deal with people in the aggregate and in which similarities between the attitudes and behavior of individuals tend to be viewed as more important than differences. . . . Large-scale activities favor the emergence of the mass because they tend to develop at the expense of communal relations. The local community comes to provide for fewer of its members' needs and therefore cannot maintain their allegiance. The rural community no longer is isolated and self-sufficient. As it becomes dependent on the city, and particularly on national markets and organizations, the rural community loses its significance and cohesion. The city does not develop the communal life that was formerly provided by the rural community. The individual who migrates to the city does not enter the community as a whole, nor is he likely to enter a subcommunity of the city. The urban subcommunity

loses its coherence as a result of the increasing scale and specialization of common activities. Instead of affiliation with a community, the urban resident frequently experiences considerable social isolation and personal anonymity.

Vidich and Bensman (1958) studied a small town in upstate New York, They argued that the townspeople's self-image as an autonomous and solidary community masked the fact of their social, political, economic, and cultural control by the mass society through centralized control of national organizations and the importance of decisions made by state government. The work of mass society theorists seems to amount to an inflation of the value of past, and a deflation of present, forms of social organization. However, as Suttles (1972: 9) points out, it is very questionable whether a "golden age when the local community was supreme" ever even existed. Mass society theorists fall into essentially the complementary error from that of rural-urban continuum theorists: they overemphasize the extent to which contemporary American society is like the ideal type of "mass society" with alienation, segmentation, separateness of roles, and homogeneity, and underemphasize its continued pluralism and the persistence and importance of "folk" or "rural" phenomena, such as solidary groupings of people who share similar values and styles of behavior.

(e) *Community Power.* Floyd Hunter's research on Atlanta, Georgia (Hunter 1953) essentially initiated the explicit study of community power structures.[3]

The primary interest here is in discussing the nature of the exercise of power in a selected community and as this community relates to the larger society. . . . I shall be using the concept of community as a frame of reference for an analysis of power relations. This is done because of a strong conviction that the community is a primary power center and because it is a place in which power relations can be most easily observed.

Because of all [the] physical activity involved in moving goods and services in the complex system designated as Regional City, it is obvious that a social order, or system, must be maintained there. Broadly speaking, the maintenance of this order falls to the lot of almost every man in the community, but the *establishment of changes* in the old order falls to the lot of relatively few.

As I became familiar with the list of forty names through the interviewing process, it became evident that certain men, even within the relatively narrow range of decision leaders with whom I was dealing, represented a top layer of personnel. Certain men were chosen more frequently than others, not only in relation to who should be chosen to decide on a project, . . . but the same men interacted together on committees and were on the whole better known to each other than to those

outside this group. Through analyzing the mutual choices made by
those interviewed, it will be shown that there is an *esprit de corps* among
certain top leaders, and some of them may be said to operate on a very
high level of decision in the community; but this will not necessarily
mean that any one of the top leaders can be considered subordinate to
any other in the community as a whole. On specific projects one leader
may allow another to carry the ball, as a leader is said to do when he is
"out front" on a project which interests him. On the next community-
wide project another may carry the ball. Each may subordinate himself
to another on a temporary basis, but such a structure of subordination
is quite fluid, and it is voluntary. [Hunter 1953: 11, 67]

Hunter's research focused specifically on key decision makers and their
interaction. Since the time of his research, the study of community power
has become an important substantive field of social research, and an arena
for debating the nature of political decision making. Scholars have concerned themselves with the formal and informal political structure, the
relations among various institutions and groups, and the political outcomes
of various structures and conflicts. Research has been conducted to support
the existence of a single core elite, differentiated or specalized elites, conflicting interest groups, and dispersed democracy in various cities and
small towns characterized as communities. These conclusions have been
related to different types of research methodology as well as to differences
in the social characteristics of the places studied (cf., e.g., Hawley and
Wirt, 1968). Walton's paper in this book provides an excellent overview
of the contributions and inadequacies of this branch of research.

(f) *Community as Social System.* The "communal organizations" approach (cf. Hillery 1969) is the most recent perspective to deal with
communities as whole entities. Scholars using it proceed from the assumption of communities as systems and concentrate on explicitly elaborating
that assumption as the major focus of their orientation. They tend to use
the systems approach of "general systems theory" (cf. von Bertalanffy 1962)
in a fairly sophisticated way, in that they look at communities as "open
systems." This means that information and influences of various kinds
flow both into and out of the community. Thus, while the focus is on the
interrelationship and interaction of local institutions that make up the
"local social system" (cf. Stacey 1969), there is also consideration of what
Warren (1963) calls horizontal and vertical linkages. Horizontal ties are
those with other similar communities, or linkages among similar organizations. Vertical ties are influences coming from more inclusive bodies, such
as federal or provincial/state governments, or those going out to units
"below" the community, such as suburbs or satellite cities.

The study of community within this overall tradition—of seeing communities as autonomous and complete territorial units—has increased our
knowledge in a number of different ways. We have gained some under-

standing of the way that social stratification, political decision making, and cultural organization operate at the local level, and of the nature of the interaction of local institutions. We have available richly textured accounts of the life styles and behavior patterns of various groups of people in different sizes and types of communities. We have some sense of the relationship between societal context ("primitive," urban-industrial) and the nature, or existence, of certain types of community.

Indeed, on the basis of this information, we can make fairly specific hypotheses about the kind of social organization that is likely to exist in a city, town, or village of a given size and economic structure within a particular societal context. In being directed toward proving that community can exist only as a territorially grounded, institutionally complete phenomenon, the research done by social scientists within this framework has indicated the nature of some important changes in society and illuminated some strong forces that serve to tie people together and perpetuate certain traditions.

However, underlying almost all of these approaches as suggested earlier, is the hidden or not-so-hidden value position not only that this is the only real or true kind of community but also that "folk," "rural," locally autonomous villages enable people to live in a more desirable way than in "urbanized" towns or cities. This bias, as was pointed out with regard to Redfield, may focus attention on some variables to the exclusion of others.

In addition, all of these approaches suffer from three major methodological problems. The first is the general problem of field research—that the findings are strongly affected by the person(s) doing the research. The second is the question of the representativeness of the community. The third problem relates to the implicit decisions made concerning which issues are considered empirical questions open to investigation and which factors are taken as given.

(1) Field Research and Investigator Bias. In field research, much of the material gathered is impressionistic, difficult to quantify, and subject to filtering by the researcher's own predilections before the perceived data are recorded; different researchers also organize their material differently, focus on different issues, etc. Moreover, each researcher's personality, sex, ethnicity, social class, etc., give that person more access to some segments of the population than to others, and make some pieces of information or some interpretations seem more believable to him or her than others. Naturally, this affects the replicability of studies. Other researches may study the same places and obtain quite different results. Such, for example, was the case with Lewis's and Avila's researches on the village studied earlier by Redfield, and Gallaher's (1961) study of "Plainville", first studied by West (1945). With the exception of the Lynds' two studies, ten years apart, of Muncie, community studies have suffered from an absence of the longitudinal or historical perspective afforded by successive research done

by the same authors. When the same community is studied by more than one researcher, there is an additional problem involving the mere fact of the community's having been studied previously and people's reactions to a second researcher (cf. Gallaher 1964).

(2) *Representativeness of the Community.* A second key methodological problem shared by all of these approaches is the question of how representative the community is of anything else (the society as a whole, communities of a particular kind, etc.). Warner and his associates are perhaps the most obviously guilty of the fallacy of generalizing from the part to the whole. They took for granted, without further investigation, that the criteria they used for the selection of towns as "microcosms" of American society were indeed characteristic of most American towns and cities. Moreover, once having made the assumption that such towns would be characterized by stability, order, and social integration, they proceeded to look for—and, in many cases, find—just those qualities. Subsequent critics have pointed out the existence of many elements of conflict and change in American society that were ignored by Warner et al. (cf. Bell and Newby 1971: 101–111).

Other researchers have been more cautious in their claims of representativeness, but often their research is misused that way by others anyway. Moreover, by their very selection of a particular town for intensive research scholars are at least making implicit assumption that generalizations can be made that will hold for similar social milieux elsewhere.

(3) *Predefinition of the Community.* The third problem of "compleat territorial community" studies is that all theory and research involves taking some things as given and assuming other things as problematic and worthy of study. In selecting an area for a "community study," there is an often unacknowledged pressure on scholars to find at least some factors which will indicate that the persons living in that area do indeed constitute a community. In other words, the community investigated is often such by predefinition rather than by empirical research. By not leaving "communityness" itself completely open to investigation, researchers make it difficult to ever completely characterize the fundamental components of a community, and hence to clearly tell a community from a noncommunity, other than on the basis of size.

I have devoted a considerable amount of space to discussion of this type of community research, largely in order to compensate for the absence of any article in this collection dealing directly with this material. Community studies such as these have provided the background from which, and in reaction to which, current research has developed. It is therefore valuable to have some sense of this literature before examining other approaches more popular in contemporary North America. These more recent approaches, in particular the next one, have arisen as attempts to refute the theories about the decline of community presented above.

(II) The Community of Limited Liability

In 1952 Morris Janowitz introduced the concept of the "community of limited liability" (Janowitz 1952). According to Suttles (1972: 48),

> Janowitz's work came at a critical juncture in the controversy over whether or not the urban neighbourhood still existed in modern urban society. As his work showed, the urban neighborhood was becoming a more specialized, a more voluntaristic, and a more partial institution.

This orientation was the major response from the mid 1950s through the 1960s to the hypotheses of the first tradition. Although scholars of both approaches would agree that urban residential areas have fewer functions, they would differ in their interpretation of this change and in the places they select for research. Scholars of the first tradition have most often studied villages or small towns, and then made predictions or generalizations about the implications of trends there for cities. Scholars in this second tradition have focused on the cities themselves, looking at particular urban residential subareas within them.

Studies of the "limited liability" kind are generally middle-range and structural-functionalist. In other words, researchers examine structures of communal solidarity and/or local institutions and suggest their functions for the people of a particular area. They may try to determine which kinds of people are served by various community structures. Such studies have resulted in three main types of findings: (a) identification of variables influencing people's use of local facilities, (b) exposition of the content of the "urban neighbor" role, and (c) description of the nature of social organization in "neighborhood" and "district" communities.

According to various studies, stage in the life cycle, value orientations and life style, and ethnicity and social class seem to be important characteristics affecting individuals' participation in neighborhoods and districts (cf., e.g., Mann 1965; Suttles 1972; Merton 1957; Gans 1962a; Michelson 1970). Similarly, the number and diversity of facilities and the aggregate characteristics of the local population seem to be important contextual factors (cf., e.g., Lee 1968; Bell and Boat 1957; Bell and Force 1956; Greer 1956). Indeed, examination of local aggregate statistics (social area analysis, factorial ecology) has become a popular subfield among mathematically minded sociologists and urban geographers as a way of locating and differentiating urban residential areas.

This type of research often faces squarely the problem of how to delimit the area that can properly be considered a neighborhood or district (and hence an object of study). Local facilities, such as elementary schools, parks, and shopping plazas, often draw their users from areas with boundaries different from one another. Residents frequently consider a one-to-three–block area as their neighborhood, but this may vary considerably (cf. Keller 1968: 97–102). Some neighborhoods are clearly defined by name and local tradition, while others may be vaguely and loosely defined in various ways by residents. Thus, one aspect of research has been the characterization of different levels of urban spatial areas. Most commonly, this has been a hierarchy consisting of neighborhood "street" community, district community (usually, though not always, a political unit such as a ward), and the municipality as a whole (cf., e.g., Jacobs 1961; Greer 1960; Suttles 1972). Much of this research on all these aspects of residential differentiation is reviewed and critically evaluated in Popenoe's paper in this collection.

Studies of neighbors and neighboring have suggested that it is usually considered permissible to call on neighbors for minor assistance (e.g., use of the telephone, borrowing of a tool) or in major emergencies, but that people and areas vary in the extent to which neighboring is broadened to include other forms of interaction (cf., e.g., Keller 1968; Pfeil 1968). Neighboring patterns have often been studied in conjunction with types of local activity, social involvement, and social organization as part of ethnographic studies similar in field work and methodology though different in theoretical assumptions from those described in the previous section. This research has tended to concentrate on suburbs and working-class inner-city residential areas in or near major cities such as Boston (e.g., Gans 1962a), London (e.g., Young and Willmott 1957), Chicago (e.g., Whyte 1955; Suttles 1968), New York (Gans 1967), and Toronto (e.g., Seeley et al. 1956; Clark 1966).

A good example of this kind of research is Lorimer's (1971) study of a "street" neighborhood in a downtown working-class district of Toronto. In his discussion of neighboring, he comments (Lorimer and Phillips 1971: 46–47):

> Often families number among their close friends one or two families living in the neighbourhood, but in general relations amongst neighbours are of a special, rather limited type. Most people who have lived in one neighbourhood for a year or two get to know by sight the other people on their street, and the longer they live in the same place the more people they become acquainted with in this way. Outside circumstances bring neighbours together on occasion; you may have to ask the man across the street to move his car, or the two of you may go outside simultaneously to check on some extra-rowdy kids. Usually it is not before circumstances require it that neighbours begin talking to each other, and when they do their conversations happen when they casually meet each other in the street. We were on speaking terms in this way with all but one of the long-time residents of Minster Lane after we had been on the street for about a year; but it was not until three years later, after I had done some canvassing for a civic election, that I came to be on speaking terms with a number of people whom I had known by sight for some time on the next street, St. John.

Most people in a neighbourhood are on closer terms than this with two or three families, often those with children who play together or those who are about the same age. Closer terms means longer and friendlier conversations on the street and occasional exchanges of small services such as taking in a parcel or keeping a key for the telephone man coming to do repairs. Even in these circumstances, however, neighbours often refer to each other by surnames rather than first names. They are likely not to exchange many visits, mostly because once someone becomes a regular visitor he (or she, as is usually the case) is moving from the rather special category of neighbour into the circle of a family's close friends. Partly because of the long-term commitment this kind of relationship usually means, partly because the styles of social life does not involve a large or constantly expanding circle of reasonably good friends, everyone is usually quite happy to stay on neighbourly terms with most neighbours. Pressure is not generally felt to convert every accessible neighbour, or every one of roughly the same age and family circumstances, into a family friend.

Using this approach, scholars have shed light on a variety of phenomena given much less attention by those working within the first tradition. For instance, they have concentrated more on the relationship between the physical and the social (e.g., what does one physical area provide that is different from another?). Scholars have indicated how individuals perceive and use physical features to define social boundaries (cf., e.g., Gutman 1966; Suttles 1968). Workers in this tradition have also identified and described forms of community and social organization within cities rather than characterizing them as "disorganized" or organized at a "mass" level.

However, causal explanations within this perspective have tended to suffer from two main problems: environmental determinism and "individualization." Environmental determinism involves attributing sole importance to physical, spatial variables (e.g., the density of housing in an area, the degree of maintenance of housing, the layout and busyness of streets) in accounting for social behavior (e.g., the amount of crime, juvenile delinquency, or drug use, the quality and frequency of neighborhood contact, etc.). Researches as diverse as Shaw and McKay's (1942) investigation of delinquency rates in Chicago from 1900 to 1940 and Jane Jacobs's (1961) consideration of urban vitality have been guilty of such explanations. Literature emerging both from social workers' concern with "social problems" and from urban planning/urban geography specialists has encouraged the perpetuation of this oversimplified explanation.

Similarly, the "social problems" approach has influenced a large number of explanations which account for social behavior patterns in terms of the individuals exhibiting that behavior. This type of explanation neglects aspects of the social structure which foster and make rational the development of behavior considered "deviant" or "problematic." Feagin's paper in this book concentrates on a critical evaluation of research on community disorganization which has largely emerged from the social problems perspective. He indicates the inadequacy of such individualized explanation and points out several other problems with traditional community disorganization research.

The struggle between this approach and the previous one has been a fairly active one. Scholars arguing for the existence of "limited liability" communities have claimed that their colleagues were biased against urban society and so were unable to perceive the development of alternative forms of social organization and community. On the other hand, the full-scale community studies people have suggested that the limited liability community is only an anachronism, a remnant of a once strong and full community now in the process of disintegration. Certainly, however, the evidence brought forth by the former has more than adequately refuted the notion of urban residents' complete isolation and disorganization.

Both of these traditions, however, have emphasized that community is a territorially bounded phenomenon in which the sharing of area and local facilities has some importance. The next approach, especially as framed by the social network analysts, arose in direct reaction to, and criticism of, both these approaches to community.

(III) Personal Community

Research on nonspatial community of limited function has been conducted under a variety of different titles and theoretical schemas. The examination of the common characteristics of institutions which "legitimately" (according to society's norms) provide solidarity has been somewhat limited to fairly abstract considerations of the nature of community and of common solidarity institutions (cf., e.g., Nisbet 1966; Mayhew 1971).

More concrete research has focused on two main phenomena: (a) informal participation in voluntary organizations and interaction with friends, and (b) social networks. Although these two kinds of research have developed from quite different origins and constitute two quite separate subfields, they both deal with what are essentially complementary aspects of individuals' solidary ties or "personal community" (Henry 1958). Here, the locus and existence of community are no longer predefined. Rather, community becomes something whose existence is open to investigation, and whose degree may be characterized as more or less strong. Also, community is assumed to be influenced by the choices of individuals rather than predetermined for them by their home's location; hence the relevance of the term *personal* community.

(a) Social Participation and Community. The social participation literature is perhaps best known for its emphasis on correlating rates of participation in voluntary organizations and interaction with friends and

kin with various social characteristics, such as social class, sex, and age, of large samples of people. More recently, researchers have examined how people select, or get recruited to, various organizations, differences in intensity and meaningfulness of involvement, and the consequences of involvement for various kinds of social support (cf., e.g., Phillips 1969).

This literature emerged largely from a theoretical concern with alienation from, and integration into, society. It is not usually considered part of the "community" literature. In fact, one way of interpreting the Gemeinschaft-Gesellschaft dichotomy has been as a distinction between "community" and "association," where association refers to rationally determined interaction in which people deal with one another in terms of a single, narrow role (e.g., shopper-clerk). However, there has been some confusion because voluntary organizations, sometimes called associations, have been characterized by scholars of the "mass society" approach as providing "*pseudo*-Gemeinschaft" (cf., e.g., Reisman 1950). However, what kind of solidarity is, in fact, provided by membership is only beginning to be researched as scholars move away from their preoccupation with "rates" of participation. What this literature needs is more of a focus on the individual and on different styles of participation and structuring of "community," as is the case in social network theory. Tomeh's paper in this collection provides a solid overview of the existing literature in this area. However, like most others in that field, she treats community as a territorial phenomenon. Community is, for her, an external concrete entity which can be related to, or affected by, participation rates. She does not deal with it as something which is in fact created by, and consists of, that very participation.

(b) *Social Network Theory and Community.* Most scholars in the social network literature, on the other hand, have treated community in precisely the manner just indicated. They have clearly focused on the nature of alternative, nonspatial forms of community, using a methodology developed largely from social anthropology, where it has been used to investigate cliques and communication structures. Social network theorists attempt to explain how urbanites select, organize, and maintain their own unique set of friends out of the number of social contacts potentially available to them. They also try to account for different patterns of social network structure and different uses of network members by various categories of people or by people in different societies. Craven and Wellman's paper in this collection provides a much needed examination of much of the burgeoning research in this area.

They point out that, contrary to many theorists of the first tradition, most urban individuals are far from isolated from one another. The great majority are enmeshed in networks of a least a few close friends and several acquaintances.

However, in addition to the struggle with their territorially grounded colleagues, scholars of this approach have also had to defend themselves against criticism that research within the network approach does not account adequately for the existence of institutions that cater specifically to members of a given network and yet have an existence separate from the members of the network. As Craven and Wellman point out, social network researchers have looked at the networks among various institutions, but not at the above-mentioned problem. The ways in which both social institutions and social relationships interrelate to form a community is one concern of the fourth tradition that we shall discuss.

(IV) Community as Society

With the exception of their disagreement about the necessity for a territorial locus, scholars of this approach have much in common with those of the first ("compleat community") approach. Thus, they would probably agree with Frankenberg's statement (1966: 238) that "all communities are societies but not all societies are communities." Within the tradition of community as society, "community" refers to segments of the population who are differentiated from others because of their common participation in specific institutions and their interaction with one another in friendship and kinship relationships. Calling a group a community in this sense also usually implies the group's consciousness of kind, a shared subculture or set of values, and internally shared norms based upon them.

This is essentially a Weberian perspective on community. Neuwirth (1969) points to a little-known piece by Max Weber in which he expounds his theory of community. Weber suggests that community formation and communal relationships result from competition for economic, political, or social interests. Communities exist among persons sharing similar social status, ethnicity, or other characteristics. Although "communities are defined in terms of the solidarity shared by their members" (Neuwirth 1969: 149), they use this as a basis for the pursuit of rational, instrumental ends. Weber argues that communities, once formed, attempt to achieve "closure" (i.e., monopolization of economic, political, and/or social advantages). To obtain it, community members may form voluntary associations or other kinds of formal social organizations.

Most of the research on communities within this tradition comes from a variety of branches of social research other than urban studies, unlike all of the other research discussed up to this point except for social participation research. There has been considerable research to indicate that ethnic and racial groups do indeed constitute communities of this kind (cf. e.g., Kramer 1970; Breton 1964). Other research has begun to adopt a similar approach with regard to groups having a common life style [e.g., the "cosmopolites" discussed by Gans (1962)], occupational and professional groups (cf., e.g., Goode 1957), age and sex groups, deviants, the disabled, and intellectuals. Indeed, research on these last five groups, together with research on ethnic and racial groups, seems to be coming together within a similar conceptualization, using the term "minority group" (cf., e.g., Abu-Laban and Abu-Laban 1973; Sagarin 1971).

Research by scholars of this approach has in some cases been picked up by urban sociologists who agree that there can be "community without propinquity" (Webber 1963) and that the loss of function for territorial communities is not the same as the loss of "community" in the society (cf., e.g. Minar and Greer 1969). In general, however, this type of research has not been brought fully into the fray of the debates in urban studies, even though it bears very directly on many of the problems introduced in the clash.

BRINGING IT ALL TOGETHER: TOWARDS A UNIFIED SOCIOLOGY OF COMMUNITY

In putting forth their approach as the only right one, some scholars in each of these traditions make the assumption that something either is or isn't a community exclusively according to their criteria. Thus, for example, if it isn't territorially grounded, it isn't a community; or if it doesn't deal with institutions, it isn't a community. Yet, as we have seen, opposing approaches can each provide valuable—and complementary—information on what constitutes a community.

Thus it seems to me much more fruitful to conceive of community as a "multidimensional ordinal variable." This phrase implies several things:

(a) that community is a *variable*. This means that things are communities not by predefinition, but rather by empirical investigation.

(b) that it is an *ordinal* variable. This means that instead of saying something either is a community or it isn't, we can talk about the *degree* to which something is a community. "Ordinal" indicates that we can have more or less "communityness" in any given situation.

(c) that it is a *multidimensional* variable. This means that there are several factors which go into making something more or less of a community, and that it is posible to be "more" of a community with respect to some factors and "less" with respect to others. What is, of course, needed is some way of ranking these factors to indicate which ones must be present to at least a minimum degree in order to call a collection of people a community.

This kind of conception seems to me to cut across these four kinds of research traditions and to provide a basis for the development of a fairly general theory of community. Using this conception, it becomes possible to plug in the research generated under each tradition as being relevant when one or another factor is present to a greater or lesser degree. For example, we can hypothesize:

(1) that to the extent that membership in an institutionally complete community of densely knit networks also involves residence in a particular locality, community members are more likely to take effective instrumental action related to their location than are persons whose residential location is associated with a community of limited liability.

(2) that competition among community groups for closure (i.e., a monopoly of social, political, and economic benefits) is mediated to the extent that urbanites are members of "multiple communities" (as discussed in the article by Craven and Wellman).

(3) that there is a tension between, on the one hand, the tendancy for ties to become diffuse rather than specific, for communities to develop common institutions and attempt closure, and for community members to want to live near one another, and, on the other hand, the tendency for urban residents to be involved in several "limited liability" communities, for specific and different functions; that resolution of this tension towards the former may be related to negative social evaluation of the category on which community membership is based or to the need for collective instrumental action in the absence of alternative ways of getting certain services; and that resolution of this tension towards the latter may be related to the degree of perceived social mobility in the society or to the extent to which societal services are provided in an individualized way (see, for example, Pahl's paper in this collection).

This type of approach assumes the potential simultaneous existence of all levels of communityness in a society. It enables researchers to look for factors that facilitate or inhibit community formation, development, and decline or those that effect changes in the relative importance of various characteristics (e.g., common location) of communities existing within a society. It also focuses attention on the relationship among the various internal components of communities, such as informal social ties, voluntary organizations, political structuring, etc. It was with this conception of integration in mind that I organized this collection, even though the material in it is drawn almost exclusively from research that is considered part of urban studies.

ORGANIZATION OF THIS COLLECTION

The first section of this book deals with what I have called the "analytic components of community." These are at least some of the factors that seem to me to deserve inclusion among the multiple dimensions making up community. They are: (1) social characteristics of the people involved (including their spatial clustering or dispersion), (2) interpersonal relationships, (3) organizational involvement, (4) social organization and institutional structure, and (5) political organization and institutions.[4] Each of these has been discussed in a separate article, and the authors of these articles themselves exemplify the different research traditions and the way that they can be applied in dealing with specific substantive problems related to the phenomena listed above.

David Popenoe is a scholar of the "limited liability community" tradition. His piece on residential differentiation focuses on the kinds of such communities that exist, the processes that affect a city's division into them. and the kinds of people who benefit most from them.

Craven and Wellman are obviously proponents of the "personal community" approach. They suggest ways of expanding knowledge through the potentialities of network analysis in clear distinction to more traditional perspectives. As pointed out earlier, Tomeh considers community as a "compleat territorial unit" even though she is dealing with phenomena which can themselves be seen as important contributors to community. Her paper brings out the broad range of information available in the social participation literature, and suggests one way of integrating it further with community research.

Feagin explicitly straddles the first and second approaches, since, as he acknowledges, the literature he deals with varies in its reference. His focus on patterns of social organization (of migrants, in disaster situations, in slums and ghettos, and in situations of collective violence) implies, however, a fairly high degree of sharing of common institutions, so that he leans toward the first approach. Walton comes down fairly emphatically as dealing with multifunctional territorial communities. Although he combines his agreement with such definitions with approval of Suttles's (1972) conception of community as a process of social differentiation, he suggests that Suttles underemphasizes the local autonomy of communities. Walton orients his discussion around three key dimensions—competition, interdependence, and competition-control—that affect the operation of the political process in American communities (i.e., urban areas and subareas).

The second section of the book looks at urbanization, which, as was surely apparent from my long discussion of the first research tradition, has often been associated with theories dealing with changes in, or the decline of, community. Tilly focuses on community within the perspective of the first approach, and outlines the forces which lead to localities (taken as predefined communities: villages, towns) acting together to achieve instrumental goals. Pahl, on the other hand, conceives of community in a way that fits within the second tradition: as a locality-grounded collectivity based on solidarity. He suggests that the likelihood that urban migrants will form communities rather than instrumental—or no—collectivities is influenced by the social organization of the cities to which they migrate.

The third section of the book deals with the ways in which communities have been planned for, and how inadequate knowledge of the several analytic components has led to problems and failures of various kinds. "Community" in "community planning" almost always refers to territorial community. Susskind deals with the planning of new towns and satellite cities; Mott, with efforts to solve some of the problems of central cities and inner-city residential areas; and Kanter, with attempts to establish communes. All three point to the importance of social organizational factors in increasing the likelihood that plans will materialize and communities survive as desired.

BUILDING COMMUNITY

In this last section, I shall discuss several controversies that have become important subjects of debate in planning for community. The most active controversies seem to revolve around (1) the viability of "participatory democracy": the scope and value of citizen participation; (2) the range of functions to be included in a community; and (3) the importance of physical design factors in promoting development of the desired kind of community.

It seems pertinent to remark, first, on the relatively infrequent use that is made of the knowledge available from the various researches discussed earlier in the paper. Certainly, each of the debates I shall discuss could benefit from some of the existing research. The existing situation is largely the fault of academics, whose information dissemination system (even within the profession) leaves much to be desired. The existing research is so diverse in approach and is located in such a wide range of social science literature that it is difficult to "get it together" either physically or conceptually. Also, it is often phrased in language that is hard for non academics to understand. The assumption that the knowledge of academics, when transmitted to students, will eventually find its way to existing community groups or lead to the development of others constitutes, at best, an indirect and chancy approach. Where knowledge *is* made available to non academics, it is usually to administrators and planners who can understand the language, and seldom to citizens' groups. As discussed by Lynd (1939) and others, this is a problem that all social scientists must acknowledge and face.

(1) The Viability of "Participatory Democracy." The phrase "participatory democracy" is one that is associated with radical or at least reformist politics. Certainly, people who move to the country to establish communes (particularly today, but usually in the past as well) have included a conception of egalitarian participation in the running of the commune as part of their ideology. Similarly, urban residential groups advocating community control of local facilities such as schools and organizing ratepayers' associations to press for things like zoning favorable to them are attempting to implement a degree of participatory democracy;

they can be viewed as relatively powerless citizens seeking to exercise a strong voice in decision making. By the same token, city planners of existing or new areas who open themselves up to inputs of information from, and involvement in the planning process by, current or potential residents of the area can be seen as participatory democracy advocates.

The above groups share a belief in the involvement of all relevant groups in the decision-making process, and differ in the degree of direct participation that they espouse. The opposing point of view or practice is represented by those few communes where a single charismatic leader makes all decisions by "social work" organizations which attempt to "help" residents of a local area by providing them with services in an individualized and segmentalized way, and by the majority of city planners, who feel that their superior knowledge enables them to know better than anyone else how communities ought to be developed or redeveloped. As Alinsky (1970: 217) commented, "This kind of planner or urban renewal expert is best exemplified by a prominent midwestern official in the general field of housing and planning who refused to meet with representatives of a broad, bona fide community organization with, 'I am not going to waste my time meeting with a bunch of ignorant slobs and field hands.'"

The various advocates of participatory democracy point to the advantages of participation for building self-confidence and expertise among persons who may not previously have had access to power. They argue that participation encourages commitment, decreases alienation, and supports the development of community in the form of solidary ties which can be activated for instrumental action (see, for example, Head 1971).[5]

Of course, it is the instrumental actions attempted and results obtained that are in many ways the most important outcomes envisioned from participatory democracy. For example, Eugster (1970) outlines her experiences as a field educator in a poor black area surrounded by wealthy suburbs. She describes how she encouraged involvement by area residents in developing and sustaining various educational projects run and controlled by the community (an adult education series of lectures, a "home study" program of tutoring school children and teens). This experience of participatory democracy stimulated the development of a politically oriented citizens' action group which began pressing for, and obtaining, other benefits and facilities for the community (including such basic ones as garbage removal service).

Participatory democracy advocates also point to the negative outcomes of current organizational structures that do not involve participation by all residents. Head (1971: 22) notes that "the concerns of citizens' participation groups represent and reflect the fact that, to a significant extent, community agencies and organizations, presumably organized for the purpose of meeting the needs of local citizens, have largely failed in achieving that goal." In many cities, the decisions of planning boards and local governments support the interests of businessmen (e.g. contractors and developers) to the disadvantage of many urban residents (e.g., small landowners and renters).

Kanter points out in her article in this book that communes controlled by a single charismatic leader can be pushed by him or her towards violence or other harmful behavior. R. E. Pahl suggests in his paper that the individualized delivery of social services inhibits the development of groups capable of instrumental collective action; Paul Mott argues that segmentation by government agencies at various levels as well as by voluntary organizations of various kinds prevents the solution of community problems that require a holistic approach. Susskind's paper points to the failures of new towns planned without the involvement of future residents, and suggests ways by which such participation can be implemented.

On the other hand, participatory democracy, given the present economic system, can tend to perpetuate the status quo, as is indicated by Repo (1972). She argues that middle-class neighborhoods will have more clout and show more expertise in getting money out of municipal governments than poorer neighborhoods. Within economically heterogeneous areas, middle-class people, with their greater verbal skills and experience in handling meetings and manipulating situations, will gain control, and may well press for facilities or changes that are contrary to the interests of working-class people in the neighborhood.

This criticism, however, underemphasizes the negative sanctions available to poor community groups (e.g., riots, violence) who have essentially little to lose by such action, and the consequent impact that active citizens' groups of poor people can have. In addition, analysis of action by local citizens' groups is relevant only to situations of redevelopment of existing areas. Where community planning refers (as it often does) to unsettled territory, there is no way for community organizers to mobilize *potential* residents (at least no one has tried it), and there is no one living there to object to various aspects of the plan.

(2) *Planned Communities—Autonomous or Dependent?* Most planners of "new towns," suburbs, and satellite cities as well as the organizers of some kinds of communes operate on the assumption that the greater the autonomy of the unit, the more desirable a place it will be to live in.[6] They also assume that such autonomy is attainable.

Lawrence Susskind points out in his paper that the impossibility of local autonomy has led to problems for new towns whose residents work elsewhere, whose industries employ people who live elsewhere, and whose facilities and population size are inadequate to satisfy the often cosmopolitan tastes of their residents. On the other hand, Kanter indicates that economically independent communes can be very impressive successes, even though the majority of contemporary North American communes are not economically autonomous and even though many communes attempting to establish economic self-sufficiency have been unable to survive. Communes with a common industry usually operate it so that jobs are rotated and/or work is done in groups, so that the work not only supports the commune but also has spiritual and social meaning as unalienated labor and as enhancement of solidarity and commitment. Nevertheless, even such communes must sell their products, purchase other things, and have various other forms of contact with nearby towns.

It is, of course, questionable whether small-scale autonomy is desirable. Certainly, in reference to the previous issue, it would make participatory democracy, more relevant, since no decisions taken elsewhere would affect the community. On the other hand, not only is this impossible in contemporary urban-industrial society but local autonomy also means isolation from many of the benefits of urban life. As Craven and Wellman point out, only large cities can sustain a variety of special-interest groups. Similarly, cultural facilities, extensive sports facilities, etc., can usually only be supported by a large population concentrated in a city.

(3) *The Importance of Physical Design Factors.* The last issue of debate is most relevant for community planning and organizing related to redevelopment of neighborhoods or districts or establishment of new towns or satellite cities. The fallacy of environmental determinism has repeatedly been made by urban planners. Their training has, until recently, concentrated on the development of well-designed, efficient plans of the physical environment (cf. e.g., Gutman 1968; Gans ˜1968), which has supported this one-sided approach.

Many of the designs of new towns, suburbs, and satellite cities conceived and executed by urban planners in North America and Britain have been based on some version of the neighborhood unit idea. As first conceived by Ebenezer Howard in 1898, this plan involved dividing up new towns into several neighborhoods of about 5000 persons each, with each neighborhood located around an elementary school (Howard 1902). It was often expected that single-family and row housing, open green space, and pleasantly designed buildings would help to remedy the social problems of the urban poor who were to be moved into sections of such towns, and would encourage the development of solidary relations among neighbors.

Obviously, such expectations were doomed to failure. People brought their social values and behavior patterns with them; only those middle-class persons who were previously sociable with their neighbors or wanted to become so were likely to do so in the new setting. Working-class persons transplanted from dense urban neighborhoods were often unhappy or adapted to the new environment in ways not expected by the planners, such as by isolating themselves at home with their nuclear families (cf., for example, Young and Willmott's [1957] research on East End working-class Londoners who moved to a new suburban housing estate).

On the other hand, the physical design of new towns has had some effects quite different from those which the planner intended. For example, Susskind suggests that planners' separation of residential areas by housing type and cost has perpetuated the traditional social-class structure. Moreover, the type of facilities included (e.g., restaurants but not pubs or night clubs, neighborhood focus around primary school) means that family-oriented middle-class adults with young children will be the ones most likely to be happy there. Working-class persons, single persons, retired persons, and families with teenagers are all likely to encounter problems when living in environments planned in this way.

NOTES

[1] Toennies's book *Gemeinschaft and Gesellschaft* was published in 1887. The dichotomy coined there has been a powerful influence on sociology ever since. "Gemeinschaft" refers to social situations of intimate relationships in which social status is ascribed, roles are diffuse, and styles of doing things are traditional. It is usually translated as "community." "Gesellschaft" is the opposite of Gemeinschaft. It refers to social situations of large-scale impersonal relationships in which social status is achieved, roles are specific, and styles of doing things are open to change and experimentation. "Gesellschaft" is usually translated as "society," sometimes as "association."

[2] A good overview of much of the research done in Britain is provided in *Communities in Britain* (Frankenberg, 1966). Bell and Newby (1971) also provide a solid critical examination of major examples of such research in the United States, Canada, Britain, and Europe.

[3] There had been research from a generalist perspective that included it as part of the examination of all aspects of local social organization, as in the work of the Lynds, Warner et al., etc. These were important antecedents.

[4] What is clearly missing is a discussion of communal economic organizations and institutions. Indeed, this kind of research occurs more frequently in anthropological than in sociological studies, perhaps because of the nature of economic organization in urban-industrial society and the norms separating economic institutions from solidarity. Nevertheless, given the pressures toward community closure in an economic sense, they deserve inclusion.

[5] Strategies of Community Organization, edited by P. M. Cox et al. (1970), is a good collection of articles outlining various approaches for implementing participatory democracy and describing specific experiences and techniques.

[6] This is similar to the underlying bias of rural-urban continuum and mass society theorists.

REFERENCES

Abu-Laban, Sharon McIrvin, and Baha Abu-Laban.
  1973 "Women and the Aged as Minority Groups: A Critique," paper presented at the annual meetings of the Canadian Sociological and Anthropological Association, May 28–31.

Alinsky, Saul D.
  1970 "Citizen Participation and Community Organization in Planning and Urban Renewal," in Fred M. Cox et al. (eds.), *Strategies of Community Organization*: 216–225.

Arensberg, Conrad M.
1939 *The Irish Countryman: An Anthropological Study.* New York: Macmillan.
————, and S. T. Kimball.
1940 *Family and Community in Ireland.* London: Peter Smith.
Avila, Manuel.
1969 *Tradition and Growth.* Chicago: University of Chicago Press.
Bell, Colin, and Howard Newby.
1971 (1972) *Community Studies: An Introduction to the Sociology of the Local Community.* New York: Praeger.
Bell, Wendell, and Marion D. Boat.
1957 "Urban Neighbourhood Types and Informal Social Relations," *American Journal of Sociology* 62 (January): 391–398.
————, and Maryanne T. Force
1956 "Urban Neighbourhood Types and Participation in Informal Social Relations," *American Sociological Review* 21 (February): 25–34.
Breton, Raymond.
1964 "Institutional Completeness of Ethnic Communities and the Personal Relations of Immigrants," *American Journal of Sociology* 70 (September): 193–205.
Clark, S. D.
1966 *The Suburban Society.* Toronto: University of Toronto Press.
Cox, Fred M., John L. Erlich, Jack Rothman, and John E. Tropman.
1970 *Strategies of Community Organization: A Book of Readings.* Itasca, Ill.: Peacock.
Davis, Allison, B. B. Gardner, and M. R. Gardner.
1944 *Deep South.* Chicago: University of Chicago Press.
Effrat, Andrew.
1970 "Sanctions and Organizational Taxonomies." Unpublished Ph.D. dissertation, Harvard University.
Eugster, Carla.
1970 "Field Education in West Heights: Equipping a Deprived Community to Help Itself," in Cox et al. (eds.), *op. cit.* 241–252.
Frankenberg, Ronald.
1966 *Communities in Britain.* Harmondsworth: Penguin.
1957 *Village on the Border.* London: Cohen and West.
Gallaher, Art, Jr.
1961 *Plainville Fifteen Years Later.* New York: Columbia University Press.
1964 "Plainville: The Twice-Studied Town," in Arthur J. Vidich, Joseph Bensman and Maurice R. Stein (eds.), *Reflections on Community Studies.* New York: Wiley, 285–304.
Gans, Herbert J.
1962a *The Urban Villagers.* New York: The Free Press.
1962b "Urbanism and Suburbanism as Ways of Life: A Re-evaluation of Definitions," in Arnold Rose (ed.), *Human Behavior and Social Processes.* Boston: Houghton Mifflin.
1967 *The Levittowners.* New York: Pantheon.
1968 *People and Plans: Essays on Urban Problems and Solutions.* New York: Basic Books.
Goode, William J.
1957 "Community within a Community: The Professions," *American Sociological Review* 22 (April): 194–200.

Greer, Scott.
  1956 "Urbanism Reconsidered: A Comparative Study of Local Areas in a
       Metropolis," *American Sociological Review* 21 (February): 19–25.
  1960 "The Social Structure and Political Process of Suburbia," *American Socio-
       logical Review* 25 (August): 514–526.
Gutman, Robert.
  1966 "Site Planning and Social Behavior," *Journal of Social Issues* 22: 4, 103–
       115.
  1968 "What Schools of Architecture Expect from Sociology," *Journal of Archi-
       tectural Education* March: 69–83.
Hawley, Willis D., and Frederick M. Wirt (eds.).
  1968 *The Search for Community Power.* Englewood Cliffs, N.J.: Prentice-Hall.
Head, Wilson.
  1971 "The Ideology and Practice of Citizen Participation," in James A. Draper
       (ed.), *Citizen Participation: Canada.* Toronto: New Press.
Henry, Jules.
  1958 "The Personal Community and its Invariant Properties," *American An-
       thropologist* 60 (October): 827–831.
Hillery, George A., Jr.
  1955 "Definitions of Community: Areas of Agreement," *Rural Sociology* 20
       (June): 111–123.
  1969 *Communal Organizations: A Study of Local Societies.* Chicago: University
       of Chicago Press.
Howard, Ebenezer.
  1902 *Garden Cities of Tomorrow.* London: Faber and Faber.
Hunter, Floyd.
  1953 (1963) *Community Power Structure: A Study of Decision-Makers.*
       Garden City: Anchor Books (Doubleday).
Jacobs, Jane.
  1961 *The Death and Life of Great American Cities.* New York: Random House.
James, Selma.
  1972 "Introduction" in Mariarosa Della Costa and Selma James, *The Power of
       Women and the Subversion of the Community.* Bristol, Eng.: Falling Wall
       Press.
Janowitz, Morris.
  1952 *The Community Press in an Urban Setting.* New York: The Free Press.
Keller, Suzanne.
  1968 *The Urban Neighborhood: A Sociological Perspective.* New York: Ran-
       dom House .
Kornhauser, William.
  1968 "Mass Society," in D. Sills (ed.) *International Encyclopedia of the Social
       Sciences* 10: 58–64. New York: Macmillan and The Free Press.
Kramer, Judith.
  1970 *The American Minority Community.* New York: Crowell.
  ———, and Seymour Leventman.
  1961 *Children of the Gilded Ghetto.* New Haven: Yale University Press.
Lee, Terence.
  1968 "The Urban Neighbourhood as a Socio-Spatial Schema," *Human Rela-
       tions* 21 (August): 241–267.
Lewis, Oscar.
  1951 *Life in a Mexican Village: Tepoztlan Restudied.* Urbana: University of
       Illinois Press.

Lorimer, James, and Myfanwy Phillips.
1971 *Working People: Life in a Downtown City Neighbourhood.* Toronto: James, Lewis and Samuel.

Lynd, Robert S.
1939 *Knowledge for What?* Princeton: Princeton University Press.
———, and Helen M. Lynd.
1929 *Middletown: A Study in Contemporary American Culture.* New York: Harcourt Brace.

Mann, Peter
1965 "The Neighbourhood," in *An Approach to Urban Sociology.* New York: Humanities Press.

Mayhew, Leon.
1971 *Society: Institutions and Activity.* Glenview, Ill.: Scott, Foresman.

Merton, Robert.
1957 "Patterns of Influence: Local and Cosmopolitan Influentials," in *Social Theory and Social Structure* (rev. and enlarged ed.). New York: The Free Press.

Michelson, William.
1970 *Man and His Urban Environment: A Sociological Approach.* Reading, Mass.: Addison-Wesley.

Minar, David W., and Scott Greer.
1969 *The Concept of Community: Readings with Interpretations.* Chicago: Aldine.

Neuwirth, Gertrude.
1969 "A Weberian Outline of a Theory of Community: Its Application to the 'Dark Ghetto'," *British Journal of Sociology* 20: 2, 148–163.

Nisbet, Robert.
1966 *The Sociological Tradition.* New York: Basic Books.

Parsons, Talcott.
1966 *Societies: Evolutionary and Comparative Perspectives.* Englewood Cliffs, N.J.: Prentice-Hall.

Pfeil, E.
1968 "The Pattern of Neighbouring Relations in Dortmund-Nordstadt," in R. E. Pahl (ed.), *Readings in Urban Sociology.* Oxford: Pergamon.

Phillips, Derek.
1969 "Social Class, Social Participation and Happiness: A Consideration of Interaction, Opportunities and Investment," *Sociological Quarterly* 10 (Winter): 3–21.

Redfield, Robert.
1941 *The Folk Culture of the Yucatan.* Chicago: University of Chicago Press.

Rees, Alwyn D.
1950 *Life in a Welsh Countryside.* Cardiff: University of Wales Press.

Reisman, David.
1950 *The Lonely Crowd: A Study of the Changing American Character.* New Haven: Yale University Press.

Repo, Marjaleena.
1972 "The Fallacy of 'Community Control'," in Bryan Finnigan and Cy Gonick (eds.), *Making It: The Canadian Dream.* Toronto: McClelland and Stewart.

Sagarin, Edward (ed.).
1971 *The Other Minorities.* Waltham: Xerox.

Seeley, John R., R. Alexander Sim, and Elizabeth W. Loosely.
  1956 *Crestwood Heights*. Toronto: University of Toronto Press.
Shaw, Clifford, and Henry D. McKay.
  1942 *Juvenile Delinquency and Urban Areas*. Chicago: University of Chicago
     Press.
Stacey, Margaret.
  1969 "The Myth of Community Studies," *British Journal of Sociology* 20, 2:
     134–147.
Stein, Maurice.
  1960 (1964) *The Eclipse of Community*. New York: Harper Torch.
Suttles, Gerald D.
  1968 *The Social Order of the Slum*. Chicago: University of Chicago Press.
  1972 *The Social Construction of Communities*. Chicago: University of Chicago
     Press.
Tönnies, Ferdinand.
  1887 (1957) *Community and Society*. New York: Harper.
Vidich, Arthur J., and Joseph Bensman.
  1958 *Small Town in Mass Society: Class, Power and Religion in a Rural Com-
     munity*. Garden City: Anchor Books, Doubleday.
von Bertalanffy, Ludwig.
  1962 "General System Theory—A Critical Review," *General Systems* 7, 7: 1–
     22.
Warner, W. Lloyd, and Paul S. Lunt.
  1941 *The Social Life of a Modern Community*. New Haven: Yale University
     Press.
  1942 *The Status System of a Modern Community*. New Haven: Yale University
     Press.
Warren, Roland L.
  1963 *The Community in America*. Chicago: Rand McNally.
Webber, Melvin.
  1963 "Order in Diversity: Community Without Propinquity," in L. Wingo
     (ed.), *Cities and Space: The Future Use of Urban Land*. Baltimore: Johns
     Hopkins Press.
Wellman, Barry.
  1968 "Community Ties and Mental Health." Toronto: Clarke Institute of Psy-
     chiatry, Community Studies Section, mimeo.
West, James.
  1945 *Plainville, U.S.A.* New York: Columbia University Press.
Whyte, William Foote.
  1955 *Street Corner Society*, 2nd ed. Chicago: University of Chicago Press.
Wirth, Louis.
  1929 *The Ghetto*. Chicago: University of Chicago Press.
Young, Michael, and Peter Willmott.
  1957 *Family and Kinship in East London*. London: Routledge and Kegan Paul.
Zorbaugh, Harvey W.
  1929 *The Gold Coast and the Slum*. Chicago: University of Chicago Press.

Analytic Components of Community

Urban Residential Differentiation: An Overview of Patterns, Trends, and Problems*

DAVID POPENOE

Rutgers University

The main causes, conditions, and social consequences of residential differentiation in urbanized communities are reviewed. A comparison is made among the forms of residential differentiation in preindustrial, industrial, and postindustrial cities and in planned and unplanned industrial cites. Major emphasis is given to the social problems and issues connected with postindustrial residential differentiation.

I. INTRODUCTION

A fundamental problem in studying and understanding modern urban communities is that internally they are highly differentiated: they consist of many different social worlds which are complexly interrelated. When one refers to an urban resident of New York, for example, does one mean a poor worker from Harlem, a rich businessman on Park Avenue, or a hippie student from the Village? They are all New Yorkers, but their lives are as different from one another as are those of any three persons in the United States. This is partly due to the fact that the residential settings in which they live are as different from each other as are any three communities in the United States. For most sociologically significant purposes these residents don't live in New York as a whole but in a limited segment of it.

This essay discusses the causes, conditions, and consequences of such *residential differentiation* in urban settings. We shall look at the basic

*I would like to thank Herbert Gans and William Michelson for their valuable suggestions and comments on an earlier draft of this paper.

patterns of residential differentiation, its main causes and social functions, how the patterns seem to be changing over time, how they vary in different international and historical settings, and, finally, at some current problems and public policy issues which are associated with this area.

Residential differentiation means the specialization of residential areas in terms of the characteristics of their inhabitants. It is one of three fundamental dimensions of a community that have been the subject of sociological analyses. The other aspects, to which the study of residential differentiation is often related, are the structures of a community as a system (such as its economic specialization or political capacities) and the relationships among people living in the community (Coleman 1970). These are discussed in other papers in this book.

II. THE SOCIAL FUNCTIONS OF RESIDENTIAL DIFFERENTIATION

It is characteristic of sociological analysis to begin with a discussion of the functions or social purposes of a phenomenon. What social purposes are served by the clustering together into local neighborhoods of persons with similar sociocultural characteristics? What social difference does it make who lives next door to you and in your local neighborhood?

It is important to note at the outset that the local residential environment, for many people, is not as important as it once was (Webber 1963; Scherer 1972; Keller 1968). It often has few economic functions (one's place of work is elsewhere) and few political functions (these are conducted on a higher level), and it is usually not especially important as a unique subculture. In addition, the social contacts of many urban residents go well beyond the local area—friends are drawn from a larger area, relatives are widely scattered, organizations are city-wide. Finally, many urban dwellers do not stay in any one area for a long time; there is a relatively high degree of residential mobility in cities. These facts tend to be especially true for persons of middle- and upper-class levels. The transcendence of one's local residential environment depends on three things: the availability of transportation and communication facilities, the means to afford them, and the desire to use them. The more technologically advanced the society, therefore, and the higher the income and educational levels, the less the importance of the local residential milieu. The neighborhood is not very important for, let us say, an upper-middle-class professional man in a metropolitan area (see Wellman 1972). Most sociologists fit into this category, and that is one reason why the importance of the residential environment is underemphasized in much of recent sociological writing.

Just as the neighborhood is least important for those with the highest geographic mobility, it is, correspondingly, most important for those with the least mobility: children (into the teen years), older people, the sick and handicapped, those who care for people in these categories (especially housewives), and the poor. For some in these categories the local environment is the *only* environment. For the young child whose life centers on the few houses close to his own, it makes a tremendous difference to him who lives next door. Similarly, the "trapped housewife" in suburbia, the older retired person, and the handicapped depend to a large degree on the local environment for their social, emotional, and sometimes physical well-being. For most people in modern societies, therefore, the residential milieu is still an important sociological unit for, in varying degrees: (1) communion with others: friendship, primary relationships, mutual aid; (2) social control; (3) sense of security and ease; (4) collective identity and sense of place; (5) socialization of children (including primary education); (6) organizational ties; church and voluntary organizations (see Suttles 1972).

A commonplace but nonetheless valid sociological generalization is that most people want to live near others who are very similar to them in important respects. In this way they tend to get the full benefit of the functions of the local neighborhood just enumerated—a wider circle of friends, agreement on norms of socialization and deviance, a greater sense of security and ease, and so on. But this is a double-edged sword. What may seem best in the short run for the individual or group can in the long run prove dysfunctional for these same individuals or groups, or for others in society. Is it "good" for neighborhood elementary schools to be single-class and single-race, for example? Is it "good" for retired persons to be living in relative isolation from other age groups? Is it "good" for housewives with young children in suburbia to have only other housewives and other young children as next-door neighbors? Further, some families do not wish to live with others just like themselves. Welfare families may not wish to be bunched with other welfare cases; blacks strive to break free of the ghetto. In cases like this the social function of residential differentiation is to separate people from one another, and in particular to contain within limited geographic areas persons the society desires to be "out of the way."

We can say that the basic social importance of living in one neighborhood rather than another is based on the significance of face-to-face contacts in social life. Each of the neighborhood functions listed above— friendship formation, socialization of children, pursuit of common interests through organizations, etc.—revolves around face-to-face contacts. Such contacts are, in turn, greatly affected by space and distance. To be with someone you must first get to him, and that may take time, effort, and money. Consequently, you tend to have more face-to-face contacts with those who are nearest to you. Three things intervene in this scheme, however. Distance is greatly modified by transportation technologies; you may be able to get to the next stop on the transit line faster than you can walk three blocks. The range of possible contacts is greatly modified by communications technology; a phone call can take the place of a visit. And finally, all social contacts are deeply shaped by social definitions and norms of behavior. You can live next door to someone yet have very limited contact; such is traditionally the case, for example, with blacks and whites living in small towns in the South. It is important to bear in mind, however, that these factors merely modify the effect of spatial proximity; they do not erase it.

III. SOME CAUSES OF RESIDENTIAL DIFFERENTIATION

The processes which lead to or "cause" residential differentiation are many and varied. One group of processes, not uncommon in the modern world, involves *negative sanction*. An example is the involuntary internment of the Japanese during the Second World War. Another is the long history of racial segregation in the United States, which continues to the present day in the form of extralegal restrictions and social norms observed in the sale and rental of property.

Some residential segregation of ethnic minorities is voluntary in character, based on a desire on the part of the minority to defend its way of life against alien customs and ideas and also to achieve greater internal solidarity. A good example is the Hasidic Jews in Brooklyn, New York.

Most residential differentiation stems from a combination of real-estate *market forces* and governmental mechanisms of *land planning*. Residential differentiation in most North American cities is largely based on such factors as the employment situation, transportation developments, and demographic trends, operating through the real-estate market, and to a small degree on government land planning programs like urban renewal and public housing (see Schnore 1965). In newly developing areas such as the suburbs, land-use planning plays a somewhat larger role.

Most modern nations in the world have a far more extensive central planning apparatus than is found in the United States. The residential character of particular areas in these nations can thus be determined to a much greater extent on the basis of long-range community considerations, often including questions of social desirability as well as economic, aesthetic, and physical factors. Land-use planning is relatively undeveloped in the United States. The most common and often the most powerful land-use control device available is the zoning ordinance, which is found only at the local levels of government (and is, therefore, ordinarily ineffective for large-area planning). The zoning ordinance has traditionally been used more as a protective than as a planning tool; its main function has been to preserve the inherent character of existing areas rather than to promote the best use of newly developing areas. In this sense, however, it has become a powerful device in maintaining existing patterns of residential differentiation (Wilhelm 1962).

The "causes" of differentiation may be sought at the micro as well as the macro level—at the level of the individual person or family making a decision about where to live. For middle-class persons, whose income level gives them a relatively free choice about housing matters, the home purchase or rental decision has become quite deliberate and rational in those modern societies where there is an adequate supply of housing. The available evidence from the United States indicates that, in general, the husband in a family will select a general area of residence with reference to its accessibility to his work and his income level, while the wife will choose the particular house within this area in terms of her own preferences and the family's needs for space (Foote et al. 1960; Rossi 1955).

The house seems to be a far more important focus of attention than the neighborhood and surrounding community in the purchase or rental decision. For families with children, however, the quality of schools is a significant consideration, and for all families an important factor is the more intangible social status characteristics that are attached to neighborhoods and areas; each family attempts to locate in the area of highest possible status within a given income level.

Households without children, such as young, single adults and older people, will not be attracted so much by schools, of course, but rather by amenities in the residential environment which cater to their special needs. As we shall discuss more fully below, this differentiation of areas in terms of different "amenity packages" as well as dwelling types has generated a type of residential differentiation which has become highly characteristic of new urban communities in advanced societies.

Persons of low income, however, don't have this kind of choice in housing. Their choice is limited to areas which are "left over" by the middle class—usually areas of relatively poor environmental and housing quality.

IV. VARIABLES OF RESIDENTIAL DIFFERENTIATION

A great amount of empirical research in the fields of sociology and social geography over the past twenty-five years has established that, in spite of the fact that many variables are used to distinguish people and groups from one another, only a very few are strong enough to provide the basis for long-term residential association among people. (This empirical work has been ably summarized in two recent works, Timms 1971 and Johnston 1971.) Much of this research was triggered by the pioneering method called *social area analysis* (Shevky and Bell 1955; Bell 1959; Bell and Greer 1962), which utilizes census data. In recent years the method of factor analysis has generated considerable empirical refinement (Berry 1971; Dogan and Rokkan 1969; Robson 1969), but the basic findings of social area analysis have held up.

We can start our discussion with those social variables which are based on *biological* properties of individuals. One such variable which is *not* very important in residential differentiation is sex. There is little clustering in urban areas along sex lines, except perhaps at the micro level of individual apartment houses. (The ratio of women to men is often higher in urban than in rural areas, however.) In blocks, neighborhoods, and subcommunities, the sexes tend to be quite highly intermixed. Most residential units contain persons of both sexes, and there is little difference in the demands made on the local environment by men and by women.

However, two other biologically rooted variables—age and race—loom very large in significance. People tend to choose friends from among their own age level, and where individuals are not connected to a family, residential differentiation in terms of age becomes quite strong. This is especially the case with two major groups in our society at the present time— young adults and senior citizens. Young adults in growing numbers are living apart from their families of origin. This has led to a marked increase in the number of single, young-adult subcommunities, especially in the newer cities of the West in the United States. Similarly, older persons who once lived with their grown children (making up an extended family) are becoming more residentially differentiated, sometimes in entirely separate and isolated communities (e.g., the desert "sun" cities).

Since most persons live in mixed-age *family* groups, however, the age variable is better expressed as *stage of the family life cycle* (Lansing and Kish 1957). The family can be said to go through a life cycle similar to the aging process, ranging from young marrieds with no children, through the child-bearing years, to older marrieds living again with no children (they having left home), and finally to the death of one marriage partner. At each stage of the life cycle there are quite different needs for space, and distinct demands on the local environment (Michelson 1970, chap. 4).

Probably the best-known variable of residential differentiation is race —at least in the United States, where residential segregation of whites and blacks has been a prominent feature of the national social structure. It is most useful to discuss race in connection with two related sociocultural variables—religion and ethnic origin—which together make up a broad variable called *ethnic status* (Gordon 1964). While ethnic status can be extremely important in accounting for residential differentiation in some cities, it is not as universally important a variable in this field as, for example, social class. This is because of the widespread differences among cities and societies in the extent to which ethnic minorities exist. Ethnicity is a very unimportant variable in accounting for residential differentiation in Oslo or Stockholm, for example.

The extent to which a minority group of a particular ethnic status is segregated physically from other groups depends, in part, on its "social distance" from the majority group. The broad principle here is that social distance is reflected in physical distance. Social distance refers, in this case, to the amount of close contact which a majority group desires to have with a minority group. (For example, to what extent they would want to be friends with a member of a minority group, or have that person as a marriage partner.) Minority groups can thus be ranked in terms of their degree of acceptance by the majority society. In general, the lower the rank of the minority group, the greater will be its degree of residential segregation—in this case, of course, mostly for involuntary reasons.

Social distance can be maintained, however, not only by physical separation, but by rigidly defined and enforced norms of social contact as well. Thus two socially distant ethnic groups can live quite near to one another with a minimum of friction when the amount and type of social contact—especially close, emotional contact—are kept under careful control. This was traditionally the situation in the American South, where blacks and whites often lived side by side with one another. This observation is also important in explaining the residential pattern in the North, where a growing body of evidence suggests that the residential segregation of blacks and white is as great as, or greater than, in the South (Lieberson 1963; Taeuber and Taeuber 1965). This fact is initially surprising, because the *social* distance between blacks and white is generally conceded to be somewhat less in the North. The more important factor at work, however, is that the norms which limit intimate social contact are much weaker in the North—and physical distance is used as a substitute. A leading sociological explanation of why racial segregation remains strong in the North, then, is as follows: In the absence of strong norms forbidding certain forms of intimate social contact, majority groups find it necessary to maintain a great amount of physical distance from blacks in order to maintain a desired social distance (Beshers 1962). In the last several years, this explanation has gained support as a result of the controversies over neighborhood schools and the busing of students.

We have not yet discussed the most powerful variable of all in accounting for residential differentiation—social class. Social class level (or social rank) often combines with the ethnic status variable, because persons of low ethnic status also tend to be of low class status. Social class is extremely important, however, even in situations of complete ethnic homogeneity.

Most neighborhoods in cities are predominantly, and come to be defined by others as, either lower-class, working-class, middle- or upper-middle-class, and so on. This seems due mainly to the fact that housing in a given area of a city is generally of a similar price or rent level, and there is a sorting of persons through the real-estate market in terms of who can pay the price (though this economic factor is supplemented by social factors. See Feldman and Tilly 1960). The poorest housing, often in the inner city, is left for those who have the lowest incomes. Newer housing, often in the suburban areas, becomes the province of upper-class families.

Income is the most widely used dimension of social class, and probably the most significant one in accounting for residential differentiation. Two other commonly used dimensions are occupation and level of education. The former was perhaps a more important variable in preindustrial cities, where special areas of the city were given over to specific occupations and people usually lived proximate to their place of business (see Sjöberg 1960 and the ensuing discussion in Section VI). In modern communities we see evidence of occupational differentiation in college towns or the areas around a university, and in business and professional neighborhoods and factory towns; yet occupations tend for the most part to be quite highly intermixed in areas of a given income level. (But see Duncan and Duncan 1955.)

Several scholars hold that education is a more powerful dimension of social class than either occupation or income in accounting for residential differentiation (Schmid 1950; Schmid, MacCannell, and Van Arsdol, Jr., 1958). Similarity of educational level is a good predictor of shared values among people, and a major ingredient of friendship formation. It is reasonable to suppose that where relatively free choice of residential location exists, education becomes an important variable.

In modern urban communities the house and neighborhood have become quite important in symbolically expressing high social status among middle, upper-middle, and upper-class families. In a fluid, impersonal, urban situation, a person's social position is not known by many with whom he comes into contact each day, and yet knowledge about social position is quite important in most social interaction (Wirth 1938). A person's "address" has become a most significant way of quickly identifying his social rank, and is a bit of information which is quickly elicited by, and given to, strangers. This has led to a great amount of status manipulation by suburban developers (as in the use of elite-sounding development names, like Wildwood Crest or Birch Tree Estates). More importantly in connection with residential differentiation, this phenomenon has generated a hardening of class lines in urban areas; the higher social classes want to protect the purity of their high-status addresses by keeping lower-class families out.

One additional sociological variable has emerged in a number of studies as having some importance for residential differentiation, though not as much as the previous ones. This is migrant status—the length of time one has lived in an area, or, alternatively, the extent to which one is considered a "newcomer" (McElrath 1970). It is often closely associated with the class and ethnic variables, and its importance is of course closely related to the amount of residential mobility in a society. Certain residential environments attract the newcomer: the newly built suburb necessarily fits into this category, while the inner-city slum has traditionally been the area of first settlement for foreign and rural immigrants to the city. These two environments have the highest rates of residential mobility in a metropolitan region. The length of time a group has lived in an area has great implications for other important aspects of community life, such as the amount of neighboring and feelings of community solidarity.

In summary, there are three main variables which account for most of the residential differentiation in urban areas: stage of the life cycle, ethnicity, and social class. This is especially true in industrialized cities in Western countries, where urban residential development is primarily a product of market forces rather than of government planning. Patterns of differentiation found in other settings, such as preindustrial cities and highly planned industrial cities, are the subject of a subsequent section.

V. THE SPATIAL PATTERN OF RESIDENTIAL DIFFERENTIATION

The focus of this section is the overall spatial pattern generated by residential differentiation. How do the separate residential clusters fit together to make up the urban pattern of subcommunities and neighborhoods? Like the topic of the last section, this too has been the subject of extensive research over the past twenty-five years (see Theodorson 1961).

The urban residential pattern is commonly analyzed using the central business district (CBD) as a reference point. The main variables of residential differentiation (class, life-cycle stage, and ethnicity) may then be discussed in terms of distance from, and pattern of distribution around, the central business district. Two major patterns of distribution were first identified many years ago: concentric zones, in which a variable is uniformly spread around the CBD at a given distance (Burgess 1925), and sectors, in which the distribution takes the form of wedge or pie-shaped sectors radiating out from the CBD (Hoyt 1939).

In modern Western cities, the farther from the CBD, the higher tends to be the social class level of residents and the more "familistic" they are in life-cycle stage (i.e., the more frequently in the stages of child-bearing and child-raising). One finds more single, older, and lower-class persons in inner-city areas, and more higher-class families in outlying suburban areas. There are two major exceptions to this, however. There still exist in many large cities bastions of upper-middle-class and upper-class residents immediately proximate to the central business district; though mostly in decline, these areas have sometimes been preserved because of topographical barriers or public action. A second exception is the high incidence of large, young families in slum areas, especially among new immigrant groups. These families, however, have traditionally moved to outlying areas as their income level rises (Gans 1962).

In their pattern of distribution around the CBD, the social class and life cycle stage variables are significantly different in many cities. The life cycle variable tends to be distributed in a concentric zonal pattern: in all directions from the CBD there is an increase in "familism" with greater distance. This is mainly related to housing density. Residential building densities tend to decrease rather uniformly by distance from the CBD (due mainly to land values, which drop as the accessibility to the center city diminishes; higher land values in the center require higher building densities if real estate development is to be profitable). In turn, those stages of the life cycle which require more dwelling space (because of larger family size) become located in the outlying areas of lower density (Johnston 1971, chap. 5).

The social class variable, on the other hand, is more sectorially distributed: some residential sectors radiating from the CBD will be of a distinctly higher class than those adjacent. This is because the wealthier families move out from the center city only in certain directions (for example, in many cities the north side of town, for reasons which are unclear, is of a higher class level than the south side). The wealthier families move to those areas which have higher residential amenity values—lakes, hills, etc. As they continue to move out ever farther from the city, the upper-middle and middle classes move in behind them, both to share the same amenities, and because the higher-class symbolic identity of the areas has been established. Once the wealthier sectors are established (it is the rich who move from the city first and often farthest), the remaining sectors are left for the settlement of lower-class persons (Berry 1965).

This schematic pattern is, in reality, modified in several important ways. The third main variable of residential differentiation, ethnic status, is typically neither sectorially nor concentrically distributed. It often distorts the general pattern in the form of large, somewhat independent clusters—the ghettos in large cities, for example.

The pattern is also distorted by industrial districts, by business districts which are secondary to the CBD, and by outlying satellite towns which become incorporated into a metropolitan area (Harris and Ullman 1945). In the case of secondary and satellite business districts, the concentric and sectorial patterns are generally repeated on a small scale with those districts at the center, but within the framework of the overall metropolitan scheme. Indeed, in the newer cities of the twentieth century, such as Los Angeles, there is no single, major CBD. Los Angeles has several separate "downtowns," each specializing in certain functions. In cities like this, the general pattern of the nineteenth-century city is duplicated several times within one metropolitan structure.

Other important distorting factors are topographic barriers to city growth (such as Lake Michigan in Chicago) and transportation routes. High-speed transportation routes, by improving accessibility to the central city in certain areas, greatly affect the uniformity of the distribution of land values and densities around a city. This creates what amounts to a sectorial pull on the concentric zones, and the distinction between the two patterns becomes somewhat blurred.

In summary, the spatial pattern of residential differentiation in metropolitan areas of the United States can be described as follows: In the outlying, low-density suburban areas live mostly families, and there is a great deal of class and racial segregation within local communities and neighborhoods. These areas are typically on the higher end of the social class ladder. The local suburban communities are often highly homogeneous in class, race, and life-cycle stage (but not necessarily in religion and ethnicity), and they often lie outside the political jurisdiction of the central city, sometimes constituting separate local governments in their own right.

The inner-city areas house a combination of the lower and working classes, racial and ethnic minorities, and persons outside of the familistic stages of the life cycle. The latter category includes students, childless couples, older persons, and young, single adults. The "missing" group in most large American cities is the middle-class family with children. The "missing" groups in most suburbs are the poor, the blacks, and the elderly (Gans 1962).

VI. SOME HISTORICAL AND INTERNATIONAL COMPARISONS

The urban residential differentiation we have been describing is principally characteristic, as we have noted, of industrial cities which have developed without political direction or planning—that is, mainly by the action of "free-market" forces. For a better understanding of residential differentiation, therefore, it is useful to examine the patterns of preindustrial cities, and those of industrial cities whose development has largely been guided by centralized government planning.

Though few cities in the world remain untouched by industrialization, preindustrial urban patterns have by no means gone out of existence, especially in the Third World. In fact, the analysis of preindustrial cities has been a significant research focus in recent years. Generalizations about preindustrial patterns are drawn from both contemporary analysis and historical documents. We should not conclude from these broad generalizations, however, that there is great uniformity in preindustrial urban patterns; if anything, preindustrial cities are more different from one another than are industrial cities.

Like industrial cities, preindustrial urban areas are often made up of people with divergent cultural traditions, and consequently exhibit rather sharp residential differentiation among ethnic and immigrant groups. Similarly, social class lines are perhaps even stronger than in the modern city. The variable which does not emerge very strongly in the preindustrial city is life-cycle stage. There seem to be few subareas in preindustrial cities which can be characterized in terms of the age or family status of the residents, independently of social class (Abu-Lughod 1969). The reasons for this include the prevalence of the extended family structure, the inflexibility of the housing market, low family incomes, and low residential mobility. These factors cause the generations to live together to a much greater degree than in the modern city, and permit much less choice in family structure and life style. Indeed, the degree to which life-cycle stage emerges as a distinct and important variable has been suggested as a measure of how "modernized" an urban social structure is (Timms 1971, chap. 4).

There is evidence which suggests that where the two variables of social class and life-cycle stage are merged in a preindustrial city, the social class variable tends to have a concentric zonal pattern around the city center; that is, the sectorial pattern of class distribution typical of the industrial city is not commonly found in preindustrial settings (Caplow 1949; Abu-Lughod 1969). In preindustrial cities, the social class level falls with distance from the center of the city (see Sjöberg 1960, 1965). The rich and the middle class live close to the centers of commercial, governmental, and religious activity for reasons of accessibility, protection, and the availability of desired utilities and other services. The poor, consequently, live in concentric zones which are peripheral to the city (and often, in medieval times, outside the city walls entirely). This pattern shows up today in many towns and cities of the Third World, where—unlike in the United States—it is often the poor who live on the hilltops in "suburban" areas. Commonly, these areas lack the city services which may exist within the city proper, such as water, sewerage, electricity, and transportation.

As our example of a planned industrial city we shall consider Stockholm, Sweden, the largest city (pop. about 1.3 million) in a country with a standard of living which is similar to that of the United States. The urban development of Stockholm has been the focus of intensive public analysis, planning, and control (Sidenbladh 1965), and it quite instructive to see how the result compares with cities in the United States which have been developed mainly by private real estate entrepreneurs (who, in turn, are guided by individual consumer decisions).

As in other industrial cities, the social class and life cycle variables emerge in Stockholm as both strong and very distinct from one another (Janson 1971). Residential differentiation of the rich and poor is quite pronounced. However, the differences between the rich and poor areas do not seem as great as in the United States because of greater class equality in Sweden; there is also characteristically a high degree of intermixing of working-class and middle-class persons, not only in each neighborhood but within each apartment building. With respect to life-cycle stage, Sweden has the highest percentage of one- and two-person households of any society in the world, due to such factors as low reproduction rates and the many older persons and young adults who live singly or in pairs. One study identified three strong life-cycle stage factors in Stockholm, young familism, established familism, and postfamilism (Janson

1972), indicating a high degree of residential differentiation in terms of the major stages of family development.

The main respect in which Stockholm differs from unplanned cities is in the overall urban spatial pattern with respect to social class (see Ödmann and Dahlberg 1970; William-Olsson 1961). Social class does not rise appreciably with distance from the center city. In this respect Stockholm more closely resembles the nineteenth-century and preindustrial patterns. The highest-class families live both in the central city area and in older, inner-lying suburbs of single-family homes. Higher-class areas in Stockholm do show a sectorial pattern, but it does not seem as clear-cut as in many American cities.

The working classes of Stockholm are much more evenly distributed within the metropolitan area than is the case in the United States. They share the inner city and close-lying suburban areas with the higher classes, but are also commonly found in the more distant and newer suburbs, many of which have been built by the government on major transportation lines at relatively high (apartment-building) densities.

In spite of the high densities which prevail in outlying suburban areas, the spatial pattern of the life-cycle variable seems to be quite similar to that found in unplanned cities. The familistic stage increases, in concentric zones, with distance from the center of the city, with the outer suburbs showing a preponderance of young families and the inner city catering disproportionately to one- and two-person households, especially those of older, often retired persons. Because of central planning, however, together with a tight housing market, one does not encounter the markedly age-homogeneous areas that are becoming common in the United States, especially for young, single adults and retired persons. While the extended family in one household is less commonly found in Sweden than anywhere on earth, the old, the young, and the middle-aged tend to live more proximate to one another (that is, within the same neighborhood and often the same apartment building) than is true in the unplanned cities of other advanced societies.

Stockholm's most striking difference from unplanned cities is the nearly complete absence of ethnic ghettos. Twenty-five years ago the population of Sweden was almost entirely homogeneous in ethnic terms, except for the Lapps and some immigrants from other Scandinavian countries. Today the population contains between 5 and 10 percent foreign born, most of whom live in Sweden's cities. This foreign population came to Stockholm at the time of a serious housing shortage. Because of that shortage (which is now mostly over), and because of government controls on the building and rental of housing, foreign immigrants were forced to scatter to many different parts of the metropolitan area. They were unable to become concentrated within single areas, blocks, or apartment buildings. The closest thing to a ghetto in Stockholm today is the high percentage of immigrants to be found in some of the most recently built suburban areas on the city's outskirts. These areas were built at the time of the highest rate of immigration of foreign labor, and provided the only sizable amount of vacant housing then on the market.

The scatteration of foreign immigrants (many into new housing units), the lack of real poverty in Sweden, and the relatively even geographic distribution of such lower-income population as does exist make Stockholm a slum-free city. Inadequate housing can still be found, but it has not been allowed to accumulate within areas—even small areas—of deterioration and blight. Furthermore, city services seem to be maintained at a high standard in all neighborhoods.

The case of Stockholm suggests that many of the trends and problems associated with residential differentiation in market-oriented societies like the United States (discussed in the next section)· are by no means inevitable. The planning and public control of urban development can make a difference.

VII. RESIDENTIAL DIFFERENTIATION IN THE UNITED STATES: TRENDS AND EMERGING PROBLEMS

Our task in this final section is to examine the dominant trends and associated social problems in the United States with respect to the three main social factors of residential differentiation: class, ethnicity, and life-cycle stage. We discussed in the last section some changes which have taken place with regard to these factors in the evolution from preindustrial to industrial urban environments. Here we shall discuss the changes involved in the evolution to *postindustrial* environments.

In order to develop an adequate grasp of social trends it is necessary to look not only at historical and comparative materials but also at the more "advanced" parts of a given society. In this section we shall concentrate on conditions in the most recently developed ·cities in the United States (e.g., Los Angeles) and in the most recently developed portions of metropolitan areas—the suburbs. These are the environments which can be referred to as postindustrial. They are characterized by a predominance of middle-class workers in service occupations (as opposed to working-class workers in industrial occupations), by automobile-oriented transportation systems (along with mass communications), and by low-density, single-family, detached dwellings (reflecting, especially, high affluence and automobile ownership) (see Popenoe 1971, chap. 13). From an evolutionary perspective, the postindustrial city is a stage of urban development as distinct from the industrial city of the nineteenth century as the latter is from the pre-industrial city.

In postindustrial urban settings we find that social class continues to be a major, perhaps the major, factor in accounting for residential clustering. In the Los Angeles area, for example, subcommunities and areas within subcommunities continue to be organized along class lines to a very marked degree (Greer and Kube 1959). However, they span a much larger geographic area than in earlier urban settings and they are more cut off from the greater community of which they are a part. This helps to account for why the Watts area of Los Angeles—a low-income, low-density, black community—was the scene of some of the earliest (and most severe) urban rioting of the 1960s. As a housing area Watts is superior to its eastern big-city counterparts. But it is as highly differentiated with respect to other areas (and internally as class-homogeneous) as any low-income area in these cities, and at the same time for reasons of geographic scale and poor accessibility it is "functionally" more isolated both from middle-class areas and from the full range of opportunities which urban living can bring. These characteristics seem to have contributed to the especially intense pressures on the citizens of Watts which triggered the violent behavior.

Of course Watts is strongly differentiated not only along class lines, but also along racial lines. The available evidence suggests that residential segregation by race has not diminished substantially in postindustrial settings; in fact, it may be more pronounced than ever. It is not entirely clear, however, to what extent racial segregation in postindustrial settings is increasingly class segregation, based on the very high degree of overlap between being black and having a low income (Banfield 1968). It is noteworthy that Oriental groups, which at one time were highly segregated in America, have become much more assimilated than blacks within postindustrial settings. At the same time, their income levels are much higher than blacks; indeed, in the case of Japanese-Americans the average income and class level are higher than for native-born Americans.

The other dimensions of the broad ethnic variable are religion and foreign heritage. Residential differentiation along these lines is significantly less in postindustrial than in preindustrial and industrial settings. The nineteenth-century city in America did perform fairly well as a melting pot in this regard. While the older cities themselves (e.g., New York City) are still quite highly differentiated in ethnic terms (Glazer and Moynihan 1963), the suburban areas around them (and the new cities in the West) contain much less residential segregation by religion and foreign heritage. The high degree to which, for example, Jews and Catholics, or Hungarians and Italians, are intermixed in many suburban areas (often living next door to one another) would have been regarded as amazing from the vantage point of an earlier time in American history (Gans 1967). This phenomenon reflects, on the one hand, the decreasing importance of institutional religion in American life, and, on the other, the rather complete assimilation of many foreign groups. The new patterns of post industrial urbanism not only reflect these larger social trends, however, but also help to shape them. When a Catholic and a Jew move side by side into a new suburban housing development (this is usually by accident rather than by design), it is reasonable to conclude, I think, that mutual understanding or a least tolerance is facilitated. At the same time, the influence of each religion over the lives of the respective families is probably weakened in the long run; minority traditions are best sustained in residential isolation. This phenomenon has become a source of particular concern in the American Jewish community.

Residential "ethnic homogenization" has not occurred, however, among groups which have remained at the lower levels of the class hierarchy, such as Mexican Americans in the Southwest. The ethnic homogenization discussed above does not indicate a weakening of class differentiation, but only that many ethnic and religious minorities have become middle-class, and that within predominantly middle-class and usually suburban settings they are increasingly intermixed.

What major problems does the continuing residential differentiation along class and racial lines create or exacerbate? The many problems associated with urban class and racial conflict are not significantly different from what they were in previous periods of urbanization; more importantly, they seem not to have diminished in the face of greater affluence and generally improved housing standards. There are three "new twists" in the postindustrial urban setting which deserve special attention, however.

First, the scale of metropolitan development combined with the preexisting pattern of rural originated local government jurisdictions in many urbanized areas means that it is quite common for rich and poor, or black and white, to fall under different local governments, as well as into different geographic subareas (see Wood 1961). In the older cities, these groups have usually been in the same government jurisdiction. The postindustrial pattern helps to give local government in metropolitan areas a surprisingly benign character in the face of all problems. Rich and poor outside the central cities seldom face one another across the political table; their local governmental structures are completely separate from one another. The political reconciliation between rich and poor or black and white could perhaps best take place at the metropolitan level, but at this level there is usually no governmental apparatus at all. Problems therefore either do not get resolved, which is often the case, or the confrontation takes place at state and national levels or through the mass media. In any event, local government becomes ever further removed from the capacity to deal with serious urban issues.

Second is the matter of the "invisible poor." In the 1950s there was widespread discussion of America as an affluent nation in which problems of poverty had been for the most part resolved. Then, in a series of events which led eventually to the War on Poverty in the Kennedy and Johnson administrations, the poor (in surprisingly large numbers, amounting to perhaps 20 to 30 percent of the nation's population) were "rediscovered" (Harrington 1962). The poor had of course been there all along; they were merely somewhat "invisible." In the smaller-sized cities of an earlier period, the poor were always near at hand (and in small villages, almost under foot). The poor and the middle and upper classes met in the market-place, in the political arena, and often in the place of business, though they lived apart. The same degree of residential differentiation on the metro-politan scale, however, means that the chances of such contacts are greatly diminished. The upper-middle-class business or professional leader who lives in a wealthy suburb may never have first-hand contact with the poor if he works near where he lives, and he may have only very slight contact with poverty if he travels to and from the city each day on a commuter train, going from rich ghetto to central business district and back again.

The third serious problem connected with the trends of class and racial-ethnic differentiation is the plight of the old central cities. The pre-industrial urban spatial pattern of the rich in the cities and the poor on the outskirts has been, as we have seen, precisely reversed. The poor have "inherited" the preindustrial and industrial urban settings, while the wealthier classes have moved on (or out) into the new postindustrial settings. While the type of person living in old center cities has changed markedly, however, the physical environment has not—except by way of deterioration. Buildings which were once adequate for persons of means with small families are internally carved up for the poor with large fami-lies; cultural facilities formerly used by the well educated become white elephants; retail shops (and entire districts), once intended for the afflu-ent, fall into decline. To make matters worse, an environment which is obsolescent and deteriorating falls under the care of persons who can least afford the cost of maintenance, resulting in a major imbalance between problems and resources. The plight of the old cities is of course greatly compounded by the fact that a high percentage of the urban poor are black, and this percentage is increasing. What is mainly a problem of poverty in most older cities of the modern world is often in the United States a dual problem of race and poverty.

It is often said that the age of cities—meaning the nineteenth-century industrial city—is over (Gutkind 1962). This statement is based on the trends that we have been discussing. Cities built in the twentieth century (at least in the United States) have assumed a distinct "noncity" pattern. The older cities are in serious economic and physical decline, and there is every indication that many of their present inhabitants don't want to live in them: the current urban poor head for the suburbs when the oppor-tunity arises, just as their predecessors did. (It is also of great significance that there are no immigrant groups on the horizon to replace the current urban dwellers when they leave the city, which creates an inner-city "vacuum" in the fields of housing, shopping, and so on.) Furthermore, governmental efforts have so far been ineffective either in stemming the economic deterioration of cities or in bringing the middle class back in significant numbers. While the "age of the cities," then, may well be coming to an end, the transitional period has generated some of the most serious domestic problems of our time.

Now let us turn to the third of the major differentiating variables. Probably the most striking trend of residential differentiation in post-industrial settings is toward increased segregation by stage in the life cycle (Greer et al. 1968). The postindustrial city can be said to be the first type of settlement in human history in which, to a relatively large degree, age groups are residentially segregated from one another, and families are segregated from persons outside the family status. Affluence, high residential mobility, and "spatial flexibility" permit local residential environments to become rather highly specialized along these lines. The three groups which are differentiating the fastest are young, single adults, families with children, and senior citizens. To some extent, families themselves are even becoming segregated into areas characterized by different stages of family development—young familism, mature familism and post familism. It is clear that each of these groups has somewhat distinct needs and interests, and that distinct residential environments can be designed specifically to cater to these differences. What is not yet clear, however, are the long-run effects which this geographic separation of ages and families has on the persons involved.

Geographic separation implies, at the very least, a weakening of daily physical contact among these various groups, in spite of the high-technology transportation to be found in postindustrial settings. Images of children without grandparents, young adults with no guidance from their elders, senior citizens split apart from their families, and trapped suburban housewives have become common in American culture, and they are all directly related to the phenomenon in question (Packard 1972). More broadly, we exhibit a growing concern about the generation gap; the latter may be a cause but is also a product of residential age differentiation.

While there are of course certain social advantages to such specialized local environments—otherwise they would not be built—the disadvantages at least deserve more public discussion and attention. There are three main ones. First, these specialized environments foster residential mobility, which already may be excessive in modern societies. As a person's age or family status changes, he often has to move to a new and sometimes distant community in order to secure the kind of housing which is best suited to his changed needs. This helps to make community living for many Americans a vast game of musical chairs. "Unnecessary" residential mobility could be diminished if persons who merely have different needs for housing space because of life-cycle changes were able to stay in the same neighborhood or community. This would require a far greater diversity of residential accommodations and neighborhood services than is to be found in the typical suburban area at present.

Second, specialization of subcommunities by life-cycle stage generates a lack of diversity in the local environment. This is especially important for those persons whose local residential environment is their principal life environment, for example, the "trapped" housewife in "suburbia." She may be surrounded by a sea of other housewives with young children, sometimes without baby-sitters (teen-agers reside in the areas for more mature families) and often without grandmothers and older persons to help with household activities. This is not to say that all suburbs are like this, or that there are not many ways in which such suburbs are more "efficient" for child raising than other kinds of communities. It does suggest that much, perhaps much of great importance, is lost in those suburbs which specialize exclusively in young families.

Third, and most intangible, is the weakening of the life cycle as a psychological and cultural reality. Anthropologists often note the sense of life's "wholeness" which is found in primitive villages, where birth and death, childhood and old age, youth and maturity, are all commingled into the daily round of life. This seems to generate a perspective and feeling of belonging on the part of persons at each life stage which is missing in modern societies. Birth and death take place away from others, usually in hospitals; residential differentiation increasingly separates childhood and old age, youth and maturity. It is true that man's spatial range has become greatly extended through technologies of transportation and communications, and that the average adult is not restricted significantly to the local residential environment. The missing cycle-of-life reality may be of greatest significance during the childhood years, therefore, when the local environment looms far greater in significance. These are of course the formative and hence most important years in a person's life.

In conclusion, residential differentiation continues to have a highly problematic character in the United States. Yet as our Stockholm comparison suggests, it is reasonable to suppose that many of these problems are mitigated in those advanced societies where housing and residential location are more subject to collective decision making and planning. One overriding public policy question about residential differentiation remains unanswered in every modern society, however. How can we assure individuals the friendliness, stability, and sense of attachment that come with homogeneous neighborhood groupings—people living with their own kind —yet at the same time foster the equality, opportunity, and balance that are associated with community heterogeneity and diversity? The sociological study of residential differentiation will, it is to be hoped, be able to shed more light on this most important issue over the next few years.

REFERENCES

Abu-Lughod, J. L.
1969 "Testing the theory of social area analysis: the ecology of Cairo, Egypt," *American Sociological Review* 34: 198–212.

Banfield, E. C.
1968 *The Unheavenly City*. Boston: Little Brown.

Bell, W.
1959 "Social areas: typology of urban neighborhoods," in M. Sussman (ed.) *Community Structure and Analysis*.
1968 "The city, the suburb and a theory of social choice," in S. Greer et al. (eds.) *The New Urbanization*.
———, and S. Greer.
1962 "Social area analysis and its critics," *Pacific Sociological Review* 5: 3–9.

Berry, B. J. L.
1965 "Internal structure of the city," *Law and Contemporary Problems* 30: 111–119.
1971 (ed.) *Comparative Factorial Ecology*. Special issue of *Economic Geography*. Worcester, Mass.: Clark University Press.

Beshers, J. M.
1962 *Urban Social Structure*. New York: The Free Press.

Burgess, E. W.
1925 "The growth of the city," in R. E. Park, E. W. Burgess, and R. D. McKenzie (eds.) *The City*. Chicago. Reprinted in G. H. Theodorson (ed.) *Studies in Human Ecology*.

Caplow, T.
1949 "The social ecology of Guatemala City," *Social Forces* 28: 113–133. Reprinted in G. A. Theodorson (ed.) *Studies in Human Ecology*.

Coleman, J. S.
1970 "Properties of collectivities," in J. Coleman, A. Etzioni, and J. Porter. *Macrosociology: Research and Theory*. Boston: Allyn and Bacon, 5–101.

Dogan, M., and S. Rokkan (eds.).
1969 *Quantitative Ecological Analysis in the Social Sciences*. Cambridge: MIT.

Duncan, O. D., and B. Duncan.
1955 "Residential differentiation and occupational stratification," *American Journal of Sociology* IX: 493–503.

Feldman, A. S., and C. Tilly.
1960 "The interaction of social and physical space," *American Sociological Review* XXV: 877–884.

Foote, N. et al.
1960 *Housing Choices and Housing Constraints*. New York: McGraw Hill.

Gans, H. J.
1962 "Urbanism and suburbanism as ways of life," in A. M. Rose (ed.) *Human Behavior and Social Processes*. Boston: Houghton Mifflin, 625–648.
1967 *The Levittowners*. New York: Pantheon Books.

Glazer, N., and D. P. Moynihan.
1963 *Beyond the Melting Pot*. Cambridge: MIT Press.

Gordon, M. M.
1964 *Assimilation in American Life*. New York: Oxford University Press.

Greer, S. et al. (eds.).
1968 *The New Urbanization*. New York: St. Martins Press.

————, and E. Kube.
1959 "Urbanism and social structure: a Los Angeles study," in M. Sussman (ed.) *Community Structure and Analysis.*

Gutkind, E. A.
1962 *The Twilight of Cities.* New York: The Free Press.

Gutman, R., and D. Popenoe (eds.).
1970 *Neighborhood, City and Metropolis: An Integrated Reader in Urban Sociology.* New York: Random House.

Harrington, M.
1962 *The Other Americans.* New York: Macmillan.

Harris, C. D., and E. L. Ullman.
1945 "The nature of cities," *Annals of the American Academy of Political and Social Science* 242: 7–17.

Hauser, P. M., and L. Schnore (eds.).
1965 *The Study of Urbanization.* New York: John Wiley.

Hawley, A.
1950 *Human Ecology: A Theory of Community Structure.* New York: Ronald.

Hoyt, H.
1939 *The Structure and Growth of Residential Neighborhoods in American Cities.* Washington: Federal Housing Administration.

Janson, C. G.
1971 "A preliminary report on Swedish spatial structure," *Economic Geography* 47: 249–257.
1972 "Social differentiation in urban areas." Stockholm: Swedish National Building Research Center. (Mimeo)

Johnston, R. J.
1971 *Urban Residential Patterns.* London: G. Bell and Sons.

Keller, S.
1968 *The Urban Neighborhood.* New York: Random House.

Lansing, J., and L. D. Kish.
1957 "Family life cycle as an independent variable," *American Sociological Review* 22: 512–519.

Lieberson, S.
1963 *Ethnic Patterns in American Cities.* New York: The Free Press.

McElrath, D. C.
1965 "Urban differentiation: problems and prospects," *Law and Contemporary Problems* 30.

Michelson, W.
1970 *Man and His Urban Environment.* Reading, Mass.: Addison-Wesley.

Ödmann, E., and G. B. Dahlberg.
1970 *Urbanization in Sweden.* Stockholm: Allmänna Förlaget.

Packard, V.
1972 *A Nation of Strangers.* New York: David McKay.

Popenoe, D.
1971 *Sociology.* New York: Appleton-Century-Crofts.

Robson, B. T.
1969 *Urban Analysis.* Cambridge University Press.

Rossi, P. H.
1955 *Why Families Move.* New York: The Free Press.

Scherer, J.
1972 *Contemporary Community: Sociological Illusion or Reality.* London.

Schmid, C. F.
1950 "Generalizations concerning the ecology of the American city," *American Sociological Review* XV: 264–281.
———, E. H. MacCannell, and M. D. Van Arsdol, Jr.
1958 "The ecology of the American city: further comparisons and validation of generalizations," *American Sociological Review* XXIII: 392–401.
Schnore, L. F.
1965 *The Urban Scene: Human Ecology and Demography.* New York: The Free Press.
Shevky, E., and W. Bell.
1955 *Social Area Analysis.* Stanford: Stanford University Press.
Sidenbladh, G. A.
1965 "Stockholm: a planned city," *Scientific American,* September 107–118.
Sjoberg, G.
1960 *The Pre-Industrial City.* New York: The Free Press.
1965 "Cities in developing and industrial societies," in: Hauser and Schnore (eds.) *The Study of Urbanization,* 213–263.
Sussman, M. (ed.).
1959 *Community Structure and Analysis.* New York: Crowell.
Suttles, G.
1972 *The Social Construction of Communities.* Chicago: University of Chicago Press.
Taeuber, K. E., and A. F. Taeuber.
1965 *Negroes in Cities.* Chicago: Aldine.
Theodorson, G. A. (ed.).
1961 *Studies in Human Ecology.* Evanston, Ill.: Harper and Row.
Timms, D. W. G.
1971 *The Urban Mosaic.* Cambridge: Cambridge University Press.
Webber, M.
1963 "Order in Diversity: Community without Propinquity," in L. Wingo, Jr. (ed.) *Cities and Space.* Baltimore: Johns Hopkins Press.
Wellman, B.
1972 "Who needs neighborhoods?" in A. Powell (ed.) *Urban Myths and Realities.* Toronto: McClelland and Stewart.
———, et al.
1972 "Community Ties and Support Systems." Toronto: University of Toronto, Center for Urban and Community Studies. (Mimeo)
Wilhelm, S.
1962 *Urban Zoning and Land Use Theory.* New York: The Free Press.
William-Olsson, W.
1961 *Stockholm: Structure and Development.* Stockholm: Almqvist and Wiksell.
Wirth, L.
1938 "Urbanism as a way of life," *American Journal of Sociology* 44: 1–24.
Wood, R. C.
1961 *1400 Governments.* Cambridge: Harvard University Press.

The Network City*

PAUL CRAVEN and BARRY WELLMAN

University of Toronto

The network approach to urban studies can be differentiated from other approaches by its emphasis on the primacy of structures of interpersonal linkages, rather than on the classification of social units according to their individual characteristics. Network analysis is also a methodology for the investigation of these structures. Substantive issues related to interpersonal ties in the city, migration, resource allocation, neighborhood, and community are examined in terms of the network structures and processes that order and integrate urban activities. Finally, a view of the city itself as a network of networks is proposed. It is the organization of urban life by networks that makes the scale and diversity of the city a source of strength rather than of chaos, while it is precisely that scale and diversity which makes the existence of a complex and widely ramified network structure possible.

The rich, and often bewildering, complexity of social life in the city is such that the sociologist who would seek to understand it has

*The advice and work of Charles Tilly and Harrison White have been seminal in the undertaking of urban network analyses as well as in the preparation of this paper. Ann Shorter's incisive editing helped us to clarify our writing. Many of the ideas in this paper were developed in informal interaction with: colleagues on the "Community Ties and Support Systems" project: Albert S. Gates, Ann Shorter, Harvey Stevens, Deborah Tannenbaum, and Marilyn Whitaker (We are additionally grateful for their assistance in preparing this paper); present (and past) colleagues at the University of Toronto: Stephen Berkowitz, (D. B. Coates), Harriet Friedmann, Leslie Howard, Nancy Howell, Graham Lowe, William Michelson, (Norman Shulman), Lorne Tepperman, (Charles Tilly), Jack Wayne, and Beverly Wellman; fellow participants in the conference on "Do Networks Matter?", held in June, 1972, in Camden, Maine, convened by Harrison White under the auspices of the (U. S.) Mathematical Social Sciences Board; Blanche Pearce of the Federation of Ontario Housing Residents' Associations, and Joel Levine of Dartmouth College. We are grateful to Elaine DuWors, Department of Sociology, University of Toronto, for typing the final manuscript. The "Community Ties and Support Systems" research project has been assisted under Province of Ontario Health Research Grant No. P.R. 196, the Laidlaw Foundation, and the Canada Council, under the auspices of the Centre for Urban and Community Studies, University of Toronto. Students in the 1973 "Urban Workshop," Department of Sociology, University of Toronto, provided penetrating critiques of an earlier draft of this paper.

always had to adopt some strategy of analysis by which to guide his inquiry. More often than not, he has approached this problem by way of a simple "sorting" strategy. He has grouped individuals and institutions into various pigeonholes, representing their individual social or organizational characteristics, so that people might be sorted into slots such as "middle-class"; institutions might be classified as "social agencies"; localities might be tagged as "suburbia." Once the units have been sorted into categories according to their independent characteristics, the sociologist classically proceeds to make sense of the classification scheme through the comparison of inhabitants of different slots. He might endeavor to find out, for example, whether "working-class suburbanites" interact more than "middle-class suburbanites," or whether "partisan" or "nonpartisan" city governments are more effective in policy implementation

In this paper we hope to show that a quite different strategy of analysis is available—one which gives priority to the way social life is organized, that is, through empirically observable systems of interaction and reliance, systems of resource allocation, and systems of integration and coordination. Sociologists who take this approach see the city not so much as a conglomeration of people and institutions but rather as a multitude of social networks, overlapping and interacting in various ways. This approach emphasizes such questions as "Who is linked to whom?", "What is the content of their relationship?", and "What is the structure of their relational network?"

The significance of these kinds of questions will be explored in the pages that follow. For the time being, we should note that matters of classification and categorization of individual social units are not completely done away with in this model; rather, they yield in importance to the structures of social interaction. Consequently, when classification is introduced it is always in the context of interactional systems, rather than in an abstract and reified way.

It remains, however, the fundamental concern of network analysis to inquire into the nature of interactional and organizational links between social units. Network studies of the city can be seen both as a perspective leading us to concentrate on certain kinds of data and certain kinds of questions, and as a methodology for the analysis of those data.

Fortunately, much data has already been collected on the kinds of interpersonal relations maintained by urbanites. In addition to analyzing simple two-person ties, sociologists have begun to look at the complex structure of social linkages in the city, examining networks of relationships between institutions as well as interpersonal networks. Using data specifically collected for network study, or recasting data collected within the framework of other approaches, these investigators can make use of mathematical techniques which help generate insights that may be nonobvious and counterintuitive. For example, matrix algebra is used to elicit information about important "indirect" ties between people or institutions not directly or obviously related to each other. (See below.)

Unfortunately, little in the way of a comprehensive overview or evaluation of urban network research has appeared to date (but see Mitchell 1969; Bott 1971; Barnes 1972; Tilly 1973). Indeed, much of the work is so recent that it has not yet found its way into the academic journals. Furthermore, many of the studies of urban ties discussed in this paper were performed before a self-conscious strategy of network analysis in urban studies had developed. While it is quite beyond our scope in this paper to provide such an overview, we shall attempt to outline the contributions such analyses have made to the elucidation of some key problems in urban studies, and to organize this paper around these issues. First, we shall discuss more precisely what is meant by the term "social network," and how such networks might be studied. Then we shall discuss some basic issues in urban studies in terms of network analysis. We shall begin with the microsociological issue of the nature of interpersonal ties in the city, and end with the macrosociological question of the social organization, integration, and coordination of the city as a whole. It is our belief: (1) that most urban phenomena can be best comprehended through the analysis of network processes, and (2) that networks enable effective use to be made of the city's size and diversity by facilitating connections between urban individuals, communities, groups, and organizations which enhance their coordinated specialized activities.[1]

WHAT IS A SOCIAL NETWORK?

A good general definition of social networks is given by Mitchell (1962: 2), who says that a network is "a specific set of linkages among a defined set of persons, with the . . . property that the characteristics of these linkages as a whole may be used to interpret the social behavior of the persons involved." For our purposes, we would have to expand this definition somewhat and point out that the units linked together to form a network need not necessarily be individual persons but may be other, larger, social units as well. They may be, for example, families, tribes, corporations, or complexes of corporations. In the case of corporations, to be sure, linkages such as interlocking directorships may appear to be between individual people, but in this context these people are representatives of corporations, and the latter are the true units of analysis.[2]

There are two widely used methods of representing social networks on paper: by means of a graph or by means of a matrix. A graph is a picture of a social network, with points on the page representing the units and lines between the points representing links. The lines may have arrowheads indicating whether the links are relationships that go in both directions or only in one "direction." For example, a relationship such as "being a brother" always goes in two directions; i.e., it is reciprocal, or symmetric.

If Joe is a brother of Tom, then Tom is a brother of Joe. Other relationships such as "being a debtor," go in only one direction; they are nonreciprocal (asymmetric). And some relationships, such as "feels close to," may be either reciprocal or nonreciprocal. Figure 1 is a graphic representation of a hypothetical social network of five individuals.

Figure 1

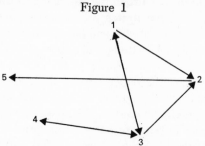

Graphic Representation of a Social Network of Five Individuals

If we assume that the points numbered one through five in Figure 1 represent people, and that the lines between them represent the relationship "feels close to," then we can interpret the graph of this network as follows: person 1 feels close to persons 2 and 3, while person 3 in return feels close to person 1. Person 2 feels close to person 5 and person 3 feels close to person 2, but neither of these relationships is reciprocated. Finally, persons 3 and 4 feel close to each other.

While graphs are useful visual representations of networks, matrix representations are more useful for mathematical analysis. The network of Figure 1 can be represented by a matrix of five rows and five columns, one row and one column corresponding to each member of the network. The presence or absence of links between members can be indicated by placing a 1 or 0, respectively, in the appropriate cell of the matrix. The diagonal cells, representing the relationships of individuals to themselves, remain empty. Using this method, the matrix representation of this network looks like Figure 2.

Figure 2

To:	1	2	3	4	5
1	–	1	1	0	0
2	0	–	0	0	1
From: 3	1	1	–	1	0
4	0	0	1	–	1
5	0	0	0	0	–

Matrix Representation of the Same Social Network as in Figure 1

Figure 3

To:	1	2	3	4	5
1	1	1	0	1	1
2	0	0	0	0	0
From: 3	0	1	2	0	1
4	1	1	0	1	0
5	0	0	0	0	0

Matrix of Indirect Paths of Length Two for the Same Social Network

We read Figure 2 as "row is related to column"; that is, the "1" in row 2 and column 5 represents the linkage extending *from* person 2 *to* person 5. The number of nondiagonal cells in the matrix is, clearly, the total number of possible linkages between the units; this quantity is equal to

$n(n-1)$, where n is the number of units. The sum of all the "1s" in the matrix is the actual number of links in the network. Using these two quantities, we can derive a "density" measure of the extent to which units in the network are linked to one another. The formula $100a/p$, where a is the actual number and p the maximum possible number of links, gives us the density of the network in the form of a percentage. This is the simplest form of a family of measures, known as "knit," "density," "mesh," etc., which represent the relative proliferation of interactional ties among members of a network.

Since density is a ratio measure, it should not be considered without also taking into account the *range* of the network, that is, the number of members. A dense network with few members may have quite different characteristics from one with equal density and many members. Thus these two measures, density and range, together constitute the basis for investigating the structural properties of networks.

So far we have considered only the case of direct linkages between network members. In Figure 1, for instance, person 1 is, in this sense, linked to person 2 but not to person 5. Bearing in mind the analogy of information flow, however, we can appreciate that there is a sense in which person 1 is indirectly linked to person 5 through the intermediary person 2. If we use the term "path" to refer to both direct and indirect linkages, then we can say that person 1 is linked to person 2 by a path with a length of one link, and to person 5 by a path with a length of two links. If we examine the graph, we will notice that there is a second linkage between person 1 and person 2, viz., a path of length two with person 3 as an intermediary. The implications of considering *indirect links*—paths with a length greater than one—will become clear when we investigate the notion of interpersonal ties in the city.

Matrix representation is a powerful tool in the consideration of paths longer than length one. By mathematically manipulating a simple matrix of the type illustrated in Figure 2, we can easily calculate the existence of paths of various lengths. To find paths of length two, we square the matrix; for paths of length three we cube it; and so on. Figure 3 is the square of the matrix in Figure 2. The cell entries indicate the number of length-two paths in our hypothetical five-person network. (See, e.g., Dorf 1969, for matrix multiplication procedures.)

Note that the diagonal cells in Figure 3 do not remain empty. For instance, one entry indicates the existence of a path of length two linking person 1 with himself. Looking back to Figure 1, we can see that this path has person 3 as an intermediary. Normally we are not concerned with such reflexive paths and exclude them from the analysis. A roughly analogous situation obtains when we find that paths of differing lengths exist between the same pair of points. In our example, we find paths of lengths one and two between persons 1 and 2. For most analytic purposes, we would concern ourselves only with the shortest path between two points (excluding longer ones from the analysis) or with the fact that a path does exist, of whatever length, between two points. Which of these options is in fact chosen depends on the nature of the analysis.

So far as the formal manipulation of network structures is concerned, we need not go much further than this for purposes of this paper.[3] We should discuss, however, the two common strategies of network research and the implications these have for analysis.

We can call the first of these the *whole-network* strategy: a depiction of *all* the linkages among *all* the units who are members of a particular population, that population having been defined beforehand by nonnetwork criteria. This population will be, at least for analytic purposes, a closed one; it might be a tribe, a school, a city, or a list of dominant corporations. Thus this approach requires that we have, first, a list of all the units in the population, and second, a list of all the direct linkages between those units. Clearly this strategy is most feasible in the case of small, visible, and clearly bounded populations, and for this reason it has been more or less the preserve of social anthropologists working in small, often isolated, societies (see, e.g., Mitchell 1969).[4]

For urban studies in the North American context, the whole-network strategy is usually impractical. The costs of mapping an entire city's population would be enormous. On the other hand, attempts to set more restrictive boundaries on the population to be studied are likely to be illegitimate because they assume a priori the existence of the very phenomena to be investigated. The establishment of a rigid classification scheme prior to empirical examination runs the risk of forcing the data to fit pre-conceived notions. If, for example, one looks for the existence of communities only within neighborhood boundaries, one will find only those communities that exist *within* the neighborhood.

A second strategy, and one quite commonly used for urban network studies, may be called the *personal-network* strategy. The word "personal" here should not be taken to imply that the unit of analysis is always an individual. Rather, the term indicates a network built from a single unit, which is, in a sense, that unit's network. The strategy involves choosing a starting unit—one individual randomly chosen from the population, for example—and asking him for a list of all the other units to which he is linked. Each of these can then be asked to supply a list, and the process can be repeated as often as necessary for the purposes of the particular research enterprise.

Most investigations, of course, do not confine themselves to starting with a single ego; rather, they study a sample of personal networks, derived from a sample of egos. As the ratio of sample to population approaches 1:1, of course, there is a convergence between the whole-network strategy and the personal-network strategy. Perhaps the major strength of the latter strategy is that it permits sampling from a large population when it would be unmanageable to study the whole network.

The kind of information we have about the structure of a network will be determined by the particular strategy we are using. In the case of the personal-network strategy, since we are dealing with a sample of the whole population it is quite unlikely that the list of Alters provided by any one of our chosen Egos will correspond exactly to any other list, so, in contrast to the whole-network strategy, we will have no single depiction of the network constituted by the whole population. In the whole-network studies, of course, the network will look the same regardless of the point at which we begin to map it. It is possible to do a thorough structural analysis when data on whole networks are available; the statistical study of personal networks inevitably forces us into a partial categorization analysis, with aspects of the networks being units of analysis.

The personal-network approach enables us, through the use of surveys, interviews, participant observations, and so on, to obtain information about a relatively large number of personal networks (see, for example, Laumann 1973; Shulman 1972; Wayne 1971). Information about the links between the alters of any given network may be elicited by asking the Ego informants to report on these links, or, more ambitiously and with the advantage of eliminating the error latent in second-hand reports, a "snowballing" approach may be taken in which each Ego's Alters are themselves approached for information about their personal networks and linkages with one another. Each person's network will then be treated as a unit of data to be subjected to statistical analysis for comparisons among networks. Some of the different approaches to the analysis of data acquired through the personal-network strategy will become apparent in our substantive discussion below.

Whereas networks, of either the "whole" or the "personal" variety, are visualized and analyzed as fixed sets of linkages among fixed social units, the actual ties between specific people are likely to vary in their content and intensity, and indeed in their very existence over time. Most network analyses provide a snapshot depiction of ties "frozen" at the moment of investigation. The persistence of ties or of the entire network structure over time is an important theoretical and empirical question which has been but scantily studied.

We shall now leave the realm of definitions, procedures, and methodological concerns in order to examine some substantive issues toward which the study of urban networks is directed.

KEY ISSUES IN STUDYING URBAN NETWORKS

The network perspective is applicable to a wide range of problems concerning the relations of individuals and collectivities in the city. In this paper, we will focus on a series of key issues in order to provide some basic insight into the usefulness of the method. The network approach is seen by the present writers not as constituting a wholesale replacement for the more traditional "categorical" approach, but rather as a fresh perspective that permits us to pose new and, we believe, important questions within the domain of urban sociology. Using the network approach, we shall attempt here to illuminate urban social structure and process and to show how data collected with a sensitivity to the existence of interpersonal ties has permitted us to take a fresh look at social life in the city.

A presentation in terms of key issues always involves some problems of organization. We have chosen to present the issues in a sequential way, so that each section represents a widening of focus to include broader and more complex questions. To start with, we inquire into the microsociological question of the nature of interpersonal ties in the city. Having established their existence and discussed their nature, we look at the ways in which these ties serve to structure the adaptation of new migrants to city life, involving them in networks of social relationships in the city. Then we examine how personal networks function in providing city dwellers with access to various tangible and nontangible resources. Our focus then shifts to the multiple communities to which urbanites belong. This involves a discussion of the importance of spatiality in network terms. Finally, we attempt an analytic overview of the city as a whole, viewed as a network of networks. Not surprisingly, as we move on to consider larger social structures, these structures reveal themselves to constitute networks of ever greater complexity.

The Nature of Interpersonal Ties in the City

Suppose we were to construct a matrix for the acquaintanceship links among the inhabitants of an idealized rural community with a population of approximately 1000. Most of the entries in such a matrix would be 1s, for by and large our villagers would be acquainted with one another, as friends, lovers, kinsmen, enemies, or merely fellow villagers. If we were now to construct a set of matrices using more restrictive criteria than acquaintanceship—such as kinship, coworkership, or exchanging mutual help—we would find fewer 1 entries in each of these new matrices, but we would probably find that people who are related in terms of any one criterion are related in terms of others as well. It is common, in our idealized village, for kinsmen to be neighbors, or to work at the same job. In so far as this is so, there is little segregation of relationships according to specific contexts; a kinsman is not a neighbor by day and an uncle by night, but rather a "neighboring uncle." Additionally, we would find that most of the residents' primary ties are contained within the boundaries of the village and the neighboring farms, the major exceptions to this rule being ties to some emigrant kinfolk and the relationships of those political and economic "brokers" whose responsibilities entail contact with "outsiders" (see Wolf 1956).

But the construction of a similar acquaintanceship matrix for inhabitants of a metropolis would yield a relatively small number of 1 entries, and a plethora of 0s. It is not so much that the city dweller has fewer acquaintances than our villagers, but rather that he has a great many more strangers. His access to many city dwellers is not through direct relations of acquaintanceship, but rather through complex networks of indirect relationships, or through formal channels. The scale of the city and the division of labor and roles within it make it far less likely that a matrix of the urbanite's neighboring relationships would be very similar to a matrix of his work relationships, his kinship relationships, or his relationships of mutual aid. These matrices might not be completely different from each other, however, for even in the most complex of large-scale cities we observe a tendency for people linked in one way to form links along other dimensions. Friends may each get jobs in the same plant or become neighbors, for example, or friendship ties may be used to gain business advantages. All the same, the networks of primary relationships for many urbanites are, to a far greater extent than for the villagers, different for each mode of relationship. As a result, an urbanite faces the relational task of coordinating and manipulating these many networks, with their diverse demands and resources.

For quite a long time, many urban scholars confused the sparsity and narrow definitions of ties in the city with their absence. In part, this arose out of a fascination with the sheer scale and complexity of the modern city, and the manifest visibility of large corporate entities as important components of it (see Wirth 1938; Nisbet 1953; Stein 1960). Complementing this was a wistful nostalgia for the idealized community of bygone days, where (so we are told) all knew one another at the village green, even if that knowledge was sometimes a vicious one (see Marx 1964; White and White 1962). In part, there was a dogged insistence upon searching for interpersonal ties on the scale of the old village community—the urban neighborhood—and an unwillingness to expand the scale of the analysis to encompass the metropolis and beyond. About the time of World War II, however, careful ethnographic and survey research into interpersonal relationships in the city began to replace the more impressionistic writings of the earlier period (see the annotated bibliography in Wellman and Whitaker 1972). Lamenting the passing of interpersonal relationships ceased to be fashionable; the dominant concern was now to trace the qualitative effects on such relationships of the characteristics of the modern city.

Among such effects has been the "unbundling" of relationships in the city, which we have seen reflected in the disparity of relational matrices for urban dwellers. Matrices based on any given particular relationship are dissimilar from those based on other kinds of relationship. People still live in neighborhoods, but (by and large) only a few of their neighbors are likely to be close friends, relatives, or coworkers. Instead, a specific neighboring relationship of low-intensity "nodding" acquaintanceship, with some visiting and non-onerous mutual aid, has developed (see Jacobs 1961; Keller 1968). To be sure, the differentiation is not complete, as there has remained some tendency for people who are close friends, relatives, or coworkers to want to live near one another. Modern transportation and communication media are not sufficient—and may never be sufficient—to overcome the costs of not having readily available personal contact. One's neighbors are not a random assortment of urbanites; on the contrary, networks of migration, and the sorting processes associated with such factors as socioeconomic status, ethnicity, life style, and life-cycle stage, make it likely that many urban neighbors will share many fundamental social attributes.

We now know that, although the people to whom they are linked may be dispersed throughout the metropolis, city dwellers remain enmeshed in intense and intimate relations of friendship, kinship, and mutual assistance. In our own research in Toronto, we have found that nearly ninety per cent of all urbanites have at least one person outside of the home to whom they feel close; most have at least four (Wellman et al. 1973). This remains true regardless of socioeconomic status, and at all stages of the life cycle. The "lonely urbanite living in a state of social disorganization" seems to be largely the invention of social pathologists in search of an object of study.

To the surprise of many sociologists, kinship has remained an important relationship for most urbanites, although the implications of the kinship tie have undoubtedly changed. Fully half of the intimates of the Torontonians in our study are kin, mostly parents, siblings, or children. Formerly, one was "stuck" with one's relatives, who lived in the same community and had normatively enforceable claims in several areas of life. To a certain extent, then, the city has had a liberating effect, as increased social and physical mobility has enabled a person to form relationships on the basis of a community of interest to a greater extent than had formerly been possible. The car and the telephone have greatly expanded the range of possible network connections. But kinship relations retain a significant appeal, partly because of their availability for assistance in times of need (see, for example, Litwak 1960a, 1960b; Adams 1968; Bott 1971). Indeed, while many urbanites have only rare contact with close kin who live far away, they still report them as a primary source of help in time of crisis (Wellman et al. 1973).

Not only has the context of the modern city occasioned a differentiation in the kinds of people constituting the urbanite's personal network, but it has also occasioned the "unbundling" of qualitatively different kinds of relationship. We have already discussed disparities in the matrices of links to friends, relatives, coworkers, and neighbors; it is necessary also to examine the nature of the interpersonal tie in terms of its content, whether it be simple sociability, financial aid, emotional support, information, coordination, and so on. In the modern city, there will be found relatively separate networks for many of these types of interaction. The urbanite consequently confronts the problem of maintaining interaction with a number of different sets of people for different reasons, having to coordinate their sometimes conflicting demands and to maintain an integrated sense of self while involved in networks having a variety of members and contents.

The maintenance of networks over time is further complicated in the city. For our pastoral villagers, the membership of a personal network is relatively stable over time. For while our villagers undoubtedly quarrel, make up, and begin and end relationships, they are confined to a relatively small population pool for the construction of these relationships, and they are constrained within this network by fairly pervasive community norms. The pool of people potentially available for network formation is many times larger in the city, and as likes, dislikes, and life situations change over the course of time, so too will personal networks. The neighboring network is subject to the most precarious temporal influences, given the high rate of geographic mobility within the city, although some former neighbors will remain in one's personal network as friends or as relatively frequently contacted acquaintances. Movement through the life cycle and change in occupation entail new needs for relationship in domestic and economic contexts. The rate of changing network memberships even in networks of greatest intimacy is extremely high; Shulman (1972), for example, found that nearly half of the Torontonians studied reported that a majority of their "intimates" had changed during a period of only one year.

In addition to this, the greater "unbundling" of relationships in the city leads to a great deal of variation in the activation of ties. Over time, and in the face of changing personal circumstances, active transactions within the network fluctuate among different members. The members called on for assistance in job seeking may not be those who are called on for financial help or for emotional support in times of crisis. Certain members may very well be called on in a number of capacities, and some are likely to occupy positions of centrality in the urbanite's interactional life; yet the scale and diversity of the city, and the multiplicity of personal networks affording access to a wide array of resources, tell against the development of dependency on a single set of intimates. Having access to many networks enhances the urbanite's ability to conduct transactions in relative privacy and secrecy so far as the members of his other networks are concerned.

This is not to deny the tendency, mentioned above, for certain kinds of links to expand beyond the concerns for which they were originally formed or activated. For example, friendship ties may be used to gain business advantages, either directly or indirectly, through reputation. And once again, the multiplicity of networks available and the large potential pool of network members that the city provides may be seen as a liberation from the constraints of the village community as much as a negative and "fragmenting" interactional context.

This is especially so when we recognize that what fragmentation and differentiation exist, however, are never complete. *Single-stranded* ties, based on links with one specific content, have a tendency to become *multistranded*, and among the multiplicity of networks in which the urbanite is involved there is likely to be one in which he is especially active, and to whose members he is especially committed. We may visualize a complex tension between the fragmentation into distinct networks that the negotiation of life in the modern city seems to entail and the sociopsychological thrust towards making single-stranded ties multi-stranded. Add to this the constant introduction of new people into the acquaintanceship sphere of the urbanite, with the concomitant potential of forming various kinds of social relationships with the newcomers, and one gains a fairly complete picture of the intricacy of interactional links in the modern city.

We recall the discussion of symmetric and asymmetric ties. Some ties, as we have seen, are by definition symmetric: if A is a brother of B, then B is a brother of A. Some are by definition asymmetric: if A is a net debtor of B, then B cannot be a net debtor of A. However, these logical distinctions tell us little about the quality of the interpersonal linkage. For A to be a brother of B does not necessarily mean that A "acts like a brother" toward B. Similarly, we cannot assume symmetry in any network ties. If A considers himself to be a friend of B, it is possible but by no means certain that B will consider himself to be a friend of A, or consider A to be his friend. Asymmetric links are especially important when we consider networks of influence, to take one example among many. Such networks have been investigated in analyses of community power (see the papers in Aiken and Mott 1970) and in studies of the dissemination of new information (e.g., Coleman, Katz, and Menzel 1957). One person influences another's decision to build a new expressway or to adopt a new medical drug. A subordinate may regularly report information to his superior, while the superior does not, and is not expected to, reciprocate in kind, although there may be another kind of reimbursement. Similarly, one person may feel close intimacy with another who in turn regards the first person only as an acquaintance. Asymmetric relationships often have fundamental inequities built into them, whether in terms of access to resources or in terms of one party's brokerage role. These matters will be explored more thoroughly when we consider access to resources through personal networks.

Let us glance here at the notion of indirect ties (reserving a fuller discussion for a later point in the paper). We note that members of personal networks are potentially linked, at one or more removes, to all the members of the networks of those persons to whom they are directly linked. Obviously, then, these indirect linkages are structured properties of the network, too. And we should note at least this implication: knowledge of the membership of a network is not a prerequisite for membership in that network. Upon meeting for the first time, members who have been up to that point only indirectly linked in the network may find that they have many friends or acquaintances in common and have been, unawares, sharing information, norms, and values for a long time.

It is the existence of such indirect ties, both symmetric and asymmetric, that enables large segments of the metropolis to be structurally organized and integrated. Although the matrix of all direct links between all urban inhabitants is quite sparse, that matrix would fill up quite quickly were we to count as linked all those who are indirectly connected via a path of length two, or one of length three, and so on (see Rapoport and Horvath 1961). Indeed, in what he has termed the "small world problem," Milgram has suggested that everyone in the world may be linked to everyone else through indirect acquaintanceship paths with an average length of about five; many, of course, would be linked to each other by many different paths (see Milgram 1967; Travers and Milgram 1969). We do not know, at the present time, what meaning this might have, either for the individual or for the world. The answer will depend, of course, on the nature of the indirect ties, and the milieu in which they are located. Nevertheless, the widespread proliferation of indirect links is of undeniable importance in the organization of life in the city, and this importance is independent of the network members' awareness of their existence.

One further element of complexity must be added to our discussion. To this point, we have been discussing links at the level of existence or nonexistence; it is this simplification that permits us to dichotomize matrix cell entries into zeros and ones. In reality, however, existing ties of the same kind vary greatly in intensity. Thus, even among one's close friends some will be closer than others. (And, of course, individuals will vary in what they mean by terms like "close.") In studying the intimate networks of Torontonians, we have found that within a personal network of up to six reported "close friends" the most important predictor of availability of support in times of trouble was the closeness ranking of the intimates (Wellman et al. 1973). Similar rankings would obtain in studies of influence; within a network of "influential" people, some would carry more influence than others, at least in specific domains (see Laumann and Pappi 1973).

Sometimes, however, as we shall see below, the weakness, rather than the strength, of interpersonal ties has its own value, in making possible broadened access to a wider range of resources and information. In this context we might recall that time-honored sociological personage, the "marginal man." In network terms, this character, having a foot in two worlds though fully a part of neither, constitutes a link between two or more otherwise more-or-less distinct network groupings. He serves to bind the different worlds together by his presence in both, making available to each the members and resources of the other. Thus, although his personal linkage to either network may be weak, and he is liable to suspicion and mistrust in both, his bridging position serves an important integrative and coordinative role, albeit at some personal cost.

Having examined in some detail the components of urban interpersonal relations in network terms, we now consider some of the structural and organizational consequences of these networks for life in the city. We begin with a consideration of migration into the city.

Networks of Urban Migration

According to the "mass society" stereotype of urban fragmentation it is the unattached, rootless, and alienated migrants to the city who are the prime movers of urban chaos. But more recent, and more painstaking, investigation has shown that, on the contrary, by and large people do not come into the city in complete isolation, but have available to them various structures and mechanisms for attaching themselves to the ongoing social process of the metropolis (see Shannon and Shannon 1968). Their use of networks in migration helps link them to the ongoing communities of the city—residential, occupational, interest-group, and the like—and thus tie them into urban structures. The use of networks by migrants is an important special case of how such ties are used in the city to gain access to resources; later in this section we shall consider such processes in a more general light.

"The migrant comes to the city with little in the way of marketable skills . . . but with kinship attachments that will enable him to survive . . . while he becomes acquainted with the simplest demands of urban life." (Shannon and Shannon 1968: 56) In the absence of such kinship attachments, the migrant to the North American city often comes under the auspices of friends or acquaintances from his former home town (see Tilly and Brown 1967). Similarly, the rising young executive transferred to a new city is taken care of, in the absence of friends or kin, by the local branch of his company (Whyte 1956).

From the outset, the migrant to the city is typically supplied with a set of interpersonal linkages that help him to manage the transition. In the vast majority of cases, these links will be in existence, and at least partially activated, even before he sets foot in the new community. Tilly and Brown stress the importance of these networks in their account of migration to Wilmington, Delaware (1967: 154):

> If, in this ordinary industrial city, such elaborate and systematic variations in patterns of migration exist, if kin groups play such a large part in the reception of newcomers, then the facts raise questions about the theory of uprooting, marginality and disorganization. Everywhere we find more persistence and proliferation of personal relations than should be there. The very groups one would expect to find disrupted by migration, for lack of security, experience, or skill in city life, show extensive contacts among kinfolk.

Few migrants arrive in the city unattached and with no place to go. Indeed, the very decision to migrate will often depend on the existence of network ties in a particular city. People decide to move to an area where they always know others, as part of a process which the Macdonalds (1963) have called "chain migration."

For example, Italian-American and Italian-Canadian migrants have tended to move into neighborhoods within the city in which their kinfolk have relocated (see, e.g., Fried 1967).[5] As a consequence of these migration patterns, networks to which new immigrants become attached tend to sort people within the city. Those in the same network, at least at the initial stages, tend to live near one another and to work at the same jobs. The aggregate effect of this network clustering is frequently the development of enclaves and "ghetto" areas within the city, based on the migrant group's common characteristics.[6] This sorting process has an impact not only on the assimilation of the migrant but on the social structure of the city as well, as distinct ethnic neighborhoods and enclaves are formed. Breton (1964) has shown how the dense concentration of culturally distinct migrants leads to the development of "institutional completeness"—the growth of a full range of institutional services geared to the particular minority. In the face of such a development, there will be little necessity (felt or real) for group members to go "outside." The structure of such enclaves is reminiscent of the dense "village" networks discussed above.

But migration is more than simply leaving the rural village to settle in the urban one. Settling in with the folks from back home is usually a temporary phase, during which skills and contacts are acquired to permit a greater independence from the old sets of ties. Many may come already so equipped, and easily move about within the city. Others learn from the friends and relatives who came before them, while still others must wait until they have developed links into new and useful networks.

So far, we have been primarily concerned with migration from abroad, or from rural or small-town locales, to the big city. Recent studies of migration from city to city, or within cities, indicate the operation of another process involving a somewhat different sorting principle. The move within the city itself may be to an area that is congruent with the urbanite's life-cycle stage, social class, or life style, with only secondary emphasis on the earlier racial, ethnic, and regional considerations (see Gans 1967; Michelson 1970, 1973). Bell (1968), for example, describes the move to the suburbs as an attempt to find a more suitable location for raising a family than the central city is perceived to be; in other words, suburbanites have chosen "familism" over such considerations as career or cosmopolitanism. This secondary migration often takes place in a context of similar network relationships as existed prior to the initial migration to the city. The timing and location of this second migration within the metropolitan area is often as affected by networks of ties to friends, kin and co-workers as was the initial migration to the city.

Finally, we must remember that as people move from city to city and from neighborhood to neighborhood, the old ties do not automatically disappear. There remain links back to the old community, the old home town, "the old country" just as there may be links forward to new communities still in the future. Some of these links remain activated, either through periodic personal visiting or through contact by telephone and letters. The net effect of this maintenance of old ties is a flow of information between country and city, old land and new. In time, some of these links may themselves be activated as the now settled immigrant becomes a link in a chain of new migration. So it is that purely personal ties between individuals serve, in the aggregate, to link city to city, region to region, and nation to nation.

Access to Urban Resources

The network processes involved in migration involve the flow of information and other resources among members of the network. But this use of networks is not restricted to migrants. The accessibility to any individual of various resources may depend on the structure and size of his personal network, and on the nature of the interpersonal linkages that make up the network. The resources involved may be tangible ones, such as information about jobs or homes, or intangibles, such as sociability or emotional support.

If we take the case of relatively tangible resources, such as Granovetter's (1973) account of how urbanites look for jobs or Lee's (1969) description of how abortionists were located, the possession of a large network of weak, far-reaching ties seems the best assurance of success. In both these cases, the "searcher" contacts those network members considered most likely either to have the desired information themselves or to have acquaintances not directly accessible to the searcher who are likely, in turn, either to have the information or to know someone who might.

Lee's study was performed when abortions were much less publicly available than they are now in North America. The abortion seeker often had to try many unproductive contacts before a productive one was finally found. Her task was sometimes simplified by the existence of informal brokers, or "specialists," with wide-ranging acquaintanceship networks of their own, who made it their business to know how an abortion might be procured. These brokers had links to networks of people who had sought abortion information in the past; the successful searcher, in turn, became part of the broker's network, which constantly expanded in this way. At times, the ex-searcher became a sub-broker in her own right, providing a link between her own personal network and that of the broker. Similar network processes often function now when users make initial "connections" with small-scale purveyors of illicit drugs.

Granovetter (1973) suggested that in the case of job seeking—and probably in the case of other relatively tangible resources as well—a loosely knit network of weak ties provides access to more varied sources of information, from a greater variety of people, than a more dense personal network that lacks extensive links beyond the common circle. For some people, being linked to a large number and broad variety of the "right" people is seen as important in its own right (see Kadushin 1966). Dense, close-knit networks, however, are more likely to provide affective resources such as sociability and support, where trust is important. Our own research has indicated that the availability of support from close friends and kin ("intimates") tends to increase as the density of the links in the intimates' networks increases (Wellman et al. 1973). So it is not only how many intimates an urbanite has that affects the availability of affective resources, but how closely linked these intimates themselves are in a personal network through which information and resources can flow. Bott, for example, argues (1971: 218) that when men and women who each maintain their own closely knit personal networks marry, "the marriage is superimposed on the previous relationships, and each partner continues to be drawn into activities with outside people." But in relationships where the partners come to marriage with more loosely knit personal networks, "they must seek in each other some of the emotional satisfactions and help with familial tasks that couples in close-knit networks can get from outsiders."

A recent study of a crime "family" has shown that its activities are associated with closely knit, strong ties among its members (Ianni with Reuss-Ianni 1972). Not all kin are members of the "family," nor are many "family" members directly linked with one another. Family members are reportedly involved in a network of more than twenty legitimate businesses as well as in illegal loan and gambling enterprises. Transactions among the disparate units in the network are possible because of the trust among the strongly tied kin members. Flows of cash, power, and influence between the formal enterprises, legal and illegal, are maintained by this network of ties, even though the various enterprises are kept strictly separate in organizational terms. Close kinship ties are maintained with those who do not choose to become members of the "family business"; the operation is not a closed corporation and it is quite easy to choose to maintain kinship ties but not business ties. Indeed, there is a great problem keeping relatives as business resources as succeeding generations are increasingly attracted to careers (or marriages) in more respectable occupational spheres.

We are now in a position to make some tentative generalizations about personal-network structures and their implications for network members. The literature indicates that relatively dense networks are generally small, and the linkages among the members quite strong. People in this kind of network usually know each other very well, share interests in common, and often tend to be similar in such social attributes as ethnicity, life style, and socioeconomic status. Loosely-knit networks, on the other hand, tend to be large, and their members less deeply involved with one another. In the place of a small and relatively homogenous group of very close friends, we tend to find a proliferation of quite different people, who have varying interests and enthusiasms but who know and remain in touch with one another. There are many more indirect links.

In general, large loosely-knit networks appear to expedite access to tangible resources, while dense networks with strong ties expedite access to more intangible, emotional resources. The issue becomes somewhat more complicated, however, in situations where there is a strong emotional content to the need for getting access to tangible resources, as in the "family business" and the search for an abortionist. Lee (1969) found, for example, that the first contacts made by searchers were often with intimates, but the pressure of having to get the information in the short time within which abortion is possible occasionally forced the searchers to contact people with whom they had only the weakest of ties. Informants made from one to nine discrete attempts to find an abortionist, and the length of the ultimately successful path varied from one to seven links. The process was expedited to some extent by the fact that some of the intimates who were contacted—notably the man involved in the pregnancy and close female friends of the searcher—"tended to be highly motivated and active in searching out the information" (1969: 77).

Once again, then, a quantitative complexity enters into the qualitative distinctions we wish to make. The notions of purely dense or loosely knit networks take on more of the status of ideal types than of accurate descriptions of the world as we inquire more closely into the various processes involved. It is probable that few urbanites are members of networks that can exclusively be characterized as either tightly knit or loosely knit, and most are members of many networks.

Personal and Multiple Communities

In theory, and in empirical fact, it is extremely unlikely that the networks of urbanites will extend throughout the city and the society in a vast undifferentiated web. There will be networks characterized by both a high density of ties between members and a relative paucity of ties outside a defined network boundary. From a network perspective, these bounded sets of links and nodes, all of whose members are connected either directly or via indirect paths of short length, are communities. In matrix terms, we would expect the union of a simple matrix of this part of the network and its square to yield very few zero cells.

In this section, we shall discuss two propositions about such network communities. First, we propose that the "personal community" of any urbanite is unique; it is a distinct function of his network relationships.

Second, we propose that, given the many different kinds of network relationships that urbanites have, and given the large scale and diversity of modern cities and the ease of transportation and communication within them, most urbanites are members of "multiple communities"; their communal lives are not describable in terms of a single all-embracing urban village.

We have defined community purely in terms of a network perspective. Knowing what we do about simpler networks, we can make some predictions about the social and psychological consequences of the particular kind of network structure that we have called a community. It is likely that sets of network members will develop high rates of interaction (intense ties) based upon their common interests or social characteristics. There is a tendency for ties formed on the basis of one kind of relationship to expand, so that relationships become multi-stranded. The high density of connections within the community facilitates the establishment of new connections therein, as common membership in the community provides a context and an opportunity for previously unconnected members to meet. Thus there is a structural tendency for the density of communities to increase over time; if we assume a finite limit to the number of discrete relationships that humans can sustain, there will be a concomitant decrease in the number of ties to outside the community.

So far, our definition of community has hinged on the existence of a single type of relationship. While some communities of interest may be viable on this simple basis, it is likely that just as ties between individuals tend to become multi-stranded, the bonds defining and holding together an entire community will tend to become more rich and complex. In this connection, we might expect an inverse relation between the number of communities the "typical" member is involved in and the qualitative complexity of any of those communities. The smaller the contextual social system, and the simpler the division of labor within it, the fewer and richer we would expect its constituent communities to be.

Psychological lore has it that when people are in frequent, positively reinforcing interaction with one another, a positive feeling grows about their interaction set, which is, consequently, reified by them (cf. Homans 1950). As communities increase in density and internal complexity, and as they become more decoupled from other social contexts, in consequence, they tend to be reified as tangible entities by insiders and outsiders alike. One common indicator of this is their acquisition of a name: "Our Crowd," "the North End," "the Military-Industrial Complex." Thus the (network) community itself becomes a category of social relations—or, more exactly, what White (1965) terms a "catnet" (i.e., category-cum-network). With the growth of the community as an entity, positive feelings toward it and identification with "it" by its members are commensurately enhanced. This in turn serves to further set the community apart, and to increase the dependence of its members on their identification with it.

Similarly, a categorically defined group of people can develop an internal network structure. This can even be true when the category aspect is a negative one, externally imposed by the (usually majority) population (Goffman 1963). Such an imposition limits the pool of potential network mates for those so labeled to the extent that a community develops, forming the network aspect of the catnet. But the further this type of community is set apart, the greater we would expect the ambivalence of its members to be, in that they are both dependent on the interactional pool that is limited to the category-cum-community and negatively identified with the stigma. A wide range of psychological mechanisms can come into play at this stage, ranging from individual withdrawal or "passing" to the reification of the community via positive identification at the collective level, e.g., "Black is beautiful." The latter represents the community's rejection of the externally applied stigma which enforced the segregation of the community in the first place, along with its retention of the structure of interpersonal ties in a positive and affiliative context.

Note that we have been careful not to define communities in spatial terms, as areas whose boundaries can be drawn on a map. In considering a community, we can just as easily be talking about a dense, bounded network of enthusiastic stamp collectors as of one of fellow residents in a particular locality. While many discussions have equated "community" with "neighborhood," we feel that it is intellectually more profitable to see the neighborhood as only a special case of community. Furthermore, *not all neighborhoods are necessarily communities;* there will be many residential localities in the city where there is little interpersonal network linkage among the inhabitants. The identification of neighborhood with community was probably more appropriate in the period before the development of widespread transportation and communication facilities; when mobility is low and communication difficult, much of one's interpersonal interaction will take place within a relatively confined geographical area.

Similarly, more than one community may exist within a given spatial neighborhood. In the West End of Boston, for example, there existed not only the Italian-American urban village studied by Gans (1962), but also sizable communities of students and medical personnel who had little or no contact with the Italians, despite their being residentially interspersed. Similar patterns have been found in Toronto neighborhoods which are in transition from one ethnic group to another.[7]

This is not to deny that there are communities which *are* locally based, i.e., neighborhoods which are also communities. Indeed, most of the extensive investigations of urban communities have been concerned with such neighborhood-communities. While this has been to some degree due to the comparative ease of conceptualization and study of such communities, one important component in the long tradition of neighborhood

"community studies" has been a yearning to rediscover the continued existence of the pastoral village within the context of the modern metropolis.[8]
The impressive body of work that has accumulated on the nature of interpersonal ties in neighborhood communities (even within the last two or
three decades—see the citations in Wellman and Whitaker 1972) attests
the survival of the identification of neighborhood with community. Numerous investigators have demonstrated that ties of kinship, friendship, and
neighboring, activated in dense local networks, have characterized many
of these geographically defined communities. However, it has become clear
that, with the exception of the most strongly-bounded neighborhood enclaves, a significant proportion of important interpersonal ties, including
those of kinship, work, friendship, influence, etc., extend beyond local
boundaries.

Greer's (1962) synthesis suggested that the neighborhood-community
is only one of many communities in which urbanites are involved. He
pointed out that residents of the same neighborhood have qualitatively
different personal networks, with some being involved almost solely in
neighborhood affairs, while others, having more metropolitan concerns,
use their homes (and their home neighborhood) almost solely as dormi-
tory, or headquarters. Furthermore, the relative proportion of predominantly neighborhood- or predominantly metropolitan-oriented people
varies between neighborhoods, so that we might construct a continuum of
neighborhood type with "urban villages" and "dormitories" at the two extremes. With the exception of the most "institutionally complete" ethnic
enclaves, it is rare to find a neighborhood that constitutes the major setting
of informal interaction for a majority of its residents.

Many city dwellers continue to use neighborhood-communities for the
fulfillment of routine needs in which ease of face-to-face contact is important (cf. Keller 1968). However, the neighborhood-community does not
exhaust the range of possible interactional contexts available to city
dwellers, and it rarely, if ever, exists in splendid isolation from other kinds
of urban communities. The urbanite's involvement in multiple communities implies limits to his involvement with any one community, and restrictions on the claim that any community can make on his allegiance and
participation.[9]

Greer (1962) argues that it is possible to map out successively larger
and more inclusive spatial areas which serve as loci of community action,
the nature of the interaction varying with the inclusiveness of the area. He
asserts that the neighborhood is predominantly a place for informal interaction, while larger local areas are the environments for more formally
organized relationships. However, each urbanite may have his own particular set of ties in his "personal community," so that we find "neighborhood actors" who participate primarily in informal local interactions and
"community actors" who are oriented to a great extent towards participation in organized local groups. Greer also has a place in his typology for

"multi-level participators": people involved in more than one locus of interaction, who can therefore act as network brokers in managing the flow of information from one area to another.

Both "locals" and "cosmopolitans," to use Merton's (1957) classification, are necessary for a community's viability. The former disseminate information within the community and enhance its solidarity, while the latter disseminate information between communities, thus linking them together. The ties that individuals have across community boundaries can serve to link communities with one another.

To recapitulate, while neighborhood communities do exist, for most urbanites they exist as only one of a multiplicity of communities in which they claim membership. The study of urban communities, therefore, must proceed from questions about the membership of people's personal networks to questions about the nature of the interpersonal linkages, and the structural characteristics of the networks. The spatiality of any given community then becomes an empirical problem. In fact, this consideration would lead us to dispense with the notion of "urban" communities, given that despatialized communities can cross city—and national—boundaries, were it not for the fact that it is the organization of the modern city that facilitates the development of such far-reaching networks (see Webber 1964; Pierce 1972).

Membership in multiple communities means membership in many different kinds of community simultaneously. These communities will vary in the extent to which the content of the linkages is affective or instrumental, and in the predominantly single-stranded or multi-stranded character of the linkages. Those communities based upon strong emotional ties will continue to have much face-to-face contact among participants. However, the development of the telephone as a personal communication system, and of the automobile as a personal transportation system, has heightened the potential viability of many communities whose members are dispersed beyond the boundaries of a single locality. One quarter of the "intimates" of the Torontonians we studied live beyond the metropolitan borders; many contacts are by telephone, with an occasional visit to reaffirm, reinforce, and, perhaps, readjust the relationship (Whitaker 1971; Wellman et al. 1973). In the face of high rates of geographic mobility, the maintenance of community ties by means other than face-to-face contact becomes increasingly prevalent. The spatial constraints on community formation and maintenance may have become so diminished that instead of "urban communities" it might be more correct to speak of "urbane communities."

Of course, the spatial limits of a community will vary with the nature of the tie. For those who are intensely linked, there may be virtually no effective boundaries at times when the instrumental or symbolic importance or complexity of the situation requires face-to-face contact, such as the death of a family member, or, in another context, an important professional gathering. Most likely, different kinds of communities will evaluate the costs of distance differently. How far will stamp collectors travel to be together, as compared with members of a religious sect? For each kind of linkage, we might posit a threshold level which varies according to the benefits accruing to the maintenance of the tie, beyond which the costs incurred by the difficulty of face-to-face contact render the maintenance of the tie prohibitively costly (see Wellman 1973).

If a person is limited to those contacts available only within his immediate locality, the nature of the ties he can establish will be limited to areas of interest common to others in the neighborhood. The development of *aspatial* communities means that he is liberated from such constraints to a great extent; he can establish contact with a variety of people dispersed over a wide area (often using existing network ties to find them), and he is better able to opt out of neighborhood-based activities which he finds uncongenial. If a person has a special passion for, let us say, modern dance, it is quite unlikely that he will find in his immediate neighborhood sufficient others who share that interest to form a viable community of interest. Ties with people who do share that interest—involving informing each other about performances by dance groups, organizing rehearsals, and, given the tendency to multi-strandedness, providing emotional support—can be maintained by telephone and by transportation within the metropolis. Such a community will certainly have at least some members who will, from time to time, meet face to face. However, members of other kinds of specialized communities may rarely meet: over-the-counter securities traders linked by computer, for example, or long-distance telephone "freaks." Those communities in which the transmission of information—rather than the sharing of emotional affect—is the predominant reason for interaction will be better able to stay linked, for the most part, by telecommunications.

Because there is always some cost to physical mobility, there are counter tendencies to the formation of radically despatialized communities. For example, if modern-dance groups were to become widely popular within a city it is probable that small communities of interest would arise in various localities, at the expense of a metropolis-wide community with no spatial clusters. In addition, there might be a tendency for those members of the community whose interest and involvement is particularly strong, and, perhaps, multi-stranded to migrate within the city so as to live near one another, thus facilitating the maintenance of their evolved ties through extended face-to-face contact. Finally, an increase in scale brings with it increases in diversity of interests, and a tendency to emphasize diversity rather than underlying commonalities. When only one small community of people with shared interests exists, the sharedness tends to be emphasized at the expense of differences within the community, so that it may be kept together. With an increase in numbers, and the consequent possibility that more than one community may be viable, fission may result on the basis of subspecialization.

In the idealized pastoral village to which cities are often compared, there was, in effect, only one community. Not only were all the villagers linked to one another, but there was a multiplicity of ties between the same people. Communities in the urban world, by contrast, have become increasingly nonlocal and specialized in character. Each urbanite is involved in a number of communities, so that the amount of time and emotional energy formerly available to one must now be spread amongst several different contexts. He is beset by the competing, and sometimes conflicting, claims of several communities. Because his personal community is composed of a multiplicity of communities in the city, his social actions will frequently entail the manipulation of several networks more-or-less simultaneously. Many or all of the members of each of his communities will not know the members of the others, so that as well as being a member of several different networks, he must serve as a link between them. The existence of multiple communities is a response to the increased scale and diversity of the city, and is facilitated by the increased availability of communication. At the same time, multiple community membership provides a fundamental mechanism for linking disparate elements of the metropolis with one another. Multiple communities, then, are both the creature and the creator of the modern urban social system.

The City as a Network of Networks

To this point, we have been concerned primarily with ties between persons. There is nothing sacrosanct, however, about the assumption that network nodes must be individuals; network linkages may equally obtain between communities, between communities and more formally organized groups, between either of these and individuals, and so on. It is just as meaningful to assert that community A is linked—directly or indirectly— to community B as it is to assert that person X is linked to person Y. The links between communities— or between other organized collectivities— may take the form of one person's multiple membership in several groups, or may be the outcome of specialization on the part of certain community members in "foreign relations" with other groups. Nevertheless, although the links may be effected through individual persons, the ties are properly between the collectivities rather than individuals.

Consider a case wherein officials of private companies in the property development industry are also members of the board of the public housing agency. Here the links are between the private corporations and the public agency. Such relationships may enable the particular companies in the private sector to acquire "inside" information so as to receive contracts for public housing work. If the major companies in the private sector are linked in a network or more formal organization which includes those who are directly represented on the public board, the property industry as a whole will have access to public-housing policy making, in the interests of the industry as a whole rather than those of any particular company. The ties give the managers of the public agency easy access to a number of "trusted" private firms to which it can subcontract its work. Here, the relevant links are clearly between the corporate entities, both public and private—although the specific linkages are people, who hold directorships on the boards of both bodies (see Craven and Lowe 1972; Lowe 1973).

The collectivities linked in such a network need not be formal organizations like corporations. Suppose the residents of a "nice" neighborhood want to prevent "undesirables" from moving in. A number of ties to other entities would be important. It might be desirable to ensure that City Hall does not rezone the area to allow the building of inexpensive housing. It would be convenient if housing inspectors were to become especially vigilant in preventing the illegal conversion of existing houses to multiple-family units or rooming houses. Real-estate agents must be encouraged to be "selective" in their choice of clientele. If "undesirables" already live close by, it would be useful for the police to take special care in seeing that the safety of the neighborhood's streets is maintained through close questioning of all who do not appear to belong there. Similarly, it would be helpful if the mass media were to develop a concern for the maintenance of "law and order" in the area.

Such eventualities might be coordinated through network ties. Perhaps an influential alderman lives in the area, already constituting a link between City Council and the neighborhood. Actual residence, however, is not a prerequisite for effective action; "knowing someone" at City Hall, at the newspaper, or in the real-estate business may be enough to exercise some control over the actions of these various collectivities. Nor do the "connections" necessarily have to be at high status levels to be effective; a resident policeman may well be able to get the police officers to whom he is directly and indirectly linked to patrol the neighborhood in the desired manner. In the case of the community, as in the case of corporations, despite the fact that individuals form the actual ties, the linkages are between collective entities—City Hall and the neighborhood community, for example.

When our units of study are collectivities and the links between them, then the internal links among members of each collectivity are of secondary interest. What is more important in the analysis are the links outward from the community, for if such links exist at all, all members of the community are connected to them, either because they themselves are links to the outside world or because they are connected, either directly or indirectly, to those who are.

We can, therefore, transform a matrix of interconnections among individuals in a population into a matrix of interconnections among communities by sorting the matrix so that fellow community members are grouped together. These communities are defined by the links among members rather than by criteria external to the networks, such as geographical mapping. We can then record a 1 in the new matrix of communities for every case in which members of different communities are linked together, or where a given individual is a member of more than one community. This matrix (Figure 4) can be analyzed like any other, bearing in mind that it is a matrix of community ties, not individual ones.[10]

Figure 4

	Individual Matrix												Community Matrix	
To:	1	2	3	4	5	6	7	8	9	10		To:	Comm. A	Comm. B
1	–	1	0	1	1	0	0	0	0	0				
2	1	–	1	1	1	0	0	0	0	0		Comm. A	1	0
3	1	1	–	1	1	0	0	0	0	0				
4	1	0	0	–	1	0	0	0	0	0	From:			
5	1	0	0	1	–	0	0	0	0	0		Comm. B	1	1
6	1	0	1	0	1	–	1	1	0	1				
7	0	0	1	0	0	1	–	1	0	1				
8	0	1	0	1	0	0	1	–	0	0				
9	0	0	1	0	0	1	1	1	–	1				
10	0	0	0	0	1	1	0	0	1	–				

The Relationship of a Matrix Showing Links Between Individuals to a Matrix Showing Links Between Communities or other Collectivities

Such matrices can be constructed for any type of relationship between communities. We should then be able to analyze, for example, information exchange among communities, comparing the process to commercial transactions, or to intercommunity friendship links. Some types of ties may appear to be more crucial than others in structuring urban relations. It should be equally possible to analyze complex relationships, composed of several different kinds of ties, among many different communities. The analytic and empirical tools necessary for such investigations are presently at an early stage of development (see Heil 1973). We can, however, suggest some hypotheses which seem, in the light of work on interpersonal ties, to be reasonable.

In such an analysis, it is likely that the very *absence* of links between communities or individuals will take on great importance in interpreting the structure of urban social processes. Recalling Milgram's (1967) argument for the pervasiveness of ties among North Americans, it is quite likely that we will find that most urban entities are directly linked to one another by at least one kind of relationship, and that even for a specific type of relationship, most urban entities are linked either directly or by a short indirect tie. This pervasive interconnectedness is in part an outcome of our assumption that only one intercommunity link is necessary for there to be a meaningful connection between the two entities. In many analyses, it may be useful to take into consideration the extent of interconnectedness, considering two communities to be more strongly tied the greater the number of links between them. Such may well be the case in studies of information dissemination or sharing of community sentiments. Yet if there is only one link, but in the person (or persons) of highly influential, powerful or central members of one or both communities, then the presence of that single intercommunity bond will be of great importance.

There is no more reason in the case of community linkages than of individual linkages to assume that ties are symmetric. In the second example above, the "nice" community A had power over the "undesirable" community B, although the intercommunity links were indirect, being mediated by the police, City Hall, and other agencies. Community B may have no links back to community A, although it is possible that ties of deference and norm-sharing do exist. In the latter case, community B might "know its place" and accept the situation. In asymmetric situations, where the networks between communities affect community access to resources, it is probable that some communities will have ties which mediate access to resources—influence, information, finances—while others may have little or none.

Other linkage systems may be based on complementarity rather than dominance: Community C is a poor neighborhood fighting City Hall. A middle-class reformist community (an aspatial community with clusters of nodes in several affluent neighborhoods) comes to its aid with financial, moral, and technical support. In return, community C donates door knockers and votes come election time.

The study of links between communities may shed some light on the controversy between those who maintain that the organization of the city is under the control of a small elite group (see the readings in Aiken and Mott 1970) and those who argue that most urbanites and urban entities act with only minimal and often semiconscious attendance to the actions of others (see Long 1958). If all communities in the city, of whatever type, are ultimately linked together directly or indirectly, then in the loosest possible sense we may characterize the city as being a network of networks. If the network ties are dense, and if one or a few communities has access to a large proportion of the available resources then the network describes in part a "community power structure." Where such a power structure exists, it is more than likely that the members of the powerful communities will share some common attributes, such as social class, occupational prestige, ethnicity, sex, and race, and that many of the intercommunity links relevant to resource manipulation will be available to them. The empirical question of whether or not such centralized elite control of networks can be said to exist points to the importance of networks in organizing urban activities, whether or not calculated organization on the part of network members is involved.

We hold that the role of networks in coordinating activity of all sorts in modern North American cities is essential to their viability. This is not only because network ties enable individuals to operate effectively on their complex urban worlds, but also because the links between individuals and communities enable the many and diverse activities that characterize the modern city to take place in such a manner that numerous individual and collective entities can coordinate with one another in relatively flexible arrangements. At the same time, solidarity is maintained among many of the elements so coordinated, and the organization of networks also facilitates the maintenance of solidarity among those units which are working together in common or complementary enterprises. Formal organizational arrangements are too inflexible and cumbersome to carry out such coordination; has there ever been a bureaucratic organization in which work has been carried out exactly, or even primarily, as the flow chart prescribes? Such formal arrangements are always supplemented—and often supplanted—by informal networks, in cities as much as in bureaucracies.

Networks provide the mechanism for linking the many specialized activities and units of the city to one another. The multiple ties that individuals and communities have provide the potential in many a situation for gaining access to a wider range of resources than would otherwise be available. The flexibility inherent in the structure of networks can accommodate situations in which a small, closely knit set of entities must act together in tight coordination, as well as situations wherein influence must be dispersed broadly through indirect links between loosely knit entities. Networks may be long-lasting or evanescent; they may consist of strong or weak ties, or a combination of both. Some network links are activated every day; others remain unanimated until the infrequent occasions when they are needed. It is the structural and processual adaptability of networks which suits them so admirably for their role as a central organizing principle in urban life.

It is the organization of urban life by networks that makes the scale and diversity of the city a source of strength rather than of chaos. And the city constitutes a receptive milieu for network processes. It provides efficient means for providing personal contact through the close working and residential proximity of large numbers of people, and through the broad availability of transportation and communication facilities. Hence the number of possible interpersonal transactions is maximized, while their cost is minimized (see Meier 1962). Thus the continued existence of large cities as centers of interaction is not an anachronistic relic of the horse-and-buggy past; rather, the city is a superior milieu for diverse network processes which continue to make it a vital center in the networks of regions, nations, and the world.

NOTES

[1]We should note that the discussion in this paper is restricted primarily to North American studies. Whether the same kind of analytic approach is applicable to urban phenomena throughout the world is an important question for further research.

[2]This, of course, is not to say that there will never be instances in which our interest is in the directors as individuals rather than in the corporations. In such a case, the individual director would in fact be the unit of analysis.

[3]Readers who want to pursue this matter are referred to Craven 1971 and other works cited there.

[4]Recently, however, the whole-network strategy has been used in the study of North American corporations and financial institutions, including as-yet unpublished work by Stephen Berkowitz, Albert S. Gates, and Michael Schwartz. Some investigations of political power structures have also used this approach (see Hunter 1953; articles in Aiken and Mott 1970; Laumann and Pappi 1973). If one has adequate information about a whole network, there are enhanced possibilities for examining the properties of the entire system through mathematical techniques. Levine (1972), to take one example, shows how major American corporations are clustered in "families" around a few institutional centers—such as the Chase Manhattan Bank and other large banks—in ways that are nonobvious on first inspection. A more traditional topic is explored by means of the whole-network approach by Coleman (1961) in his study of interpersonal ties in Midwestern high schools. He demonstrates that these ties may be grouped into discernible cliques associated with characteristics of the students involved, such as social class, and with their norms, such as liking sports.

[5]See also the British data discussed in Young and Willmott (1962) and Granovetter (1972).

[6]"Ghetto" is put in quotation marks here since the term technically refers to an area walled off and controlled by a hostile authority. We note that in the situations cited here the community might to a large extent be separated from the surrounding populace by the closed nature of the network connections among members of the group, with few activated links to the "outside."

[7]The study was performed by students in the Urban Workshop, Department of Sociology, University of Toronto.

[8]See, for example, Nisbet's (1953) and Stein's (1960) laments for what Stein calls "the eclipse of community."

[9]Greer (1962) discusses at great length what he calls "the community of limited liability."

[10]Our analysis here was clarified at a conference attended by Wellman on "Algebraic Models of Social Structure," held in May, 1973 in Cambridge, Mass., and led by Harrison White and associates.

REFERENCES

Adams, Bert.
   1968 Kinship in an Urban Setting. Chicago: Markham.

Aiken, Michael, and Paul Mott (eds.).
   1970 The Structure of Community Power. New York: Random House.

Barnes, J. A.
   1972 Social Networks. Reading, Mass.: Addison-Wesley.

Bell, Wendell.
   1968 "The city, the suburb, and a theory of social choice," in Scott Greer et al.
      (eds.) The New Urbanization. New York: St. Martin's Press, 132–178.

Bott, Elizabeth.
   1971 Family and Social Network (2nd ed.). London: Tavistock Publications.

Breton, Raymond.
   1964 "Institutional completeness of ethnic communities and the personal rela-
      tions of immigrants," A.J.S. 70 (September); 193–205.

Coleman, James.
   1961 The Adolescent Society. New York: The Free Press.
   ———, Elihu Katz, and Herbert Menzel.
   1957 "The diffusion of an innovation among physicians," Sociometry 20 (De-
      cember): 253–270.

Craven, Paul.
1971 "The use of egocentric network properties as predictor variables," in "Community Ties and Support Systems" Project, Working Paper No. 1. Toronto: Centre for Urban and Community Studies, University of Toronto.
————, and Graham Lowe.
1972 "Social and economic aspects of O.H.C." Paper presented at the annual convention of the Ontario Housing Tenants Association, Toronto.

Dorf, R. C.
1969 *Matrix Algebra.* New York: Wiley.

Fried, Marc.
1967 "Functions of the working-class community in modern urban society," *Journal of the American Institute of Planners* 33 (March): 90–103.

Gans, Herbert.
1962 *The Urban Villagers.* New York: The Free Press.
1967 *The Levittowners.* New York: Pantheon.

Goffman, Erving.
1963 *Stigma.* Englewood Cliffs, N.J.: Prentice-Hall.

Granovetter, Mark.
1972 "The development of friendship structures." Unpublished paper. Baltimore: Department of Social Relations, Johns Hopkins University.
1973 "The strength of weak ties," *American Journal of Sociology* 78 (May): 1360–1380.

Greer, Scott.
1962 *The Emerging City.* New York: The Free Press.

Heil, Gregory.
1973 "Structure in social networks." Unpublished paper. Cambridge, Mass.: Department of Sociology, Harvard University.

Homans, George.
1950 *The Human Group.* New York: Harcourt, Brace and World.

Hunter, Floyd.
1953 *Community Power Structure.* Chapel Hill: University of North Carolina Press.

Ianni, Francis, with Elizabeth Reuss-Ianni.
1972 *A Family Business.* New York: Russell Sage Foundation.

Jacobs, Jane.
1961 *The Death and Life of Great American Cities.* New York: Random House.

Kadushin, Charles.
1966 "The friends and supporters of psychotherapy: on social circles in urban life," *American Sociological Review* 31 (December): 786–802.

Keller, Suzanne.
1968 *The Urban Neighborhood.* New York: Random House.

Laumann, Edward.
1973 *Bonds of Pluralism.* New York: Wiley.
————, and Franz Urban Pappi.
1973 "New directions in the study of community elites," *American Sociological Review* 38 (April): 212–230.

Lee, Nancy Howell.
1969 *The Search for an Abortionist.* Chicago: University of Chicago Press.

Levine, Joel.

1972 "The sphere of influence," *American Sociological Review* 37 (February): 14–27.

Litwak, Eugene.
1960a "Occupational mobility and extended family cohesion," *American Sociological Review* 25 (February): 9–21.
1960b "Geographical mobility and extended family cohesion," *American Sociological Review* 25 (June): 385–394.

Long, Norton.
1958 "The local community as an ecology of games," *American Journal of Sociology* 44 (November): 251–261.

Lowe, Graham.
1973 "The role of the state in the Canadian economy: a case study of the interface between Ontario Housing Corporation, Central Mortgage and Housing Corporation and Toronto's builder-developer industry." Unpublished paper. Toronto: Department of Sociology, University of Toronto.

Macdonald, John, and Leatrice Macdonald.
1963 "Chain migration, ethnic neighborhood formation, and social networks," *Milbank Memorial Fund Quarterly* 42 (January): 82–97.

Marx, Leo.
1964 *The Machine in the Garden.* New York: Oxford University Press.

Meier, Richard.
1962 *A Communications Theory of Urban Growth.* Cambridge, Mass.: M.I.T. Press.

Merton, Robert.
1957 "Patterns of influence: local and cosmopolitan influentials," in *Social Theory and Social Structure* (rev. and enlarged ed.). New York: The Free Press, 387–420.

Michelson, William.
1970 *Man and His Urban Environment.* Reading, Mass.: Addison-Wesley.
1973 "Residential mobility as a deficit compensating process." Paper presented to the annual meeting of the Canadian Sociology and Anthropology Association, Kingston, Ontario. May.

Milgram, Stanley.
1967 "The small-world problem," *Psychology Today* 1 (May): 62–67.

Mitchell, J. Clyde.
1969 "The concept and use of social networks," in J. Clyde Mitchell (ed.) *Social Networks in Urban Situations.* Manchester: University of Manchester Press, 1–50.

Nisbet, Robert.
1953 *The Quest for Community.* New York: Oxford University Press.

Pierce, John.
1972 "Communications," *Scientific American* 227 (September): 30–41.

Rapoport, Anatol, and W. Horvath.
1961 "A study of a large sociogram," *Behavioral Science* 6: 279–291.

Shannon, Lyle, and Magdaline Shannon.
1968 "The assimilation of migrants to cities," in Leo Schnore (ed.) *Social Science and the City: A Survey of Urban Research.* New York: Praeger (paper text edition), 49–75.

Shulman, Norman.
1972 "Urban social networks." Doctoral dissertation. Department of Sociology, University of Toronto.

Stein, Maurice.
  1960 *The Eclipse of Community*. Princeton, N.J.: Princeton University Press.
Tilly, Charles.
  1973 "General introduction," in Charles Tilly (ed.) *An Urban World*. Boston:
       Little, Brown (in press).
  ————, and C. Harold Brown.
  1967 "On uprooting, kinship, and the auspices of migration," *International
       Journal of Comparative Sociology* 8 (September): 139–164.
Travers, Jeffrey, and Stanley Milgram.
  1969 "An experimental study of the small-world problem," *Sociometry* 32
       (December): 425–443.
Wayne, Jack.
  1971 "Networks of informal participation in a suburban context." Doctoral
       dissertation. Department of Sociology, University of Toronto.
Webber, Melvin.
  1964 "The urban place and nonplace urban realm," in Melvin Webber, et al.
       (eds.) *Explorations in Urban Structure*. Philadelphia: University of Penn-
       sylvania Press, 79–153.
Wellman, Barry.
  1973 "The network nature of future communities." Paper presented at the
       annual meeting of the Society for the Study of Social Problems, New
       York. August.
  ————, and Marilyn Whitaker (eds.).
  1972 *Community-Network-Communication: An Annotated Bibliography*. Mon-
       ticello, Ill.: Council of Planning Librarians.
  ———— et al.
  1973 "Community ties and support systems," in Larry Bourne, Ross Mac-
       Kinnon, and James Simmons (eds.), *The Form of Cities in Central
       Canada*. Toronto: University of Toronto Press (in press).
Whitaker, Marilyn.
  1971 "The users and uses of different modes of communication," in "Com-
       munity Ties and Support Systems" Project, Working Paper No. 2. Toronto:
       Centre for Urban and Community Studies, University of Toronto.
White, Harrison.
  1965 "Notes on the constituents of social structures." Unpublished paper.
       Cambridge, Mass.: Department of Social Relations, Harvard University.
White, Morton, and Lucia White.
  1962 *The Intellectual Versus the City*. Cambridge, Mass.: Harvard University
       Press.
Whyte, William H., Jr.
  1956 *The Organization Man*. New York: Simon and Schuster.
Wirth, Louis.
  1938 "Urbanism as a way of life," *American Journal of Sociology* 44 (July):
       3–24.
Wolf, Eric.
  1956 "Aspects of group relations in a complex society: Mexico," *American
       Anthropologist* 58 (December): 1065–1078.
Young, Michael, and Peter Willmott.
  1962 *Family and Kinship in East London* (2nd ed.). Harmondsworth, Middle-
       sex: Penguin.

Formal Voluntary Organizations: Participation, Correlates, and Interrelationships

AIDA K. TOMEH

Bowling Green State University

The purpose of this paper is to give an overview of the literature on formal voluntary organizations in the urban community. The theoretical approaches that guided much of the research in this area are identified as social structural, social psychological, and organizational. Basic findings suggest that formal participation, including church membership, is a characteristic of urban life. Population characteristics, attitudes, informal interaction, and community involvement are all related to formal membership. Moreover, formal organizations attempt to integrate individuals with the larger community, and such groups, in urbanizing areas, facilitate modernization.

The role of formal associations in community life has been the subject of scholarly research for many years. As early as 1835, de Tocqueville noted that one of the most striking features of American society was the way in which people at the local level joined together in formal associations to meet specific goals or solve community problems. Such groups are numerous and diverse and involve large numbers of individuals (Wilensky 1961b: 215; Rose 1967: 218).[1]

The formal or voluntary association may be interpreted as an organizational invention that aids in the continuing transitional process of urbanization by combining blends of primary and secondary social experiences. Some writers argue persuasively that intermediate organizations facilitate modernization (Eisenstadt 1956a; Geertz 1962; Little 1965), contributing to the stability of modern societies by providing social units intermediate between the individual and the community (cf. Tannenbaum 1951 on labor unions; Rose 1965 on voluntary organizations as intermediate groups). (In this paper, the term "community" is used in a very general sense to refer to a form of secondary social organization composed of commercial, industrial, familial, cultural, and other constituent units in a given habitat, which, through their interaction, create a complex behavioral system.)

Formal organizations seem especially effective as institutions supportive of social change, in that they function to adapt the social structure to changing conditions. Sometimes such groups develop counter associations when threats to established patterns become increasingly difficult to ignore. As these associations gain momentum and approach success, they become the foci of social movements (Turner and Killian 1972) and thus constitute one of the most important levers of social and cultural change in modern society.

Other associations support the normative order, reinforcing important values, help to distribute power at the grass roots level, and help members to control an important part of their environment. In addition, some organized groups together provide a type of "cultural pluralism" (Rose 1954: 58) in which varied interests may be supported within the same society. Such groups enable minorities to achieve greater cohesion and self-expression and to take some action toward realizing their aims in society. Obviously, some of these associations are active in social reform or social change. For instance, the local branches of the NAACP have brought a large number of cases of discrimination into the courts and established legal precedents that have made the laws and the courts more protective of minority groups. Similarly, occupational groups (e.g., labor unions, trade associations, business and professional groups) exert their influence on the community, if necessary by striking in order to obtain benefits for their members and defend their occupational interests.

A variety of other groups provide opportunities for self-expression and exchange of ideas and experiences within a limited field of interest (e.g., athletic clubs, hobby clubs, fraternal lodges, book clubs). Other organized groups such as service clubs (e.g., Rotary, Kiwanis, Lions) integrate the business and professional interests of the community in addition to providing a means for self expression. In one way or another, then, formal organizations and their diversified activities comprise a conspicuous feature of American community life.

This paper attempts a survey of the major theoretical propositions and empirical findings on formal associations in the community. One of our purposes is to examine the major theoretical approaches that have guided much of the scientific research on formal organizations. A related issue is that of conceptualization in this field; hence the various meanings of the concept, measurement procedures, and alternative criteria for differentiating organizations into distinct types are discussed and a presentation of empirical studies to illustrate the use of such concept follows. Later sections of the paper deal with research on rates of participation, characteristics of group members, the relationship between formal and informal involvement, and the role of voluntary associations in other societies.

Theoretical Concerns and Conceptualization

The field of formal organizations is still in an early stage of development. Most theoretical analysis in this area is at the level of developing a conceptual framework and speculating about possible theoretical propositions.

The study of participation in formal organizations involves three identifiable theoretical approaches:

(1) Focus on the nature and structure of industrial society. The emphasis here is on the functions, and pervasiveness, of the formal group. On this level, formal associations are seen as contributing to society by supporting the normative order or seeking to change it and implement important values. At the same time, such organizations may contribute to social stability as adaptive mechanisms for traditional institutions, and their importance is further noted in terms of the role they play in various societal processes such as the distribution of power, decision making, opinion formation, and socialization.

(2) The social psychological approach. In this context formal associations are viewed as integrative for the personality systems of their members. Thus, the function of the association on the personal level is to provide the individual with affectual support and other satisfactions formerly available to him in such traditional groups as the family, neighborhood, and church. More generally, the association allows individuals to transcend their immediate life situations and serves to integrate them with the broader community and society. Rose (1962a) argues that the voluntary organization has a psychological effect on its members in counteracting the feelings engendered by the mass society. By providing meeting time for discussion of strategies and techniques for attaining the goals of the organization, the voluntary organization contributes to a reduction of social helplessness among its members, offers members a sense of belongingness and a partial escape from boredom, and supports those caught in the disorder of social change.

While the above two approaches involve different levels of analysis, both stem from a functional theoretical orientation in that formal associations are considered to be integrative for both society and the individual and to provide a direct way for individuals to initiate change (cf. Rose 1954: 61, 1962a; Greer and Orleans 1962: 635; Rossi 1961; Erbe 1964: 213; Babchuk and Edwards 1965; Jacoby 1965; Tomeh 1969).

(3) Examination of associations within the framework of organizational theory, with a focus upon the association as the unit to be studied (cf. Young and Larson 1965; Clark 1968; Laskin and Phillett 1965; Motz et al. 1965; Warriner and Prather 1965; Harp and Gagan 1971). When viewed from this angle, the research problem becomes that of studying associational participation as a variable in community structure. More specifically, this approach considers of interest the structure of the association, the different processes of operation, the impact of the social setting upon the organization, the pattern of relationships within the association, and the interrelationships of various structural, organizational, and ideological features.

Unfortunately, sociologists have applied organizational theory more widely in their studies of large-scale organizations and other relevant institutions than in their analyses of voluntary groups. This is somewhat surprising, since a large volume of organizational activity in the modern community actually occurs within voluntary associations, a fact which strongly justifies their inclusion as significant parts of community social structure. Moreover, they provide a ready-made supply of organizations necessary for comparative analysis.

Since a wide variety of formal organizations exists, it is important to indicate what is meant by the term, "Formal organization," how the concept of membership participation is measured empirically, and what criteria are used for distinguishing various types of formal associations. In doing so, we will attempt to review studies which deal with these issues in order to clarify conceptual analysis of formal associations and aid in suggesting theoretically fruitful lines of empirical investigation.

Before specifying the points of disagreement relative to the inclusiveness of the concept, let us sketch the general meaning of the term. "Formal groups" and "voluntary associations" have been used interchangeably to mean organizations in which membership depends on the free choice of the individual while severance rests at the will of either party. Such groups, which may be small or large, are usually nonprofit in nature and are organized to pursue mutual and personal interests of the members so as to achieve common goals. Authority and duties are delegated and collective objectives are defined. Offices are filled by election or selection and periodic and/or frequent meetings are generally held at a regular meeting place. The units defined above are designated variously as formal groups, organizations, associations, clubs, societies, or special-interest groups.

The urban milieu is widely sprinkled with such groups; indeed, they seem to be proliferating at such a rate and to constitute such a solid part of urban living that some students have questioned the inclusiveness of the concept. For example, formal groups ranging from churches, labor unions, and certain types of profit-making organizations to fraternal groups, civic groups, and athletic teams are often grouped together in analysis. Sometimes an index of social participation is constructed on the basis of membership in these diverse groups when in effect they serve very different purposes. Thus, there is little consensus among researchers regarding the operational definition of voluntary groups. This is particularly true with regard to church membership.

In some studies, church is included as a voluntary association because it typically has the greatest number of members in the community and therefore addresses itself to an important sector of man's social living (Hagedorn and Labovitz 1967 include church membership along with fraternal, neighborhood, and sports involvement as indicators of social participation), or because church activity has become secularized to such an extent that it can be subsumed, at least partially, under general associational activity. In other studies, church is treated as a formal group but separated from other voluntary groups (cf. Axelrod 1956; Tomeh 1969), on the grounds that membership in church may not be as voluntary as a scientific definition of "free will" might allow, in that people perhaps maintain their religious affiliation involuntarily on account of the affiliation of their parents. And in other treatments of voluntary associations, church affiliation and activity are often relegated to a separate "religious" category and not treated as indicators of participation (cf. Wright and Hyman 1958; Hyman and Wright 1971; Bell and Force 1956a. The latter exclude church but include church-related groups.).

The other major formal group which poses a similar problem in terms of classification is the labor union. It is the voluntary nature of the labor union which is questionable. Some maintain that the worker by virtue of his occupation is expected if not required to join a union; under such circumstances, there is not much choice in his membership and the labor union is excluded as a voluntary group. Others include labor unions on the grounds that membership represents a significant type of social participation (cf. Spinard 1960 on documentation of union participation).

Similarly, the participation dimension with respect to formal organizations has been measured in various ways: number of affiliations in formal groups, frequency of attendance, duration of each membership, amount of time spent at each association meeting, and frequency with which officership is assumed (cf. Komarovsky 1946; Dotson 1951; Scott 1957; Reissman 1956; Foskett 1955; Bell and Force 1956a, 1956b; Freeman et al. 1957; Hagedorn and Labovitz 1967 for studies using one or another measure of participation).[2] Underlying most of these investigations, however, is the asumption that associations are like one another in a number of attributes. It is further assumed that participation in voluntary associations involves the same set of motivations whether it is participation in an administrative organization, for example, or in a professional one. This has not been demonstrated. What has been established is the nature and scope of participation in such groups.

In view of the conceptual problems raised above, Evan (1957) proposes an alternative perspective for examining the concept of participation in voluntary groups. His conceptual framework points to four classes of problems for research: (1) motivation of members for belonging to different voluntary organizations, (2) change in motivation for participation in the course of membership in different formal groups, (3) differences in the structure of various groups, and (4) change in the structure of such groups over a period of time. Thus, in analyzing participation patterns in voluntary associations, this orientation sheds light on the motivational orientation of the participant while taking into account the organizational structure of the formal group. Although such a research proposal requires a longitudinal rather than the customary cross-sectional design, the procedure lends itself to further analysis of such problems as apathy and group behavior in a modern complex society.

Palisi (1968) is also critical of the voluntary group concept. He points out that the rationale behind the definition of voluntariness is not adequately stated. Moreover, the lack of consensus about the classification of economic, political, and religious organizations as voluntary or nonvoluntary suggests that this type of classification is rather vague. Palisi calls, therefore, for a study of the social forces behind formal voluntary associations. Here the emphasis is on the differential social forces and pressures influencing members to participate (e.g., type of community, social class, family structure) rather than on the traditional concept of voluntariness.

Unfortunately, the guidelines proposed by Evan and Palisi have not influenced further research in the area of formal group membership. Other attempts to adequately conceptualize formal group membership have been presented in the form of a typology. Thus, Gordon and Babchuk (1959) differentiate three types of organizations according to the function they perform for the individual or the community or both. (1) Expressive groups are organized to control deviant behavior through socialization and the integration of the adult personality. Members of these groups (interest and hobby groups, recreational clubs, senior citizens groups, etc.) engage in activities that provide immediate gratification and affectual support and implement special interests for the individual. (2) Instrumental groups are organized to cope with the external environment. These groups (job-related associations, farmer organizations, business groups, labor unions, professional groups, PTAs, political organizations, civic groups, etc.) are concerned with activities designed to maintain the normative order or seek to change it by achieving some condition affecting nonmembers outside of the organization. (3) "Mixed" groups, incorporating both expressive and instrumental functions, provide certain privileges for the members in addition to social facilities. Examples of these groups are church-related organizations, fraternal-service groups, Masons, American Legion groups, and the like (cf. Booth et al. 1968 for more descriptive details; Rose 1954: 52; Parsons 1951; Parsons et al. 1953; Lundberg et al. 1934 for similar typologies).

Babchuk and Gordon's (1962) work is especially relevant for ranking organizations in relation to each other and for dealing with member identification with the organization (see also Jacoby and Babchuk 1963; Moore 1961). On a theoretical level, Harp and Gagan (1971) state that instrumental formal groups, with their more inclusive goals and broader membership base, will result in a greater involvement of community members (cf. Babchuk and Edwards 1965; Smith 1966b; Clark 1968). However, although a number of writers are concerned with the instrumental/ expressive differentiation, this classification of associations has been used in only a few additional research reports to date (c. Moore 1961; Jacoby 1965; Dackawich 1966; Ross and Wheeler 1967, 1971; Booth 1972).

A less popular but equally valuable approach to the study of formal group membership is the Warriner-Prather (1965) typology, which focuses on the internal structure and central activities of organizations rather than on the question of participation and community function. The voluntary association, rather than the person or society, becomes the unit of analysis. In essence, the typology differentiates four types of groups on the basis of the rewards each provides for members: (1) pleasure in performance: folk dance clubs, textile painting clubs, discussion groups, etc., (2) sociability: the happy-hour club, social circle, birthday club, etc., (3) ideological symbolism: church, other religious organizations, etc., and (4) production: the Humane Society, the League of Women Voters, service clubs, etc. The authors claim that these four types of associations are distinct types of social organization and that each represents a distinct form of social integration. However, more work needs to be done with large samples in order to discover recurring characteristics of the types, clarify the meaning of differential rates of participation in voluntary associations, and examine the rates of membership in each of the types for different segments of the population. In any event, there appears to be some merit in the above typology, at least enough to provide the basis for a more systematic comparison and integration of findings obtained in studies on formal vs. informal groups and other organizations, which are presently not adequately related to each other.

On the whole, the Gordon-Babchuk (1959) and Warriner-Prather (1965) typologies represent a sociologically significant way of classifying associations (cf. also Blau and Scott 1962, for classification system based on prime beneficiary). These distinctions may be more useful for sociological research than the traditional systems of classification which attempt to classify formal groups in accordance with the institutional sector of society in which they exist; that is, organizations are categorized as religious, occupational, recreational, athletic, educational, political, economic, civic, fraternal, etc. (cf. Hausknecht 1962; Laskin 1961: 14). The latter method of classification is hardly grounded on sociological theory.

Rates of Membership and Participation

The theoretical approaches and conceptualizations discussed above provide a framework for the empirical study of formal organizations, though theoretical knowledge on the subject is far from complete. In this section, we will review the principal studies on rates of membership that sought to elucidate the scope of participation and the extent to which individuals in a modern society seek organizational membership.

Unfortunately, some of the empirical investigations on rates of affiliation are not very consistent, due to differences in samples, methodological procedures, definitional criteria, and nature of the problems selected for analysis. In fact, even studies using probability samples vary considerably in their findings. To illustrate, a variation ranging between 53 and 84% is reported in the affiliation rate of formal group membership (cf. Wright and Hyman 1958; Hyman and Wright 1971; Axelrod 1956; Tomeh 1969; Scott 1957; Bell and Force 1956b; Babchuk and Booth 1969). Some of these studies include church and labor unions; others exclude them.

Perhaps of greater consequence for interpreting the meaning of membership is the degree of involvement of persons who are members. With the exception of a few studies, results indicate that a large percentage of those who belong to voluntary associations belong only in name and assume a rather passive role (cf. Axelrod 1956; Scott 1957; Bell and Force 1956b; Dotson 1951).

When church affiliation is examined, research shows that membership and participation in church, although still not universal, are more widespread and intensive than in other formal groups (cf. Bultena 1949; Lenski 1961; Warren 1963: 192; Tomeh 1969; A Social Profile of Detroit 1952; Bushee 1945; also Goode 1966 on church attendance and class). Thus, if church membership is indicative of social integration, then church as an institution represents an integral part in society by virtue of the greater numbers of associations focused around religious institutions than any other formal group as well as the apparent high affiliation with religious organizations.

When church membership is considered in conjunction with membership in other formal groups, one may conclude that associational membership is characteristic of urban dwellers. Nonetheless, a small minority of urbanites remain relatively isolated from organizational activities as represented by churches, clubs, and associations, and enjoy none of the benefits of integration that formal membership affords. This is not to imply that such individuals are not integrated in society in some other way.

Correlates of Membership and Participation

While knowledge of the extent of affiliation in formal groups is generally important for an understanding of contemporary social life, it is also essential to know what kind of people do or do not join these groups. We will examine differentials in participation in terms of demographic characteristics such as SES, age, sex, and other related variables believed to be important, in addition to attitudinal factors that may make the above patterns more meaningful.

1. *Socioeconomic Status* In all, most of the studies (cf. Mather 1941; Komarovsky 1946; Bushee 1945; Scott 1957; Reissman 1954; Tomeh 1969; Grusky 1964; Wilensky 1961a, 1961b; Gerstl 1961; Hagedorn and Labovitz 1967, 1968; Foskett 1955; Freeman et al. 1957; Hausknecht 1962; Martin 1952; Axelrod 1956; Wright and Hyman 1958; Hyman and Wright 1971; Phillips 1969; Booth et al. 1968; Hodge and Treiman 1968) indicate that the various indices of social class (i.e., education, occupation, and income) are related to organizational affiliation. At least one conclusion seems warranted, viz., that persons of higher SES are more likely to participate in formal organizations than are their counterparts in low SES groups.[3] The same is true with respect to church membership (cf. Lenski 1961; Goode 1966). Another conclusion that early and recent studies seem to document is that persons having higher SES are likely to join groups that differ categorically from those joined by persons of lower SES. For example, upper-class individuals tend to be overrepresented in historical societies and country clubs; middle-class persons predominate in civic-oriented groups (the Rotary Club, Kiwanis Club, Chamber of Commerce) or youth-serving groups; and working-class persons are overrepresented in fraternal organizations and veterans' associations (Bell and Force 1956a; Komarovsky 1946; Babchuk and Booth 1969; Hagedorn and Labovitz 1967; Booth et al. 1968).

While social structural variables (interaction opportunities, institutional models, nature of the situation) and social psychological variables (socialization, roles) may account for a large portion of the social class differences in membership participation (cf. Booth et al. 1968; Blum 1964; Hausknecht 1964; Brager 1969; Axelrod 1956; Wilensky 1961a; Foskett 1955; Phillips 1969), psychological variables (apathy, anomie, authoritarianism) may also be important determinants of people's levels of participation.[4] Future research directed toward examining class-linked boundaries to organizational participation needs to consider these variables simultaneously in order to explain empirically the connection between SES and organizational membership.

2. *Age and Life-Cycle Stage* When age is related to membership in formal organizations, research shows a tendency toward a linear relationship, i.e., an increase in membership as the person passes through adolescence, young adulthood, and adulthood, until fifty or sixty years of age, when membership begins to decline (cf. Hausknecht 1962; Babchuk and Edwards 1965; Lane 1959). Although this relationship is generally true, there seems to be some ambiguity in the pattern of participation and the

boundaries of age (cf. Babchuk and Booth 1969; Axelrod 1956; Bell and Force 1956a; Scott 1957; Foskett 1955), as well as in the influence of sex (Babchuk and Booth 1969).[5]

Different theoretical propositions are offered to explain differential participation by age. From the point of view of role theory, differences in participation by age are explained in terms of one's position in the social system, which necessitates a particular behavioral pattern (Foskett 1955). Proponents of the integration theme argue that the usual age differentiation reflects the integration of the young in society as they assume career and family responsibilities, whereas with the approach of old age a gradual detachment from society takes place. This is not to imply that older people in society are not integrated in other ways (cf. Pihlbland and McNamara 1965; Videbeck and Knox 1965; Rose and Peterson 1965).

Studies of the participation of children or adolescents show that many more working-class and lower-class adolescents affiliate with groups than one would expect from the membership rates for adults of this class level (Baeumler 1965). This and other research suggest that participation is family linked (cf. Anderson 1943; Hodge and Treiman 1968), though the same pattern does not hold in Babchuk and Gordon's (1962) study.[6] At any rate, what is important in all these studies is the fact that participation is not considered independent of that of parents or siblings.

It is found that children affiliate in expressive organizations and adults in instrumental and/or instrumental-expressive organizations; as an individual reaches old age his participation in instrumental groups declines and his involvement in expressive groups increases (Babchuk and Gordon 1962). Thus, there appears to be a cycle of associational-type participation which parallels the life cycle.

The family per se is not an institution that facilitates involvement in formal group membership, except for those groups in which participation is based upon family interests (cf. Booth and Babchuk 1969). It appears that the presence of young children in the family has a depressing effect upon the wife's membership or attendance in groups but not upon the husband's (cf. Wilensky 1964: 311, 1961b; Harry 1970). Nonetheless, marriage and joint spouse membership tend to increase participation in voluntary associations, especially after children leave home (Sussman 1955; Hausknecht 1962; Babchuk and Booth 1969; Schmidt and Rohrer 1956).

3. *Sex*   Evidence on male-female differences in voluntary group participation is more or less consistent with the exception of a few studies (Hausknecht 1962: 31–32), viz., male affiliation rate is higher than female (cf. Scott 1957; Palisi 1965; Dotson 1951; Babchuk and Booth 1969) but that commitment of time is about the same (cf. Booth 1972).

An interesting sidelight is that when type of group is analyzed more men than women affiliate in instrumental groups, whereas the reverse is true of expressive groups (including church-related organizations). In instrumental groups men dominate the leadership scene and in expressive groups women are in control (Booth 1972; Babchuk et al. 1960). These distinctions could at least in part be attributable to differences in early sex-role socialization as well as to differential experience and opportunities in later life.

4. *Race* Much has been written and said about the organizational membership of blacks as compared to whites. Perhaps the most prevalent interpretation of black-white differences is based on SES, in that blacks are found predominantly in the lower socioeconomic groups and hence are less likely to be affiliated with formal organizations (cf. Wright and Hyman 1958; Hyman and Wright 1971 for empirical evidence). This conclusion is reached without considering the membership rates of blacks and whites at comparable SES levels. Studies which take this factor into account show higher participation rates for blacks at all social class levels, especially lower class (cf. Babchuk and Thompson 1962; Orum 1966; also Renzi 1968 for further evidence on black voluntary participation; Dackawich 1966; Ross and Wheeler 1967, 1971).

For whatever reasons, blacks have indeed become joiners. The rise of a wide range of black associations in recent years indicates that voluntary associations are not the preserve of the white middle class.

An explanation for the higher organizational participation of blacks is stated by Babchuk and Thompson (1962). Following Myrdal's (1944: 952) theoretical orientation, they claim that since blacks are not allowed to gain prestige and power in the organizational life of American society (i.e., the work sphere), they compensate by increased rates of participation and exaggerated tendencies to establish new associations. It is also argued that the greater affiliation of blacks may be related to the looser ties that characterize their extended family structure, especially in the lower class. Whatever the case may be, the response of blacks to segregation appears to be quite the opposite of indifference and apathy.

5. *Religion* Research findings on the relationship between religious preference and organizational membership are on the whole consistent. Among those religiously affiliated, Protestants are more frequently members of associations (other than church) than Catholics (cf. Hausknecht 1962; Bell and Force 1956a; Scott 1957; Wright and Hyman 1958).

The apparent membership differential by religious affiliation is partly a function of the structural and ideological aspect of each religion, which facilitates or impedes participation in voluntary associations. To begin with, the organizational structure of the Protestant church is rather flexible and allows more individual freedom and free inquiry. Moreover, the Protestant ethic has historically been identified with individualistic competitive patterns of thought and action. This orientation facilitates the participation of Protestants in voluntary associations.

By contrast, the structure of the Catholic church is relatively rigid, and members of the Catholic faith are bound to the authority of their religious leaders. Moreover, ideologically Catholics have more often been associated with a collectivistic, working-class pattern of thought and action historically opposed to the Protestant ethic and the spirit of capitalism. As a result, strong religious indoctrination in the traditions of the Catholic church has impeded the participation of Catholics in voluntary groups.

However, the Catholic church responded to the attraction of secular associations by promoting a large number of Catholic organizations in an effort to keep the voluntary associations tendency within a Catholic framework. Thus, when the two religious groups are compared with respect to membership and activity in *religious* associations, Catholics show higher levels of participation. The relationship is not appreciably affected when variables like class, vertical mobility, etc., are controlled (cf. Lenski 1961; Curtis 1960; and Bruce 1971 on effects of occupational mobility on church participation. Also Argyle 1959 for a review on church membership and the correlates of church attendance). In a comparative sense, the Jewish group shows a low level of religious participational membership. According to Lenski (1961), the vigor of Jewish communalism more than compensates for the weakness of the religious associations.

The difference between Protestants and Catholics continues to hold when the two kinds of membership, i.e., church and voluntary associations, are interrelated. Involvement in the Catholic church is only *mildly* linked with increased involvement in voluntary associations, while involvement in the Protestant church is *strongly* linked with increased involvement in voluntary associations. Lenski (1961) maintains that Protestant churches act as a training ground for participation in voluntary associations because they have a tendency to extend the interests of individuals beyond the limits of family and kin, thus weakening the bonds of the extended family and stimulating formation of and participation in voluntary associations.

The relationship of the Catholic church to the kin group seems to be different. The Catholic stand is more nearly a complementary relationship than a competitive one. While the explanation offered above is plausible, there is still much about Protestant/Catholic variability in church participation that needs to be explained. Intergenerational stability in religious affiliation may be a crucial variable in understanding Protestant vs. Catholic patterns of church participation (cf. Hodge and Treiman 1968 for a similar concern).

Available evidence, then, suggests that religious affiliation per se plays an important part in determining membership participation in formal groups including church. Thus religion, like race, defines the boundaries of group membership, though the implications are different for the two categories.

6. *Residential and Occupational Mobility*   Available data on the re-

lationship between residential mobility and voluntary association membership are not very consistent. Some studies indicate a positive correlation between length of residence and affiliation in organizations (cf. Freeman et al. 1957; Tomeh 1969; Zimmer 1955), whereas Wright and Hyman (1958), using data from the Denver survey, show no systematic relationship between length of residence at the same address and incidence of affiliation with voluntary associations, and in Scott's study (1957), length of residence had a significant effect upon participation only in conjunction with other variables like age and marital status.

Other studies also show some variability in their results. Litwak's (1961) study based on a survey of white married women from a suburb in Buffalo, New York, indicates that when individuals are negatively oriented toward their neighbors, they increasingly use voluntary associations the longer they are in the neighborhood. On the other hand, those positively oriented toward the neighborhood exhibit the highest degree of club affiliations at the stage of moderate mobility, while at the most settled stage club membership declines but never reaches the low membership rate of the least settled stage. The theoretical assumption underlying these results is that neighborhood orientation and stage of move relate to neighborhood integration via the use of voluntary associations.

Another study based on a white married female population (Windham 1963) indicates that wives who had always lived in Pittsburgh belonged to more organized groups, attended more meetings, and held more positions of power in organizations than wives born in other cities or in rural areas. With continued residence in the community, participation rates of migrants and nonmigrants tended to become more nearly equal. Although comparisons between this study and others based on more representative samples cannot readily be made, at least some inferences can be drawn regarding the role of early background on subsequent behavior and the effects of migration on the social organization of the community hosting the migrants. Research on social participation of migrants in urban areas indicates that the kinds of associational ties which migrants have and the rate at which they participate in associations vary with the degree of their assimilation into city life (cf. Zimmer 1955). Interurban or intracity migrants usually have only minor social adjustments to make and hence attain the participation rates of nonmigrants of similar demographic characteristics in a short period of time. Those who come from rural areas take longer than urban migrants to become as socially active in voluntary associations as nonmigrants with similar demographic characteristics (Zimmer 1955).[7]

The above illustrative studies suggest that where data can be grouped similarly in terms of the different categories of residential mobility, where a differentiation is made between the very recent newcomer and all others, and where samples are similar in type of population, there may be more consistency in the findings. Implicit in all these analyses, however, is the assumption that at different times during a period of residence voluntary associations may act as a mechanism for integration in the community.

Occupational-mobility, unlike residental mobility, is only vaguely related to membership in voluntary groups, unions, and church (cf. Curtis 1959, 1960; Vorwaller 1970; Bruce 1971). Nonetheless, it is worth pointing out the theoretical implications involved.

It is reasoned that some of the effects of occupational mobility may be related to status insecurity and/or differential socialization (Litwak 1960). The mobile person not only breaks ties with individuals of his former stratum, but may also have difficulties in forming new ties with members of the class he moves into (Blau 1956; Wilensky and Edwards 1959).

Of course, there are consequences other than disruption of ties, isolation, and low rates of formal participation that may ensue among mobile individuals. Blau (1956:292; also Litwak 1961), for example, suggests that mobile persons may overparticipate in certain types of groups so that new ties will be formed; as a result their participational level will increase compared to that of nonmobile individuals on the same status level. Blau refers to this pattern as "overconformity." As time goes on, the differential in participation between mobile and nonmobile persons will disappear when a point of "acculturation" is reached (Blau 1956; Vorwaller 1970). Which of these hypothetical patterns is exhibited in a given situation may be a function of the type of mobility or type of formal group, or may reflect the measure of participation itself.

7. *Size of Community and Place of Residence* The effect of urbanization on organizational membership and participation is another concern for students of formal organization. Findings on rural-urban differences are contradictory (cf. Wright and Hyman 1958; Hausknecht 1962; Babchuk and Thompson 1969). However, the noticeable resemblance between urban and rural communities in terms of affluence, education, and mobility is a sign which points toward greater similarity in their rates of organizational membership than the reported associational differences.

Within a city, a question of considerable importance posed by the deconcentration or suburbanization of the urban community is the effect of centrifugal movement on the formal participation of residents in community activities. Previous studies have presented information on one segment of the total population without supplying comparable data on other parts of the population, or have chosen as samples parts of the population that are small and not representative (Martin 1953; Axelrod 1956; Wright and Hyman 1958). With the exception of one study (Zimmer and Hawley 1954), interaction does seem to be higher in the suburbs (cf. Tomeh 1969; Carlos 1970 on church membership), but it must be stressed that the greater interaction of suburban residents is a function of population characteristics such as homogeneity of residents as well as of place of residence (cf. Tomeh 1964, 1969; Gans 1961, 1962).

Thus, researchers in this field have examined associational membership in many widely different situations and in many parts of the country: large and small cities (cf. Hausknecht 1962; Wright and Hyman 1958), suburban and inner areas (cf. Zimmer and Hawley 1959; Tomeh 1969), partial and total populations (cf. Axelrod 1956; Tomeh 1969; Bell and Force 1956a, 1956b; Scott 1957; Freeman et al. 1957; Reissman 1954), single cities and on adults as a whole (cf. Hyman and Wright 1971), specific social classes (cf. Babchuk and Gordon 1962; Dotson 1951), ethnic groups (cf. Palisi 1965, 1966; Lopata 1964; Vrga 1971), military personnel (cf. Garbin and Langhlin 1965), and racial groups (cf. Babchuk and Thompson 1962; Ross and Wheeler 1967, 1971; Dackawich 1966; Orum 1966; Renzi 1968).[8]

Although much knowledge has been gained from the above various investigations, little is known about how the homogeneity or heterogeneity of a population affects interaction patterns in a given type of organization in terms of interpersonal relations, influence, style of leadership, consensus, or the like. These concerns are, unfortunately, not pursued even though they may be highly relevant to understanding the internal dynamics of organizations.

Finally, although there are many analyses of the correlates of membership, few of these are multifactional or multivariate[9] (cf. Freeman et al. 1957; Erbe 1964; Harp and Gagan 1971; Hodge and Treiman 1968; Olson 1972). In most instances, moreover, survey results are repeated and the theoretical propositions tested are grossly simplified. As a result not many sophisticated hypotheses have emerged. Further empirical investigations should make use of statistical procedures that permit an analysis of newly discovered variables in terms of their effect upon known relationships.

While all the preceding differences in participation according to demographic variables seem plausible and coherent with respect to one another, there is a continuing lack of information on attitudinal factors in relation to formal group participation. The inclusion of these additional dynamic factors will undoubtedly broaden the scope of formal participation research and allow a more complete analysis of the factors related to this phenomenon. More sophisticated generalizations may then be developed that are more meaningful and applicable, especially for those interested in improving membership participation patterns or changing participational levels.

In general, research dealing with attitudes has indicated that member participation is related to satisfaction, a feeling of control, optimism, confidence in society, a sense of predictability, and feelings of happiness and adjustment (cf. Beal 1956; Rose 1959; Hausknecht 1962; Phillips 1967, 1969; Segal et al. 1965; Smith 1966a). Dynamic analyses, however, are relatively few.

Sources of Affiliation

Studies on the nature of affiliation processes are rather limited, and what is available concerns the effect of informal contacts on participation in formal organizations. The conceptual framework for dealing with this relationship is based on exchange theory as synthesized by Katz and Lazarsfeld (1955). In their work on small groups and mass communications, they report that personal influence is one of the most important intervening variables in explaining consumer choice in marketing, fashions, movie going, and opinion formation regarding public affairs. The theoretical assumption is that a primary-group relationship is of central importance for predicting behavior in different situations.

With regard to affiliation with an association, Booth and Babchuk (1969) show that persons with several friends and relatives often become members through informal contacts, whereas those with smaller personal networks become members through formal leaders, or themselves initiate the contact which results in membership.[10] Secondary sources like the mass media are utilized in the affiliation process only as an impetus.

Personal influence seems to be more important for joining expressive than instrumental groups (see Booth and Babchuk, 1969). In a sense, a personalized pattern of affiliation becomes an extension of a web of highly personalized informal relations (see Babchuk and Gordon, 1962).

Although these studies (Babchuk and Gordon 1962; Booth and Babchuk 1969; also Jacoby 1966) show that the number and kind of personal contacts one has play an important role in one's associational activities, nothing is known in a comparative sense of the influence on an individual's organized activities of other informal groups, like those among neighbors and co-workers. Thus, the term "personal influence" is used in a broad sense, thereby obscuring the effect of other types of informal groups.

Furthermore, there are sources of influence other than informal groups that make individuals decide to join associations, such as self-interest, previous experience, active recruitment on the part of an organization, events or specific circumstances, and so forth. An assessment of these different influences is relevant not only for ranking their relative importance but also for observing the differential impacts of organizational participation on those recruited from different sources. It is, therefore, important to develop a theoretical framework based on a typology of individuals recruited to formal organizations, taking into account their previous experience and attitudes prior to joining (cf. Sills 1957 on an empirically derived classification).

Formal vs. Informal Interaction

In examining relationships between formal group participation and other forms of social participation, the literature suggests that individuals with high participation in a given type of social activity are also likely to be active in other activities as compared with individuals with low participation. Findings suggest that persons with many friends have higher levels of social participation than those with fewer friends (cf. Axelrod 1956; Scott 1957; Wright and Hyman 1958; Greer 1956; Caplow and Forman 1950; Williams 1958; Jacoby 1966; Babchuk and Thompson 1962; Palisi 1965, 1966).[11] This general phenomenon is referred to as the "cumulative effect" of social participation. A number of theoretical explanations are offered for this. Reisman (1958: 378), for example, makes reference to a dynamic concept of energy expansion in the presence of interest and motivation. This point of view, however, is in contrast to a zero-sum conception of energy as a fixed quantity to be expended in one activity or another. Palisi (1965, 1966) argues that relationships between different forms of social participation reflect the social structure of the group or society in terms of cultural influences, values, attribution of different statuses to various roles, background factors affecting self-perception and expectations, and so forth.

Others maintain that when different forms of social participation are generated by basically the same interest, a person may be inclined to pursue more than one source of activity. On the other hand, when different types of social participation fulfill different needs, a person may find that a choice has to be made in confining himself to some one activity. For example, people who join a formal group which provides leisurely activities will join any other group which caters to similar interests. What is important here is a consideration of the similarity and/or dissimilarity of functions of various forms of social participation which purport to explain the conditions under which the "cumulative effect" applies (cf. Weiss 1970; Tomeh 1974 for a similar viewpoint and further evidence).

As for the relationship of family participation to organizational membership, the works of Wirth (1938) and other pre-1950 sociologists suggest that the notion of substitution is applicable. The contention is that formal voluntary associations are prevalent in the city due to the fact that the individual has become alienated from the family. That is, urbanites join various formal groups in order to fulfill affiliative needs previously satisfied within the domain of the family. Palisi's (1965, 1966) studies on the Italian-American community indicate that family participation is inversely related to formal group membership because activities with the immediate family impede membership participation in formal groups. Both Palisi and Wirth imply a need for affiliative activities satisfied within the family and/or in formal groups depending on attractiveness of alternatives and total time available in which to satisfy these needs. However, Palisi explains the inverse relationship in some social activities in terms of the cultural definitions, norms, and social structure of the group or society, whereas Wirth implies a general decline of primary group relationships and the isolation of the individual in the urban city.

An any rate, a distinction should be drawn among the different types of informal participation—relatives, neighbors, friends, and co-workers— and an analysis made of how such interactions are individually related to differing degrees of formal membership. Such an analysis might be valuable for understanding the interrelationships between social structures and substructures as well as for predicting and modifying social participation.

Community Involvement and Associational Membership

Other studies relate associational membership to social involvement and/or community involvement. Hausknecht (1962) contends that the voluntary association acts as a link between the immediate situation of the individual and the larger society. Accordingly, he finds that membership in formal groups leads to greater factual knowledge of the immediate local environment and of the broader society encompassing it. Even with the variable of education controlled, group members, more so than nonmembers, tend to be linked with the broader community through the reading of books and magazines (cf. Allardt 1960 for similar results on a Finnish sample). Group members are also more likely than nonmembers to take part in community activities.

Furthermore, studies show that involvement by individuals in voluntary associations, community affairs, and churches will in turn mobilize them to become politically active (cf. Maccoby 1958; Zimmer and Hawley 1959; Wright and Hyman 1958; Hastings 1956; Olsen 1972). These studies also support the social pluralism theory, which argues that active involvement in voluntary groups, churches, and other organizations tends to bring individuals into contact with the larger community and provides them with the resources necessary for effective political action.

From another perspective, contemporary mass society theorists view voluntary organizations as mechanisms to reduce alienation and moderate extremist behavior (cf. Kornhauser 1959; Arendt 1951; Rose 1954). A special function is thus attributed to the voluntary organization as a socializing agent to restrain hostile reactions and promote social control. Research undertaken within this framework has generally shown that participants in voluntary organizations are consistently less alienated, even with social class differences controlled (cf. Erbe 1964; Rose 1962b; Meier and Bell 1959; Neal and Seeman 1964).

However, there is also the possibility that participation and mass behavior are directly related independent of alienation. On this point, research shows that those participating in voluntary organizations are most likely to be active in politics even when variations in social class and alienation are held constant (Erbe 1964). Organizational involvement, moreover, remains as an effective predictor of political activity, while alienation is not.

Perhaps what needs to be demonstrated is whether participation in voluntary groups engenders among the alienated and nonalienated alike a sense of constraint against mass extremist behavior more broadly defined than political apathy as a mass reaction. For example, the anticipation of various mass society theorists that participation in intermediate organizations exerts restraint against mass reaction is not borne out in Nelson's study of business owners (1968; also see Pinard 1968 on participation and mass movements).

With findings as disparate as the above, it is difficult to judge the comprehensiveness of the integration hypothesis to the effect that participation in formal groups is likely to retrain rather than support certain forms of mass behavior. It must be noted, however, that Nelson (1968) examines the integrative effects of participation in work-related organizations of an economic subgroup such as the small business owner. Thus, if further research shows that participation for other occupational and marginal groups in society does not promote attitudes and behaviors indicative of integration, then one cannot ignore the importance of subgroups in society and the conflict they may engender (cf. Coser 1964; Gusfield 1962).[12]

To reflect on this issue further, associational membership in ethnic groups is not always integrative. This is especially true when associations provide too firm an anchorage in the original culture, thereby hindering the acculturative process of minority groups (cf. Gordon 1964). In fact, ethnic minorities, aided by their organizations, are beginning to represent separate political forces in society (cf. Levy and Kramer, 1972). Moreover, social bargaining and factionalism among minority groups may indicate the existence of certain forms of conflict (cf. Shibutani and Kwan 1965). The presence of conflict is not necessarily dysfunctional, however, unless it continues to be a source of strain and tension in society or in the community (cf. Lopata 1964; Vrga 1971 on assimilation of ethnic groups in the community via voluntary organizations). At any rate, the integrative functions of such groups on the level both of society and the individual need to be interpreted with care.

Voluntary Organizations in a Cross-Cultural Perspective

In European societies, the increase in voluntary associations has been mostly along the lines of cooperatives, church-sponsored societies, political parties, and labor unions (cf. Rose 1954; Gallagher 1957 for data about France). The rigidity of the social structure is not conducive to the growth of a large number of reform or welfare associations. In this respect, associations seldom play a vital role in community life and appear, in fact, to be oriented toward the prevention of change rather than its integration and mediation (cf. Curtis 1971 on formal participation in Canada, Great Britain, Germany, Italy, and Mexico).

Contrastingly, Japan presents the unique situation of a non-Western but industrial country in which associations form an important part of the social structure (Norbeck 1962, 1972). It is reported that much of the economic and social life of the rural resident is conducted through associations. Among urban residents, common-interest associations (e.g., labor unions, schoolteacher groups, women's leagues) are abundant and have considerable power with regard to the economic and social affairs of the community. Many other groups which primarily deal with pleasurable activities are adjuncts of industrial concerns and other large economic enterprises and religious sects. The growth of voluntary associations in Japanese society is attributed both to modern urban conditions and to cultural changes.

In developing societies, a wide variety of secondary associations exists. In the urban areas of West Africa, Little (1957) finds that some associations are traditional, serving mainly tribal or kinship needs and catering largely to the poor and unskilled. Some incorporate modern goals of mutual aid and benefit as well as status- and class-oriented activities related to occupation. Many of the associations help new members adjust to the newly urbanized life of the city, thus serving as partial substitutes for traditional agencies of socialization (cf. Banton 1968).

The experience of other developing areas is no different from that of West Africa in terms of the urban context that presents new avenues and opportunities for the growth of new types of associations (cf. Douglas 1972 on Malaysia; Pye on Burma in Southeast Asia; Banfield 1958 on an Italian town). Unions, political organizations on a modest level, and credit and loan groups can be found, but the most common groups are those which provide either temporary or permanent aid and guidance for those who need to make the adjustment to city life or to urban bureaucratic structures (cf. Breese 1966). An important function of voluntary associations in such cities is their capacity at times to maintain a stable base for traditionalists living in a nontraditional milieu by merging traditional and modern activities, training individuals in skills they can apply more widely in city life, and making the adjustment process from one kind of social universe to another less difficult (cf. Anderson 1971; Hamer 1967 on Southwestern Ethiopia; Meillassoux 1969 on Bamako; and for studies on other societies see Eisenstandt 1956b on Israel; Anderson and Anderson 1959 on a Danish urban community; Dotson 1953 on a Mexican city; Rossides 1966 and Card 1968 for Canadian community studies).

Summary and Conclusions; Future Research

A great deal of the research on formal group participation has involved a functional orientation; only a few studies utilize an organizational framework. The functional approach operates on two levels of analysis—the structural and the social psychological. On the societal level, the emphasis is on the role and function of the formal group, which is viewed as an integrative force in the urban society. On the personal level, the voluntary group is seen as providing the individual with affective support and helping him integrate with the larger community (cf. Rose 1954, 1962a; Greer and

Orleans 1962; Rossi 1961; Erbe 1964; Babchuk and Edwards 1965; Jacoby 1965; Tomeh 1969).

The organizational approach focuses on the association itself as the unit of analysis. From this perspective, the problems of interest relate to the organization of the association, processes of operation and interaction, types of leadership, patterns of influence, internal effects of social change, and so forth (cf. Young and Larson 1965; Clark 1968; Laskin and Phillett 1965; Motz et al. 1965; Warriner and Prather 1965; Harp and Gagan 1971). It must be noted in passing, however, that organizational theory has generally been applied in studies dealing with large-scale organizations, bureaucratic structures, and other such units rather than formal groups. This discrepancy in present research is unfortunate, particularly in view of the fact that a tremendous amount of organizational interaction within the modern urban community takes places in formal groups. Also, the sheer number of such groups would be a valuable resource for purposes of comparative analysis.

The empirical findings on membership participation differ widely. The lack of consensus stems from differences in sample selection, use of secondary data, differing methodological procedures, and other related problems. Although it is impossible to come up with an exact figure, cited research shows that the majority of urbanites are members of at least one formal group other than church. Church, however, continues to attract the highest membership (cf. Lenski 1961; Tomeh 1969; Warren 1963). These observations lead to the conclusion that in a highly urbanized community in which secondary types of relationships and multiplicity of interests are maximized, participation in formal organizations is widespread. Thus, insofar as membership participation is an index of integration in society, only a small minority of urban dwellers have none of the benefits of integration that formal affiliation affords. This is not to imply that individuals in society are not integrated in other ways. Unfortunately, the studies on formal membership do not reveal what form of social organization are found among those who lack such affiliation. Possibly the social and psychological functions that associations perform for those who are affiliated are assumed for nonmembers by other types of social institutions.

For the most part, empirical investigations directed at distinguishing individuals who participate in formal groups from those who do not participate are limited to analyses of population characteristics. In general, the findings indicate that participation in voluntary organizations is high among high-SES groups, males, married persons, Protestants, and blacks. Results with respect to age, length and place of residence, and size of community are not very consistent. Furthermore, the variation within the different categories of most of the demographic variables is rather wide.

It is important to note that only a few of the above analyses utilize multivariate or multifactorial techniques (cf. Harp and Gagan 1971; Hodge and Treiman 1968; Olsen 1972; Freeman et al. 1957; Erbe 1964). Thus variables that appear to be consistently important, like SES, life-cycle stage, etc., are not always held constant in studies of other factors, though these variables may account for whatever relationships are found with respect to the latter.

Moreover, the effects of the heterogeneity or homogeneity of the voluntary group membership population are generally neglected, although this characteristic may affect patterns of interaction, types of leadership, and degree of consensus, within the organization. The level of participation within an organization has not been treated as an attribute of the organization. Finally, the structural characteristics of formal groups have been examined from the standpoint of the occupants of roles, while the structure of the organization in the community is seldom regarded as itself a variable within a comparative community context.

In contrast to the preponderance of research on demographic characteristics, studies relating membership to attitudinal and psychological factors are few. What is known is that membership in formal groups is associated with feelings of satisfaction and well-being, optimistic attitudes, a sense of predictability, etc. (cf. Beal 1956; Rose 1959; Hausknecht 1962; Phillips 1967, 1969; Smith 1966a). The study of such dynamic variables undoubtedly contributes to further understanding of the phenomenon of participation, but additional research is needed in order to determine the nature of the casual relationship. Thus, for example, if membership in formal groups tends to generate positive feelings, then such involvement may have the effect of reducing psychological or emotional problems. In any event, a serious attempt must be made to consider structural and attitudinal variables simultaneously in order to explain or predict formal participation and assess its consequences. Unfortunately, past research is more or less one-sided.

Perhaps the first question that needs to be answered concerns the motivations and personality characteristics of those who join groups. Studies addressing themselves to this question show that personal influence (cf. Jacoby 1966; Babchuk and Gordon 1962; Booth and Babchuk 1969) and personality (cf. Smith, 1966a) play a very important role in determining the extent of one's associational activities. Such efforts have also been limited, and other types of influence on decision-making relative to affiliation (such as reference groups, self-interest, previous experience, specific events, etc.) have been inadequately treated in terms of a research strategy or a theoretical typology.

Some of these issues are important, moreover, because of their implications for the nature of the community, in that the type of association an individual encounters is related to the associational structure of the local community. The community is, among other things, the locus for the function of providing opportunities for social participation of various kinds. In this respect, communities differ greatly in the pattern of associational activities which they afford. For example, a community with a long history of varied formal groups as well as a large associational membership may facilitate the formation of new voluntary groups, whereas the presence of a community in which formal groups are less important may be a factor in their dissolution or a barrier to membership participation. Communities may also vary with respect to type of formal organization. In some communities economic and political groups are likely to predominate, whereas in others interest groups and recreational clubs are prevalent. This suggests that communities differ with regard to sources of affiliation, which difference in turn may affect membership rates or affiliation processes. Pursuit of these and other similar concerns may lead to more integration of the functional and organizational approaches (see Ross 1972 for a theoretical start on voluntary association theory.)

Investigation of a number of other problems might provide a stronger connection between the two approaches. An example of what is needed is an understanding of the factors operating in the dissolution of voluntary associations or the conversions of such groups to nonvoluntary groups. Of equal importance is a comprehension of the factors involved in nonparticipation and membership eligibility, motivations for affiliation, attitudes toward membership, relationships between various formal and informal structures, the extent to which voluntary groups can tolerate a distinct informal structure, and so on. Research is scarce in these areas of interest. Another problem of theoretical importance, discussed earlier, is the need to delineate the inclusiveness of the concept of voluntary groups.

Voluntary organizations, finally, perform various functions for the community—educational, religious, recreational, cultural, welfare, and the like. Some groups are clearly organized with the express purpose of pursuing some area of interest or concern on behalf of others in the community, thus acquiring an interest in the influencing of community affairs or of important decisions on policy matters. To that extent, formal voluntary groups are a vital part of the social structure and play a crucial mediating role in the relations between social units in the community as well as provide a link between the individual and his community. Even in newly urbanizing areas voluntary groups play a very important role in facilitating further modernization by adapting the social structure to modern requirements and assisting individuals to adjust to urban community life.

NOTES

[1]According to Wilensky (1961b), bibliographical data compiled by sociologists and others show, for example, 80,000 local trade unions, 100,000 different women organizations, 1,500 national trade associations, and 4,000 Chambers of Commerce.

[2]Other studies on formal groups, particularly those conducted in rural communities, have used the Chapin (1947: 196–197) Social Participation Scale—i.e., membership attendance, contributions, committee membership, and offices held—or some variant of

it as an operational definition of participation (cf. Anderson 1946: Mayo 1951; Mayo and Marsh 1951; Hay 1950; Martin 1952).

[3]This same relationship is obtained in rural communities (cf. Hay 1950; Brown 1953) as well as in other countries (cf. Zetterberg 1960, a national sample of Swedes; Allardt and Pesonen 1960, a survey of a large Finnish industrial city; Rokkan 1959, a national sample on Norway; Dotson 1953, on a large Mexican city).

[4]Explanations offered by various investigators interested in accounting for social class differences in participation involve considerations of anomie (cf. Bell 1957; Simpson and Miller 1963), authoritarianism (cf. Eysenck 1951), sectarianism (cf. Dynes 1957), and apathy (cf. Dean 1960, 1961).

[5]Zimmer and Hawley (1959) report the usual difference between younger and older individuals relative to membership, but no significant differences among the age groups in the city's fringe. This calls attention to the importance of place of residence and to the socioeconomic status of the suburb, which diminishes the influence of age on membership. Thus, the correlation between age and participation may be a spurious product of their relationship to other major variables (e.g., SES) which determines one's participation.

[6]The difference may be that slum children whose parents are affiliated display a greater tendency toward affiliation than those whose parents are not.

[7]In the general context of residential mobility, home owners participate more in voluntary associations than non–home owners (Hausknecht 1962; Scott 1957). The relationship holds regardless of SES and level of urbanization of the region, although Wright and Hyman (1958) indicate that home ownership as a determinant of membership is related to social stratification. The explanation for the relationship is that home ownership is associated with a stability and predictability vis-à-vis others in the area. Hausknecht (1962) contends that home ownership involves a major economic investment and hence owners have a stake in the neighborhood and wider community, and it is in this sense that the home owner is integrated in society. If the data are analyzed along the lines of occupational involvement (Wilensky 1961a), or different levels of mobility stage (Litwak 1961), however, the participation differential between renters and home owners may be greatly reduced.

[8]Other researchers have investigated relationships between formal group membership and major institutional variables, like family status of the area (see Bell and Force 1956b), cohesion of the neighborhood (see Litwak 1961), managerial training policies of major firms, status crystallization (see Lenski 1956), and environmental pressures impinging on the structure of the association itself (cf. Rose 1955; Simpson and Gulley 1962).

[9]Multifactorial and multivariate analysis are statistical techniques for handling problems involving a large number of variables. These techniques begin with a matrix of intercorrelations which gives results on a number of interrelationships simultaneously. The aim in multifactorial analysis is to reduce a large number of operational indices to a smaller number of conceptual variables. The aim in multivariate analysis is to identify variables as determiners of other variables and specify how effective they are.

[10]Hodge and Treiman's (1968) findings show that for both males and females membership in voluntary organizations is strongly influenced by the parents' level of organizational participation.

[11]Brown (1954) in his rural sample finds that people who are most active in formal groups are most likely to engage in informal activities such as visiting, giving parties, etc. Similarly, studies based on non-American samples show positive relationships between leisure activities and club membership (cf. Allardt et al. 1958 on a Finnish youth sample).

[12]Such a pursuit requires a clarification of the relationship among various definitions of integration, as well as of their common relation to participation (cf. Landecker 1951 on different types of integration).

REFERENCES

Allardt, Erik, and P. Pesonen.
1960 "Finland," *International Social Science Journal* 12 (Quarter 1): 27–39.
————, Pentti Jartti, Frina Jyakila, and Yrjo Littunen.
1958 "On the Cumulative Nature of Leisure Activities," *Acta Sociologica* 3, No. 4: 165–172.

Anderson, Robert.
1971 "Voluntary Associations in History," *American Anthropologist* 73 (February): 209–222.
————, and Gallatin Anderson.
1959 "Voluntary Associations and Urbanization: A Diachronic Analysis," *American Journal of Sociology* 65 (November): 256–273.

Anderson, Walfred A.
1943 "The Family and Individual Social Participation," *American Sociological Review* 8 (August): 420–424.
1946 "Family Social Participation and Social Status Self-Rating," *American Sociological Review* 2 (June): 253–258.

Arendt, Hannah.
1951 *The Origins of Totalitarianism*. New York: Harcourt, Brace.

Argyle, Michael.
1959 *Religious Behavior*. Glencoe, Ill.: The Free Press.

Axelrod, Morris.
1956 "Urban Structure and Social Participation," *American Sociological Review* 21 (February): 13–18.

Babchuk, Nicholas, and Alan Booth.
1969 "Voluntary Association Membership: A Longitudinal Analysis," *American Sociological Review* 34 (February): 31–45.
————, and J. Edwards.
1965 "Voluntary Associations and the Integrative Hypothesis," *Sociological Inquiry* 35 (Spring): 149–162.
————, and C. Wayne Gordon.
1962 *The Voluntary Associations in the Slum*. University of Nebraska Press.
————, Ruth Marsey, and C. Wayne Gordon.
1960 "Men and Women in Community Agencies: A Note on Power and Prestige," *American Sociological Review* 25 (June): 399–403.
————, and Ralph V. Thompson.
1962 "The Voluntary Associations of Negroes," *American Sociological Review* 27 (October): 647–655.

Baeumler, Walter.
1965 "The Correlates of Formal Participation Among High School Students," *Sociological Inquiry* 35 (Spring): 235–240.

Banfield, Edward C.
1958 *The Moral Basis of a Backward Society*. Glencoe, Ill.: The Free Press.

Banton, Michael.
1968 "Voluntary Associations," 1. Anthropological Aspects, in *International Encyclopedia of the Social Sciences* 16. New York: Macmillan and The Free Press, 357–362.

Beal, George M.
1956 "Additional Hypotheses in Participation Research," *Rural Sociology* 21 (September–December): 249–256.

Bell, Wendell.
1957 "Anomie, Social Isolation and the Class Structure," *Sociometry* 20 (June): 105–116.
———, and Maryanne T. Force.
1956a "Social Structure and Participation in Different Types of Formal Associations," *Social Forces* 34 (May): 345–359.
1956b "Urban Neighborhood Types and Participation in Formal Associations," *American Sociological Review* 21 (February): 25–34.

Blau, Peter M.
1956 "Social Mobility and Interpersonal Relations," *American Sociological Review* 21 (June): 290–295.
———, and W. Richard Scott.
1962 *Formal Organizations*. San Francisco: Chandler.

Blum, Alan.
1964 "Social Structure, Social Class and Participation in Primary Relationships," in Arthur B. Shostak and William Gombrey (eds.), *Blue Collar World*. Englewood Cliffs, N.J.: Prentice-Hall, 195–207.

Booth, Alan.
1972 "Sex and Social Participation," *American Sociological Review* 37 (April): 183–192.
———, and Nicholas Babchuk.
1969 "Personal Influence Networks and Voluntary Association Affiliation," *Sociological Inquiry* 39 (Spring): 179–188.
———, Nicholas Babchuk, and Alan B. Knox.
1968 "Social Stratification and Membership in Instrumental-Expressive Voluntary Associations," *Sociological Quarterly* 9 (Autumn): 427–439.

Brager, George.
1969 "Organizing the Unaffiliated in a Low Income Area," in Amitai Etzioni (ed.), *A Sociological Reader on Complex Organizations*. New York: Holt, Rinehart, and Winston, 375–383.

Breese, Gerald.
1966 *Urbanization in Newly Developed Countries*. Englewood Cliffs, N.J.: Prentice-Hall.

Brown, Emory J.
1953 "The Self as Related to Formal Participation in Three Pennsylvania Communities," *Rural Sociology* 18 (December): 313–320.
1954 "Informal Participation of Active and Inactive Formal Participants," *Rural Sociology* 19 (December): 365–370.

Bruce, James.
1971 "Intragenerational Occupational Mobility and Participation in Formal Associations," *Sociological Quarterly* 12 (Winter): 46–55.

Bultena, L.
1949 "Church Membership and Church Attendance in Madison, Wisconsin," *American Sociological Review* 14 (June): 384–389.

Bushee, Frederick.
1945 "Social Organizations in a Small City," *American Journal of Sociology* (September): 117–226.

Caplow, Theodore, and Robert Forman.
1950 "Neighborhood Interaction in a Homogeneous Community," *American Sociological Review* 15 (June): 357–366.

Card, B. Y.
1968 *Trends and Changes in Canadian Society*. Toronto: Macmillan.

Carlos, Serge.
1970 "Religious Participation and the Urban-Suburban Continuum," *American Journal of Sociology* 75 (March): 747–759.

Chapin, F. Stuart.
1947 *Experimental Designs in Sociological Research.* New York: Harper and Brothers.

Clark, T. N.
1968 *Community Structure and Decision Making: Comparative Analysis.* San Francisco: Chandler.

Coser, Lewis.
1964 "Durkheim Conservatism and Its Implications for his Sociological Theory," in Kurt Wolff (ed.), *Essays on Sociology and Philosophy.* New York: Harper and Row, 211–232.

Curtis, James.
1971 "Voluntary Association Joining: A Cross-National Comparative Note," *American Sociological Review* 36 (October): 872–880.

Curtis, Richard G.
1959 "Note on Occupational Mobility and Union Membership in Detroit: A Replication," *Social Forces* 38 (October): 69–71.
1960 "Occupational Mobility and Church Participation," *Social Forces* 38 (May): 315–319.

Dackawich, John.
1966 "Voluntary Associations of Central Area Negroes," *Pacific Sociological Review* 9 (Fall): 74–78.

Dean, Dwight.
1960 "Alienation and Political Apathy," *Social Forces* 38 (March): 185–189.
1961 "Alienation: Its Meaning and Measurement," *American Sociological Review* 26 (October): 753–758.

Dotson, Floyd.
1951 "Patterns of Voluntary Associations Among Urban Working Class Families," *American Sociological Review* 16 (October): 687–693.
1953 "A Note on Participation in Voluntary Associations in a Mexican City," *American Sociological Review* 18 (August): 380–386.

Douglas, Stephen.
1972 "Voluntary Associational Structure in Malaysia: Some Implications for Political Participation," *Journal of Voluntary Action Research* 1 (January): 24–37.

Dynes, Russell.
1957 "The Consequence of Sectarianism for Social Participation," *Social Forces* 35 (May): 331–334.

Eisenstadt, Samuel N.
1956a "Sociological Aspects of Economic Adoption of Oriental Immigrants in Israel: A Case Study of the Problems of Modernization," *Economic Development and Cultural Change* 4 (April): 269–278.
1956b "The Social Conditions of the Development of Voluntary Associations: A Case Study of Israel," *Scripts Hierosolynitana* 3: 104–125.

Erbe, William.
1964 "Social Involvement and Political Activity," *American Sociological Review* 29 (April): 198–215.

Evan, William.
1957 "Dimensions of Participation in Voluntary Associations," *Social Forces* 36 (December): 148–153.

Eysenck, J. J.
1951 "Social Attitude and Social Class," *British Journal of Sociology* 2 (September): 198–204.

Foskett, John.
1955 "Social Structure and Social Participation," *American Sociological Review* 20 (August): 431–438.

Freeman, Howard K., Edwin Novak, and Leo C. Reeder.
1957 "Correlates of Membership in Voluntary Associations," *American Sociological Review* 22 (October): 528–533.

Gallagher, Orvoell R.
1957 "Voluntary Associations in France," *Social Forces* 36 (December): 153–160.

Gans, Herbert.
1961 "Planning and Social Life: An Evaluation of a Friendship and Neighbor Relations in Suburban Communities," *Journal of the American Institute of Planners* 27 (May): 134–140.
1962 "Urbanism and Suburbanism as Ways of Life: A Re-Evaluation of Definitions," in Arnold Rose (ed.), *Human Behavior and Social Processes*. Boston: Houghton Mifflin Company, 625–648.

Garbin, A. P., and Vivian L. Laughlin.
1965 "Military Participation in Voluntary Associations," *Sociological Inquiry* 35 (Spring): 227–234.

Geertz, Clifford.
1962 "The Rotating Credit Associations: A Middle Rung in Development," *Economic Development and Cultural Change* 10 (April): 241–265.

Gerstl, Joel E.
1961 "Leisure and Occupational Milieu," *Social Problems* 9 (Summer): 56–68.

Goode, Erich.
1966 "Social Class and Church Participation," *American Journal of Sociology* 72 (July): 102–111.

Gordon, Milton.
1964 *Assimilation in American Life.* New York: Oxford University Press.

Gordon, Wayne C., and Nicholas Babchuk.
1959 "A Typology of Voluntary Associations," *American Sociological Review* 24 (February): 22–29.

Greer, Scott.
1956 "Urbanism Reconsidered: A Comparative Study of Local Areas in Metropolis," *American Sociological Review* 21 (February): 19–25.
———, and Peter Orleans.
1962 "The Mass Society and the Parapolitical Structure," *American Sociological Review* 20 (October): 634–646.

Grusky, Oscar.
1964 "The Effects of Succession: A Comparative Study of Business Organizations," in Morris Janowitz (ed.), *The New Military.* New York: Russell Sage Foundation, 83–111.

Gusfield, Joseph.
1962 "Mass Society and Extremist Politics," *American Sociological Review* 27 (February): 19–30.

Hagedorn, Robert, and Sanford Labovitz.
1967 "An Analysis of Community and Professional Participation Among Occu-

pations," *Social Forces* 46 (June): 484–491.
1968 "Participation in Community Associations by Occupation: A Test of Three Theories," *American Sociological Review* 33 (April): 272–283.

Hamer, John H.
1967 "Voluntary Associations as Structures of Change Among the Sidamo of South Western Ethiopia," *Anthropological Quarterly* 40 (April): 73–91.

Harp, John, and Richard J. Gagan.
1971 "Scaling Formal Voluntary Organizations As An Element of Community Structure," *Social Forces* 49 (March): 477–482.

Harry, Joseph.
1970 "Family Localism and Social Participation," *American Journal of Sociology* 75 (March): 821–828.

Hastings, Phillip K.
1956 "The Voter and the Non-Voter," *American Journal of Sociology* 62 (November): 302–307.

Hausknecht, Murray.
1962 *The Joiners.* New York: Bedminster Press.
1964 "The Blue Collar Joiners," in Shostak and Gombery (eds.), *Blue Collar World.* Englewood Cliffs, N.J.: Prentice-Hall, 207–215.

Hay, Donald.
1950 "The Social Participation of Households in Selected Rural Communities of the North East," *Rural Sociology* 15 (June): 141–148.

Hodge, Robert, and Donald Treiman.
1968 "Social Participation and Social Status," *American Sociological Review* 33 (October): 722–741.

Hyman, Herbert, and Charles R. Wright.
1971 "Trends in Voluntary Association Memberships of American Adults: Replication Based on Secondary Analysis of National Sample Surveys," *American Sociological Review* 36 (April): 191–206.

Jacoby, Arthur.
1965 "Some Correlates of Instrumental and Expressive Orientations to Associational Membership," *Sociological Inquiry* 35 (Spring): 163–175.
1966 "Personal Influence and Primary Relationships: Their Effect on Associational Membership," *Sociological Quarterly* 7 (Winter): 76–84.
——, and Nicholas Babchuk.
1963 "Instrumental and Expressive Voluntary Associations," *Sociology and Social Research* 47 (July): 461–471.

Katz, Elihu, and Paul Lazarsfeld.
1955 *Personal Influence.* Glencoe, Ill.: The Free Press.

Komarovsky, Mira.
1946 "The Voluntary Associations of Urban Dwellers," *American Sociological Review* 11 (December): 686–698.

Kornhauser, W.
1959 *The Politics of Mass Society.* Glencoe, Ill.: The Free Press.

Landecker, Wenner.
1951 "Types of Integration and Their Measurement," *American Journal of Sociology* 55 (January): 332–340.

Lane, Robert E.
1959 *Political Life: Why People Get Involved in Politics.* Glencoe, Ill.: The Free Press.

Laskin, Richard.
1961 *Voluntary Organizations in a Saskatchewan Town.* Saskatoon, Canada: Center for Community Studies.
————, and Serena Phillett.
1965 "An Integrative Analysis of Voluntary Associational Leadership and Reputational Influences," *Sociological Inquiry* 35 (Spring): 176–185.
Lenski, Gerhard E.
1956 "Social Participation and Status Crystallization," *American Sociological Review* 21 (August): 458–464.
1961 *The Religious Factor.* Garden City: Doubleday and Company.
Levy, Mark, and Michael Kramer.
1972 *The Ethnic Factor.* New York: Simon and Schuster.
Little, Kenneth.
1957 "The Role of Voluntary Associations in West Africa Urbanization," *American Anthropologist* 59 (August): 579–596.
1965 *West African Urbanization: A Study of Voluntary Associations in Social Change.* Cambridge: Cambridge University Press.
Litwak, Eugene.
1960 "Occupational Mobility and Extended Family Cohesion," *American Sociological Review* 25 (February): 9–21.
1961 "Voluntary Associations and Neighborhood Cohesion," *American Sociological Review* 26 (April): 258–271.
Lopata, Helena Z.
1964 "The Function of Voluntary Associations in an Ethnic Community: Polonia," in Ernest Burgess and Donald Bogue (eds.), *Contributions to Urban Sociology.* University of Chicago Press, 203–223.
Lundberg, G., M. Komarovsky, and M. McInery.
1934 *Leisure: A Suburban Study.* New York: Columbia University Press.
Maccoby, Herbert.
1958 "The Differential Political Activity of Participants in Voluntary Associations," *American Sociological Review* 23 (October): 524–532.
Martin, Walter.
1952 "A Consideration of the Formal Association Activities on Rural-Urban Fringe Residents," *American Sociological Review* 21 (August): 687–694.
1953 *The Rural-Urban Fringe: A Study of Adjustment to Residence Location.* Eugene, Oregon: University Press.
Mather, W. C.
1941 "Income and Social Participation," *American Sociological Review* 6 (June): 380–383.
Mayo, Selz C.
1951 "Social Participation Among the Older Population in Rural Areas of Wake County, North Carolina," *Social Forces* 30 (October): 53–59.
————, and C. Paul Marsh.
1951 "Social Participation in the Rural Community," *American Journal of Sociology* 57 (November): 243–247.
Meier, Dorothy, and Wendell Bell.
1959 "Anomie and Differential Access to Life Goals," *American Sociological Review* 24 (April): 189–202.
Meillassoux, Claude.
1969 *Urbanization of an African Community: Voluntary Associations in Bamako.* Seattle and London: University of Washington Press.

Moore, Joan W.
1961 "Patterns of Women's Participation in Voluntary Associations," *American Journal of Sociology* 66 (May): 592–598.

Motz, A. B., Wayne C. Rohrer, and Patricia Dagilaitis.
1965 "American Sociological Regional Societies: Social Characteristics of Presidents," *Sociological Inquiry* 35 (Spring): 207–218.

Myrdal, Gunner, Richard Sterner, and Arnold Rose.
1944 *An American Dilemma.* New York: Harper and Brothers.

Neal, Arthur, and M. Seeman.
1964 "Organizations and Powerlessness," *American Sociological Review* 29 (April): 216–226.

Nelson, Joel.
1968 "Participation and Integration: The Case of the Small Businessman," *American Sociological Review* 33 (June): 427–438.

Norbeck, Edward.
1962 "Common Interest Associations in Rural Japan," in Robert J. Smith and Richard K. Beardsley (eds.), *Japanese Culture: Its Development and Character.* Chicago: Aldine, 73–83.
1972 "Japanese Common Interest Associations in Cross-Cultural Perspective," *Journal of Voluntary Action Research* 1 (January): 38–41.

Olsen, Marvin.
1972 "Social Participation and Voting Turnout: A Multivariate Analysis," *American Sociological Review* 37 (June): 317–333.

Orum, Anthony M.
1966 "A Reappraisal of the Social and Political Participation of Negroes," *American Journal of Sociology* 72 (July): 32–46.

Palisi, Bartolomeu.
1965 "Ethnic Generation and Social Participation," *Sociological Inquiry* 35 (Spring): 219–226.
1966 "Patterns of Social Participation in a Two-Generation Sample of Italian-Americans," *The Sociological Inquiry* 7 (Spring): 167–178.
1968 "A Critical Analysis of the Voluntary Association Concept," *Sociology and Social Research* 52 (July): 392–405.

Parsons, Talcott.
1951 *The Social System.* Glencoe, Ill.: The Free Press.
——, R. F. Bales, and E. A. Shils.
1953 *Working Papers in the Theory of Action.* Glencoe, Ill.: The Free Press.

Phillips, Derek.
1967 "Social Participation and Happiness," *American Journal of Sociology* 72 (March): 479–488.
1969 "Social Class, Social Participation and Happiness: A Consideration of Interaction, Opportunities, and Investment," *Sociological Quarterly* 10 (Winter): 3–21.

Pihlblad, C. Terence, and Robert L. McNamara.
1965 "Social Adjustment of Elderly People in Three Small Towns," in Arnold Rose and Warren Peterson (eds.), *Older People and Their Social World.* Philadelphia: F. A. Davis Company, 49–73.

Pinard, Maurice.
1968 "Mass Society and Political Movements: A New Formulation," *The American Journal of Sociology* 78 (May): 682–690.

Pye, Lucian W.
 1962 *Politics, Personality and Nation Building*. New Haven: Yale University Press.
Reisman, David.
 1958 "Leisure and Work in Post-Industrial Society," in Eric Larrabee and Rolf Meyersohn (eds.), *Mass Leisure*. Glencoe, Ill.: The Free Press, 363–388.
Reissman, Leonard.
 1954 "Class and Social Participation," *American Sociological Review* 19 (February): 76–84.
Renzi, Marrio.
 1968 "Negroes and Voluntary Associations," *Research Reports in the Social Sciences* 2 (Spring): 63–71.
Rokkan, S.
 1959 "Electoral Activity, Party Membership, and Organizational Influence." *Acta Sociologica* 4 (Quarter 1): 25–37.
Rose, Arnold M.
 1954 *Theory and Method in the Social Science*. University of Minnesota Press.
 1955 "Voluntary Associations Under Conditions of Competition and Conflict," *Social Forces* 34 (December): 159–163.
 1959 "Attitudinal Correlates of Social Participation," *Social Forces* 37 (March): 202–206.
 1962a "Reactions Against the Mass Society," *Sociological Quarterly* 3 (October): 316–330.
 1962b "Alienation and Participation: A Comparison of Group Leaders and the Mass," *American Sociological Review* 27 (December): 834–838.
 1965 *Sociology*, 2nd ed., rev. New York: Knopf.
 1967 *The Power Structure: Political Process in American Society*. New York: Oxford University Press.
 ———, and Warren A. Peterson (eds.).
 1965 *Older People and Their Social World*, Philadelphia: F. A. Davis Company.
Ross, Jack.
 1972 "Toward a Reconstruction of Voluntary Association Theory," *British Journal of Sociology* 23 (March): 20–32.
 ———, and Raymond Wheeler.
 1967 "Structural Sources of Threat to Negro Membership Associations in a Southern City," *Social Forces* 45 (June): 583–586.
 1971 *Black Belonging*. Westport, Conn.: Greenwood Publishing Company.
Rossi, Peter H.
 1961 "The Organizational Structure of an American Community," in Amitai Etzioni (ed.), *Complex Organizations*. New York: Holt, Rinehart and Winston, 301–312.
Rossides, Daniel W.
 1966 *Voluntary Participation in Canada: A Comparative Analysis*. Toronto: Canadian Association for Adult Education.
Schmidt, John Frank, and Wayne C. Rohrer.
 1956 "The Relationship of Family Type to Social Participation," *Marriage and Family Living* 18 (August): 224–230.
Scott, John C., Jr.
 1957 "Membership and Participation in Voluntary Associations," *American Sociological Review* 22 (June): 315–326.

Segal, Bernard, Robert Weiss, and Robert Sokal.
1965 "Emotional Adjustment, Social Organization and Psychiatric Treatment,"
    American Sociological Review 30 (August): 548–556.

Shibutani, Tamotsu, and Kian M. Kwan.
1965 Ethnic Stratification. New York: The Macmillan Company.

Sills, David.
1957 The Volunteers. New York: The Free Press.

Simpson, Richard, and Max H. Miller.
1963 "Social Status and Anomie," Social Problems 10 (Winter): 356–364.

Simpson, Robert L., and William H. Gulley.
1962 "Goals, Environment Pressures, and Organizational Characteristics,"
    American Sociological Review 27 (June): 344–350.

Smith, David Horton.
1966a "A Psychological Model of Individual Participation in Formal Voluntary
    Organizations: Application to Some Chilean Data," American Journal of
    Sociology 72 (November): 249–266.
1966b "The Importance of Formal Voluntary Organizations for Society," Soci-
    ology and Social Research 50 (July): 483–491.

A Social Profile of Detroit.
1952 Report on the Detroit Area Study. Ann Arbor: University of Michigan
    Press.

Spinard, William.
1960 "Correlates of Trade Union Participation," American Sociological Review
    25 (April): 237–244.

Sussman, Marvin B.
1955 "Activity Patterns of Post-Parental Couples and Their Relationship to
    Family Continuity," Marriage and Family Living 17 (November): 338–
    341.

Tannenbaum, Frank.
1951 A Philosophy of Labor. New York: Knopf.

Tomeh, Aida K.
1964 "Informal Group Participation and Residential Patterns," American Jour-
    nal of Sociology 70 (July): 28–35.
1969 "Empirical Considerations on the Problem of Social Integration," Socio-
    logical Inquiry 39 (Winter): 65–76.
1974 "On the cumulative nature of social participation and mass media in
    Lebanon." International Journal of Contemporary Sociology, forthcoming.

Turner, Ralph, and Lewis Killian (eds.).
1972 Collective Behavior, 2nd ed. Englewood Cliffs, N.J.: Prentice-Hall.

Videbeck, Richard, and Alan B. Knox.
1965 "Alternative Participatory Responses to Aging," in Arnold M. Rose and
    Warren A. Peterson (eds.), Older People and Their Social World. Phila-
    delphia: F. A. Davis Company, 37–49.

Vorwaller, Darrel J.
1970 "Social Mobility and Membership in Voluntary Associations," American
    Journal of Sociology 75 (January): 481–495.

Vrga, Djuro, Jr.
1971 "Differential Associational Involvement of Successive Ethnic Immigra-
    tions: An Indicator of Ethno-Religious Factionalism and Alienation of
    Immigrants," Social Forces 50 (December): 239–248.

Warren, Roland.
1963 *The Community in America.* Chicago: Rand McNally and Company.
Warriner, Charles, and Jane Prather.
1965 "Four Types of Voluntary Associations," *Sociological Inquiry* 35 (Spring): 138–148.
Wilensky, Harold L.
1961a "Orderly Careers and Social Participation: The Impact of Work History on Social Integration in the Middle Class," *American Sociological Review* 26 (August): 521–523.
1961b "Life Cycle, Work Situation, and Participation in Formal Associations," in R. W. Kleemier (ed.), *Aging and Leisure.* New York: Oxford University Press, 213–242.
1964 "Work, Careers, and Social Integration," in S. N. Eisenstadt (ed.), *Comparative Social Problems.* New York: The Free Press, 306–319.
———, and Hugh Edwards.
1959 "The Skidder: Ideological Adjustments of Downward Mobile Workers," *American Sociological Review* 24 (April): 215–231.
Williams, James.
1958 "Close Friendship Relations of Housewives Residing in an Urban Community," *Social Forces* 36 (May): 358–362.
Windham, Gerald.
1963 "Formal Participation of Migrant Housewives in an Urban Community," *Sociology and Social Research* 47 (January): 201–209.
Wirth, Louis.
1938 "Urbanism as a Way of Life," *American Journal of Sociology* 44 (July): 1–24.
Wright, Charles, and Herbert H. Hyman.
1958 "Voluntary Association Membership of American Adults: Evidence From National Sample Surveys," *American Sociological Review* 23 (June): 284–294.
Young, R. C., and O. F. Larson.
1965 "A New Approach to Community Structure," *American Sociological Review* 30 (December): 926–934.
Zetterberg, Hans L.
1960 "National Pastime: Pursuit of Power," *Industria International.* Stockholm: 105–107, 156–168.
Zimmer, Basil.
1955 "Participation of Migrants in Urban Structures," *American Sociological Review* 20 (April): 218–224.
———, and Amos Hawley.
1959 "The Significance of Membership in Associations," *American Journal of Sociology* 65 (September): 196–201.

Community Disorganization: Some Critical Notes*

JOE R. FEAGIN

University of Texas (Austin)

In recent years numerous discussions of urban communities have given great weight to themes of disorganization and disorder. This paper critically examines several important conceptual, procedural, and substantive issues inherent in most treatments of community disorganization. To illustrate such fundamental problems as "overgeneralization" and dominant group bias five specific topics—migration, disasters, slums, ghettos, and collective violence—were selected for intensive analysis.

In recent years most popular and many scholarly discussions of urban communities have given great weight to themes of disorganization and disorder. Stress on community problems often seems to be the order of the day, whether the "community" being discussed is a few hundred black families in a ghetto setting, a large white-collar suburb, or an entire metropolitan area. Yet in spite of this growing emphasis social science analysts have not spent as much time as one might have expected grappling with the important conceptual and empirical issues involved in discussions of disorganization. It is my intention in this exploratory paper to point up a few of these critical issues, providing some preliminary spadework for future conceptual and empirical analysis.

Although it is not the purpose of this paper to develop a comprehensive conceptual framework for the analysis of community, a few comments on

*This paper is a revised version of a paper presented at the 1972 American Sociological Association meetings in New Orleans, Louisiana. I would particularly like to thank Charles Tilly, Robert Perrin, S. Dale McLemore, David Perry, Charles Bonjean, Alejandro Portes, Marcia Effrat, and Andy Effrat for their useful comments on an earlier version of this paper.

definitions will provide a useful starting point. With only mild exaggeration Bell and Newby (1972: 27) have argued that every sociologist "has possessed his own notion of what community consists of, frequently reflecting his ideas of what it *should* consist of." Indeed, Hillery's (1955) review of nearly one hundred definitions of community still stands as the only systematic attempt to sift out essential characteristics. In spite of the fact that an incredibly diverse assortment of characteristics was found to be associated with the term "community," Hillery's elaborate classification indicated that three basic defining characteristics have often been distinguished: a limited geographical area, normative sharing, and social interaction. While the delineation of community in these terms is little more than a beginning, particularly because of the vagueness of notions like "limited geographical area," it is already in advance of definitional analysis in regard to community disorganization. Apparently, only two or three analysts have recently sketched out the critical aspects or characteristics of community disorganization. Working at a rather abstract level, Bernard (1968: 163) has suggested that the disorganization of a community be viewed as "a state in which one or more of the several subsystems, for whatever reason, fail to function at some specified expected level of effectiveness, or it may be defined as the processes that lead to such a state, or it may refer both to the processes and to the state." Basic to this view is the idea that disorganization entails a serious malfunction in a subsystem of a community's social system. Of importance too is the emphasis on disorganization as both a process and as a state.

Coleman (1971), on the other hand, seems to have developed his view of community disorganization in a less abstract way, by reviewing how the concept of community disorganization has actually been used by students of society and by examining examples often cited. Coleman (1971: 659) has distilled "the two elements of community disorganization pointed to by many authors." He terms the two types "disintegration" and "conflict." First, there is the category of phenomena which involve a lack or deterioration of social norms or consensus. By implication the lack or deterioration of social ties or orderly social arrangements emphasized by other authors would also fall under this rubric. "Disintegration" is a term often used to denote this type of community disorganization. Yet other phenomena are described in the language of disorganization because the collective patterns of behavior involved (e.g., collective violence) are regarded as challenging established structures of power and resources in communities, disorderly behavior which makes evident divergent values and perspectives. "Conflict"" is a term often used to describe this type of community disorganization. Yet value or perspective conflict is not the main characteristic of collective violence which leads many to view it in disorganization terms. For many, collective violence on the part of dissenting minorities is seen as distinctively irrational and abnormal and thus, as a very serious example of community disorganization; and many also link disintegration of social ties and norms among minorities, seen as an earlier phase, to the emergence of radicalism and collective violence. The relevance of these two perspectives to the general definitions of community which were reviewed by Hillery seems fairly clear. Those typical definitions depicted community organization in terms of normative consensus and social interaction. And many authors, including those reviewed by Coleman, have assessed community disorganization in terms of a breakdown in normative and social integration.

In addition, some observers of community life have used disorganization terminology not only where they see social disintegration or conflict, but also where they note deviant organization. Certain behavior patterns found in some segments of urban communities have been regarded as radically different from conventional behavior and thus, as examples of pathological organization. In his critical review of the cultural and family disorganization literature Valentine (1968: 23) noted the tendency for social scientists to leap "from social statistics, which are deviant in terms of middle-class norms, to a model of disorder and instability." This has particularly been true in the case of conventional portraits of slum and ghetto communities, with combinations of the disintegration and deviant organization perspectives being common. Of course, technically speaking, there is a certain contradiction in the terms used by many analysts, since, as Nisbet (1970: 263) has pointed out with regard to such frequently cited examples of disorganization as prostitution and organized crime, "a great deal of so-called disorganization in society is anything but that."

Thus, it seems that there are three broad reasons the language of community disorganization has been used in the analysis of community phenomena reflecting concern with disintegration, conflict, and deviant organization. The conventional approach to community disorganization, particularly the approach which deals with concrete community problems, assesses to what extent certain presumptively pathological conditions exist in a particular geographical area, and if they seem serious, depicts that situation in the terminology of community disorganization. Analysts of community change have been particularly captivated by the widely used language of disorganization.

There are several important procedural, conceptual, and substantive issues inherent in most treatments of community topics using this language, including such issues as generalizing from a part to the whole, dominant group bias in interpretation, overlays or layers of organization and disorganization, and the tendency to gloss over or to be unaware of empirical counter-evidence. I will return to these issues in a general way in the concluding section, but first I would like to examine the way in which these issues arise in regard to a number of specific community problems often discussed in terms of disorganization. Given the diverse assortment of phenomena depicted in these terms, it has been necessary to be selective. Somewhat arbitrarily, thus, I have chosen to limit the discussion which follows to urban communities and to examine migration, disasters, slums, ghettos, and collective violence in order to illustrate some important procedural, conceptual, and substantive issues.

The topics of migration and disasters have been chosen to illustrate primarily (but not exclusively) the disintegration perspective; in the literature the "community" of interest here has often been of town or city size, although the impact of these factors has also been assessed frequently in regard to subareas of cities. The topics of slums and ghettos will be reviewed in order to illustrate both the disintegration and deviant organization perspectives, with the "community" of interest usually being a subarea of a city. Collective violence has been selected to illustrate primarily the conflict aspect of disorganization theorizing, with "community" in the literature referring sometimes to subareas of cities and sometimes to the larger context. As will be seen, however, it is not impossible to make rigid distinctions between these three disorganization perspectives, since many social analysts have blended all three perspectives in developing interpretations.

DISORGANIZATION: DISINTEGRATION

Disintegration of orderly social arrangements and the weakening of social norms by a variety of disruptive factors have been of paramount interest to many recent observers of the urban scene, including some who would go so far as to characterize urban society as chaotic and exploding (e.g. Hauser 1969). Take, for example, urban migration, often seen as the culprit lying behind much community disintegration and disorganization. The image of the migrant to urban areas who has a severely disruptive effect on community order and plays a significant role in the weakening or disappearance of norms and orderly social arrangements at the point of destination is still a powerful one in evaluations of community problems. Cornelius (1970: 98) has underlined the importance of Louis Wirth, the "Chicago School" or urban sociology, and folk-urban analysts such as Redfield in generating views of urban life and of migrant assimilation which emphasize disorganization:

> The resulting description emphasized the anomic, disintegrative, disorienting, depersonalizing features of urban life and entry into the urban environment, manifested in psychological maladjustment, poorly defined

social roles, breakdown of traditional value systems and controls on deviant behavior, the weakening of family and kinship ties, and the decline of religious life. . . . Such conditions are assumed necessarily to accompany exposure to the urban environment, and then incidences of various forms of personal and social pathology in areas heavily settled with in-migrants . . . are listed as indicators.

After tracing the origin and character of disorganization theories in North American sociology, Cornelius demonstrates the use of similar disorganization theories in assessing the adaptation and political behavior of migrants to Latin American cities. Similarly, Nelson (1970: 396) has documented the disintegration assumptions in research on migration to Latin American cities:

> It is often assumed that many or most of the newcomers have been torn from a tightly structured rural society and plunged into a bewildering, impersonal, and harsh environment with few or no sources of support and guidance. Shock and isolation produce personal disorientation and political anomie.

With regard to migration to North American cities specific emphasis has been placed on deviant organization and conflict effects as well as on disintegrating effects. The impact of migration on urban crime and collective violence, as well as on the evolution of family organization in areas settled by migrants, has been stressed. For example, Coleman (1971: 703) seems to accept a combined interpretation of the disorganizing tendencies of migration: "The flow of blacks and Puerto Ricans into large cities is great, and these migrants initially have no stake in the city, no reason for not committing crime other than the fear of getting caught." For some it has been an easy step from this view of crime and migration to the parallel view that normless and tieless migrants contributed greatly to the collective violence in urban ghettos during the last decade (see Skolnick 1969; Fogelson and Hill 1968; Lupsha 1969). Moreover, Frazier's (1957: 630ff) view of the disintegrating effects of migration on typical black families— the breakup in urban areas of family patterns adapted to rural areas—has been widely influential. Referring to the breakup of migrating black families, Moynihan and Glazer (1963: 52) have underlined the cataclysmic effects of migration:

> Migration, uprooting, urbanization always create problems. Even the best organized and best integrated groups suffer under such circumstances. But when the fundamental core of organization, the family, is already weak, the magnitude of these problems may be staggering.

Other writers (Moynihan 1965; Forman 1971) have similarly accepted or developed this line of argument, and some have suggested that one negative result of continuing migration was the development of a pathological type of family organization, female-headed families, thus combining disintegration and deviant organization perspectives.

Yet conventional wisdom about the comprehensive disintegrating and disorganizing effects of migration per se has been brought into question in recent years by the evidence and analysis of a number of researchers. Reviewing the literature relevant to U.S. cities, Tilly (1968: 155) has recently made a convincing case for questioning many of the misconceptions which pass for wisdom in regard to migration:

> As for problems directly produced by migration, my main message has been that they have been seriously misunderstood and exaggerated. Migrants as a group do not notably disturb public order, their arrival does not lower the quality of the city's population, they place no extraordinary demands on public services, and they do not arrive exceptionally burdened with personal problems.

For example, looking at the available literature on crime and migration, Tilly found that black migrants had lower delinquency rates and imprisonment rates than native residents of the area studied. Moreover, examination of family disorganization revealed that recent migrants "were less likely than the rest to have broken families, and this is especially true within the nonwhite population" (Tilly 1968: 148). In addition, conventional assumptions about recent migrants fueling ghetto revolts in the United States have been contradicted by empirical evidence on the characteristics of rioters indicating native birth or long-term residence (Tilly 1968; Fogelson and Hill 1968; Lupsha 1969).

Nor was Tilly the first to question conventional views of disorganization and migration; a few years before, in a brief but neglected assessment, Wilensky and Lebeaux (1965: 123–124) had questioned the presumed disruptive effects of migration. Citing a few scattered pieces of empirical research, they suggested that geographical mobility was central to the urban scene, but "not necessarily disruptive." Both Tilly (1965) and Wilensky and Lebeaux have noted the critical importance of kinship and friendship networks in the assimilation of migrants into a new urban milieu. The great importance of informal and formal social networks, aspects of social organization, in the period between migrant departure and complete urban adjustment has frequently been neglected in studies of migrants and urban problems.

With regard to disorganization theories of urban migration as applied to Third World countries, particularly Latin American countries, a number of analysts have begun to piece together data which raise serious questions about images of disintegration and disorder. Mangin (1970: xvi) has suggested that, while much literature has focused on the destructive effects of migration, "the remarkable thing is the efficient way so many peasants have adapted and contributed to city development." In the first systematic review of several dozen empirically based studies bearing in some way on cityward migration, with emphasis on Latin American cities, Cornelius (1970: 103ff) concluded that the evidence did not support the view of urban migration as severely frustrating, socially disorganizing, or politically alienating. Cornelius (1970: 106) also noted that several studies indicated significant political (organization) activity among in-migrants, although not of the revolutionary kind many disorganization theorists would expect. Reviewing Third World urban migration, Nelson (1970: 396) came to the similar conclusion that there was virtually no evidence that recent migrants tend to be distinctively "radical or violence-prone" and that disorganiza-tion-revolution theories have gone wrong by neglecting data indicating that many or most urban migrants have prior urban exposure and receive extensive settling-in help from family, friends, and employers.

In sum, then, recent reviews of the evidence raise serious questions about disorganization theories of urban migration. The assumed disinte-grating and disorganizing effects of migration, especially with regard to social isolation, weakening of norms, family character, crime, collective violence, and political radicalism, need much further examination. The supposed connections between migration and community disorganization are actually not well established, although one needs to exercise caution in generalizing from the limited data available. At the very least, firm con-clusions about migration as disorganizing to communities should be avoided; much research yet remains to be done.

While I am most conversant with urban migration as an example of growing research evidence contradicting conventional perspectives on community disintegration, other topics which have commonly been dis-cussed in the language of disintegration also seem to be attracting revisionists. For example, recent disaster research reports have taken issue with conventional notions about the impact of external factors such as disasters on urban communities. In a fashion similar to discussions of urban migration, disasters have been cited as major examples of cataclysmic events precipitating panic, a breakdown in orderly social arrangements and law and order, a lack of family and other co-ordinated action, and the disappearance of goal-oriented behavior. For example, Bernard (1962: 349), who seems aware of some of the contradictory evidence cited below, has depicted disasters as important examples of community disintegration and disorganization. Dynes (1970: 7–8) has summarized popular and scholarly disaster perspectives which at the community level include the image of a social jungle:

People, hysterical and helpless, gradually shed the veneer of civilization and exploit others. It is said that looting is common, and that outside authority is perhaps necessary in order to inhibit these resurgent primitive urges. It is assumed that many will flee from the disaster area in mass panic, leaving the community stripped of its human and natural resources.

However, in recent monographs Quarantelli and Dynes have summarized research on disasters, much of it conducted by the Disaster Research Center at Ohio State University, which seems to contradict the exaggerated emphasis in conventional wisdom on community disintegration. Thus, Quarantelli and Dynes (1972: 67–70) found little evidence of irrational panic in face of impending hurricanes and similar disasters: "It appears that the major problem in an emergency is getting people to move, rather than preventing panic and disorderly flight."

The image of random or uncoordinated behavior in communities where disasters occur is also contradicted by the evidence. Quarantelli and Dynes (1972: 68) conclude from their data that:

> In general, disaster victims react immediately to their plight. Individuals first seek help from family and friends, then from larger groups such as churches. . . . The pattern of self-reliance and informal mutual help covers all forms of disaster behavior.

Informal social networks and channels continued to play a critical role in such situations; Dynes (1970: 8) concluded that "what people have learned about social life in the past is not suddenly discarded as a result of such events."

In addition to this meaningfully patterned behavior, researchers have found little in the way of serious breakdowns in social norms. Looting or other criminal behavior during disasters has been remarkably infrequent. Quarantelli and Dynes (1972: 68) found no declarations of martial law and no "instance in which a person left an important emergency post out of anxiety." In sum, then, the image of extensive disintegration in the wake of disaster has not been substantiated by field research.

DISORGANIZATION: DISINTEGRATION AND DEVIANT ORGANIZATION

Yet another example of inaccuracy and exaggeration in conventional wisdom about the urban scene can be seen in the numerous discussions of the disintegrating and disorganized character of social life in "slum" communities: the breakdown of traditional norms and values, the lawlessness, the quest for immediate gratification, the deterioration of family and kinship ties, the social isolation and anonymity. For many conventional observers a major example of disintegration, viewed both in continuing process and present structure terms, has been the urban slum community. For many, too, the slum has been the repository of deviant and undesirable types of social organization, such as prostitution and organized crime. More often than not, these two somewhat distinctive disorganization perspectives have been conjoined in slum analyses.

Essentially negative portraits of the poor, especially of the poor in United States cities, have been part of the lore of social scientists for a number of decades:

> The slum is a distinctive area of disintegration and disorganization.
>
> Over large stretches of the slum men neither know nor trust their neighbors. Aside from a few marooned families, a large part of the native population is transient: prostitutes, criminals, outlaws, hobos.
>
> The slum gradually acquires a character distinctively different from that of other areas of the city through a cumulative process of natural selection that is continually going on as the more ambitious and energetic keep moving out and the unadjusted, the dregs, and the outlaws accumulate (Zorbaugh 1929: 128–129).

Although several decades have elapsed since Zorbaugh wrote these sentences, crucial elements of this perspective have persisted into the present period. Thus, Forman (1971: 103, 127ff) adopts a perspective which virtually equates the slum and its inhabitants with pathology and disorganization, stressing family disorganization, gambling, prostitution, drugs, and psychological abnormality. And Hunter (1968: 20–93) seems to be more or less in the Zorbaugh tradition when he accents the key elements of the slum problem: social isolation, alienation, run-down housing, cultural limitation, migration, crime, and broken families.

Views of poor communities which accentuate negative or pathological traits have been particularly influenced by the culture-of-poverty generalizations of anthropologist Oscar Lewis (1965). The culture-of-poverty perspective emphasizes the transgenerational character of the defective subculture of those residing in slum areas, particularly in Latin America and in the United States, and fits nicely with other approaches viewing the slum in disorganization terms. The widespread acceptance of this view can be seen in the legitimacy given to it even in the government publications. A recent scholarly publication, *Growing Up Poor* (Chilman 1966), has in effect given United States government sanction to the culture-of-poverty portrait, with its special emphasis on personal disorganization and sociopsychological issues: superstitious and rigid thinking, impulsive parental

behavior, inadequate childrearing practices, lack of ability to defer gratification, little emphasis on educational achievement, poor impulse control,
little value placed on neatness, little expressed affection. For many
observers enumeration of characteristics such as these has served to sum
up in a general way the character of slum life.

In spite of this dominant emphasis on disorganization and defective
subcultures, from time to time a few social scientists have challenged key
aspects of the conventional wisdom. Some time ago, Whyte tried to stem
the rush to judgment among those writing in the Zorbaugh tradition.
Linking conventional wisdom about the disorganizing effects of urbanization in general, as expressed by Louis Wirth and others, to these views of
the slum, Whyte noted:

> If the city represents the highest development of individualization and
> hence of social disorganization, some scholars have thought to find in
> the slums the most striking manifestations of these phenomena that
> exist in the city (Whyte, 1943: 34).

Whyte (1943: 37) continued by arguing that his field study of the poor in
Boston revealed substantial evidence of extensive and meaningful social
organization, particularly primary organization, among the families he
studied: "Here people live in family groups and have built up an elaborate
social organization." Moreover, Whyte concluded by questioning the conventional view of non-middle-class organization (e.g., political machines
and organized crime) as community disorganization.

Whyte's call for serious consideration of social networks and organization among the poor went virtually unheeded for several decades. It was
not until the 1960s that a number of research studies began to demonstrate
the existence of meaningful social integration and organization among the
poor, studies moving away from the dominant concern with pathology.
More has been found among the poor than disintegration and crime-
oriented organization. In *The Urban Villagers* (1962) Gans reported
finding an urban village among the Italian poor in Boston. Complex and
intimate social networks were quite important in the integration of the
West End of Boston, extensive social organization that put meaning into
day-to-day existence. Similarly Fried and Gleicher (1961) have pointed
to the significance of informal networks and internal social structure in
providing residential satisfaction for poor urbanites. More recently, in his
study of a complex Chicago slum area, Suttles (1968: 3) rejected the labels
of "disorganization" and "value rejection," concluding that the area studied
was "intricately organized" and that the overwhelming majority of the
residents were "quite conventional people." While Suttles' analysis is

limited by its focus on street life and adolescent males, it provides additional evidence of the integrative importance of peer groups and social networks among the urban poor.

Moreover, a few recent studies (e.g., Lane 1968) have shown that the number of secondary organizations, particularly voluntary associations, in urban areas of extreme poverty in the United States is more substantial than disintegration theorists might expect. Indeed, those operating from an extreme disintegration point of view might be hard pressed to explain the emergence of the substantial number of protest organizations, including tenants' group and welfare rights organizations, during the last decade in the United States.

A number of analysts have recently questioned the conventional wisdom which exaggerates disintegration and deviant organization in the slum areas of Latin American cities. Cornelius (1970: 114–115) has argued that the traditional emphasis on disorganization has caused Latin American researchers to overlook the critical informal associational activity in poor areas, including areas settled by poor in-migrants. Squatter settlements in Latin American cities have shown a considerable amount of informal interaction and nonassociational groupings:

> This pattern appears to have developed most strongly in the Brazilian *favelas*, where numerous forms of *both* associational and non-associational group activity have been observed, including mutual aid networks, credit cooperatives, *ad hoc* systems for distribution of water and electricity, cooperative marketing arrangements, group activity to raise money to buy illegally occupied land, and a variety of recreational groupings (Cornelius, 1970: 115).

This richness of social organization has been documented not only for Brazil but also for other Latin American slum areas, including those in Venezuela and Guatemala. Mangin (1970: xxix) reported that research in Peru revealed the readiness and ability with which residents of poor communities responded to new opportunities for gaining political power, including providing participants in and leadership for political organization. Pointing to the widespread organization found in a number of recent studies, Mangin (1970: xxvii) argued that perspectives such as those emphasizing a culture of poverty overemphasized "internal conditions, personality factors, and the like" and underemphasized "external economic conditions." Valentine's (1968: 55–60) argument in regard to culture-of-poverty perspectives such as that of Oscar Lewis was even more direct, since Valentine found in Lewis's own research evidence of substantial community organization and cosmopolitanism in poor areas, rather than overwhelming disorganization and pathology.

This research on urban slums in the United States and Latin America, taken together with studies of social integration among the working-class poor in European cities (e.g., Young and Wilmott 1957), points up an important difference between (1) a perspective which shows awareness of the physical, economic, and psychological difficulties faced by poor urbanites and at the same time seriously recognizes the presence of integrative norms, social networks, and other "positive" social phenomena (strengths) to be found among poor urbanites, and (2) a perspective which views the *typical* poor urbanite as a malintegrated isolate, criminal, or moral derelict, a person so caught up in social or personal disorganization that he or she cannot cope with everyday life or respond to economic and political opportunities if these appear. Lest the reader misconstrue this as a Pollyanna-type argument and jump to the opposite conclusion that all is well among the poor, I would hasten to add that much research (e.g., Gans 1962; Ryan 1971) indicates that economic and political deprivation, shaped in the main by factors outside the slum, is also a fact of life for most slum residents. Yet these critical environmental aspects of slum existence have received much less attention than they deserve. As with migration and disasters, much additional research is needed before we can accurately generalize about the complexity and overlays of life in slum communities.

At a time when a number of scholars have begun to look beyond the conventional portrait of slum disorganization, most are still writing one-sided accounts of life in black communities in the United States. Until recently few had raised questions about the widespread use of the language of disorganization in regard to ghetto dwellers. Authors as diverse as Frazier (1957), Myrdal (1964), Clark (1965), Rainwater (1966), and Moynihan (1965) have given emphasis to disintegration and deviant organization themes (e.g., social isolation, widespread family disorganization, lack of integration, nondeferred gratification, fleeting friendships, anomie) in regard to black ghettos. Some inclination toward black pathology and disintegration themes can be found even among some scholars who have been skeptical about the general slum-as-disorganization perspective. Fried and Levin (1968) have questioned whether black ghettos have the same patterns of community and family cohesiveness as other working-class slums; and Clinard (1966: 60) has suggested that the outstanding characteristic of the typical black slum resident "is the high degree of instability in his family life."

Indeed, one of the most prominent social science discussions in recent years has focused on the lack of social integration, normative consensus, and cohesion in black ghetto areas. Central in discussions of community disintegration or deviant organization have been the character and structure of black families. Influenced by Frazier (1957), Moynihan, in his now-famous *The Negro Family* (1965: 5), argued that "at the heart of the deterioration of the fabric of Negro society is the deterioration of the Negro family. It is the fundamental source of the weakness of the Negro community at the present time." He then proceeded to suggest that the typical black American family was a broken or disintegrated family, and in turn tied that disintegration to other problems of black communities. Moynihan dramatically accentuated the "tangle" of pathology and crumbling social relations which in his view characterized black communities. In a fashion similar to many writing in the Frazier-Moynihan tradition, Coleman (1971: 703) has also accented in passing the "abnormality" of black areas, "the absence of integration, the absence of any processes that produce a common bond of identity."

The policy impact of this disintegration and pathology emphasis in the social science literature on ghettos can be traced in prominent government reports, such as the *Report of the National Advisory Commission on Civil Disorders*. Under a conventional heading of "Unemployment, Family Structure, and Social Disorganization," this report (National Advisory Commission on Civil Disorders, 1968: 7) used a variety of disorganization codewords:

> The culture of poverty that results from unemployment and family breakup generates a system of ruthless, exploitative relationships within the ghetto. Prostitution, dope addiction, and crime create an environmental "jungle" characterized by personal insecurity and tension.

In examining the conventional ghetto portrait it becomes clear that much of what has been asserted about slum life in general has also been applied to black ghetto life. As with the case of the more general slum discussions, a major difficulty with this portrait is that there is a growing amount of contradictory evidence. At best, images of ghettos depicting life and people there solely in terms of pathology and disintegration are gross exaggerations. Increasingly, research in the 1960s and 1970s has raised serious questions about these conventional images. Elsewhere Perry and I (1972: 460) have reviewed the small but expanding literature on ghetto family life and social structure and have suggested, in regard to *typical* ghetto residents and relative to dominant group patterns,

> that there is a socially significant, healthy, and diverse primary family structure, there is a high level of kinship interaction which is also quite intense, and there is a high level of friendship and neighboring [in ghetto communities]. Hence, there is evidence which suggests that the internal structure . . . of the ghetto is not necessarily an environment which atomizes the person in an alienated state with no friends or organizational support from family or relatives.

Reviewing the literature on secondary organization, participation, and cosmopolitanism, we have also averred (1972: 460) that the typical black ghetto resident's everyday work is probably not one in which he,

> like the turtle, is encapsulated and, when threatened, will not leave his shell. We discovered that he has as much, if not more contact with the news media than white urbanites; he participates as much [as] if not more than white urbanites in voluntary organization; and he can be as cosmopolitan [as] if not more cosmopolitan than white urbanites when it comes to traveling around the city and interacting with persons of other social identities.

Documentation for these arguments can be found in monographs by Meadow (1962), Babchuk and Thompson (1962), Feagin (1966), Podell (1968), and Wellman (1971).

To take the widely discussed issue of the black family, we have seen recently a significant expansion of research efforts directed at a better understanding of the strengths and weaknesses of black families, research efforts triggered by the public debate. Moynihan fostered the view that the typical black family was disorganized, that female-headed or matriarchal families predominated, and that black males did not contribute greatly to the support of their families. However, the argument that discussions of ghetto family life focusing on disorganization are replete with misconceptions has received support in a number of recent studies. For example, Hill (1971), drawing on government statistics and a few other sources, reached some provocative conclusions: (1) that most black families were male-headed; (2) that most intact black families were not matriarchal, but egalitarian or patriarchal in decision-making structure; (3) that black husbands were not peripheral wage earners, but the main providers in most families; (4) that the extent of family desertion had been greatly exaggerated; and (5) that there was surprising emphasis on the importance of education among low-income black families. Other recent research studies have corroborated this image of the average black family as male-headed and egalitarian (or patriarchal), rather than as female-headed and matriarchal (Billingsley 1968; Hyman and Reed 1969; Mack 1972).

In addition to themes of social disintegration and family disorganization, one also finds a special emphasis in many ghetto analyses on a variety of types of pathological or deviant organization, as can be seen in the references of the National Advisory Commission on Civil Disorders (1968: 7) to prostitution, narcotics, and crime. This type of disorganization emphasis can be found not only in discussions of black ghettos but also in discussions of other types of slums as well, so much so that the "jungle" portraits of these areas often blend together discussions of disintegration with discussions of types of organization deviant from conventional or dominant group standards. Indeed, social phenomena such as family disorganization have been examined by analysts using both the disintegration and pathological organization perspectives.

While I do not have the space here to consider all the ramifications of this pathological organization issue, several points are important to note. In the first place, while criminal behavior and organization may exist to a disproportionate degree in slum and ghetto areas (a conclusion which may be shaky in light of recent research on white-collar crime), it seems to be exaggerated in many assessments of day-to-day life in these areas. It is too easy to move from characteristics of a minority of residents of a given urban community, however unconventional and colorful, to ungrounded generalizations about areas in general. Second, the quick typification of slum and ghetto areas in pathological organization terminology, with its frequently accompanying overtones of character flaws and individual blame, tends to play down the intimate relationship between non-middle-class social organization in these areas and the larger social system surrounding them. In most cases it remains to be demonstrated in what ways a given type of non-middle-class organization or pattern of behavior is pathological, nor is the standard of reference (i.e., what is normal and why) clearly specified. While I do not mean to suggest that one could not specify meaningful standards for social pathology (e.g., phenomena demonstrably harmful to the residents of a given community), it would be relatively difficult to demonstrate that the patterns of behavior commonly viewed as disorganized or pathological are not in fact adaptive-functional sociocultural arrangements. We still have a great need for additional (and preferably comparative) research along the lines of Merton (1957: 72), who, in a pioneering research study, showed the "functional equivalence" of certain types of quasi-legal behavior in poor areas. As Nisbet (1970: 263) has recently asserted, "there may in fact be no disorganization at all, in any empirical sense of the term, behind the rise of delinquent, criminal, or other problem behavior."

DISORGANIZATION AND CONFLICT

In addition to social disintegration, the other major type of disorganization which Coleman (1971) differentiated was community conflict. For Coleman the accent seemed to be on the divergent norms, values, or perspectives which open conflict made evident, leading to situations of community disorder and "paralysis." Not surprisingly, recent developments in United States cities, particularly the collective violence of black Americans and college students, have catapulted violent conflict into many discussions of disorganization and community problems. That urban violence here, as well as that in urban areas of other countries, has reflected divergent values and perspectives seems undeniable on the basis of existing data. However, many who have viewed collective violence in negatively toned disorganization terms have had more in mind than a clash of perspectives frustrating unified community effort. Many have viewed collective violence as a stage of community disorganization flowing from an earlier stage of disintegration, which in turn resulted from social change such as cityward migration; and many have expressed the view that open attacks on established arrangements can be consigned to the category of uniquely pathological, abnormal, or irrational behavior.

However, a few researchers—particularly those recently engaged in empirical research on collective violence—have begun to question conventional views of violent conflict. In discussing migration I referred to a few researchers who had questioned the common model: change → disintegration → violent conflict. This model views violent conflict or political radicalism as a developmental stage flowing from an earlier stage of community disintegration. Among the change factors often seen as underlying disintegration would be migration. Yet in regard to ghetto violence in United States cities, we have already seen that research on rioters indicated recent migrants played a minor role in the development of rioting (Fogelson and Hill 1968; Feagin and Hahn 1973). Cornelius (1970) and Nelson (1970), reviewing the scattered empirical data on Third World cities, similarly concluded that weight of evidence was against theories linking migrants, disintegration, and radical political action. Problematic too in some disintegration → violent conflict linkages are assumptions about the disintegrating and disorienting world of the slum, questionable assumptions in light of the evidence previously considered.

In addition, the change → disintegration → violent conflict model seems to have provided the backdrop for much traditional analysis depicting collective violence in terms of abnormality, pathology, and irrationality. Criticizing theories of Le Bon (1952), Smelser (1962), and Brown (1965), Skolnick (1969: 332) and his associates summed up elements of the traditional social science view:

> Under this conception, the routine processes of any given society are seen as stable, orderly, and predictable, operating under the normative constraints and cumulative rationality of tradition. The instability, disorder, and irrationality of collective behavior, therefore, are characteristic of those groups that are experiencing 'social strain'—for example, the unemployed, the recent migrant, the adolescent.

Skolnick (1969) and his associates were among the first to question the contrast between the rational-normal state and irrational-pathological dissidents. They argued that conventional popular and social science approaches were less than adequate because of the inconsistency of the terminology (not viewing the violent behavior of authorities as such), because of such lack of attention to recurrent patterns (viewing collective violence of dissidents as irrational and formless, when in fact there has been a good bit of structure and pattern), and because of inadequate attention to the power-authority context of collective action. Moreover, critically assessing the influential perspectives of Smelser (1962) and Gurr (1970), Nardin (1971) underscored the ideological character of much social science theorizing. Referring to the influential work of Smelser, he noted that "the policy implications of the theory of collective behavior, where drawn, are never in the form of advice to reformers or the discontented, but only to the 'agents of social control'" (Nardin 1971: 28). Objecting to social science vocabularies with no provision for irrational social control by the state or rational violence by dissidents, Nardin (1971: 29) argued that

> Like Smelser's, Gurr's theory begins with the distinction between legitimate or normal and illegitimate or abnormal political behavior. As does Smelser, Gurr tends to associate the behavior of political authorities with the former category and the behavior of partisans with the latter. Given this conceptualization of the nature of political violence, Gurr, like Smelser, writes largely from the point of view of the authorities.

Because of this dissatisfaction with the traditional perspective, Skolnick, Nardin, Tilly, and a number of others engaged in empirical research on collective violence have begun to move away from the common (change → disintegration or strain → collective violence) model to a new (power-political process → collective violence) model. Drawing on empirical data on violence in European cities, Tilly (1969) has been one of the most articulate advocates of this latter model. Tilly has argued that the weight of evidence points toward the normality of collective violence in the life histories of Western societies. Arguing that neither a universal aggressive instinct nor pathological moments or men was necessary to explain the occurrence of collective acts of destruction, Tilly suggested that "historically, collective violence has flowed regularly out of the central political processes of Western countries" (1969: 4). An essential point in Tilly's analysis is that collective violence has often emerged in the history of societies where social groups found themselves locked into a struggle for power. Groups moving up in the structure of power have engaged in various collective actions, including violence, in an attempt to gain power, while other groups already in power have fought by whatever means necessary—including particularly the use of the established police forces—to maintain their advantage in power and resources. Nardin (1971: 36) has also developed a political process perspective, arguing that collective violence of dissidents has arisen not out of the failure of the state to control those enduring strain but out of real conflicts of only partly reconcilable interests. From this perspective government is a party to community conflict.

A more adequate approach to violent conflict in urban communities might bring organization, rather than disorganization or disintegration, to the center of the explanatory framework. Within cities there have always been unequal distributions of power, wealth, and other resources; these distributions have been a fundamental component of community organization. Obserschall (1973: 33) underscored this crucial point:

> Social conflict arises from the structured arrangement of individuals and groups in a social system—from the very fact of social organization. . . . Some are better off, and others are worse off. Those who are favored have a vested interest in conserving and consolidating their existing share; those who are negatively privileged seek to increase theirs, individually or collectively.

Not only has violent conflict flowed out of this distributional structure, but much collective violence has also been characterized by other social patterns—by goal-oriented activity, by normative consensus among dissidents (and police forces), and by the use of preexisting social networks (Nardin 1971; Feagin and Hahn 1973). While many problems in the character and structure of community conflict of a violent type can be resolved only by further research, the proponents of the political process → collective violence model have already raised very basic questions about traditional popular and social science conceptualizations.

CONCLUSION

Even this brief review of a few topics often discussed in the language of disorganization and disorder points up a number of persisting conceptual and empirical dilemmas recurring in the analyses of those concerned with community issues. One important analytical problem is the tendency to overgeneralize. The inclination to depict whole communities as disorganized or disintegrating may be partially explained by the tendency to jump from characteristics of a part to characteristics of the whole. A conspicuous example of this leap can be seen in the conventional discussion of widespread family disorganization in black communities. Even if one accepts the common (if yet to be demonstrated) view that female-headed families are distinctively pathological, a view used to buttress general images of ghetto deterioration, one cannot accurately generalize from statistics which show a minority of ghetto families to be female-headed to the conclusion that *the* black family is unstable or disorganized or that family disintegration is a defining characteristic of black ghettos. Thus the black family might more accurately be viewed, even from a middle-class point of view, as integrated or "healthy." This tendency to overgeneralization and exaggeration is not limited to discussions of black ghettos; it is sometimes characteristic of discussions of slums, migration, and disasters too. A careful analyst should not jump from the characteristics of limited segments of communities under analysis—even characteristics which might plausibly be demonstrated to be pathological—to a characterization of entire communities in pathological terms.

Yet another problem in numerous discussions of disorder and disorganization is the problem of class or dominant group bias. Valentine has underlined the point that even where it is empirically verified for segments of communities, *different* organization in urban communities should not be regarded as *disorganization*. Too often there has been a leap

> from social statistics, which are deviant in terms of middle-class norms, to a model of disorder and instability. Such reasoning effectively eliminates consideration of possible cultural forms that . . . might have their own order and functions (Valentine, 1968: 23).

This general point about middle-class or dominant group bias in popular and social science treatments of social pathology and disorganization is not new. Several decades ago, Mills (1963) made a similar argument in his article on the ideology of social pathologists. While Mills's critique may apply somewhat more directly to those who work in a relatively unsophisticated way with community problems and less to many social science analysts working with community disorganization, his argument that analysts of pathological organization and behavior patterns are inclined to accept the norms of dominant groups as standards for evaluation is still quite relevant.

Indeed, if terms like "disorganized" and "pathological" are to retain any social science utility, much conceptual and definitional work remains to be done. The ideological use of pathological terms to characterize disliked or non-middle-class patterns of social behavior will no longer suffice. Thus, in order to designate certain patterns or organizations as pathological, one might reasonably be required to demonstrate that they are in fact harmful to, or dysfunctional for, the community in question. If this operation were further specified and applied to commonly cited examples of social pathology such as broken families or the "rackets," it might well turn out that these cases were not pathological, but rather adaptive-functional (albeit different) structures. Indeed, many decades ago Durkheim (1966) emphasized the problem of defining social pathology and concluded that one could not talk of pathology until one had a clear idea of what normalcy was for a given set of social units.

By way of conclusion, I would like to emphasize three of the more serious consequences of the tendency among popular and social science analysts to leap too quickly to the rhetoric of disorganization and abnormality in discussing community issues such as those reviewed in this paper. In the first place, much social analysis has been so preoccupied with disorganization that the order and integration of the communities or subcommunities being examined has been neglected or unrecognized, even though there may have been important similarities between that order (networks, families, goals, norms, values, etc.) and that which can be found elsewhere. This neglect of internal organization needs to be remedied by much additional research, whether the concern is with slums, ghettos, or communities hit by disasters. Moreover, the central theme of a more adequate conceptual approach might well be *organization*, with (1) continuity of social structure (as in the case of migration), (2) normative and organizational similarities between various socioeconomic groups, (3) different (but adaptive-functional) sociocultural structures, and (4) overlap of a similar-different sociocultural structures being crucial topics for analysis.

Secondly, the conventional terminology tends to play down external factors. A number of researchers have recently accentuated the importance of the external structural and organizational context of community problems often dissected in disorganization terms. In evaluating the deficiencies of disintegration theories of migration, Cornelius (1970: 115–116) questioned the traditional neglect of certain theoretically critical variables external to the migrants. Noting the absence of research on the governmental context, a major environmental variable, he called for more extensive research on the actions of established elites, government administrators, and power holding groups in shaping the circumstances and adaptive responses or urban migrants. And both Tilly (1969) and Nardin (1971) raised this issue of the broader sociopolitical context in reviewing the topic of collective violence by dissidents.

One of the most serious consequences of the rather pervasive disorganization pathology perspective, and the community analysis flowing from it, has been the effect on policy making and public action. The operation of the bias can often be seen in the process of definition of community problems. Skolnick and Currie (1970: 1–16) emphasized this selectivity issue by suggesting the question, "Why have certain community problems been given far more attention than others?" They further criticized the tendency to accept dominant values and power structures as given and to select as community problems only those social maladjustments recognized as such by dominant groups. The research studies by Gans (1962) and Fried (1963) on the grief which city officials brought into the lives of poor Italian Americans as a result of defining (inaccurately) their area of the city as a disorganized, pathological slum area, and subsequently bulldozing it in the name of urban renewal, remain as major examples of research illustrating the serious policy consequences of the disorganization perspective.

While it is the case that many researchers working in the area of community studies are aware of the intrusion of dominant group bias into conceptual analysis, critical arguments such as those made by the revisionists discussed in this paper have not affected research operations as much as one might have expected. Most analysts of community problems are still more likely to focus on the characteristics and behavior of victims of society, rather than on the perhaps more critical problem of the surrounding sociopolitical system. I would like to stress that many of the disorganization topics discussed here seem to cry out for more thorough empirical research, including solid (if not prestigious) descriptive analysis, as well as new conceptual approaches. Beyond that, there is the need to pay more attention to those who have admonished us to look beyond the relatively unresistant and easily researched units of communities to the problematic character of dominant values and power structures.

REFERENCES

Babchuk, Nicholas, and Ralph V. Thompson.
1962 "The Voluntary Association of Negroes," *American Sociological Review* 27 (October): 647–655.

Bell, Colin, and Howard Newby.
1972 *Community Studies.* New York: Praeger.

Bernard, Jessie.
1962 *American Community Behavior,* rev. ed. New York: Holt, Rinehart, and Winston.
1968 "Community Disorganization," in David Sills (ed.), *Encyclopedia of the Social Sciences,* Vol. III. New York: Macmillan, 163–168.

Billingsley, Andrew.
1968 *Black Families in White America.* Englewood Cliffs, N.J.: Prentice-Hall.

Brown, Roger.
1965 *Social Psychology.* New York: The Free Press.

Chilman, Catherine S.
1966 *Growing Up Poor.* Washington, D.C.: U.S. Government Printing Office.

Clark, Kenneth B.
1965 *Dark Ghetto.* New York: Harper and Row.

Clark, S. D.
1962 *The Developing Canadian Community,* 2nd ed. Toronto: University of Toronto Press.

Clinard, Marshall B.
1966 *Slums and Community Development.* New York: The Free Press. .

Coleman, James S.
1971 "Community Disorganization and Conflict," in Robert K. Merton and

Robert A. Nisbet (eds.), *Contemporary Social Problems*, 3rd ed. New York: Harcourt, Brace, Jovanovich, 657–708.

Cornelius, Wayne A.
1970 "The Political Sociology of Cityward Migration in Latin America: Toward Empirical Theory," in Francine M. Rabinowitz and Felicity M. Trueblood (eds.), *Latin American Urban Annual*. Beverly Hills, Cal.: Sage Publications, 95–147.

Durkheim, Emile.
1966 *The Rules of Sociological Method*, 8th ed. Trans. by Sarah A. Solovay and John H. Mueller. New York: The Free Press.

Dynes, Russell R.
1970 *Organized Behavior in Disaster*. Lexington, Mass.: D. C. Heath.

Feagin, Joe R.
1966 *The Social Ties of Negroes in an Urban Environment*. Cambridge, Mass.: Harvard University. Unpublished Ph.D. dissertation.
——, and Harlan Hahn.
1973 *Ghetto Revolts*. New York: Macmillan.

Fogelson, Robert M., and Robert B. Hill.
1968 "Who Riots?" in *Supplemental Studies for the National Advisory Commission on Civil Disorders*. Washington, D.C.: U.S. Government Printing Office, 217–248.

Forman, Robert E.
1971 *Black Ghettos, White Ghettos, and Slums*. Englewood Cliffs, N.J.: Prentice-Hall.

Frazier, E. Franklin.
1957 *The Negro in the United States*, rev. ed. New York: Macmillan.

Fried, Marc.
1963 "Grieving for a Lost Home," in Leonard J. Duhl (ed.), *The Urban Condition*. New York: Basic Books, 151–171.
——, and P. Gleicher.
1961 "Some Sources of Residential Satisfaction in an Urban Slum," *Journal of the American Institute of Planners* 27: 305–315.
——, and Joan Levin.
1968 "Some Social Functions of the Urban Slum," in Bernard J. Frieden and Robert Morris (eds.), *Urban Planning and Social Policy*. New York: Basic Books, 60–83.

Gans, Herbert J.
1962 *The Urban Villagers*. New York: The Free Press.

Glazer, Nathan, and Daniel P. Moynihan.
1963 *Beyond the Melting Pot*. Cambridge, Mass.: Harvard University Press.

Gurr, Ted R.
1970 *Why Men Rebel*. Princeton: Princeton University Press.

Hauser, Philip M.
1969 "The Chaotic Society: Product of the Social Morphological Revolution," *American Sociological Review* 34 (February): 1–18.

Hill, Robert B.
1971 *The Strengths of Black Families*. New York: Emerson Hall Publishers.

Hillery, George A.
1955 "Definitions of Community: Areas of Agreement," *Rural Sociology* 20 (June): 111–123.

Hunter, David R.
1968 *The Slums.* New York: The Free Press.

Hyman, Herbert H., and John S. Reed.
1969 "Black Matriarchy Reconsidered: Evidence from Secondary Analysis of Sample Surveys," *Public Opinion Quarterly* 33 (Fall): 346–354.

Lane, John.
1968 "Voluntary Associations Among Mexican Americans in San Antonio, Texas." Austin, Texas: University of Texas. Unpublished Ph.D. dissertation.

Le Bon, Gustave.
1952 *The Crowd.* London: Ernest Benn.

Lewis, Oscar.
1965 *La Vida.* New York: Random House.

Lupsha, Peter A.
1969 "On Theories of Urban Violence," *Urban Affairs Quarterly* 4: 273–295.

Mack, Delores E.
1971 "Where the Black-Matriarchy Theorists Went Wrong," *Psychology Today* 4 (January): 24, 86–87.

Mangin, William.
1970 "Introduction," in William Mangin (ed.), *Peasants in Cities.* Boston: Houghton Mifflin Co., xiii-xxxix.

Meadow, Kathryn P.
1962 "Negro-White Differences Among Newcomers to a Transitional Urban Area," *The Journal of Intergroup Relations* 3: 320–330.

Merton, Robert K.
1957 *Social Theory and Social Structure,* rev. ed. Glencoe: The Free Press.

Mills, C. Wright.
1963 "The Professional Ideology of Social Pathologists," in Irving L. Horowitz (ed.), *Power, Politics and People: The Collected Essays of C. Wright Mills.* New York: Ballantine Books, 525–552.

Moynihan, Daniel P.
1965 *The Negro Family: The Case for National Action.* Washington, D.C.: U.S. Government Printing Office.

Myrdal, Gunnar.
1964 *An American Dilemma,* Vol. 2. New York: McGraw-Hill.

Nardin, Terry.
1971 "Theories of Conflict Management," *Peace Research Reviews* 4 (April): 1–93.

National Advisory Commission on Civil Disorders.
1968 Report of the National Advisory Commission on Civil Disorders. Washington, D.C.: U.S. Government Printing Office.

Nelson, Joan.
1970 "The Urban Poor: Disruption or Political Integration in Third World Cities?" *World Politics* 22: 393–414.

Nisbet, Robert A.
1970 *The Social Bond.* New York: Knopf.

Oberschall, Anthony.
1973 *Social Conflict and Social Movements.* Englewood Cliffs, N.J.: Prentice-Hall.

Perry, David C., and Joe R. Feagin.
1972 "Stereotyping in Black and White," in Harlan Hahn (ed.), *People and Politics in Urban Society*. Beverly Hills, Cal.: Sage Publications, 433–463.

Podell, Lawrence.
1968 *Families on Welfare in New York City*. New York: Center for the Study of Urban Problems, City University of New York.

Price, Daniel O.
1971 "Rural-Urban Migration and Poverty: A Synthesis of Research Findings, With a Look at the Literature." Austin, Tex.: Report submitted to Office of Economic Opportunity.

Quarantelli, E. L., and Russell R. Dynes.
1972 "When Disaster Strikes It Isn't Much Like What You've Heard About," *Psychology Today* 5 (February): 67–70.

Rainwater, Lee.
1966 "The Crucible of Identity: The Negro Lower-Class Family," *Daedalus* 95: 172–216.

Ryan, William.
1971 *Blaming the Victim*. New York. Random House Vintage Books.

Skolnick, Jerome.
1969 *The Politics of Protest*. New York: Simon and Schuster.
———, and Elliott Currie (eds.).
1970 *Crisis in American Institutions*. Boston: Little, Brown and Co.

Smelser, Neil J.
1963 *Theory of Collective Behavior*. New York: The Free Press.

Suttles, Gerald D.
1968 *The Social Order of the Slum*. Chicago: University of Chicago Press.

Tilly, Charles.
1965 *Migration to an American City*. Wilmington, Del.: Agricultural Experiment Station and Division of Urban Affairs, University of Delaware.
1968 "Race and Migration to the American City," in James Q. Wilson (ed.), *The Metropolitan Enigma*. Cambridge, Mass.: Harvard University Press, 136–157.
1969 "Collective Violence in European Perspective," in Hugh D. Graham and Ted R. Gurr (eds.), *Violence in America*. New York: Bantam Books, 4–44.

Valentine, Charles A.
1968 *Culture and Poverty*. Chicago: University of Chicago Press.

Wellman, Barry.
1971 "Crossing Social Boundaries: Cosmopolitanism among Black and White Adolescents," *Social Science Quarterly* 52 (December): 602–624.

Whyte, William F.
1943 "Social Organization in the Slums," *American Sociological Review* 8 (February): 34–39.

Wilensky, Harold L., and Charles N. Lebeaux.
1965 *Industrial Society and Social Welfare*. New York: The Free Press. Paperback.

Young, Michael, and Peter Willmott.
1957 *Family and Kinship in East London*. Baltimore: Penguin Books.

Zorbaugh, Harvey W.
1929 *The Gold Coast and the Slum*. Chicago: University of Chicago Press.

The Reconciliation of "Subjective" and "Objective" Data on Physical Environment in the Community: The Case of Social Contact in High-Rise Apartments*

WILLIAM MICHELSON

University of Toronto

Expanding traditional sociological conceptions of community to include environmental considerations in community research, this paper stresses the importance of documenting both subjective and objective environmental concerns, as well as reconciling such differences as are presented and details precedence. Some recent data on the nature of social contact in high-rise "communities" illustrate this approach.

The city is an active arena of actions and decisions. As Norton Long (1958) pointed out some years ago, a multitude of actors and groups with distinct interests and points of view assembles around urban issues, milling and lobbying—sometimes winning, sometimes losing. The input of some of these actors is based on administrative experience and

*I wish to express my particular debt to Anna-Rose Spina, David Belgue, John Nelson Stewart, Don Rogers, June Steele, Les Cseh, and Chris Cotterell, for various elements of the data presented. Cathy Hogue, Beverly Thompson, and Mina Auciello helped with the typing. I am grateful to Alan Armstrong, Andrew and Marcia Effrat, and Herbert Gans for comments on an earlier draft of the paper. However, the paper is my own product, and I stand responsible for its shortcomings. This is a revision of a paper presented at the 1973 Meeting of the American Sociological Association.

of others on succinct measures of efficiency. The input of still others is based on subjective belief and perception.

The customary practice in the recent past was to base community decisions as much as possible on "hard" economic or econometric types of information. This practice, however, attracted considerable opposition, since it appeared to ignore many real human characteristics and needs, which were more difficult to measure. A strong movement at present is to counter this cold-blooded trend with more subjective, emotionally alive arguments, advanced particularly by persons who are actually exposed to a problematic situation.

I do not advocate the exclusive adoption or rejection of either of these extremes. However, I see a danger at present in the possibility of throwing the baby out with the bath water, so to speak, because subjective proposals by first persons are not always realistic or beneficial in terms of solving the problem at hand. The experience of being poor, for example, does not always equip someone with the solution for abolishing poverty, and many poor people appear to want nothing more than to acquire the technological tools of their opponents. (A frequent complication is arrogant self-certainty on the part of competing groups in the urban arena. All of them cannot be absolutely correct, but most of them act as if they are.)

The challenge I see is not to denigrate but to enhance the prospect of those affected by decisions about communities, through the production and demonstration of factual evidence to document the subjective side of arguments on important community matters: *better* data of a subjective nature must exist to force an accommodation with the more customary economic data.

Furthermore the parallel presentation of objective and subjective data (or in any case data representing considerably different approaches to the subject) cannot help but create a more general context; this creates the possibility of explaining the reality involved to a greater extent than is possible with either type of data alone. This "confrontation" of differing types of data, when successful, tends to force community issues away from the realm of rhetoric and into one of explicit explanation, which is more likely to serve as a basis for accommodative planning.

My concentration in this paper is on one aspect of the community which is seldom treated explicitly—its physical environment. Although Robert Park's original formulation (1925) of "community" emphasized those aspects of behavior which could be understood with reference to the *social* commonalities of people sharing identifiable, local geographic areas, it takes no stretch of either the theoretical or practical imagination to realize the validity of exploring those aspects of behavior best understood with reference to prominent features of the *physical* environment within or relevant to local communities (cf. Michelson 1970). Although most social phenomena can be explained with reference to other social, cultural, and psychological phenomena and relatively few of them owe great explanatory debt to factors in the physical environment, it is clear that without this reference we lack *full* explanation. Many of the issues now wracking communities and studied by community theorists (such as urban renewal, residential density, and highway planning) concern the social impact of the physical environment. What, then, is the precedent for the gathering of factual information, both subjective and objective, as input to the kind of fruitful confrontation I envisage on community issues concerning physical environment?

Fortunately, recent years have seen the growth of major efforts within the social sciences to document the subjective side of reality concerning urban physical environment. While neither perfect methodologically nor particularly additive substantively, this research effort has at least become credible. I should like to first review the nature of some of these subjective approaches in the area of community environment, and then contrast them briefly with somewhat "harder" approaches to the same subject area. Then I should like to present an example from my current research on life in high-rise apartments (physical artifacts thought to "poison" traditional social relations among people in local communities). This will illustrate the contrast between data reporting subjective impressions of community as opposed to that from more objective measures of reality, the juxtaposition of the two positing an explanation which is considerably less value laden than the conclusions customarily drawn by the proponents of the two sides on the particular issue concerned.

SUBJECTIVE RESEARCH ON PHYSICAL ENVIRONMENT

I should like to review briefly the precedent for subjective documentation concerning physical environment in the community. I shall discuss first which questions are being asked within this research tradition[1] and second, what types of methods are being brought to bear.

(i) *What is the meaning of a plan, procedure, or place?* A number of studies have investigated just what a proposed building, plan, or procedure (such as planning or zoning) might mean to the people who are potentially affected by one or more of them. Werthman (1965), for example, investigated what planning meant to people who lived in planned communities. While many benefits thought missing in communities which grow without central direction are expected as the consequence of initial planning, he found that the one shared meaning given to planning was that it protected residents from development unknown to them at the time they moved in. Planning was felt to protect one from having a glue factory or gas station across the street—and little else. Hence, community controversies which focus on planning issues might benefit from somebody's knowledge of what planning means to the people arguing about it.

At a very microscopic scale, Rosengren and DeVault (1970) investigated the meanings accorded different rooms in a maternity hospital by the users of the hospital—meanings not irrelevant to the status position and to the prognosis of the person involved. Very small-scale physical phenomena such as these can play major roles in the lives of people sharing local facilities and in part forming self images based on them.

At a somewhat larger scale, Lee (1970a) and Keller (1968) have examined what neighborhoods, taken as entities, mean to people and what they do not mean; Strauss (1961) has gone so far as to investigate the meaning of the pattern of the entire metropolis to the people who individually explore and use its component parts. His thoughts emphasize the importance of local areas which individual people actually use in forming their impression of the whole city.

Still other researchers have looked at the meaning of specific types of environment such as landscapes (Sonnenfeld 1966), shopping centres (Downs 1970), and old-age homes (Lawton 1972), which serve as foci for community discussion.

Whether micro or macro, however, these studies indicate that significant groupings of people share images and meanings within the city, although all people are not subjected to the same environmental stimuli nor do all subgroups agree on the meaning of all aspects of the environment.

(ii) *How do shared images arise?* Once it is clear that shared images and meanings are attached to specific aspects of environment relevant to communities, a second question is how these images come about. Lee (1970a) and Strauss (1961), for example, went on to ask what artifacts (discernible institutions, uniformity in design) compose neighborhoods and metropolitan areas and cause them to be perceived as such. Lee has also explored relationships between the types of images held by people and such factors as the subjects' sex and present location within a city (1970b).

Some authors have written on how children acquire the images they gain about space (Beck 1970), while others have investigated how adults gather images on specific environmental contexts, for example high-rise apartments (Reed 1972), large natural open spaces (R. Lee 1972), and pollution as a problem (Swan 1972).

(iii) *What are the dimensions of perceived environment?* Other researchers have investigated the conceptual components within environments that lead to their being observed or ignored by members of the public. For example, Kevin Lynch's exploratory work (1960) in Boston, Los Angeles and Jersey City established the importance of such concepts as "focal points" and "edges." It illustrates, for example, that *built* artifacts serve to identify and bound local areas with social and emotional connotations. Somewhat later, Appleyard (1964) used highly detailed and sophisticated methodological tools to ascertain what actually attracts the attention of motorists exposed to different physical stimuli. Wohlwill (1966) pointed to such components of environment as stimulation, novelty, complexity and variation in the process of attracting attention among the public.

(iv) *To what extent do subjective reactions to environment help account for the different behavior of subgroups within the population?* A study by Orleans (1967), for example, in Los Angeles documented graphically that different ethnic subgroups within the population had markedly greater knowledge of the metropolis in which they lived than did others. This was attributable in large part to the relative affluence of these groups and their ability to use private and public transportation in efforts to learn more about the opportunities in their environment. The importance of local community in the lives of different subgroups is hence partly a function of their ability (or their inability) to be mobile over a large area of the city. Ladd (1970) demonstrated racial differences in urban territorial behavior, attributable to the racially segregated living quarters in which children are raised.

(v) *What cultural rules of spatial positioning and behavior take form within given social systems?* Hall (1966) and Sommer (1969), for example, have contributed widely heralded work showing that the distances people put between each other for specific purposes are a direct function of their culture. The former, for example, points out the "minuets" precipitated when diplomats from different cultures talk with each other; the one with the notion that conversationalists should be very close to each other advances, while the other diplomat continually retreats in defence of his ideas of spatial separation. Hall and Sommer have applied this approach to such local, everyday settings as university libraries and classrooms and high-rise apartments. In every case, they have documented regularities in spatial behavior which occur in less explicit form within local communities and which follow prescriptions seldom written on paper.

(vi) *To what extent is territorial behavior a natural propensity?* Still other authors have investigated whether the way we treat territory is instinctive, representing basic needs or even innate drives. Ardrey's popular work (1966) on the subject suggests that territorial behavior, ranging from family privacy to national belligerence, can be traced to roots in animal behavior. Stea, a psychologist whose work is generally more hard-nosed than Ardrey's, attributes (1970) many of our attitudes relating to territory to such normal requirements as defense, sexual attraction, and display. Others have applied subjective notions such as territoriality to specific and problematic environmental contexts, such as the psychiatric ward and the benefits from privacy therein (Esser 1970). A recent application of these considerations to local communities, although one which is highly general, was made by Suttles (1972, esp. Part 3).

(vii) *What is the social organization of environmental decision making?* Others again, in trying to understand nonobjective bases of environmental manipulation, ask what types of people become concerned and active in cases which result in decisions about community environment. Decisions are not always made on the basis of dry fact, and it is generally important to know who exercises influence leading to the making of decisions. Although there is considerable precedent for such studies regarding the community more generally, their value regarding even non-heated environmental issues is not always recognized. A number of authors, for example, in trying to understand how decisions are made in the pollution and environmental control arena, turn to identification of the protagonists and their motives for entering the public arena (cf. Burch et al, 1972: pp. 257–331; Tognacci 1972). This explains perhaps more than any cost benefit analysis how decisions are finalized.

Another group of researchers ask how those within established administrative structures operate with respect to environmental issues in the community. Sewell (1971), for example, investigated the environmental attitudes within public bureaucracies of public health officers on the one hand and engineers on the other, finding considerable difference in ideology between them. Studies of this sort help demonstrate why many well-intended initiatives do not reach successful conclusions (see also Craik, 1970a).

Obviously, then, there is now some precedent for research on a wide variety of questions providing documentation on the subjective side of our continuum, even if the answers so far are on widely differing conceptual planes, with little cumulation of results. Such a variety of questions pursued naturally implies that a wide variety of methods have been used.

Methods have indeed varied. While much work has incorporated the relatively standard sociological technique of interviewing, some of it has not. But even when interviewing, researchers have used a variety of unconventional approaches. As Craik (1970b) has pointed out, interview situations may differ both in how researchers decide to ask their questions and in the format by which they receive responses.

A number of researchers, for example, have received fruitful returns by having respondents record their impressions in map format (Gould 1966; Orleans 1967; Goodey 1972). Others have found pictorial material (photographs, drawings, etc.) useful as a stimulus for information on people's thoughts concerning community environment (Peterson 1967; Sonnenfeld 1966; Canter and Thorne 1972; Michelson 1966). Still others have used variations of attitude tests—paired comparisons (cf. Rushton 1969), the semantic differential (Lowenthal and Riel 1972), and Likert-type scaling (Craik 1970b). Researchers have even built scale models of possible local environments as a stimulus for subjective responses from people (Pyron 1972).

A variation on interviewing techniques was pioneered by Lynch (1960) when he had respondents stroll along routes within a city which he had an interest in studying with a tape recorder in hand, recording their spontaneous impressions and perceptions of the local environment as they went.

Other researchers have relied on careful observational techniques. Barker, for example, has spent more than a generation in a manageably small town in the midwestern U.S., carefully recording what he sees in specific buildings and locales which he calls behavior settings (1968). Sommer (1969) has used observational techniques regularly when examining the spatial rules operative in classrooms, libraries, cafeterias, and the like.

In many studies in which subjective information concerning local environment is accumulated, strict sampling methods have been employed in which the basic unit has been the environmental context of the person being studied, rather than the traditional social context. The reason for this approach is obvious, but it differs from traditional practice within sociology, as applied to more traditional community studies.

OBJECTIVE RESEARCH APPROACHES

Although the focus to this point has been on the precedent for and the important questions answered by approaches to subjective phenomena concerning people's interface with their community environment, there is also abundant research activity concerning the documentation of exactly what happens in this man-environment interface in a strictly objective manner, nearly devoid of interpretation. At very low levels of scale, for example, precise methods are being developed to record human behavior; researchers investigating the flow pattern and attractions of places like museums have placed sensors at frequent, regular intervals under rugs, to record exactly the circulation of persons in space (Bechtel 1970). Machines as well have been devised to record the exact patterns of eye movement in given spatial contexts; data received from such methods go far beyond expressed verbal sentiment in documenting people's reactions to a stimulus.

At a somewhat broader level, like that attributed earlier to Strauss (1961), interview and questionnaire methods have been used to an increasing degree to gather information about people's regular daily activity. A world-wide community of researchers (acting relatively independently) has discovered the utility, for the partial solution of social planning and physical planning problems, of so-called time and activity budgets (cf. Michelson 1973). The approach in this case is to ask people not what they think, feel, or perceive, but rather exactly what they did during a finite period close enough to the time and appropriate enough to the method of recording so that distortion in reporting is minimized.[2] Gathering information about people's daily activity, broken down into meaningfully small segments, this approach amasses coincident data on what people do (available quantitatively in terms of length of time), where this takes place, and with whom. This approach, for example, could enable researchers interested in learning how much time fathers spend with their children (and whether or not it has anything to do with the local community) to gather facts on this subject. It enables simultaneous assessment of activity, spatial content, and social structure. Measures such as this are now being taken extremely seriously in governmental plans to establish systems of national social accounts, to complement the traditional systems of economic accounts.

These are, of course, examples of extensions of "hard" methods of data gathering to the research context of physical environment. They run parallel to the more subjective approaches explored above. The more macroscopic or far flung the phenomenon they seek to assess, the less likely these techniques may be to record the objective behavior directly. There is almost always some degree of inexactness in measuring what is desired. But the major difference from the subjective approach is the attempt, however imperfect, to gather data on tangible movements, activities, and behaviors in contrast to images, beliefs, attitudes, feelings, rules and propensities.

However, the crucial question, as suggested at the outset, concerns the juxtaposition of the two methods on any single problem as well as the resulting potential benefit. Without forcing a confrontation between subjectively and objectively supported positions on environment, it is difficult to expect representatives of government to act rationally either for or against such value-charged beliefs affecting local communities as (1) we should emphasize road building because automobiles give people gratification, (2) we should emphasize high density, mixed developments on short blocks in order to stop crime in the streets (cf. Jacobs 1961), and (3) the world is flat, or otherwise.

PERSPECTIVES ON ENVIRONMENT

Although the various answers to the discrete questions posed in the previous section may not add up at this time to a unified body of knowledge, they fit into a short series of perspectives with rather well-defined relationships to one another, illustrated by Diagram 1.

At the centre of our concern are two phenomena, one or both of which may be present depending on our focus: (1) local behavior to be explained with reference to the physical environment, and (2) a decision to be made reflecting the fit between a social-behavioral context and a physical environment potentially available for construction and use which affects the community, directly or indirectly.

In its most general and dramatic form three filters act to designate the fit between our central concern and the environment. When analyzing environment as it currently exists, one uses these filters as a way of explaining, apart from social labels (e.g., social class, marital status, etc.), why a particular behavior does or does not occur within the given environmental context. When, on the other hand, one wishes to start with behavior and plan for an appropriate future setting, one uses these filters as a way of screening out inappropriate design alternatives. The three filters as sketched in Diagram 1 are opportunity, perception, and culture.

There is little belief these days that physical environment *determines*

Diagram 1 General Factors Mediating the Fit of Behavior and Environment

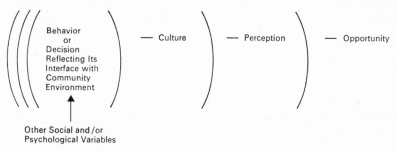

behavior to any extent other than with respect to the effects of noise. Instead, spatial arrangements are thought to be permissive. Activities can take place within the spatial framework permitted by the built environment but the construction of an environment providing opportunity for an activity to ensue does not guarantee that it will in fact. Nonetheless, if a design is such that it is physically impossible for an activity to take place, then all the desire in the world will not enable that activity to occur in that particular place. Good discussions, for example, are rare in rooms where the chairs are nailed down facing an authority figure in the front, while the same group appears transformed once located in surroundings where people may face one another. Similarly, in communities, it may be hard for people to buy indigenous local goods without some kind of outlet, but the presence of the outlet does not mean people will buy there. Hence a first question concerning desired behavior and a physical environment, before any consideration of cultural influences or perception, is whether it is possible or likely for a behavior or activity to occur within the opportunity structure represented by the physical environment (Michelson 1971).[3]

A second filter is perception. Do people perceive physical artifacts as intended? For example, something of a waste problem occurred at a recent world's fair because the special, architect-designed waste containers were too beautiful to have been perceived for what they were by great numbers of people. To take another example, one great problem in the design of new neighborhoods in communities is that people frequently do not perceive the unity and the internal logic of these units as much as do their designers, who restrict their attention to unit boundaries on a drawing board. People must perceive a local area as a community before the latter can exercise any of its expected social effects. Whether for world's fairs, newly built neighborhoods, or indeed mental hospitals, universities, or a whole host of other settings, there is considerable evidence that people's behavior is in a significant degree a function of what they do or do not perceive in a given environment (cf. Proshansky, Ittelson, & Rivlin 1970). Nonetheless, perception is relevant for the subsequent appearance of a given behavior *only* if environment provides the necessary opportunity for it to occur.

Finally, culture suggests what should happen in a specific environment context, given sufficient opportunity and appropriate perception. One school of researchers has concentrated on the norms within given cultures for how people distribute themselves in space (Hall 1966; Sommer 1969). Various design alternatives either support or violate these norms, having relatively fine-grain effects on the resultant behavior. Another cultural approach has emphasized the symbolism (learned early in life) which is associated with particular types of buildings and spaces (Barker 1968; Rapoport, 1969). According to this perspective, for example, when entering a room having the symbols of a place of worship, one assumes a set of behavior considerably different from that which occurs in response to the symbols of a lounge or a bar. This suggests that behavior within units identified as local communities may vary greatly from culture to culture. However, to continue the logic of the diagram, cultural influences are a relatively unimportant influence on environmental behavior if the desired behavior has no physical opportunity to occur and if the relevant symbols are not perceived.

While I have accorded an order of primacy among opportunity, perception, and cultural influence with respect to behavior in the context of local environment, this particular order is specific in its application to *whether* a desired behavior takes place in a given setting. If, on the other hand, one wishes to know *why* a particular observed behavior is found there, then the closer one gets to the centre of the diagram, the greater the explanatory power adhering to a given filter. Hence the order of primacy regarding observed behavior would be reversed.

The major point of this section, however, is that the many discrete research efforts, incorporating both subjective and objective approaches, fall into several perspectives which complement each other in explaining the interface of behavior and local environment. Other writers have used somewhat different language, but the thrust is a common one. Buttimer, for example, speaks of the interaction between sociological space, interaction space, the symbolic level, the affective level, and the purely morphological (1972: pp. 285). Sonnenfeld suggests that environment has both "elements" and "qualities" (1972: pp. 268). Kates speaks of direct stimulus and symbolic meaning (1966). Goodey speaks of the behavioral process as distinct from the perception process (1972). Finally, Proshansky, Ittelson, and Rivlin, after reviewing various earlier attempts to conceptualize the interface between man and environment, described environment as simply "objective" and "subjective" (1970: pp. 27–28). We can be certain in any case that it is at least that.

THE CASE OF SOCIAL CONTACT IN HIGH-RISE APARTMENTS

I was very concerned with the popular conception that the resident of a high-rise apartment is out of contact with other people, a challenge and threat to observers who believe that interaction with others, preferably on the basis of residential proximity, is a requisite of good mental health and citizenship. To assess this matter requires examining the extent to which this physical artifact (the high-rise apartment) affects the nature of one's social contact, whether in the form of a traditional locality-based community or some alternative. This, in turn, requires both relatively subjective and objective data—the former in terms of beliefs about the characteristics of neighbors and neighboring in a high-rise, and the latter in terms of the pattern of actual behavior.

The study from which these data are drawn is a longitudinal study, with the primary purposes of establishing the degree of self-selection present in the choice of essentially contrasting environments (cf. Bell 1968) and then the subsequent influence, if any, on behavior exercised by the spatial constraints of the home environment.[4] We focused on people who were about to move to high-rise apartments, on the one hand, and to single family homes, on the other. Each housing subgroup also consisted of people locating in the city center and of people moving to far suburban locations, omitting those in an intermediate belt. All housing units selected for study were in the greater Toronto area.

Sampling followed the logic of the natural experiment, focusing upon families who were in a normal course of events undergoing the specific move in which we were interested. Table 1 indicates the breakdown of our sample according to the housing types and locations which served as sampling criteria. So as to achieve a sample of people whose actions represented some effective degree of choice, a further control in the sampling was on the price on homes and apartments purchased and on the rental level of apartment homes rented. The control assured a sample of middle- to upper-income respondents, the spatial constraints on whose behavior could nonetheless be applied to the eventual benefit of persons of lower income, since the latter would be even less likely to have the resources to

Table 1   Characteristics of the Sample According to Housing Types and Locations Which Served as Sampling Criteria

High-Rise Downtown	109 (14.3%)
Single House Downtown	94 (12.4%)
High-Rise Suburb	286 (37.6%)
Single House Suburb	272 (35.8%)
a. New—209	
b. Resale—63	

adapt to these constraints. We also controlled the sample with respect to stage in the life cycle, studying only families with both spouses present and in the child-bearing years, of whom some had children and some did not; this control was undertaken both to minimize superfluous variation in the data and also to help answer nagging policy questions about a subsegment of the population thought to have some of the more serious housing problems.

At this point long interviews[5] have been held at three intervals in the moving and settlement cycle: immediately upon having chosen the new housing and before moving, approximately two months after moving, and one year and two months after moving. We expect to gather terminal (for us) data at a period four years and two months following the move. At each interview point interviews were held within the family separately with the wife (primary respondent), with the husband whenever possible, and with one child (pre-selected by random procedures) if one aged from ten to seventeen years was present.

This paper reports only data from the first phase of the study (just before the move) and for the wife only. Furthermore, it concentrates only on the high-rise low-rise comparison, as the threat to "community" is thought to come from high-rise residence.

Although the structure of the paper stresses the necessity to reconcile subjective and objective data, a preface to our findings must acknowledge that, operationally, these polar opposites may be difficult to realize in pure form. While, for example, we sought information reflecting respondents' description beliefs, it is possible that what they say is merely a reflection of belief in the ultimate veracity of what they read in the newspaper. On the other hand, there are instances in which the reporting of hard, factual material is distorted by respondents' interpretation of what happens rather than what really occurs. Although these dangers are ever-present, it is nonetheless a desirable objective to seek data from the two approaches, weighing, comparing, and if necessary, reconciling the answers forthcoming. Certainly, discrepant pictures of the same reality must be reconciled even if operationally impure.

To get information on the perceived characteristics of future neighbors in high-rise apartments and in homes, we asked the respondents to compare their own economic and educational level with those of their hypothetical new neighbors. One significant difference between the respondents moving to single homes and those moving to high-rise apartments, regardless of their present residence, was the percentage of "don't know" answers regarding the education of their future neighbors. This is shown in Table 2. Although the percentage of "don't know" answers is considerably higher with respect to education than with respect to the economic level of post-move neighbors, in both cases people moving to apartments were less likely to identify the characteristics of their new neighbors.

Table 2 Perceptions of Socioeconomic Characteristics, with Associated "Don't Know" Answers, of Post-Move Neighbors by Housing Change

| | POST-MOVE NEIGHBORS | | | |
| | Education | | Economic Level | |
HOUSING CHANGE	Percentage "Don t Know" Answers	Percentage of Balance Stating "More than Self"	Percentage "Don t Know" Answers	Percentage of Balance Stating "Higher than Self"
House to House	53.7%	40.3%	21.0%	29.5%
House to Apartment	64.5	31.3	25.9	7.5
Low-Rise to House	43.6	30.8	16.4	17.8
Low-Rise to Apartment	53.8	23.3	25.6	22.4
Apartment to House	37.5	50.0	8.9	29.3
Apartment to Apartment	52.1	22.8	20.7	19.2
	(N = 73)		(N = 102)	

In terms of those able to make such an identification, the overall trend was consistent with Bell's findings (1968): people expected their new neighbors to be socioeconomically similar to themselves. This is shown in Table 2. However, people moving to houses were more likely than those moving to apartments to imagine their new neighbors as being superior to themselves, demonstrating a stronger minority feeling among the homeowners that they were moving up with the Joneses. The only exception to this pattern among all the categories of movers was among those moving from various forms of low-rise multiple housing, and the difference represented in that exceptional case is extremely small.

Hence, while most people experienced no great upward mobility in their housing move, those moving to high-rise apartments seemed less concerned with this issue and had fewer perceptions that their neighbors would be anything except in the same boat in terms of socioeconomic status.

We asked also about the personal traits which respondents attributed to their pre-move neighbors, to their post-move neighbors and to themselves. Respondents were presented with the set of cards stating twenty-seven personal traits and were asked first to identify those they thought would apply to their pre-move neighbors, then those they thought might apply to their new neighbors, and finally those which might apply to themselves. As Table 3 indicates, those moving to high-rise apartments were considerably less likely to attribute traits to their new neighbors. Although this indicates no great preoccupation with community on the part of people moving to a high-rise, it does not in itself indicate the nature of personal contact expected after the move.

Table 3 Trait Knowledge of Post-Move Neighbors for Each Change in Housing Type

CHANGE IN HOUSING TYPE	NUMBER OF TRAITS ATTRIBUTED TO NEIGHBORS Percentage in Each Category			N
	0 to 3	*4 to 10*	*11 or More*	
House to House	44.4%	39.3%	16.3%	209
House to Apartment	49.2	42.0	8.6	69
Low-Rise to House	36.5	45.2	18.4	93
Low-Rise to Apartment	45.3	45.2	9.5	95
Apartment to House	26.5	46.8	26.5	64
Apartment to Apartment	39.4	49.0	11.7	231
			Total	761

Somewhat more important implications of this phenomenon may be seen from data concerning the similarity which people see between their own traits and those of their expected new neighbors. Table 4 indicates even greater differences between those moving into houses and those moving into apartments. When it comes to the personal characteristics of their new neighbors, people moving to houses, particularly from other forms of dwelling, see considerably more points of similarity between themselves and their neighbors than do those moving to high-rise apartments.

Table 4 Trait Similarity with Post-Move Neighbors for Each Change in Housing Type

CHANGE IN HOUSING TYPE	NUMBER OF TRAITS PERCEIVED AS HELD IN COMMON Percentage in Each Category			N
	0 or 1	*2 to 5*	*6 or More*	
House to House	39.2%	33.5%	27.3%	209
House to Apartment	43.4	36.2	20.3	69
Low-Rise to House	29.0	37.7	33.3	93
Low-Rise to Apartment	46.3	35.8	17.9	95
Apartment to House	21.9	40.7	37.5	64
Apartment to Apartment	36.4	40.2	23.4	231
			Total	761

The qualitative nature of the traits attributed to residents of apartments as compared to those in houses is indicated in Table 5. Whether based on the characteristics of the pre-move neighbors or on the characteristics of their post-move neighbors, there was greater consensus about traits thought to apply more to neighbors in single-family-home areas than about those applying to neighbors in apartment settings. The former are thought more likely to be proud of property appearance, neat, living for the family, and handy. Those currently living in single homes think that their neighbors in addition are efficient, while those moving to houses see their new neighbors as child-oriented. In contrast, apartment people see their neighbors in a much more limited and less positive fashion. Those now living in high-rise apartments are more likely to see their neighbors as withdrawn, sloppy, and living for the present. Those moving to apartments anticipate their new neighbors will also live for the present but, in addition, will be modern and lively—a somewhat more optimistic but nonetheless extremely limited picture.

Table 5 Personal Characteristics Attributed to Neighbors Living in Single Houses Compared with Apartments

TRAIT	NEIGHBORS IN SINGLE HOUSES		NEIGHBORS IN APARTMENTS	
	Attributed to:		Attributed to:	
	Pre-Move Neighbors	Post-Move Neighbors	Pre-Move Neighbors	Post-Move Neighbors
1. Proud of Property Appearance	X	X		
2. Neat	X	X		
3. Living for the Family	X	X		
4. Child-Oriented		X		
5. Efficient	X			
6. Handy	X	X		
7. Withdrawn			X	
8. Sloppy			X	
9. Live for the Present			X	X
10. Modern				X
11. Lively				X

Tables 6 through 9 illustrate graphically people's orientation concerning the relationship of their personal traits to those of their current and future neighbors, according to the type of move they are about to make. Table 6 shows that the general orientation among persons moving from *one house to another* is that the characteristics of their current neighbours, their future neighbors, and themselves are generally similar. In contrast, those moving from *homes to apartments,* as illustrated in Table 7, while showing less awareness of the characteristics of their post-move neighbors, nonetheless show a greater affinity between themselves and their current neighbors (in homes) than between themselves and their future neighbors (in high-rise apartments). Table 8, depicting the comparison of those moving from *one high-rise apartment to another,* shows a pattern quite similar to those moving from one home to another, with two minor exceptions: the neighbors are known slightly less well, and the future neighbors are seen with somewhat more positive eyes than are older neighbors. Table 9, however, depicting the viewpoints of those moving *from apartments to homes,* shows a considerably greater similarity between self and future neighbors (in homes) than between self and current (apartment) neighbors on all positive traits, with the reverse true for negative traits.

Evidence of a subjective nature, then, would indicate that people moving to high-rise apartments expect or have noticed a degree of ill-defined *socioeconomic* similarity between themselves and their neighbors but marked *personal* dissimilarities. This fact, plus the substantive nature of the traits which people attribute to apartment dwellers, would suggest strongly the perceptual basis for lack of contact among apartment dwellers. This is quite consistent with the pattern established in a local public housing context, within which people moving in thought they would have little in common with their new neighbors, expected little personal contact, and then subsequently saw very little of them in fact (Hartman 1963). In short, one has scant evidence that those moving to high-rise apartments expect community contact.

Our data also enabled us to investigate the actual behavior of our respondents as it occurred in the physical context in which they lived before their moves, which in turn allowed an attempt to juxtapose objective reality with their perceptions. We asked, for example, about the three people to whom our respondents felt closest personally inside their pre-move neighborhood. Table 10 indicates the frequency with which these local contacts were seen. It shows that there are considerable differences in the same direction that would be expected following from the perceptions of neighbor contact: those living in houses see their local friends more frequently than those living in apartments. Nonetheless, it would also appear that the most sociable people among those living in any type of housing are those moving *to* high-rise apartments, not to houses. However,

Table 6

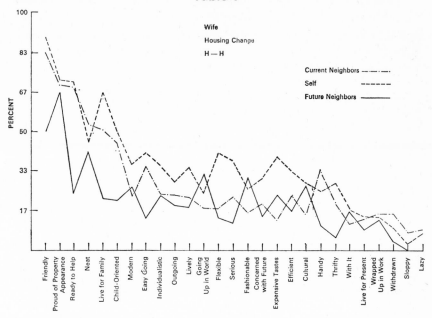

Wife
Housing Change
H — H

Current Neighbors ——·——·
Self ———————
Future Neighbors —————

Table 7

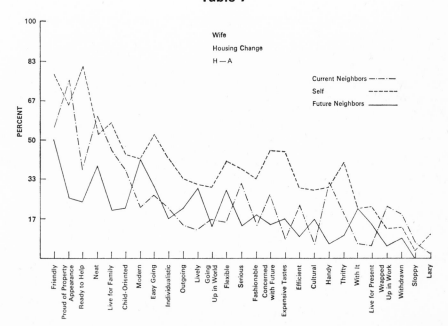

Wife
Housing Change
H — A

Current Neighbors ——·——·
Self ———————
Future Neighbors —————

Table 8

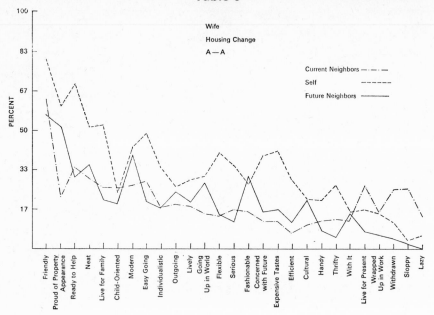

Table 9

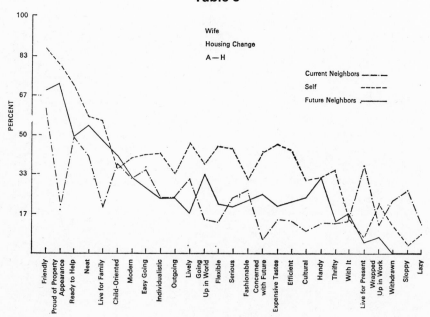

these attributes prove spurious once location is controlled. Those moving to the suburbs are initially more sociable in this instance than those moving downtown, regardless of housing types.

Table 10 Frequency of Neighborhood Contacts by Housing Change

| | FREQUENCY OF CONTACT Percentage of Total Contacts for Each Group | | |
HOUSING CHANGE	Once Per Week or More	Several Times Per Month or Less	N
House to House	65.13%	34.87%	671
House to Apartment	72.41	27.59	174
Low-Rise to House	62.28	37.72	289
Low-Rise to Apartment	70.61	29.39	228
Apartment to House	45.25	54.75	179
Apartment to Apartment	59.80	40.20	602

Total Number of Contacts (Maximum of three per respondent)   2143

We also investigated the frequency of contact, measured the same way, with close friends who lived *outside* our respondents' local neighborhoods. There was no evidence whatever to differentiate our respondents according to their housing type, either before their move or after.

Reference to the three persons thought closest outside one's neighborhood does not approach exploration of the *extent* of contact patterns. Nonetheless, even further doubt is cast upon actual differences in behavior between these subgroups when other measures of contact behavior are introduced. For example, Table 11 was created from time budgets reported by our respondents. There were no differences attributable to housing types with respect to the average minutes on weekdays which were devoted to visits, parties, or feasts. On Sundays, those living in apartments were, if anything, the more sociable people in this respect. With respect to a second measure of time, the average number of minutes spent in a day with persons not residing in the respondents' household, again the scores of those living in apartments, particularly those moving from one apartment to another, are high (certainly not low, as hypothesized from subjective materials). This is true both for weekdays and for Sundays, but the difference is more clearly noticeable for the former.

Table 11   Average Minutes Per Day Spent on Different Activities and with Types of People Present by Housing Change

	Persons not Residing in Household		Receiving Visits or Parties with Friends and Relatives, Attending Receptions	
	Daily	Sunday	Daily	Sunday
House to House	137	134	40	87
House to Apartment	162	138	29	68
Low-Rise to House	129	148	33	78
Low-Rise to Apartment	112	185	37	66
Apartment to House	155	173	25	96
Apartment to Apartment	280	164	36	99

When one looks, as in Table 12, at how people project their current patterns,[6] there is no clear difference which would indicate that people moving to houses will have significantly more intensive contact patterns than those moving to apartments. If anything, those initially living in apartments expect to have even more contact after their move than before —more so than those initially living in other types of dwellings. Those changing either from an apartment to a home or the reverse expect to increase their contact somewhat more than those remaining in the same type of housing.

Table 12   Expected Frequency of Contact with New Neighbors by Housing Change

Housing Change	More Contact with New than with Old Neighbors	No Change	Less Contact with New than with Old Neighbors	N
House to House	26.4%	64.3%	9.3%	193
House to Apartment	33.8	60.0	6.2	65
Low-Rise to House	35.7	52.4	11.9	84
Low-Rise to Apartment	47.1	41.4	11.5	87
Apartment to House	59.0	36.1	4.9	61
Apartment to Apartment	48.9	48.4	2.7	219
Total				709
No Answer				52

To this point, then, the data indicate that the subjective differences according to housing type which people record about neighbors are not accompanied by similar patterns of actual contact in current housing. Indeed, depending on how one measures such actual contact, the reverse may even be true.

I suggested at the outset that a fruitful purpose might be served by attempts at reconciling discrepancies between the two forms of data. What accounts for the discrepancy observed here?

One way of answering this question is to explore other aspects of the contact patterns described, to ask if the contact patterns of home- and high-rise dwellers fail to differ significantly and regularly in the direction expected in ways other than frequency and duration.

We explored, first, where people tended to see their friends. There were no differences worth recording among apartment dwellers and home dwellers or according to their post-move residences.

We investigated as well under what circumstances people first made the acquaintance of their friends. This time some significant clues were disclosed. Table 13 indicates that those living in high-rise apartments are far less likely to have met their local friends within the neighborhood than are those living in any other type of housing. Although they did not make the acquaintance of these people uniformly at any other single place, they were much more likely to have met them through mutual friends, at work, at school, or during childhood. In contrast, those living in houses had met their local friends primarily within the neighborhood.

Table 13 Where First Met Neighborhood Contacts by Housing Change

| HOUSING CHANGE | WHERE FIRST MET % of Total Number of Places for Each Housing Change | | | | | | N |
	During Child-hood	High School, University	Through Mutual Friends	At Work	In Neighbor-hood	Other	
House to House	4.9%	1.3%	9.8%	4.5%	64.3%	15.2%	468
House to Apartment	4.4	2.7	13.3	8.0	56.6	15.0	113
Low-Rise to House	6.1	2.8	15.0	5.6	57.2	13.3	180
Low-Rise to Apartment	9.2	1.3	17.6	14.4	45.1	12.4	153
Apartment to House	15.7	13.0	25.0	9.3	18.5	18.5	108
Apartment to Apartment	12.2	5.2	14.9	17.2	31.6	18.9	402
Total Number of Places							1424

Table 14 goes further in indicating that those living in apartments and particularly those moving to apartments, regardless of their current residence, are much more likely than are those living in or moving to houses

Table 14   Relationship of Most Frequent Contact by Housing Change

HOUSING CHANGE	RELATIONSHIP % of Total Contacts for Each Housing Change			N
	Family or Relative	Neighbor	Friend	
House to House	37.0	34.4	28.6	189
House to Apartment	39.9	20.0	40.0	65
Low-Rise to House	32.4	26.5	41.0	83
Low-Rise to Apartment	27.7	22.9	49.4	83
Apartment to House	42.7	23.0	34.4	61
Apartment to Apartment	32.1	23.4	44.5	218
Total				699
No Answer				62

to consider these local contacts "friends," rather than "neighbors," regardless of the actual proximity of their residence.

There is a difference, then, in the *formation* of the friendship patterns of those moving to apartments and those moving to houses.

What, then, *explains* these differences in contact patterns? The answer appears to be quite simple. There are significant differences between the categories of environment in terms of the percentage of women within each category who hold jobs. Among those moving to downtown apartments, 78% of wives work, while 47% who are moving to suburban apartments do so, in contrast to no more than 30% among all categories of those moving to single family houses. The work variable, in fact, explains, at this point in the paper, all the foregoing variables concerning contact patterns much more directly than environmental factors. While work status is also related to the number of children a woman has, and while, in addition, children frequently serve as a catalyst to the creation of adult friendships, it is nonetheless working status which is the dominant explanatory variable in the present set of data. Indeed, when one examines similar data for husbands, the influence of the wife's working status is great in explaining the friendship pattern of the husbands as well.

Furthermore, it is a *combination* of location and housing type (i.e., the downtown high-rise apartment dweller) which displays the greatest influence of the working wife. A suburban apartment is frequently a compromise between family needs in situations where the wife works but where there are also children in the family.

In any case, the "objective" picture is one of lack of isolation among apartment dwellers. They are no more isolated, according to the various measures here, than are those living in other types of dwellings. There are, however, different *paths* to friendship as a consequence of the wife's family-employment status, which in turn tends to coincide largely with the selection of housing and location—so much so that in practical terms these factors must all be considered simultaneously. Women living in high-rise apartments by and large meet even their local friends through *communities of interest* rather than through *territorially based neighborhoods*. While they have friends in their local areas, the local area itself is not a factor in originally making acquaintances.

This would indicate quite clearly that the ideas put forward by Webber (1963) and Wellman (1971), to the effect that people may increasingly have *personal* communities not based on residential proximity, are valid. It would indicate as well that this notion, called "community without propinquity" by Webber, is not distributed randomly among the population but appears within particular social and physical contexts within the city.

Furthermore, by the law of averages, people living in high-rise apartments are likely to know a considerably smaller percentage of their neighbors than do those living in single-family areas, where the pool realistically available for friendship may include only about one dozen families (cf. Gans 1967).

As a consequence, people give no credit to their apartment buildings for the existence of the friendships they have. The buildings and the neighbors are given less than positive marks for sociability and personal compatibility. Thus, people tend to have negative associations connecting high-rise buildings and social contacts as a consequence of the path which led to their particular local friendships, largely a consequence of their personal family-employment status and associated nonlocal community of interests. That people hold these buildings as antisocial while at the same time not suffering a deficit of social contact, local or otherwise, is both understandable and logical.

To understand the community today requires this reconciliation: localities have more or less relevance to personal contacts, depending on the context, while people's personal contact patterns may or may not have a basis in locality.

It is potentially fruitful, therefore, to investigate the basis for the existence of two understandable points of view concerning the reality of a community situation, rather than to continually promulgate just one of them. The brunt of this paper was to put forward the necessity, as well as the precedent, for measuring both subjective and objective factors on any environmental situation facing local communities and to place them into a mutually explanatory framework, in that process robbing them of their emotional intensity. This does not in itself guarantee a satisfactory resolution, but it may speed that end in the absence of practical or political forces to the contrary.

NOTES

[1]At this point, concentration on the types of questions being asked is more illuminating than focusing on the rather tentative and scattered answers that have emerged to date.

[2]A valuable test of the validity of such methods was done by Carlstein et al (1968).

[3]This is basically the same notion as that advanced by Studer, who uses the term "behavior contingent environment" (1970).

[4]We sought as well, from a policy point of view, to study the social implications of major trends in housing and the types of facilities and services which might be needed to optimize each of these alternatives, regardless of their absolute desirability. Principle sponsor for this study is the Central Mortgage and Housing Corporation (Canada), and further assistance has been received from the Canada Council.

[5]Interviewing was subcontracted to York University Survey Research Centre, as were the first two phases of coding. Phase III was coded by Recon Ltd., Toronto.

[6]This question is clearly neither fully objective nor subjective, but it deals with people's expected changes in factual pattern, rather than with qualitative description of a purely hypothetical relation.

REFERENCES

Appleyard, Donald et al.
1964 *The View from the Road*. Cambridge, Mass.: MIT Press.
Ardrey, Robert.
1966 *The Territorial Imperative*. New York: Atheneum.
Barker, Roger G.
1968 *Ecological Psychology*. Stanford, Cal.: Stanford University Press.
Bechtel, Robert.
1970 "Human Movement and Architecture," in Harold Proshansky et al. (eds.), *Environmental Psychology*. New York: Holt, Rinehart and Winston, 642–645.
Beck, Robert.
1970 "Spatial Meaning and the Properties of the Environment," in Harold Proshansky et al. (eds.), *Environmental Psychology*, 135–141.
Bell, Wendell.
1968 "The City, Suburb, and a Theory of Social Choice," in Scott Greer et al. (eds.), *The New Urbanization*. New York: St. Martin's Press, 132–168.
Burch, William et al.
1972 *Social Behavior, Natural Resources, and the Environment*. New York: Harper and Row.
Buttimer, Anne.
1972 "Social Space and the Planning of Residential Areas," *Environment and Behavior* 4 (September): 279–318.
Canter, David, and Ross Thorne.
1972 "Attitudes to Housing: A Cross Cultural Comparison," *Environment and*

Behavior 4 (March): 3–32.

Carlstein, Tommy et al.
1968 Individars Dygnsbanor i Nàgra Hushallstyper. Lund: Institute for Cultural Geography and Economic Geography, University of Lund.

Craik, Kenneth.
1970a "The Environmental Dispositions of Environmental Decision-Makers," *The Annals* 389 (May): 87–94.
1970b "Environmental Psychology," in Kenneth Craik et al., *New Directions in Psychology* 4. New York: Holt, Rinehart and Winston, 1–121.

Downs, Roger M.
1970 "The Connotative Structure of an Urban Shopping Centre," *Environment and Behavior* 2 (June): 13–39.

Esser, Aristide H.
1970 "Territoriality of Patients on a Research Ward," in Harold Proshansky et al. (eds.), *Environmental Psychology*, 208–214.

Gans, Herbert J.
1967 *The Levittowners*. New York: Pantheon Books.

Goodey, Brian.
1972 "Displays for Mating," *Design and Environment* 3 (Summer): 46–53.

Gould, Peter R.
1966 On Mental Maps. Ann Arbor: University of Michigan, Inter-University Community of Mathematical Geographers, discussion paper No. 9.

Hall, Edward T.
1966 *The Hidden Dimension*. Garden City, N.Y.: Doubleday.

Hartman, Chester.
1963 "The Limitations of Public Housing: Relocation Choices in a Working-Class Community," *Journal of the American Institute of Planners* 24 (September): 283–296.

Jacobs, Jane.
1961 *The Death and Life of Great American Cities*. New York: Random House.

Kates, Robert W.
1966 "Stimulus and Symbol," *Journal of Social Issues* 22 (October): 21–28.

Ladd, Florence C.
"Black Youths Share Their Environment: Neighborhood Maps," *Environment and Behavior* 2 (June): 74–99.

Lawton, M. Powell.
1972 "Some Beginnings of an Ecological Psychology of Old Age, "in Joachim F. Wohlwill and Daniel H. Carson (eds.), *Environment and the Social Sciences: Perspectives and Applications*. Washington, D.C.: American Psychological Association, 114–125.

Lee, Robert G.
1972 "The Social Definition of Outdoor Recreation Places," in William Burch et al., *Social Behavior, Natural Resources and the Environment*. New York: Harper and Row, 68–84.

Lee, Terrence.
1970a "Urban Neighbourhood as a Socio-Spacial Scheme," in Harold Proshansky et al. (eds.) *Environmental Psychology*, 349–370.
1970b "Perceived Distance as a Function in the City," *Environment and Behavior* 2 (June): 40–51.

Long, Norton.
1958 "The Local Community as an Ecology of Games,"*American Journal of Sociology* 64 (November): 251-261.

Lowenthal, David.
1972 "Research In Environmental Perception and Behavior," *Environment and Behavior* 4 (September): 333–342.

——, and Marquita Riel.
1972 "The Nature of Perceived and Imagined Environments," *Environment and Behavior* 4 (June): 189–208.

Lynch, Kevin.
1960 *The Image of the City*. Cambridge, Mass.: MIT Press and Harvard University Press.

Michelson, William.
1966 "An Empirical Analysis of Urban Environmental Preferences," *Journal of the American Institute for Planners* 32 (November): 355–360.

1970 *Man and His Urban Environment: A Sociological Approach*. Reading, Mass.: Addison-Wesley.

1971 "The Case of the Equine Fountain," *Design and Environment* 2 (Winter): 28–59.

1973 "The Advent of Multi-dimensionality in Conceptions of the Quality of Urban Life." Paper prepared for a conference, "The City in History: Idea and Reality," University of Michigan, Ann Arbor, Michigan.

Orleans, Peter.
1967 "Urban Experimentation and Urban Sociology," in his *Science Engineering, and the City*. Washington, D.C.: National Academy of Science.

Park, R. E. et al.
1925 *The City*. Chicago: University of Chicago Press.

Peterson, George L.
1967 "A Model of Preference: Qualitative Analysis of the Preception of the Visual Appearance of Residential Neighborhoods," *Journal of Regional Science* 7 (1): 19–32.

Proshansky, Harold et al.
1970 *Environmental Psychology*. New York: Holt, Rinehart and Winston.

——, William H. Ittelson, and Leanne G. Rivlin.
1970 "The Influence of the Physical Environment on Behavior: Some Basic Assumptions," in Harold Proshansky et al., *Environmental Psychology*, 27–37.

Pyron, Bernard.
1972 "Form and Diversity in Human Habitats: Judgemental and Attitude Responses," *Environment and Behavior* 4 (March): 87-120.

Rapoport, Amos.
1969 *House Form and Culture*. Englewood Cliffs, N.J.: Prentice-Hall.

Reed, Paul.
1972 Situated Interaction: Normative and Non-Normative Bases of Patterned Social Behaviour. Toronto, University of Toronto, Centre for Urban and Community Studies, Research paper No. 55.

Rosengren, William, Spencer, De Vault.
1970 "The Sociology of Time and Space in an Obstetrical Hospital," in Harold Proshansky et al., *Environmental Psychology*, 439–455.

Rushton, Gerald.
1968 "The Scaling of Locational Preferences," in Kevin R. Cox and Reginald

G. Golledge, *Behavioral Problems in Geography: A Symposium*. Evanston, Ill.: Northwestern University, Studies in Geography, No. 17, 197–227.

Sewell, W. Derrick.
1971 "Environmental Perception and Attitudes of Engineers and Public Health Officials," *Environment and Behavior* 3 (March); 23–49.

Sommer, Robert.
1969 *Personal Space*. Englewood Cliffs, N.J.: Prentice-Hall.

Sonnenfeld, J.
1966 "Variable Values in Space and Landscape: An Inquiry into the Nature of Environmental Necessity," *Journal of Social Issues* 22 (October): 71–82.
1972 "Social Interaction and Environment," *Environment and Behavior* 4 (September): 267-277.

Stea, David.
1970 "Space, Territory, and Human Movements," in Harold Proshansky et al. (eds.), *Environmental Psychology*, 37–42.

Strauss, A. L.
1961 *Images of the American City*. New York: The Free Press.

Studer, Raymond G.
1970 "The Dynamics of Behavior-Contingent Physical Systems," in Harold Proshansky et al. (eds.), *Environmental Psychology*, 56–76.

Suttles, Gerald D.
1972 *The Social Construction of Communities*. Chicago: The University of Chicago Press.

Swan, James A.
1972 "Public Responses to Air Pollution," in Joachim F. Wohlwill and Daniel H. Carson (eds.), *Environment and the Social Sciences: Perspectives and Applications*. Washington, D.C.: American Psychological Association, 66–74.

Tognacci, Louis N. et al.
1972 "Environmental Quality: How Universal is Public Concern?" *Environment and Behavior* 4 (March) 73–86.

Tognacci, Louis N. et al.
1972 "Environmental Quality: How Universal is Public Concern?" *Environment and Behavior* 4 (March) 73-86.

Webber, Melvin.
1963 "Order in Diversity: Community Without Propinquity", in Lowden Wingo (ed.), *Cities and Space*. Baltimore: The Johns Hopkins Press, 23–54.

Wellman, Barry.
1971 "Who Needs Neighborhoods?" in J. A. Draper (ed.), *Citizen Participation: Canada*. Toronto: New Press, 282-287.

Werthman, Cart et al.
1965 "Planning and the Purchase Decision: Why People Buy in Planned Communities." Berkeley: Institute of Regional Development, Centre for Planning and Development Research, University of California, Preprint No. 10.

Wohlwill, Joachim F.
1966 "The Physical Environment: A Problem for a Psychology of Stimulation," *Journal of Social Issues* 22 (October): 29–38.

The Structural Bases of Political Change in Urban Communities[*]

JOHN WALTON

Northwestern University

The field of urban politics is vast and rapidly increasing. Students of a number of disciplines with a plethora of specific interests work within its hazy boundaries. The purpose of this essay is to attempt a contemporary synthesis of the field by linking a set of social structural changes to a variety of patterned political outcomes. Concretely a number of trends affecting urban social organization are summarized with three dimensions. Next the political consequences of change along each of these dimensions are discussed in some detail. Finally, the variable effects produced by the interplay among dimensions are dealt with in a way that gives rise to some data-based speculation about the future of urban politics. In addition to advancing a number of researchable hypotheses, it is hoped that the essay will sensitize the reader to some of the more fundamental issues that loom ahead.

Writing about the condition of urban communities in the United States becomes increasingly difficult precisely because so much

*The ideas developed in this paper are the product of a number of influences. Too numerous to mention by name are, first, my students in a Fall 1972 Seminar on Political Sociology who contributed to the sometimes tortuous process of rendering clarity to the framework developed here. Second are my colleagues at the Northwestern University Center for Urban Affairs who, through a series of continuing seminars, have substantialy expanded my knowledge of the field. My friend Mike Aiken could be cited on most of these pages for the ideas he got me thinking about. Other friends and congenial reviewers include Dick Berk, Peter Rossi, Allan Schnaiberg, and, particularly, Terry Clark who provided me with a very detailed set of comments on an earlier draft. Finally, in her capacity as Special Issue Editor, Marcia Effrat made a number of useful, substantive suggestions and saved me the embarrassment of public disclosure of my spelling competence.

writing is being done on the topic. As is often the case in social science, the profusion of research, theorizing, and commentary on urban affairs has served less to provide us with a coherent body of established interpretations than to raise ever new sets of interrelated questions. Complexities engendered by the diversified and exponentially increasing research literature are further clouded by the normative judgments commentators attach to the "facts" of the urban condition. In the 1920s and 1930s, for example, urban sociologists decried the city as unfit for healthy social life: conducive to segmentalized personalities, social pathology and disorganization (Simmel 1950; Wirth 1938; Mills 1943). During the 1950s and 1960s others countered this pessimistic appraisal with portraits of greater community organization and life-style adaptation than had been believed to exist earlier (Janowitz 1952; Gans 1962; Greer 1956 and 1962). Yet, within a few years the city was again being described in the vocabulary of "crises" centered on poverty, racial segregation, and atrophying public services: ungovernable and unliveable (Williams 1967; Ficker and Graves 1971; Hadden et al 1971; Cohen 1970; Milgram 1970). And just as we come full circle we are informed anew that the urban crisis is largely overrated, affecting only a small minority of the inner city poor who bring troubles on themselves through shortsightedness, while "the overwhelming majority of city dwellers live more comfortably and conveniently than ever before" (Banfield 1968: 3).

Certainly urban communities are changing, but one must wonder if they are oscillating so rapidly between such extremes. Obviously part of the disparity in these views stems from the different values and purposes of separate observers. Another explanation lies in the fact that they address somewhat different features of the urban landscape, not to mention the different types of cities from which observations are generalized. Nevertheless, there are substantial overlapping areas of disagreement that force questions concerning just where we are and where we are likely to be headed. Such questions prompt this essay.

One way to gain closure on these issues is to shift attention from the broad outlines of the urban condition to more specific processes, particularly ones that seem to be at the root of matters in the sense that they are more the causes than the results of the larger phenomenon. This, of course, is a theoretical decision. To explain general aspects of city life one investigator might choose to focus on demographic change and ecological patterning, while another would concentrate on the distribution of economic goods and services. Such theoretical choices are rarely pretentious claims that all is to be explained from a given starting point. Rather, they reflect the investigator's strategic bet that more can be explained from this standpoint than from another. In that vein the present discussion will center on the political process and, particularly, on that process as the crucial allocative link between social structural change and the eventual distribution of privileges and burdens.

Yet, so far, this does not really clarify matters. The field of urban or community politics is extremely varied. Students of sociology, political science, law, history, and economics work within its hazy boundaries. Typical objects of inquiry include such disparate problems as voting and referenda, power and decision making, public expenditures, local government organization, political participation, collective violence, public policy in education, law enforcement, development, health, and poverty. Few, if any, successful efforts have been made to bring together these strands of inquiry in a theoretically unified conception of community politics. And no small part of the problem is a persistent suspicion that the notion of "community" these days has little content or utility. In short, the idea of "community politics" raises a dual ambiguity of scope and content.

These problems are raised not to discourage further thinking, but to clarify the purposes of this essay. These are, first, to define the terms entailed by the notion of urban community politics. Second, to identify the principal social structural trends or changes that influence urban community politics. Third, to reduce these changes to a more manageable set of dimensions that integrate seemingly disparate aspects of the political process. And, finally, to suggest some projections and hypotheses concerning the directions in which urban politics are moving. No paradigm or agenda for research will be offered since such efforts are justifiably ignored by scholars with their own agenda. To the extent that the framework is persuasive, others may find new ways of organizing the field and posing their own questions.

THE CONCEPTS OF COMMUNITY AND POLITICS

Vexing indeed is the word "community." As Bloomberg (1966: 360) suggests, it is a staple of everyday language: "The term 'community' itself may not be used as much in the everyday rhetoric of American public life as 'peace with justice' or 'brotherhood,' but it surely runs a close second." In the academic world comparable deference is shown, with both the American Sociological Association and the Society for the Study of Social Problems having established a community section at the "cabinet level" of the organizations. Ironically, but for the resistance of Congress, Richard Nixon's administrative reorganization plan for the federal government would have created a Community Development Division as one of four "super cabinet" organizations.

Whether in spite of or because of its frequent usage, the notion of community seems to impart multiple imagery and little unique content. Typically it is used interchangeably with terms designating a neighborhood (e.g., "the West Side community"), a city (e.g., "the Bay Area community"), an association (e.g., "the medical community"), a symbolic reference group (e.g., "the community of scholars"), an institution (e.g., "the prison community"), and many others. To add to this confusion others suggest that the term is an anachronism in modern society that has witnessed "the eclipse of community" (Stein 1960).

This definitional problem is not new. Hillery (1955) found in the sociological literature alone some ninety-four definitions among which there was considerable disagreement, although sixty-nine of these included, at least, the ideas of a territorial area characterized by social interaction and a common tie. Reflecting these themes more succinctly Sjoberg (1964: 114–115) states,

> A community is a collectivity of actors sharing a limited territorial area as the base for carrying out the greatest share of their daily activities. This definition implies that persons interact within a *local* institutional complex which provides a wide range of basic services, yet it also takes into consideration the fact that the community is not necessarily a self-sufficient unit.

In a more recent discussion Schnore (1967) suggests that the above definition raises a number of issues about the nature of communities that still require clarification. It should be emphasized, he goes on, that the term (1) refer to an identifiable area, (2) not apply to aggregates such as occupational groups, (3) nor to institutions such as prisons or hospitals, and (4) be reserved for areas in which daily interaction is possible. Accordingly,

> I shall regard "the community" as *the localized population which is interdependent on a daily basis, and which carries on a highly generalized series of activities in and through a set of institutions which provides on a day-to-day basis the full range of goods and services necessary for its continuity as a social and economic entity.* (Schnore 1967: 95)

As formal definitions go each of these is adequate. Both stress such key elements as territorially localized population, activities carried out in common within the territory, a set of local institutions serving its needs, and interdependence though not necessarily self sufficiency. But these formal definitions necessarily obscure much of the nature and dynamics of communities. For example, they convey little about the multiple levels of community organization, the variability in community integration and interdependence or the interplay between local and extralocal factors that create the environment in which a community develops and acquires (or loses) an identity. It is precisely such omissions that permit the frequent and erroneous equation of community and city in the literature on "community power structure," "comparative community studies" and so forth. That is, generalized treatments of the community typically begin with definitions similar to the foregoing but end up comparing attributes of the geopolitically defined concept of city (urbanized area) by recourse to census data (Bonjean 1971; Schnore 1967). This, of course, papers over the fact that consistent application of the concept of community would doubtless reveal that most cities embody a number of more and less well defined communities. With the exception of urban ethnographies (e.g., Gans 1962; Liebow 1967; Suttles 1968; Zorbough 1929) and quantitative techniques like social area analysis (Shevky and Bell 1955), the tendency has been to hypostatize the dimensions of community organization and thereby abandon the study of community as it is sociologically defined. The problem here is more than a methodologically expedient "loose fit" between the concept and its operational definition, since what is most distinctive about communities (i.e., segmented life-spaces and life-styles) becomes totally emasculated.

Counteracting this trend in ways that promise substantial theoretical gains is the brilliant new book of Gerald Suttles (1972) *The Social Construction of Communities*. Suttles' main thesis is that communities do not now, nor have they ever existed as isolated and autonomous entities. Rather, they come into being and acquire their identity in *response to* impingements from the larger societal environment.

> First, total societies are not made up of a series of communities, but communities are units which come into being through their recognition by a wider society. Community, then, presumes some type of supra-community level of organization. Second, the community is not a little society but a form of social differentiation within total societies, and the problem is how appropriate this type of social differentiation is in modern societies. (Suttles 1972: 257)

Suttles sets on its head the romantic (Gemeinschaft) notion of autonomy. With regard to local integration, he goes on to distinguish four levels of community organization (local networks and the face-block, the defended neighborhood, the community of limited liability, the expanded community of limited liability). For present purposes, however, the key point is that the community, "as a territorial basis for associational selection," comes into being and changes in response to external influences among which big government and big business are the most crucial in the contemporary setting. Suttles may underemphasize the extent to which local characteristics become "functionally autonomous" and feed back into the interplay between community and society, but the distinctive merit of his approach is that it forces us to look at this interactional node.

In what follows, then, we shall employ the foregoing definitions of community in conjunction with Suttles' view of community as a process of social differentiation. Understanding that, attention will be confined to "urban communities" or the city-suburb complexes that make up metropolitan regions. To avoid inconsistency this is not necessarily the Standard Metropolitan Statistical Area (SMSA) of the Census Bureau (which is likely to be larger), but a region behaviorially defined by the extent to which populations depend upon and organize their routine activities around a common set of closely related institutions (e.g., governments, employers, shopping centers, etc.). Obviously a metropolitan region embracing multiple urban communities gradually shades off into localities less closely tied to the center, and any "cut-off" point is somewhat arbitrary and not as necessary here as in studies based on some form of statistical mapping.

Finally, this discussion focuses on the politics of urban communities. As alluded to earlier, the political process is to be understood as an allocative link between social structures that generate resources and their eventual distribution. More specifically we shall conceive of the political process as the interplay between authoritative public bodies and the persons or institutions (including other governmental units) that attempt to influence the policies or decisions of those bodies.

SOCIAL TRENDS AND THE CHANGING ENVIRONMENT OF URBAN POLITICS

If communities and their politics are to be understood as selective responses to intrusive influences from the larger societal environment, then a first order of business is to identify the most important of these influences. What are the key social trends in contemporary American society that variously shape and alter the character of urban communities? From a wide array of important influences five general processes will be discussed.

1. Urbanization

The United States is rapidly becoming a nation of city dwellers. According to the 1960 census 70 percent of the population was "urban" (i.e., lived in localities of 2500 or more persons), up from 64 percent in 1950 and about 40 percent in 1900. Of that 70 percent, "Nearly two-thirds of the people lived in Standard Metropolitan Statistical Areas (SMSA), i.e. cities of 50,000 or over, the counties in which they are located, and adjoining counties which meet stated criteria of economic and social integration with the central city" (Taeuber 1968: 28). Early reports from the 1970 census indicate that the proportion of Americans living in Metropolitan Areas has moved up several percentage points in the last decade. The phrase "rapid urbanization" is, of course, relative; cities in many of the developing countries are growing at a much faster rate (Davis 1965). Nevertheless, a dramatic shift toward urban living is one of the most fundamental facts of contemporary societies.

2. Suburbanization

On closer examination, however, it appears that in many of the older and larger urban areas this population increase is occurring exclusively in the suburbs, with the central cities either holding their own or actually losing ground. Among the fifteen largest cities of 1950, all had come to represent a reduced proportion of the total population within their Metropolitan Area (SMSA) by 1970, with the drop averaging around 20 percent. Illustratively, in 1950 the population of Chicago accounted for 70 percent of the Metropolitan Area; by 1970 it contributed only 48 percent although its absolute loss in population was only 300,000 or about 11 percent. The city of Houston doubled in absolute size during the same period but dropped from 54 percent to 45 percent of the Metropolitan Area. Most of 1950's fifteen largest cities (the only exceptions being Houston and Los Angeles) lost small increments in absolute size, but *all* lost ground *relative to* the suburbs and urban fringe. Again among the fifteen, only two still embodied more than half of the Metropolitan Area population in 1970, i.e., Milwaukee (51 percent) and New York (68 percent) U.S. Bureau of the Census, 1970). It should be emphasized that newer and smaller central cities, particularly in the southwestern and western regions, are still likely to be growing and experiencing *less* unbalanced growth vis-a-vis the suburbs. Nevertheless the main effect is clear; rapid urbanization is better understood as the rapid growth of suburbs and fringe areas within the larger Metropolitan Area.

3. Social Polarization

The foregoing trends would be of secondary importance if they involved no more than an even-handed spatial reorganization of the population. The fact is, however, that they represent a tendency toward greater social differentiation along lines of race, class, and status. We are reminded of the now familiar statement from President Johnson's Commission on Civil Disorders, "This is our basic conclusion: our nation is moving toward two societies, one black, one white—separate and unequal . . . a white society principally located in suburbs, in smaller central cities and in peripheral parts of large cities and a Negro society largely concentrated within large cities" (U.S. National Advisory Commission on Civil Disorders, 1968: 407). But, once again, the data require careful scrutinizing and suggest that this is a rather sweeping oversimplification. The fact is that there have always been black suburbs and that between 1950 and 1960 the black population in suburbs of northern and western cities not only increased faster than in earlier decades, but also increased faster than the white population (Farley 1970: 513–516). Nevertheless, this recent shift in the *proportionate* rate of increase of black over white suburban populations has effected only a very slight *overall* change in the racial composition of suburbia (from roughly 2.2 perceñt to 4 percent between 1960 and 1968 (Farley 1970: 514)), since the numerical base for the percentage increase was miniscule to begin with. Three further qualifications should be noted. First, the black population of southern suburbs is decreasing rapidly, although its present level (roughly 10 percent) is still higher than in northern and western regions. Second, illustrating the heterogeneous character of suburbia and the duplication of city-born patterns of racial segregation, the suburban localities into which blacks have moved tend to be older areas experiencing population succession, new developments intended for black occupancy, and impoverished enclaves (Farley 1970: 525). Third, while these trends go on in the suburbs, central cities continue to become *more* polarized racially owing to the fact that their black populations are also increasing significantly while white populations are generally declining (the only exception to this pattern is found in the West, with white populations of central cities also increasing but at a substantially reduced rate by contrast to black resulting, therefore, in a growing polarization).

Summarizing the question of urban social differentiation along racial lines, central cities are generally becoming more segregated and, while there has been a slight overall increase of suburban black population, this tends to be distributed in segregated neighborhoods. In the main, therefore, and notwithstanding suburban heterogeneity, "Cities and their suburban rings are becoming more dissimilar in racial composition..." (Farley 1970: 526). As Gans (1968) observes, "Today, the predominantly Negro city is still far off in the future, and the all-Negro city is unlikely." Nevertheless, this is the trend in the midst of which urban communities and their politics are engulfed.

Beyond the racial dimension, urban social differentiation also operates along class and status lines. Although race, class, and status are correlated, they are not isomorphic. Poor and less educated whites continue (sometimes of necessity) to live in central cities, while economically mobile blacks (outside the South) move to the suburbs. Adding further variety to this pattern are the growing number of working class suburbs (Berger 1960; Dobriner 1963; Gans 1967). Yet, again, the main effect of recent social change has been to increase city-suburban differentials in education, income and occupational skill. Although there appears to be substantial variability in this trend by region, racial composition, and age of cities, Schnore (1972) reports that the bulk of the evidence supports the "evolutionary hypothesis" whereby older and larger cities increasingly house the poorer, less educated, and less skilled residents of the Metropolitan Area. This trend, based on comparisons of the censuses of 1950 and 1960, appears to have continued. In Chicago, for example, 1970 census data show that on a five item socioeconomic status scale (including median family income, median home value, median rent, percent high school graduates, and percent professional or managerial) constructed for 85 city neighborhoods and 137 suburbs, the central city contributed only one of the top 25 neighborhoods and 22 of the bottom 25. In 1960, only 24 city neighborhoods were above the median and by 1970 that had fallen to 20, with the majority losing in relative scale location (*Chicago Sun-Times*, December 17, 1972: 7). One consequence of this shift was a reported increase in the racial segregation of public schools (*New York Times*, December 17, 1972). Given all of these changes it is not surprising that a recent Gallup Poll reported that only 13 percent of its sample now prefer city living, down from 22 percent in 1966 (*Chicago Sun-Times*, December 17, 1973: 23).

4. Economic Polarization

Because social processes are highly interdependent, trends in differentiation observed with respect to population, race, class and status are apt to be reflected, as cause and effect, in the economy. Thus, relative to the total Metropolitan Area, the central city generally represents a declining proportion of the labor force and the available jobs—these are not the same due to commuting (Neenan 1972). Paralleling Schnore's evolutionary interpretation, it also appears that older and larger cities are experiencing a net (as opposed to relative) loss of employment, especially in the manufacturing and retail trades (Birch 1970). So far the wholesale trade and services have been less prone to suburban flight, since the advantages of a centralized location may be more critical for these enterprises. The upshot of these sectoral differentials may be an increasing specialization and imbalance in city economies. Finally, there is some indication that older Metropolitan Areas are, as a whole, losing in total employment (Birch 1970). Illustratively, in 1972 the total number of jobs in New York City fell by 73,000 (or 2 percent), the third consecutive year for such losses that added up to 257,200, setting the city's employment level back to 1960 standards. Although some New York suburbs gained jobs, the larger Metropolitan Area witnessed a net loss (*New York Times*, December 31, 1972: 1). Conversely, while the city of Chicago was slowly losing jobs (some 300,000 between 1960 and 1970; 70,000 between 1970 and 1972) and was surpassed in total employment by the suburbs in 1972 (1.35 versus 1.28 million), the Metropolitan Area had a net gain (*Chicago Sun-Times*, December 31, 1972: 9).

Ironically, just as the central cities find themselves in increasing financial difficulties due to the flight of affluent residents and businesses and a declining tax base, they are confronted on the other side by escalating demands for public services such as mass transit, education, welfare and environmental control. This irony is compounded by the fact that the demand for many city services (e.g., mass transit, highways, police, etc.)

is stimulated by contiguous suburbs and their commuters who use those services. The question of whether the suburbs thus exploit the cities or indirectly bear a share of the tax dollar costs has been argued both ways and may yet be unsettled (Kasarda 1972; Neenan 1972). Nevertheless, in terms of both public and private economic resources the gap between city and suburb is widening (Thompson 1965).

5. Vertical Integration

A final trend of particular importance for the politics of urban communities has less to do with the sheer distribution of people and resources than with the networks within which they are organized. Warren (1963) has suggested that communities may be viewed as organized along two axes, the horizontal axis referring to linkages among local community institutions and the vertical axis designating connections between community and extracommunity instituions. Accordingly, Warren (1963: 53) notes that the "... great change in community living includes the increasing orientation of local community units toward extracommunity systems of which they are a part, with a decline in community cohesion and autonomy." American communities, and most notably urban communities, are becoming increasingly interdependent with metropolitan, state, and national institutions, both public and private, as a result of the twin processes of external intervention and local aspiration. These processes take many concrete forms, among which the spread of big government and big business is the most dramatic. In the public arena,

> Along with changing budgetary priorities and activities, there has been a redistribution of the responsibilities for conducting these activities. In 1902, for example, local governments clearly dominated in most domestic functions such as education, highways, public welfare, parks and recreation, natural resources, and police protection. By the 1960's, however, local governments found themselves sharing these activities to a far greater extent with state and federal governments. (Mitchell, 1968: 269)

Federal programs in housing, education, poverty, model cities, and revenue sharing, in conjunction with political-legal reforms such as reapportionment and antidiscrimination legislation, all have combined to reshape the character of local communities.

Similarly, the local impact of national corporations is becoming more pervasive. As a result of the merger movement, branch plants, and absentee ownership, the reins of economic control increasingly lie outside the local community. Further, these vertical linkages extend far beyond government and business to include voluntary associations (Warren 1956; Turk 1970), political interest groups (e.g., civil rights groups, the National

League of Cities, etc.), and such pervasive, if neglected, institutions as organized crime, which has decentralized in the best administrative tradition of other venerable American institutions.

DIMENSIONS OF URBAN COMMUNITY POLITICS

So far this discussion has sought to clarify the nature of urban communities and to specify several of the most fundamental social trends affecting their organization. With that behind us we may now turn to the central question of politics and political change. Stated briefly, attention now shifts to the questions: what are the key dimensions of urban community politics, how do the earlier documented social changes affect these dimensions separately and in combination, and, ultimately, in what directions are the politics of urban communities moving—what can we expect in the near future?

For purposes of analysis we shall conceive of the urban political process as shaped and altered by changes along three key dimensions: segmentation, interdependence, and competition-control (or decentralization-centralization). Certainly one could add other dimensions, but these three adequately summarize the impact of major social trends and fit the heuristic purposes of this discussion. *Segmentation* refers to the process by which communities become differentiated from one another on the basis of social characteristics, life-styles, and economic resources. Segmentation is preferred to the term "social differentiation" which is multidimensional and may imply any of a variety of patterns of intra- and intercommunity distribution of people and resources. That is, "social differentiation" would embrace any pattern of community organization, while the notion of segmentation is directional, implying greater nucleation or polarization. *Interdependence* is also a directional concept, referring to more or less coordination between various levels of community organization as well as between the community and the larger society. Finally, *competition-control* refers to the leadership or decision making process and, particularly, the extent to which it is either *centralized* among a few actors, enabling community-wide policy imposition, or *decentralized* among many, requiring coalition formation. The notion competition-control is preferred to "power structure," since it implies variability and the suggestion that power is always negotiated, never total. Consistent with the foregoing conception of politics, competition-control focuses on the intersection of local and extralocal pressures on allocative decision making. The political correlates of each of these dimensions will be discussed first. Subsequently we shall turn to the more complex issues of how the interplay between the dimension affects the political process.

Segmentation and Politics

From the most general standpoint, trends toward social and economic polarization are reflected in the political sphere by greater segmentation of interests and interest group constituencies with conflicting ambitions. This is most clearly evident in the differences between the political interests of central cities and suburbs, although, as we shall see, there are also important differences within cities and suburbs.

Acknowledging the fact that socioeconomic (Schnore 1963) and political (Walter and Wirt 1971) characteristics of suburbs vary widely and that some city-suburb differentials may be declining, it still remains the case that, in the aggregate, suburbs are appreciably more prone to support the Republican Party than are central cities. For example, Walter and Wirt (1971: 757), report that while cities and suburbs fluctuated in the extent to which they separately supported Republican presidential candidates between 1948 and 1964, their differences in party preference remained a fairly constant 15 percent (e.g., in 1956 the city-suburban Republican vote was approximately 50 percent versus 65 percent; in 1964 it was roughly 26 percent versus 39 percent). Similarly, a study of 154 representative American suburbs indicated that 52 percent consistently voted Republican against 32 percent consistently Democrat. And, further, suburban Republican preferences increased at successively lower level contests (president-congress-mayor). Finally, as would be expected, the more residential and more affluent suburbs were the most staunchly Republican, the Democrat preference coming from older, industrial and less affluent suburbs (Wirt 1965).

Yet, party preference is only the tip of the iceberg since, typically, the alternatives presented by the two major parties represent ambiguous policy choices of vague locality reference. Locally salient issues reflect more substantial political cleavage. In the matter of public schools, for example, sharp differences were found in the proportion of central city versus suburban public (school and government) officials favoring the more equalitarian form of metropolitan district reorganization. Interestingly, it was also found that while this schism was less pronounced in smaller metropolitan areas, suburban residents, and particularly their public officials, were much more strongly opposed to change than their city counterparts (Zimmer and Hawley 1967).

Regarding the likelihood of metropolitan cooperation across a broad range of services, Williams (1967) makes a useful distinction between "life-style services" (e.g., education, police, zoning, etc.) and "system-maintenance services" (e.g., a metropolitan telephone system, health services, sanitary districts, etc.). The suburbs, he reasons, will oppose metropolitan centralization of life-style services but support integration of system-maintenance services, particularly as communities within the

Metropolitan Area become more specialized (or segregated). One study of twenty-one municipalities in the Oklahoma City Metropolitan Area provides support for this speculation. Among local officials more favorable attitudes were expressed toward the integration of system-maintenance-type services (health, libraries, transportation, water, refuse, parks and recreation) than toward life-style-type services (planning and zoning, fire, urban renewal, education, police), and a factor analysis of these attitudinal data reflected a relatively clean separation of the two types of services (Kirkpatrick and Morgan 1971).

Similar results derive from a study of Philadelphia city and suburban residents. Concerning a regional air pollution control authority (a system-maintenance service), 78 percent of the central city residents surveyed favored the idea as compared to a respectable 64 percent of suburbanites. However, with respect to area-wide government, 61 percent of the Philadelphians supported the proposal as opposed to only 18 percent of the suburbanites (Williams et al. 1965).

In light of these consistent findings a "deviant case" analysis proves most illuminating. That is, in some Metropolitan Areas central city and suburbs have combined to support city-county consolidation or "metro-government." Do these cases contradict the hypothesis that social and economic polarization lead to segmented and conflicting political interests? Interestingly, they do not. Hawkins (1967) studied the universe of (fifteen) city-county consolidation referenda between 1945 and 1964. Although he found suburbs less favorable toward consolidation than cities, the differences were not regularly associated with social rank (education and occupational status). Rather, "The almost uniform positive correlations . . . suggest that as social differences increasingly favor the fringe there is an increasing tendency for the fringe to vote *for* city-county consolidation" (Hawkins 1967: 333, emphasis in original). Further, in cases where the referenda were defeated (nine of the fifteen) there was no substantial difference between the proportion of opposition votes delivered by cities and suburbs. While, on the surface, these findings appear inconsistent with the preceding discussion, on closer examination it turns out that *all* of the consolidation referenda were initiated in counties of southern states. And this is most important given the fact (reported earlier) that southern Metropolitan Areas demonstrate less socioeconomic polarization than older and larger areas of the North (cf. Schnore 1972). Indeed, our general thesis appears further confirmed by the fact that only in the less socially and economically segregated (polarized) Metropolitan Areas did the question of consolidation even come to a vote in these years.

In related studies, the Miami-Dade County area successfully adopted metropolitan government partly on its efficiency merits, but, more fundamentally because of the relative absence of segmented communities and crystallized political interests (Sofen 1966). In Jacksonville, Florida an interesting variation on this theme took place. Here signs of racial and economic polarization appeared earlier than in most southern cities, result-ing in an estimated 44 percent black population in the city by the mid-sixties. According to the study of Sloan and French (1971), white political leaders successfully campaigned for metropolitan government in order to reconstitute a white majority in the Jacksonville city-Duval county area and thus retain their own control.

So far we have argued that the social and economic polarization of cities and suburbs has led to segregated communities that pursue conflict-ing self-interests. No discussion of this point would be complete without mention of the Wilson and Banfield (1964) "public-regardingness" thesis. From selected referenda in Chicago and Cleveland, Wilson and Banfield show that upper-income suburban voters often side with low-income city residents in supporting welfare services that are generally less favored or opposed by middle-income groups. From this they conclude the existence of a "public regarding ethos" whereby certain subcultures, defined by both income and ethnicity (Anglo-Saxon and Jewish), tend to suppress their own self-interest for the benefit of the larger public. Though far from de-finitive, the evidence Wilson and Banfield offer cannot be ignored, particu-larly when other studies produce parallel findings (cf. Hahn 1968; Hawkins 1967). Clearly there are some instances of affluent liberal com-munities taking positions that are not in their own immediate interest, whether we call this public virtue or "conscience money"—representing as it does a much smaller absolute tax bite for upper than for middle incomes. Nevertheless, the limits of this virtue are rather narrow. In their own data Wilson and Banfield demonstrate that public-regarders are somewhat more enthusiastic about general welfare expenditures that derive from regres-sive sales taxes as opposed to property taxes. Second, most of the welfare projects that public-regarders supported (e.g., county hospitals, court houses, welfare buildings, etc.) represented no tangible threat to the life-style values of their own communities. And, finally, when it comes to the latter type of issue, the bulk of the evidence seems to support a "private-regarding" ethos across income and ethnic categories.

Before leaving the general topic of this section it should be stressed that segmented political interests not only distinguish city and suburb, but also cut across intra-urban and intra-suburban communities. Several studies discussed earlier (e.g., Walter and Wirt 1971; Williams 1967; Kirkpatrick and Morgan 1971; Hawkins 1967; Wilson and Banfield 1964) demonstrate this variability particularly with respect to the socioeconomic and political heterogeneity of suburbs. On certain political issues older, less affluent, industrial suburbs are apt to resemble typical central city communities in their politics, just as middle-class city enclave communities will follow suburban patterns. Moreover, studies of migrants to the suburbs indicate that a "transplantation," as opposed to a "conversion," theory provides the best explanation of their political interests; political preferences acquired over a lifetime become transplanted in the suburban milieu, more than they are altered by new surroundings (Wood 1958; Greenstein and Wolfinger 1958–59; Campbell et al. 1960; Millett and Pittman 1958). In at least one respect, however, the transplantation theory requires qualification. Supporting evidence is based largely on party preference and may underestimate the impact of suburban socialization, particularly with regard to locality-relevant issues of the type former city residents have never had the need to form an opinion about.

Within the city a similar pattern of segmented political interests is found. Illustrative are studies, such as those of Greer (1972), growing out of the social area analysis tradition and focusing on the political consequences of ecological differences between urban communities. Greer (1956) analyzed patterns of political participation and interest in central city communities of comparable social rank and segregation, but differing in their degree of urbanization (or familism). In this controlled comparison urbanization was associated with distinctive differences in social behavior, notably segmented interests and less community participation. By contrast the "less urban" communities were characterized by greater homogeneity and community-oriented activities. In a more general vein this work suggests that the less urban community may be more readily mobilized for political action.

Finally, turning to segregated inner city communities, the black and brown ghettos, evidence indicates that in terms of income and employment the gap between these communities and the larger urban society is widening (Williams 1967). Among the more evident political consequences of this trend are militant separatist movements, increasingly in conflict with police and local officials, and campaigns for community control, particularly of neighborhood schools that do battle with working-class community groups. Thus the "social order of the slum" emerges as a response to persistent conflict and tension engendered by the larger trends of segregation and inequality (Suttles 1968; Molotch 1972). Understandably there is the temptation of folk wisdom to draw casual inferences from these conditions to the incidence of rioting and collective violence. Presumably the most segregated and deprived ghettos are the most prone to civil disorders. But here the data fail to support conventional thinking; measures of social and economic deprivation or differentiation are not systematically associated with the incidence of urban riots. Although the evidence in this area is mostly negative, several studies do agree that city size, percentage of nonwhite and nonsouthern location are among the few reliable predictors. (Spilerman 1970; Downes 1970; Jiobu 1971). How these are interrelated and sequentially linked to other factors remains a matter for subsequent investigation, but even the available evidence indicates that trends toward social and economic polarization are somehow related to ghetto violence as a form of political, or at least "pre-political," protest (Berk and Aldrich 1972).

Interdependence and Politics

We have already opted for Suttles' (1972) interpretation of the community as a territorial basis for associational selection created in response to conditions of the larger society. So, too, community politics must be understood as shaped in large part by the interdependence between local and extralocal institutions. Discussion of this dimension of urban community politics requires less detailed analysis than the foregoing since the political consequences of increasing interdependence generally have the effect of creating new bases of *potential* political competition within and between communities. Perhaps the most common illustration of this is the observation, replicated in a variety of situations, that federal intervention in local politics may effect greater democratization (Vidich and Bensman 1958; Presthus 1964; D'Antonio 1966). The scenario producing this effect is easily sketched. Federal intervention (e.g., subsidies, poverty programs, civil rights legislation) is typically directed at remedying local problems that have remained intractable due to a lack of resources or will. Federal intervention introduces new resources into the community in the form of expenditures or legal powers and, while existing elites may successfully coopt many of these, a greater or lesser amount typically devolves on formerly powerless groups. An initial toehold on power may expand substantially as a result of a new conferred legitimacy as well as the successive introduction of additional external resources. For example, many local political groups established first in response to civil rights legislation were successively reconstituted and expanded as urban renewal, model cities and poverty programs came requiring local participation (Kramer 1969). Although many of these programs entail minimal resources and are often short-lived, at the very least they have the effect of politicizing new interest group constituencies and providing them a training ground in the ways of local politics.

In addition to promoting competition within communities, federal intervention also encourages competition among communities and cities for a larger share of the largesse. Aid to education and services such as welfare and mass transit are the clearest illustrations of increased struggle among city hall, state capitol, and Washington. In these struggles local groups have sought to manipulate federal programs in their own interests. For example, federal highway programs that benefit chiefly suburban commuters have been assailed by central cities in an attempt to break the "highway trust" by diverting funds for subsidies to mass transit systems. Conversely, local governments and citizen groups have, for the most part, actively resisted and undermined federal directives on school bussing and public housing.

The most recent and well documented excursion of the federal government into local community politics was the War on Poverty. Although, as

we shall discuss shortly, the impact of federal poverty programs varied
from one city and community to another, their general effect was to create
new political constituencies among the formerly disenfranchised. With
reference principally to New York City, Bell and Held (1969: 173–174)
conclude about these programs

> A number of extraordinary changes are taking place in American life.
> . . . There is, first, the *increasing "politicization"* of society, particularly
> in urban affairs. . . . The classical effects of politicization are clear: the
> decision points are visible rather than dispersed. The consequences are
> plain, for people know "whose ox will be gored." There is an over-
> concentration on law and legislation, and an increasing burden on
> administration. *All of this, inevitably, increases the potential for group
> conflict.* . . . Second, a group of *"new men"* have come into the political
> system, specifically among the blacks. . . . Finally, we have seen the
> emergence, in a formal way, of the idea of *"group rights"* as the means
> whereby disadvantaged groups, particularly blacks, *can establish their
> claims* in the system (emphasis added).

Kramer's (1969) comparative study of five San Francisco Bay Area
city-county localities is noteworthy in that it demonstrates significant variability in the vitality and effectiveness of programs across cities and their
subcommunities or "target areas." Communities more effective in delivering
services were smaller and more consensual. Localities that effectively promoted community organization and participation (as opposed to service
delivery in the short run) were larger and typically had prior experience
with federal programs or the civil rights movement. Within the city of
San Francisco remarkable variation occurred at the community level ranging from sedate, service-oriented Chinatown to the tumultuous, organizational or power-oriented Western Addition. Obviously, it was the latter
orientation that mounted the strongest challenge to local political control.
In a comparative study of fifty United States cities Vanecko (1969) gen-
eralizes some of these results. Community Action Agencies (CAA) that
emphasized organization and participation, rather than service delivery,
accomplished greater institutional change in the sense of responsiveness
to the needs and demands of the poor (i.e., numbers of the poor served by
programs). Further city characteristics associated with this approach included percentage of nonwhite, percentage of poor, and nonsouthern location. Commenting on the specific resources that poverty agencies provided
these communities, Vanecko (1969: 629) notes,

> Since such agencies exist primarily in cities with relatively high levels
> of political activity in poor neighborhoods, their effectiveness is in
> extending or complementing the activity and involvement of the resi-
> dents of poor neighborhoods. We can only speculate at this point, but
> the critical additions that CAA's provide may be protection from active
> resistance to the efforts of neighborhood residents, integration of the

activities which may be somewhat diffuse, legitimacy for suspect activities, moral support, and perhaps simplest of all, financial backing.

It should be noted here that there are significant parallels between both the city characteristics and extralocal influences conducive to community organization politics and riot politics. It will be recalled that several studies found percentage of nonwhite and nonsouthern location among the predictors of riot cities. Further, Spilerman (1970: 643) notes that since much of the leadership for redressing racial inequality comes from the federal government, ghetto communities ". . . now base their expectations regarding future improvements in status largely on the cues coming from Washington." Stated more generally, *community organization and civil disorders may be interpreted as kindred forms of political action occurring in similar urban localities as a result of similar extralocal influences.*

Among the many additional varieties of interdependence one would have to include the increasing proliferation of overlapping governmental authorities which combine to fragment locality-based political control (Wood 1964; Danielson 1965). Similarly, in the private sector, the increasing number of absentee-owned corporations dilutes local control in ways we shall mention below. However, to avoid any impression that the effects of interdependence include, invariably, greater political competition, it should be recognized, first, that at the "lower end" many cities may be so ineffectual or elite-controlled that federal programs have either little impact or *further reinforce privileged* groups (Stinchcombe 1968; Lowi 1970). Second, at the "upper end" welfare policies of different federal administrations may work broader changes quite apart from local participation (Sheppard 1969). Nevertheless, within these limits, the growing interdependence between urban communities and extralocal institutions is clearly the most potent force in altering contemporary political relationships, and, generally, alters them in the direction of greater competition and potential conflict (Kesselman 1972).

Competition-control and Politics

The third dimension of this schema involves the local leadership or decision making process. In the foregoing sections we have focused on political cleavage from the standpoints of community segregation and interdependence particularly as these processes differentiated new *constituencies* and *potential* competition. Here we turn to the more pointed concern of how power is distributed among local *elites,* the structural correlates of various power arrangements, and the forces behind change in the distribution of power *between* elites and nonelite interest groups.

Fortunately, in this area there exists not only a vast literature of community studies (Clark 1968a; Hawley and Witt 1968; Aiken and Mott 1970), but also a number of recent analyses which attempt to codify and compare results from large samples of cities (see Table 1). Further, these analyses have focused on the dual objectives of, first, determining those city characteristics associated with different patterns of power distribution, and, second, assessing the extent to which those patterns are related to different consequences or "outputs," typically in the sense of local programs and public expenditures. Our strategy here will be to review both phases of this research in light of the social and economic trends discussed earlier This will allow some inferences concerning the directions of change in local leadership patterns and their consequences.

Table 1 presents a notational summary of five comparative studies listed in chronological order. The five differ somewhat methodologically: numbers 1, 2, and 4 are based on codification and secondary analysis of other studies, while numbers 3 and 5 entail original field research. Moreover, although each of the five focuses on the conceptually similar dependent variable concentration-dispersion of power, only numbers 1 and 4 operationalized that variable in the same way. However, these methodological differences are an asset for present purposes since they provide alternative measures that "triangulate" on the same phenomenon, thereby enhancing the confidence that can be placed on convergent results. Finally, it should be noted that this summary is an expansion of Clark's (1972) earlier endeavor which may be consulted for additional parallels.

Since each of the studies listed in Table 1 contains its own "methodological costs and benefits" (Grimes et al., 1971) that temper generalization, attention here will focus only on the right-hand column summarizing convergent findings.

Interestingly, from the standpoint of theories of "social differentiation" and "increasing scale," measures of population size, economic diversity, and industrialization do not conform to predicted associations with decentralized power arrangements; with only one exception the studies find no relationship. On the positive side of the ledger, dispersed (or "pluralistic") power structures are found in cities that are older, have a high proportion of absentee owned corporations, high unemployment, racially and ethnically heterogeneous populations, and nonsouthern location. Variables inversely related to decentralized power (i.e., associated with more concentrated power arrangements) include population increase, reform ("good") government, and higher socioeconomic status (in terms of education, occupation and income).

Recognizing that these findings are tentative, what theoretical speculation and further testing do they suggest? In terms of the framework developed in this paper *nearly all of those variables values or scale locations associated* (positively or negatively) *with decentralized power structures simultaneously characterize the evolving central city, and, conversely, variable values associated with centralized power structures characterize younger cities and modal suburbs.* Stated differently, the trends in urbanization, social and economic polarization, and inter-

Table 1   Notational Summary of Five Large Sample, Comparative Studies Relating Community Characteristics to Decentralized Arrangements of Power

	1. Walton (1966,1970)	2. Gilbert (1968,1972)	3. Clark (1968b,1972)	4. Aiken (1970)	5. Grimes, Bonjean and Lineberry (1971)	Sum
A Size and Age						
1. Population Size	0	0	+	0	$\left\{{+\atop o}\right\}$	0
2. Population Increase	−	−		$\left\{{-\atop o}\right\}$	$\left\{{-\atop o}\right\}$	−
3. Age of City	+			$\left\{{+\atop o}\right\}$		+
B. Economic Characteristics						
4. Economic Diversity	0	0	+	0	$\left\{{-\atop o}\right\}$	0
5. Industrialization	0		0	$\left\{{+\atop o}\right\}$	+	0
6. Absentee Ownership	+			+		+
7. Unemployment		+		+		+
C. Political Characteristics						
8. Reform Government Nonpartisan Elections	±	−	−	−		−
City Manager	0	+		−		−
9. Party Competition	+					
10. Voluntary Association Activity			±			
D. Social Characteristics						
11. Socioeconomic Status	$\left\{{-\atop o}\right\}$	±		$\left\{{-\atop o}\right\}$	$\left\{{-\atop o}\right\}$	−
12. Population Heterogeneity		+		+	+	+
13. Non-South	+	+		+		+
Number of Studies or Cities Compared	55,61	166	51	57	17	

Legend: + = Positively associated with decentralized power arrangements.
          − = Negatively associated with decentralized power arrangements.
          0 = No association found.
          ± = Mixed findings for different indicators of a single concept.
          $+/-\atop o$ = Tending in + or − direction but weak association.
          blank = Variable not investigated.

dependence tend generally to move in the direction of greater decentralization of power at the local level in a manner akin to Schnore's (1972) "evolutionary sequence." Reading the data in the opposite direction this means, of course, that less "evolved" localities (i.e., younger, growing, southern and western, less polarized internally, reform government, and high-status cities and suburbs) more typically host cohesive, concentrated elite leadership. Although the generalization is not totally surprising, it does suggest the irony that our "crisis ridden" central cities may also represent our crucibles of democracy.

Yet, this still does not answer why such a generalization should obtain. Returning to our framework, a very general explanation may be derived. Namely, those cities increasingly subject to the differentiation of potential interest group constituencies through the processes of segregation and externally conferred resources, do in fact generate organizational modalities to compete for influence. This suggests the simple proposition that *to the extent that a locality is characterized by segregated and/or interdependent communities, its political process is more organized and competitive.* Related theorizing by Aiken (1970), Mott (1970), and Aiken and Alford (1970a) has pushed this line of reasoning further by suggesting that the structural characteristics of competitive power arrangements may be interpreted as jointly reflecting organizational density (power centers) and collaboration (interfaces). Thus, structural characteristics are linked to the more crucial local organizational structure and, in turn, "... the greater the number of centers of power in a community and the more pervasive and encompassing the interfaces, the higher the probability of innovation in a given issue arena" (Aiken and Alford 1970a: 633). While most of this reasoning is speculative and the notion of local organizational structure requires further specification (cf. Turk 1970), the evidence to date suggests that this may be the most productive avenue of subsequent inquiry.

Until recently a much neglected issue in the study of community power structures was what difference they made; that is, whether different decision-making styles were associated with different policy outcomes. Three interesting studies bear indirectly on this issue by linking some of the city characteristics already discussed to levels of local government activity. Lineberry and Fowler 1967) found that reform governments tend to tax and spend *less* than traditional city governments. In a groundbreaking exploration of interdependence between local and nonlocal organizations, Turk (1970) demonstrated that a higher level of activity occurred in poverty agencies in those cities with *greater* extralocal integration. And, as alluded to already, Aiken and Alford (1970a, 1970b) have shown that the length and level of involvement of urban renewal, poverty, and public housing activities in a large sample of American cities are positively associated with organizational differentiation, experience and interorganizational networks (or collaboration). To a greater or lesser extent each of these studies suggests that certain conditions, themselves positively associated with decentralized power, are also related positively to higher levels of governmental "outputs" (i.e., duration and coverage of programs, levels of expenditure, etc.).

Fortunately, we are not limited to drawing the logical inference from these studies—that decentralized decision making leads to higher levels of "output." Three further studies bear directly on that issue. In Clark's (1968b) analysis of urban renewal and general budgetary expenditures and Aiken's (1970) review of public housing, urban renewal, and poverty and model cities programs, decentralized decision making was consistently associated with more active programs. The picture is not altogether clear, however, since Grimes and associates (1971) found a negative relationship between their measure of power dispersion and expenditures generally and educational expenditures specifically. Noteworthy, though, was the fact that fifteen of the seventeen cities in this study were southern and, conceivably, decentralized only by southern standards. If, on a continuum with the Aiken and Clark cities, these fell toward the more centralized end, as seems possible, all of the results would coincide. For the moment, then, the bulk of the evidence (i.e., five of six pertinent reports) indicates that decentralized power, the structural correlates of which have already been specified, leads to greater governmental "outputs." Both Clark and Aiken qualify their findings, noting that they apply to less volatile, or "fragile," types of programs and to ones that were initiated chiefly by the federal government. Clark (1972: 309) goes further to distinguish between "public goods" versus "separable goods" and hypothesizes that the former may be more readily implemented by centralized power arrangements and the latter by decentralized ones.

THE INTERPLAY OF SEGMENTATION, INTER-DEPENDENCE, AND COMPETITION-CONTROL

So far we have assessed the political consequences of change along these three dimensions of community organization more or less in isolation. To complete the logic of this analysis and provide some hint as to the general directions of political change in urban communities, we must consider the ways in which these dimensions affect one another. Recognizing the fact that, given three directional variables which may be uniquely ordered in combinations of two and three, the number of logically possible patterns of reciprocity quickly becomes complex. Consequently, we shall deal only with a subset of what appear to be the most meaningful linkages empirically.

In the main *segmentation and interdependence* appear to be inversely related. As communities become increasingly tied to extralocal institutions many of the old supports for social and economic segmentation are undermined, and this process typically gives rise to political conflict via renewed efforts to maintain local "integrity" (i.e., homogeneity). More specifically, since communities have always been affected in one-way or another by the larger society of which they formed a differentiated segment, it is the nature or quality of these interdependent ties that is presently changing so as to make them more salient.

> Without external allies the local community and its defended boundaries are in a precarious position. Not only are such allies essential to

its defense, but their opposition or realignment may be fatal to the
neighborhood's sense of integrity and self-determination. In recent
years there is reason to believe that it is the changing posture of these
external allies rather than any marked decline in their own internal
defensiveness and solidarity which has so panicked many communities.
With the passage of federal and state open housing laws and the
desegregation of some local schools, a number of community groups
righteously felt themselves betrayed. The growing role of the federal
government in constructing housing and in providing mortgage money
threatened to be another blow to a long-term alliance in which the construction industry, real estate men, local government, and the federal
authorities had implicitly endorsed the existing composition of local
communities. (Suttles 1972: 245–246).

In a similar vein many of the large corporations moving out of the
central cities find their operations hampered by exclusionary residential
patterns and are able to apply leverage for change.

Suburban counties and municipalities need the revenue of the employers. The employers need employees. Employees need housing they
can afford, accessible to their jobs. The interests of these diverse groups
may come together in a way that brings pressure to bear . . . towards
"opening up" the suburbs. (Rubinowitz 1973: 10).

Although a wide variety of similar external influences (e.g., the civil rights
movement, court decisions, fair employment practices, etc.) could be cited
as trends subverting social and economic polarization, it should also be
recognized that until recently local and nonlocal forces have combined to
create the marked patterns of segregation documented earlier. If we are
now witnessing the beginnings of a reversal, this is only the beginning of a
political conflict that will continue to be played out into the foreseeable
future.

The relationship between *segmentation* and *competition-control* is best
illustrated by the movement for decentralization or "community control"
of public services, notably of neighborhood schools, but also in the areas
of police, health, welfare, etc. Inspired in part by the emphasis on community participation in federal poverty and model cities programs, the
community control movement has flourished best in ghetto communities
that come to regard their local institutions as controlled by alien powers.
Black community control, of course, represents no more than the aspiration for political power over local institutions long enjoyed by white
citizens, particularly in the suburbs. Consequently, community control is
both an ideological and a power struggle among differentiated communities contributing to more competitive urban politics. Interestingly, while
some observers feel that decentralization may be an effective strategy for
improving public services in certain areas (Fantini and Gittell 1972; Bell
and Held 1969), a growing number of critics (including psychologist

Kenneth Clark, who early advocated community control of New York City schools—(*New York Times,* June 9, 1972) now believe that the movement is self-defeating, since it minimizes the impact of external resources and produces community organization on a scale incompatible with effective political action vis-a-vis centralized urban and national authorities that control the crucial resources for long-term structural change (Kristol 1968; Wilson 1968; Suttles 1972).

Without prejudging this complex issue, it would appear that the progressive segmentation of urban areas has led to intracommunity cohesiveness and politicization and intercommunity competition. In those areas where patterns of segregation are breaking down (e.g., the "inner suburbs") the reverse should be true.

On the third pairwise comparison of dimensions, we have already suggested that the relationship between *interdependence and competition-control* tends to be directly covariant; greater interdependence leads to greater competition and vice versa. For example, a review of the community power literature indicates that to the extent that communities become interdependently tied to extralocal institutions, their political processes become more competitive (Walton 1968). Nevertheless, local arrangements of power play a crucial and autonomous role in this process. Illustratively, Crain and associates (1969) studied the effects of externally induced pressures for school desegregation in fifteen cities and concluded that the key variable in successful desegregation was the existence of a "civic elite," that is, a coordinated leadership group representing public and private institutions committed to the preservation of a viable central city. Similarly, Greenstone and Peterson (1968) found that the impact of the federal poverty program varied substantially across four cities according to the degree political power was centralized. Generally speaking, the more centralized elite cities (Chicago and Philadelphia) reflected a pattern of *less* citizen participation in decision making and *greater* allocation of poverty funds. Conversely, in the less centralized cities (New York and Los Angeles) the poverty program induced *greater* citizen participation and competition, albeit with *less* expenditure of funds. A similar pattern may be inferred from Kramer's (1969) study of the poverty program in the San Francisco Bay Area in light of separate analyses of political power in San Francisco (Wirt 1970) and Oakland (Hayes 1972).

Moreover, just as similar federal programs have different consequences in different city political systems, so, too, different programs affect local leadership groups in different ways. Most studies of the poverty program indicate that, to a greater or lesser extent, it "shook up" local arrangements of power, at least temporarily, by fostering participation and/or politicization of the poor and disenfranchised. In New York City, Bell and Held (1969) conclude that substantial redistribution of influence was accomplished largely because Mayor Lindsay employed the program as a form of patronage to create a new power base among liberals and minorities. In the Bay Area, however, "The effects on city politics of resident participation were ... minimal. Although *a new center of minority influence was established* in each community, the CAP (Community Action Program) did not appear to disrupt the prevailing structure and balance of power in any significant way" (Kramer 1969: 257; emphasis added). By contrast to these directionally consistent influences of the poverty program, federal programs in urban renewal (Rossi and Dentler 1961; Greer 1965), transportation (Colcord 1967), model cities under "planned variation" (Shopshire 1972), and recently enacted revenue sharing, all appear to fortify prevailing local arrangements of power by providing new resources independent of special political constraints (Lowi 1969).

All of this suggests, first, that the political consequences of interdependence are variable and, second, that if its main effect is to promote greater political competition, newly emergent interest groups have scarcely begun to challenge the pattern of institutionalized inequality. And the present federal administration, however motivated, appears intent upon closing off many of the avenues of influence that momentarily appeared promising from the normative standpoint of participatory democracy (i.e., categorical aid programs as opposed to revenue sharing, active enforcement of school and housing desegregation, and the recently dismantled programs of O.E.O. and H.U.D.)

CONCLUSION

The bulk of this essay has endeavored to construct a manageable framework for organizing and interpreting urban community politics. I have summarized a set of important social trends by three "dimensions" and have sketched some of those changes along them that shape local politics in specified ways. Finally, we discussed the interplay among the dimensions and attempted to underscore some of the *variable* political consequences stemming from different combinations of factors.

The framework may be regarded alternatively as a provisional synthesis and a set of hypotheses. That is, many of the suggested linkages require further evaluation. Illustratively, at a high level of abstraction interdependence and competition are alleged to be directly correlated. Nevertheless, at least two key intervening variables affect this association: local leadership structure (centralized—decentralized) and the nature of the external influence (e.g., status quo maintaining urban renewal or politicizing poverty programs). Consequently, the relevant property space for this association alone becomes manifold and similar exigencies apply to other hypothesized relationships. While this may smack of undue equivocation, it is intended to unpretentiously emphasize the complexity of these phenomena, how much we do and do not know, and where we might successfully probe in the future. And that kind of message appears more useful than the familiar and casual extrapolation of single trends that invariably point to "crises" wherever we turn. If we know nothing else about sociological processes, we know that they are highly interdependent and variable, requiring the kind of multidimensional contingency models of explanation suggested here.

With that in mind, these concluding paragraphs may be productively devoted to some inferential leaps from the framework into the future of urban politics. Most fundamentally it seems that we are not witnessing an "eclipse of community" or even necessarily a decline in community autonomy as a result of trends on the national level. Communities, as defined here, are permanent features of social organization and will certainly persist just as they will change in response to the changing character of external influences that so shape their destinies. Further, as Suttles (1972: 258) notes, community autonomy and interdependence do not conform to a zero-sum relationship: "More direct administrative relationships between local and national levels or organization may give local residents and their representatives a louder, not a smaller voice in determining the services which come to them." As we have seen, these alternatives depend very much upon the particular community of reference (e.g., a ghetto as opposed to an affluent, exclusionary suburb) and the nature of the intrusive relationship (e.g., blockbusting or federally subsidized sewers). Rather than an eclipse or decline of communities, we are more likely to see a great deal of *persistence* along with some *realignment* of locality organization in response to ties of interdependence. For example, communities are apt to become increasingly organized in response to "vertical stimuli" in the form of absentee-owned corporations shaping the local economy, federal housing law disrupting community "integrity," state services such as transportation and education bringing the community into closer social proximity with its surroundings.

Unquestionably these changes and what they portend for local values and life-styles will not evolve according to some principle of entropy or natural harmony. Increasing community conflict is to be expected, and conflict directed in the same vertical channels that inspire the "problem." A ready index of heightened conflict and politicization is the extent to which local disputes become *legal* issues and, moreover, legal issues based on "life-style" values. Certainly the bussing controversy is prototypical, but more revolutionary legal battles lie ahead. The *Serrano* decision in California, which held that state methods for financing public schools based on local property taxes "invidiously discriminate" against the poor living in communities with fewer resources, provides an opening wedge for the redistribution of public resources according to extralocal, statewide criteria (Greenbaum 1971; Myers 1971). Legal advocates of open housing point to an arsenal of methods for attacking segregated residential communities lodged in federal agencies and subsidy programs (Rubinowitz, 1973). We can anticipate a substantial escalation in this kind of conflict over the distribution of privileged services and, of course, this is simply one area illustrating what was earlier described as an "evolutionary" movement toward more competitive political processes, notably in older and larger central cities.

These developments lead to another prediction, namely that the growing incidence of conflict will increasingly take place in the suburbs and other communities that have benefited from the effects of polarization. Finally, we turn to supracommunity forms of organization. Just as civil rights workers in Selma saw their ranks swollen by northern volunteers, so antibussing rallies in Memphis are crowded by the Michigan faithful. Both ghetto and suburban communities are likely to attempt to link community control strategies with supraterritorial alliances as they come to recognize the extralocal origins of their concern and instrumentalities for influence.

If it is difficult in most circumstances to separate one's personal values from their analysis; it becomes impossible when we begin to project into the future. Summarizing these discursive observations from a personal standpoint, at least five species of political change can be anticipated; greater conflict and competition, channeled along vertical lines, resorting to legal methods, occurring in more privileged surroundings, and organized along supraterritorial lines. The speed with which these changes will come about depends very much upon sanctions from the top. While many, perhaps most, of the federal programs of the mid-sixties either reinforced the status quo of privilege (Lowi 1969) or only marginally improved the lot of the disadvantaged, a new era was heralded in the perceived rights and expectations of powerless urban groups. And that seed remains despite recent moves to curtail "great society" programs in favor of a "new federalism" that would erase small gains in participatory democracy by turning federal resources back to the unconstrained, self-interested use of local groups(e.g., through general revenue sharing). The seed will grow, slowly for the moment, as larger trends continue to move in the direction of an exacerbated urban problem. It would be foolhardy to predict any imminent reversal in historic patterns of increasing inequality. What can be predicted with some certainty, however, is the likelihood that conflict in urban politics will increasingly take the form of class and racial struggles aimed at the elimination or the maintenance of those structures of privilege that have occupied our attention here. By contrast to earlier periods of our urban history the political struggle ahead will center increasingly on group rights and quality-of-life issues as opposed to individual rights and quantitative rewards. It will increasingly focus less on "service delivery" in absolute terms than on the *distributional* consequences of prevailing institutional arrangements. And whether these developments arise in the short or the long run, urban sociologists will be on hand to chronicle their effects to the extent that they focus attention on those points of reciprocal influence between the community and the national society.

REFERENCES

Aiken, Michael.
1970 "The Distribution of Community Power: Structural Bases and Social Consequences," in Michael Aiken and Paul E. Mott (eds.), *The Structure of Community Power*. New York: Random House, 487–525.
————, and Robert R. Alford.
1970a "Community Structure and Innovation: The Case of Urban Renewal," *American Sociological Review* 35 (August): 650–665.
1970b "Comparative Urban Research and Community Decision-Making," *The New Atlantis* 1 (Winter): 85–110.
————, and Paul E. Mott (eds.).
1970 *The Structure of Community Power*. New York: Random House.

Banfield, E. C.
1968 *The Unheavenly City: The Nature and Future of Our Urban Crisis*. Boston: Little, Brown.

Bell, Daniel, and Virginia Held.
1969 "The Community Revolution," *The Public Interest* 16 (Summer): 142–177.

Berger, B.
1960 *Working-Class Suburb: A Study of Auto Workers in Suburbia*. Berkeley: University of California.

Berk, Richard A., and Howard E. Aldrich.
1972 "Patterns of Vandalism During Civil Disorders as an Indicator of Selection of Targets," *American Sociological Review* 37 (October): 533–547.

Birch, D. L.
1970 *The Economic Future of City and Suburb*. New York: Committee for Economic Development.

Bloomberg, W.
1966 "Community Organization," in Howard S. Becker (ed.), *Social Problems: A Modern Approach*. New York: Wiley, 359–425.

Bonjean, C. M.
1971 "The Community as Research Site and Object of Inquiry," in Charles M. Bonjean, Terry N. Clark, and Robert L. Lineberry (eds.), *Community Politics: A Behavioral Approach*. New York: Free Press, 5–15.

Campbell, Argus, Philip E. Converse, Warren E. Miller, and Donald E. Stokes.
1960 *The American Voter*. New York: Wiley.

Chicago Sun-Times.
1972a December 17:7.
1972b December 31:23.

Clark, T. N. (ed.).
1968a *Community Structure and Decision-Making: Comparative Analyses*. San Francisco: Chandler.
1968b "Community Structure, Decision-Making, Budget Expenditures, and Urban Renewal in 51 American Communities," *American Sociological Review* 33 (August): 576–593.
1972 "The Structure of Community Influence," in Harlan Hahn (ed.), *People and Politics in Urban Society*. Beverly Hills: Sage, 283–314.

Cohen, H.
1970 "The Constraints," from "Governing the Megacentropolis: a Symposium," *Public Administration Review* 30 (September/October): 488–497.

Colcord, F. C.

1967 "Decision-Making and Transportation Policy: A Comparative Analysis," (Southwestern) *Social Science Quarterly* 48 (December): 383–397.

Crain, R. L.
1969 *The Politics of School Desegregation: Comparative Case Studies of Community Structure and Policy-Making.* New York: Anchor Ed.

Danielson, M. N.
1965 *Federal-Metropolitan Politics and the Commuter Crisis.* New York: Columbia University.

D'Antonio, W. V.
1966 "Community Leadership in an Economic Crisis: Testing Ground for Ideological Cleavage," *American Journal of Sociology* 71 (May): 688–700.

Davis, K.
1965 "The Urbanization of the Human Population," in *Cities.* New York: Knopf, 3–24.

Dobriner, W.
1963 *Class in Suburbia.* Englewood Cliffs, N.J.: Prentice-Hall.

Downes, B. T.
1970 "A Critical Reexamination of the Social and Political Characteristics of Riot Cities," *Social Science Quarterly* 51 (September): 349–360.

Fantini, Mario, and Marilyn Gittell.
1972 *Decentralization: Achieving Reform.* New York: Praeger.

Farley, R.
1970 "The Changing Distribution of Negroes within Metropolitan Areas: The Emergence of Black Suburbs," *American Journal of Sociology* 75 (January): 512–529.

Ficker, Victor B., and Herbert S. Graves.
1971 *Social Science and Urban Crisis: Introductory Readings.* New York: Collier-Macmillan.

Gans, H. J.
1962 *The Urban Villagers: Group and Class in the Life of Italian-Americans.* New York: The Free Press.
1967 *The Levittowners: Ways of Life and Politics in a New Suburban Community.* New York: Random House.
1968 "The White Exodus to Suburbia Steps Up," *The New York Times Magazine* (January 7).

Gilbert, C. W.
1968 "Some Trends in Community Politics: A Secondary Analysis of Power Structure Data from 166 Communities," (Southwestern) *Social Science Quarterly* 48 (December): 373–381.
1972 *Community Power Structure: Propositional Inventory, Tests, and Theory.* Gainesville: University of Florida.

Greenbaum, W. N.
1971 "Serrano vs. Priest: Implications for Educational Equality," *Harvard Educational Review* 41 (November): 501–534.

Greenstein, Fred I., and Raymond E. Wolfinger.
1958–59 "The Suburbs and Shifting Party Loyalties," *Public Opinion Quarterly* (Winter): 473–482.

Greenstone, J. David, and Paul E. Peterson.
1968 "Reformers, Machines, and the War on Poverty," in James Q. Wilson (ed.), *City Politics and Public Policy.* New York: Wiley.

Greer, S. A.
1956 "Urbanism Reconsidered: A Comparative Study of Local Areas in a

Metropolis," *American Sociological Review* 21 (January): 19–25.
1962 *The Emerging City: Myth and Reality.* New York: The Free Press.
1965 *Urban Renewal and American Cities: The Dilemma of Democratic Intervention.* Indianapolis: Bobbs-Merrill.
1972 *The Urban View: Life and Politics in Metropolitan America.* New York: Oxford.

Grimes, Michael D., Charles M. Bonjean, and Robert L. Lineberry.
1971 "Structural Correlates of Leadership Arrangements in Seventeen Communities." Paper presented at the annual meetings of the Southwestern Social Science Association (March).

Hadden, Jeffrey K., Louis H. Massotti, and Calvin J. Larson (eds.).
1971 *Metropolis in Crisis: Social and Political Perspectives* (2nd ed.). Itasca, Ill.: Peacock.

Hahn, H.
1968 "Northern Referenda on Fair Housing: The Response of White Voters," *Western Political Quarterly* 21 (September): 483–495.

Hawkins, B. W.
1967 "Life Style, Demographic Distance, and Voter Support of City-County Consolidation," (Southwestern) *Social Science Quarterly* 48 (December): 325–337.

Hawley, Willis D., and Frederick M. Wirt (eds.).
1968 *The Search for Community Power.* Englewood Cliffs, N.J.: Prentice-Hall.

Hayes, E. C.
1972 *Power Structure and Urban Policy: Who Rules in Oakland?* New York: McGraw-Hill.

Hillery, G. A.
1955 "Definitions of Community: Areas of Agreement," *Rural Sociology* 20 (June): 111–123.

Janowitz, M.
1952 *The Community Press in an Urban Setting: The Social Elements of Urbanism.* Chicago: University of Chicago Press.

Jiobu, R. M.
1971 "City Characteristics, Differential Stratification and the Occurrence of Interracial Violence," *Social Science Quarterly* 52 (December): 508–520.

Kasarda, J. D.
1972 "The Impact of Suburban Population Growth on Central City Service Functions," *American Journal of Sociology* 77 (May): 1111–1124.

Kesselman, M.
1972 "Research Perspectives in Comparative Local Politics: Pitfalls and Prospects," *Comparative Urban Research* 1 (Summer): 10–30.

Kilpatrick, Samuel A., and David R. Morgan.
1971 "Policy Support and Orientations Toward Metropolitan Political Integration Among Urban Officials," *Social Science Quarterly* 52 (December): 656–671.

Kramer, R. M.
1969 *Participation of the Poor: Comparative Case Studies in the War on Poverty.* Englewood Cliffs, N.J.: Prentice-Hall.

Kristol, I.
1968 "Decentralization for What?" *The Public Interest* 11 (Spring): 17–25.

Liebow, E.
1967 *Tally's Corner: A Study of Negro Street Corner Men.* Boston: Little, Brown.

Lineberry, Robert L., and Edmund P. Fowler.
1967 "Reformism and Public Policies in American Cities," *American Political Science Review* 61 (September): 701–716.

Lowi, T. J.
1969 *The End of Liberalism.* New York: Norton.
1970 "Apartheid U.S.A.," *Trans-action* 7 (February): 32–39.

Milgram, S.
1970 "The Experience of Living in Cities," *Science* 167 (March 13): 1461–1468.

Millett, John, and David Pittman.
1958 "The New Suburban Voter: A Case Study in Electoral Behavior," (Southwestern) *Social Science Quarterly* (June): 33–42.

Mills, C. W.
1943 "The Professional Ideology of Social Pathologists," *American Journal of Sociology* 49 (September).

Mitchell, Joyce M., and William C. Mitchell.
1968 "The Changing Politics of American Life," in Eleanor Bernert Sheldon and Wilbert E. Moore (eds.), *Indicators of Social Change: Concepts and Measurements.* New York: Russell Sage, 247–294.

Molotch, H.
1972 *Managed Integration: Dilemmas of Doing Good in the City.* Berkeley: University of California.

Mott, P. E.
1970 "Configurations of Power," in Michael Aiken and Paul E. Mott (eds.), *The Structure of Community Power.* New York: Random House, 85–100.

Myers, P.
1971 "Second Thoughts on the Serrano Case," *City* (Winter): 38–41.

Neenan, W. B.
1972 *Political Economy of Urban Areas.* Chicago: Markham.

New York Times.
1972a June 9:1.
1972b December 17:32.
1972c December 31:1.

Presthus, R.
1964 *Men at the Top: A Study in Community Power.* New York: Oxford University Press.

Rossi, Peter H., and Robert Dentler.
1961 *The Politics of Urban Renewal.* New York: The Free Press.

Rubinowitz, L. S.
1973 "A Question of Choice: Access of the Poor and the Black to Suburban Housing," *Urban Affairs Volume VII.* Beverley Hills: Sage.
     Housing," *Urban Affairs Volume VII.* Beverley Hills, Cal.: Sage.

Schnore, L. F.
1963 "The Social and Economic Characteristics of American Suburbs," *The Sociological Quarterly* 4 (Spring): 122–134.
1967 "Community." Neil J. Smelsen (ed.), in *Sociology: An Introduction.* New York: Wiley, 81–150.
1972 *Class and Race in Cities and Suburbs.* Chicago: Markham.

Sheppard, H. L.
1969 "Some Broader Reality Frameworks for Anti-Poverty Legislation," *Social Science Quarterly* 50 (December): 487–493.

Shevky, Eshref, and Wendell Bell.
1955 *Social Area Analysis*. Stanford, Calif.: Stanford University.
Shopshire, J. M.
1972 "Some Perspectives on Federal Decentralization and Revenue Sharing with Several Implications for Community Politics." Northwest University mimeo.
Simmel, G.
1950 "The Metropolis and Mental Life." From Kurt Wolff (ed.) *The Sociology of Georg Simmel*. New York: The Free Press.
Sjoberg, G.
1964 "Community," in Julius Gould and William L. Kolb (eds.), *A Dictionary of the Social Sciences*. New York: The Free Press, 114–115.
Sloan, Lee, and Robert M. French.
1971 "Black Rule in the Urban South?" *Trans-action* 9 (November–December): 29–34.
Sofen, E.
1966 *The Miami Metropolitan Experiment: A Metropolitan Action Study* (2nd ed.). Garden City, N.Y.: Anchor.
Spilerman, S.
1970 "The Causes of Racial Disturbances: A Comparison of Alternative Explanations," *America Sociological Review* 35 (August): 627–649.
Stein, M. R.
1960 *The Eclipse of Community: An Interpretation of American Studies*. Princeton, N.J.: Princeton University.
Stinchcombe, J. L.
1968 *Reform and Reaction: City Politics in Toledo*. Belmont, Cal.: Wadsworth.
Suttles, G. D.
1968 *The Social Order of the Slum: Ethnicity and Territory in the Inner City*. Chicago: University of Chicago.
1972 *The Social Construction of Communities*. Chicago: University of Chicago.
Taeuber, C.
1968 "Population: Trends and Characteristics," in Eleanor Bernert Sheldon and Wilbert E. Moore (eds.), *Indicators of Social Change: Concepts and Measurements*. New York: Russell Sage, 27–74.
Thompson, W. R.
Cities," in Philip M. Hauser and Leo F. Schnore (eds.), *The Study of*
1965 "Urban Economic Growth and Development in a National System of *Urbanization*. New York: Wiley, 431–490.
Turk, H.
1970 "Interorganizational Networks in Urban Society: Initial Perspectives and Comparative Research," *American Sociological Review* 35 (February): 1–19.
U.S. Bureau of the Census.
1970 *Statistical Abstracts of the United States 1970*. Washington, D.C.: U.S. Government Printing Office.
U.S. National Advisory Commission on Civil Disorders.
1968 Report of the National Advisory Commission on Civil Disorders. Washington, D.C.: U.S. Government Printing Office.
Vanecko, J. J.
1969 "Community Mobilization and Institutional Change: The Influence of the Community Action Program in Large Cities," *Social Science Quarterly*

50 (December): 609–630.

Vidich, Arthur J., and Joseph Bensman.
1958 *Small Town in Mass Society*. Princeton, N.J.: Princeton University.

Walter, Benjamin, and Frederick M. Wirt.
1971 "The Political Consequences of Suburban Variety," *Social Science Quarterly* 52 (December): 746–767.

Walton, J.
1966 "Substance and Artifact: The Current Status of Research on Community Power Structure," *American Journal of Sociology* 71 (January): 430–438.
1968 "The Vertical Axis of Community Organization and the Structure of Power," (Southwestern) *Social Science Quarterly* 48 (December): 353–368.
1970 "A Systematic Survey of Community Power Research," in Michael Aiken and Paul E. Mott (eds.), *The Structure of Community Power*. New York: Random House, 443–464.

Warren, R. L.
1956 "Toward a Typology of Extra-Community Controls Limiting Local Community Autonomy," *Social Forces* 34 (May): 338–41.
1963 *The Community in America*. Chicago: Rand McNally.

Williams, Oliver P.
1967 "Life Style Values and Political Decentralization in Metropolitan Areas," (Southwestern) *Social Science Quarterly* 48 (December): 299–310.
———, Harold Herman, Charles S. Liebman, and Thomas R. Dye.
1965 *Suburban Differences and Metropolitan Policies: A Philadelphia Story*. Philadelphia: University of Pennsylvania.

Williams, W.
1967 "The Crisis Ghetto," *Trans-action* 9 (September): 33–42.

Wilson, James Q.
1968 "The Urban Unease: Community vs. City," *The Public Interest* 12 (Summer): 25–39.
———, and Edward C. Banfield.
1964 "Public-Regardingness as a Value Premise in Voting Behavior," *American Political Science Review* 58 (December): 876–887.

Wirt, F. M.
1965 "The Political Sociology of American Suburbia: A Reinterpretation," *The Journal of Politics* 27 (August): 647–666.
1970 "Alioto and the Politics of Hyperpluralism," *Trans-action* 7 (April): 46–55.

Wirth, L.
1938 "Urbanism as a Way of Life," in Albert J. Reiss, Jr. (ed.), *On Cities and Social Life*. Chicago: University of Chicago.

Wood, R. C.
1958 *Suburbia: Its People and Their Politics*. Boston: Houghton and Mifflin.
1964 *1400 Governments*. Garden City, N.Y.: Anchor.

Zimmer, Basil G., and Amos H. Hawley.
1967 "Opinions on School District Reorganization in Metropolitan Areas: A Comparative Analysis of the Views of Citizens and Officials in Central City and Suburban Areas," (Southwestern) *Social Science Quarterly* (December): 311–324.

Zorbaugh, H.
1929 *The Gold Coast and the Slum*. Chicago: University of Chicago.

Community
and
Urbanization

Do Communities Act?*

CHARLES TILLY

University of Michigan

ECLIPSE OF COMMUNITY?

We Westerners are inclined to consider the community a normal base for solidarity, a natural unit of collective action. Kinship groups, associations, firms, churches and a number of other groups in which we pass our lives all seem less natural, or less likely, or both. It isn't hard to find plausible justification. The European social life within which today's fundamental Western institutions grew up accented the community. A kinship system which singles out the nuclear family as its residential unit and builds relationships within a kindred (a kin group whose own boundaries shift from person to person), for example, seems an unreliable basis for solidarity or collective action. A matrilineage, one imagines, would do better. More important, the relatively homogeneous and predominantly peasant population of Europe did, indeed, organize a lot of its social life around village institutions.

Yet today's communities appear to lack solidarity. They act together rarely, if at all. Sociologists have often dealt with this contrast between a presumably solidary past and a presumably unsolidary present by postulating a decay in the strength of communities. The decay is supposed to result from the rising scale, complexity and mobility of social life. The dominance of the city caps all these trends. The results of scale, complexity and mobility count as *decay* because solidarity is, of course, the natural, healthy state of mankind. So, at least, goes the doctrine.

*National Science Foundation grant GS-2674 has supported the research behind this paper. Ronald Aminzade, Bruce Fireman, and Marcia Effrat gave cogent criticism to an earlier draft, and Louise Tilly made some helpful proposals for its revision. The section on Sicily contains some fragments of my paper, "Town and Country in Revolution," presented to the Research Conference on Communist Revolutions, St. Croix, V.I., January 1973, which was sponsored by the Planning Group on Comparative Communist Studies, American Council of Learned Societies.

When Maurice Stein wrote a general essay on the evolution of American communities during the twentieth century, he called it *The Eclipse of Community*. Few people, so far as as I know, found the title strange. Yet the actual evidence and argument in the book don't show us a process of decline. The book portrays American communities as experiencing urbanization, industrialization, and bureaucratization and consequently being drawn more and more decisively into national networks of power and communication. The closest it comes to displaying an *eclipse* is in suggesting that communities are becoming less autonomous than they used to be. That is a far cry from decay, decline, and disintegration. An organization can easily become more active and influential in its own sphere as it loses autonomy. Industrial firms, for example, often go through that very cycle when they merge into conglomerates and cartels. A philosophy which values organizational autonomy for its own sake will treat that change as a loss. But the language of withering, of decay, is misleading when applied to a shift in the external relations of a group, if the group continues to function on its own ground.

Ferdinand Tönnies gave an early and influential form to the idea of decay. In his contrast of *Gemeinschaft* and *Gesellschaft*:

> Both village and town retain many characteristics of the family; the village retains more, the town less. Only when the town develops into the city are these characteristics almost entirely lost. Individuals or families are separate identities, and their common locale is only an accidental or deliberately chosen place in which to live. But as the town lives on within the city, elements of life in the Gemeinschaft, as the only real form of life, persist within the Gesellschaft, although lingering and decaying. (Tönnies 1963: 227)

Gemeinschaft, he tells us, is solidary, total, natural. *Gesellschaft* is solitary, partial, contrived.

Robert Ezra Park proposed a similar distinction: on the one hand, the simple, natural interdependence of homogeneous rural communities and of some social worlds within the city; on the other hand, the created, complex, specialized interdependence of true urbanites. He was more precise than Tönnies about the mechanisms involved:

> In a great city, where the population is unstable, where parents and children are employed out of the house and often in distant parts of the city, where thousands of people live side by side for years without so much as a bowing acquaintance, these intimate relationships of the primary group are weakened and the moral order which rested upon them is gradually dissolved. (Park 1952: 33)

Park did not, to be sure, share Tönnies' distaste for *Gesellschaft*. He found adventure in the flux and diversity of the city. Yet his fundamental theory fell into the same line as that of Tönnies.

If that seemed dubious, we would only have to look at the mirror image of the theory produced by Park's son-in-law, Robert Redfield. The anthropologist's models of folk and urban communities are more manageable than Tönnies' models, but they have a similar tone. Redfield summed them up in a book dedicated to Park, *The Folk Culture of Yucatan*. He conceived of a continuum from the isolated, homogeneous *folk* community to the mobile, heterogeneous *urban* community; movement along that continuum produced disorganization, secularization and individualization. The ideal folk community was therefore small, personal, sacred, homogeneous, isolated, organized. The ideal urban community was large, impersonal, secular, heterogeneous, widely connected, disorganized. The contact with cities and with the rest of the world which transforms a community from one to the other, in Redfield's analysis, is essentially a process of disruption, disintegration and decay.

In our own day, the retrospective quest for community continues. Critics of the last decade have delighted in lambasting Park, Redfield, and Louis Wirth. The usual weapon is the demonstration that people in big, dense settlements lead active social lives, have a lot to do with their kinsmen or neighbors, and so on. (For reviews, see Wellman and Whitaker 1971; C. Tilly 1973b: ch. 2.) Left at that point, the demonstration resembles the attack on Marx which consists of pointing out that highly industrial countries, contrary to Marx's expectation, had few revolutions in the twentieth century. In fact, either Marx or Park could have the basic process right and yet make erroneous forecasts. The demonstration leaves the main question moot: did the growth of large cities reduce the richness and intensity of everyday social relations? Does it now?

Nevertheless, one intriguing notion has grown out of the last decade's work on the question. It is that urbanites substitute nonspatial communities for spatial communities: people lived pre-metropolitan life, the argument says, in small-scale territorial groupings; metropolitan residents build viable sets of social relations which are dispersed in space.

Melvin Webber's "non-place urban realm," despite its ugly label, provides us with a fine example of that line of argument. As Webber says:

> The idea of community . . . has been tied to the idea of place. Although other conditions are associated with the community—including "sense of belonging," a body of shared values, a system of social organization, and interdependency—spatial proximity continues to be considered a *necessary* condition.
>
> But it is now becoming apparent that it is the accessibility rather than the propinquity aspect of "place' that is the necessary condition. As accessibility becomes further freed from propinquity, cohabitation of a territorial place—whether it be a neighborhood, a suburb, a metropolis, a region, or a nation—is becoming less important to the maintenance of social communities. (Webber 1964: 108–109)

If Webber is right, a simple, strong critique of the classic formulation follows. Those who saw decay, eclipse, and disintegration of community life with the growth of cities were probably concentrating too hard on *territorial* communities, and failing to notice the nonterritorial forms which replaced them.

A neat escape, if it works. The trouble is that even in big cities people continue to act collectively at times on the basis of common territory: the people of a neighborhood resist urban renewal, white homeowners band together to resist black newcomers, disputes over the operation of schools bring geographical groupings clearly into view. Perhaps we can dispose of these cases as exceptions, or as residues of the past. Still, their very existence identifies the need for a better understanding of the conditions under which collective action on a territorial basis occurs. The rest of this paper explores those conditions.

The Questions, and Some Tentative Answers

Do communities act? We'd better be sure which of the many uses of "communities" and "act" we have in mind. Suppose we treat as a community any durable local population most of whose members belong to households based in the locality. We leave the extent and character of bonds among them an open question. That means taking the other horn of the dilemma from the one chosen by Webber; he chooses to make solidarity define communities and to leave the extent of territoriality problematic; we choose to make territoriality define communities and to leave the extent of solidarity problematic.

Suppose we consider collective action to be any application of pooled resources on behalf of the population as a whole. It is then no trick to distinguish degrees of collective action. They depend on the extent and immediacy of (1) the pooling of resources, and (2) the involvement of members of the community in the application of the pooled resources. A city administrator's expenditure of tax revenues on a new water cooler in the name of citizenry would fall near the zero end of the scale; the massing of every man, woman, and child in front of the city hall (the "resources" now being the time and energy of the citizens) would score near 100.

If these are to be our definitions, then our starting question isn't a very useful one. Of course communities act. At least some communities act some of the time. The worthwhile questions lie further along the way:

1. Among all kinds of social groups, what determines the degree of collective action in any particular period and place?

2. Given a certain degree of collective action, what affects the likelihood

that *communities*, rather than other kinds of social groups, will be the actors?

3. Did the urbanization of the world transform these relationships? Is it transforming them now?

These are among sociology's grandest and oldest questions . . . and no easier to answer for having often been asked.

My reflections on the grand old questions mix conceptualization, common sense, and empirical generalizations drawn from observation of urbanization, migration, and collective action over the last few hundred years in Europe and North America. To orient the discussion, let me propose three general answers:

1. The extent of a group's collective action in any particular period and place is mainly a function of (a) the current extent of its mobilization; (b) its current power with respect to other groups; (c) the lightness of the repression ordinarily applied to its actions; and (d) the current uncertainty that the claims it is making on other groups will be honored.

2. In general these conditions are more likely to apply to *communities* when (a) communities are homogeneous with respect to the main divisions of power at a regional or national level; (b) the cost of communication rises rapidly as a function of distance; and (c) control over land (as compared with the other factors of production) is valuable but unstable.

3. In general, urbanization raises and then lowers the power-homogeneity of communities, the value of control over land, and the instability of control over land; it also lowers the distance-cost of communications more or less continuously. Its short-run effect on community collective action will therefore vary with the relative pace of these diverse changes; but in the long run urbanization shifts the balance away from the communities as collective actors.

As stated, these answers are obscure and partly tautological. The plausibility and utility of the arguments are obviously going to depend a good deal on the meanings we assign to words such as mobilization, power, repression, and cost. There we need crisp concepts. After a brief interlude for conceptualization, the remainder of this essay will go into explicating, illustrating, elaborating, modifying and—to some extent—defending the three broad answers.

A Garland of Concepts

A group can't exert collective control over resources without both social relations and some minimum of common identity. Not all organized groups exert collective control over resources, however. The process of acquiring collective control over resources is *mobilization*; the process of losing collective control over resources, demobilization. If a group applies pooled resources to common ends, it is carrying on *collective action*. By definition, then, an unmobilized group does not act collectively. Do communities act, then? Well, sometimes they do, since communities sometimes acquire collective control over resources, and they or their agents sometimes apply those resources to common ends; in those cases, they mobilize, and they carry on collective action.

Let's consider the place of solidarity in all this. In the study of collective action, two alternative ideas of group solidarity are appealing. First, we might consider solidarity to be the average strength of existing ties among members of the group and might take "strength" to mean the extent of effective claims any pair of individuals have on one another. (Where the claims are unequal, we could reasonably take the lesser of the two sets as the measure for the pair of individuals—thus saying that where everyone owes his life, if requested, to the king, but the king owes nothing to any individual, king-subject solidarity is low.) Then it is clear that extensive collective action can occur when solidarity is low. Coercion will do the job. So will the creation of a specialized organization which stores and disposes of pooled resources. Either or both of these tends to work well if the resources in question are liquid and concentrated: money, movable property, services of specialists. Solidarity, on the other hand, is likely to be important, or even essential, where the resources in question are fixed and dispersed. If many individuals in a group have to take risks, sacrifice friendship or yield land, solidarity will have to be high. Overall, then, we shouldn't expect to find a very close connection between the extent of a group's solidarity and the extent of its collective action.

The alternative conception of solidarity is as the extent to which individuals are willing to make commitments to other members of the group on the basis of common membership alone. If I, a Greek, meet a new Greek, and because he's Greek I prepare to do him favors, we have some evidence that solidarity among Greeks is high. If this sort of solidarity is high, the group in question probably has a great potential capacity for collective action, all other things being equal. However, this sort of solidarity may be high in a group whose members are widely dispersed and have little contact with each other, so there is no reason to expect a close connection between collective action and solidarity by this definition, either.

How should we conceptualize *power*? Power is a function describing the return a group receives when applying varying amounts of resources externally for collective ends. Most groups will receive a greater return if they apply more resources, but they differ greatly in the return they receive per additional unit of resources applied. We might fabricate three power functions, as in Figure 1. Group A receives a low, constant return on re-

Figure 1

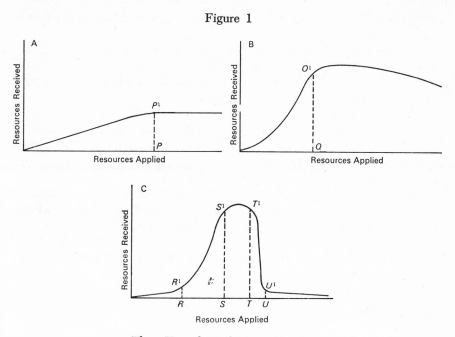

Three Hypothetical Power Functions

sources applied up to a point at which it no longer makes any difference how large the input is: the output is always the same; the marginal return is therefore declining. (So long as it was stuck with that schedule, such a group would obviously do better never to exceed the expenditure P in any particular burst of collective action.) Group B experiences an accelerating rate of return up to point Q, but then finds the rate declining to become slightly negative. Group C gets very little return for small applications of resources up to point R, a rapidly accelerating return from R to S, and an increasingly negative return from T to U. A is, I expect, a common circumstance where the groups in question are well-established and the means of exchange among them highly formalized. B looks more like a characteristic political interchange in which a little gets you nothing but success breeds success—up to a point. And C could describe a tighter political situation in which a group has to make a good deal of noise to be heard at all and is likely to be crushed if it makes a hullabaloo.

To be sure, to turn these speculations into operations we would have to (1) measure inputs and returns with a precision and comprehensiveness no political analyst has achieved for any group so far, and (2.) devise a way of equating different kinds of resources: in this particular system, do 1,000 votes equal 5,000 demonstrations? What is more, power is easier to describe for a pair of units whose interaction we can observe over a determinate period of time than for a larger set of groups. But we can ascribe an overall power position to a group by averaging and weighing its interactions with all other groups.

Repression, in this line of analysis, is closely related to power. Repression occurs when the effect of another group's action is to raise the cost of collective action to the group whose behavior we are analyzing. (Governmental repression is an important special case; it consists of actions by agents of the government which raise the cost of collective action to (1) some specific group, or (2) all groups.) The cost of collective action to a group, finally, is the extent to which its members forego other available and desired uses of the resources in question as a consequence of the employment of the resources in collective action.

These concepts, by extension, lend themselves easily to the analysis of power struggles, collective violence, and revolution. That is, indeed, where they came from (see Lees and Tilly 1973, Rule and Tilly 1972, Shorter and Tilly 1973, Snyder and Tilly 1972, C. Tilly 1972a, 1972b, 1973a). We have no need to make that set of connections here. We have defined a range of conditions a population can meet:

GROUP———▶MOBILIZING/DEMOBILIZING———▶
COLLECTIVE ACTION———▶POWER.

We have not taken up the classic sociological question: where do organized groups come from? We assume their existence. Implicitly, we have also defined an elementary model of collective action:

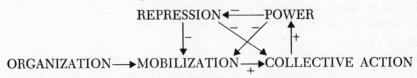

The model represents the mobilization of a group as a function of its organizational structure and of the type and extent of repression to which it is subject. In its present form, of course, the model is not very helpful on that score, since it doesn't specify which sorts of groups mobilize easily, and so on; later sections of this essay will take up part of that question. The model further indicates that the main effect of repression on collective action occurs via the effect on mobilization. Other groups—and especially governments—act to remove resources from the collective control of the group in question and to raise the cost of putting new resources under collective control.

The model also indicates that continuous collective action tends to increase the power (i.e., the marginal return from the collective application of resources) of the group, and that an increase in power tends to demobilize the group, since it can achieve its desired return with lesser expenditures of resources. That is a debatable conclusion, since groups often form new demands in the process of satisfying old ones. Nevertheless, the overall tendency is probably for the acquisition of power to demobilize a group: the professional managers begin to take over, individuals begin to use the acquired connections for their own ends, and so on.

Likewise, the model neglects several obvious, important complications, such as the probability that the repression-mobilization relationship is curvilinear: a small amount of repression stimulates mobilization, a large amount crushes it. For the most part, this paper ignores those important complications. The model, finally, fails to specify the relationship between organization and mobilization. That is my paper's principal topic.

The Bases of Collective Action

Collective action, then, consists of a group's application of pooled resources to common ends. Most collective action consists of making claims on other groups. There are exceptions: a religious brotherhood which spends its time together in common worship is engaging in collective action; so is a family which strikes off into the wilderness to start a new farm. Few groups, however, can meet their day-to-day requirements for resources without somehow calling on other groups.

Markets routinize these transfers. A market is a specialized device which requires special conditions. It can hardly operate without great concentration of property rights in any particular unit of land, labor, capital, technique, or commodity. In seventeenth- and eighteenth-century Europe (and more so in the rest of the world) the notion that the full range of land, human labor, and their products should be for sale at the discretion of a single owner was a revolutionary idea. A great many people who exercised common rights in land and labor resisted the landlords, merchants, and officials who acted on such notions. The standard European land occupation, in which villagers tore down fences of recently-enclosed fields and reasserted their former rights to forage, graze, glean, or hunt, expressed this resistance eloquently.

Even where markets prevail, such diffuse, valuable and/or risky resources as personal loyalty, willingness to kill or be killed, advice on major decisions, and support in political contests are frequently the subject of claims, but most of those claims are made outside the market. The market is important, yet it is not necessarily the fundamental mediator of claims or the model for all others.

Why do groups ever make claims on other groups? In general, because some or all of their members believe the group (1) needs resources currently controlled by another group in order to pursue an established collective objective, and (2) has a right to those resources. The basis for that right may range from a general principle (such as freedom to assemble without harassment) to a specific, established usage (such as the villagers' long-established opportunity to glean in a landlord's fields once the harvest is in). Newly mobilizing groups tend to base a high proportion of their claims on general principles; obviously, they rarely have the opportunity to invoke established usage. These principled claims, moreover, tend to be *offensive*—marking out rights, guarantees, privileges which other groups have never conceded to them before.

Long-mobilized groups, on the other hand, tend to make the bulk of their claims in terms of time-honored usage. Many such claims are quite routine—the government calls for this year's conscripts, the landlord calls for this month's rent. Long-mobilized groups, however, are also likely to produce *defensive* claims in response to the unacceptable claims of another group. In the first half of the nineteenth century, the well-organized tailors of many European cities found themselves threatened by the spread of cheap machine-produced goods; they fought off the declining wages and lengthening hours by means of strikes for maintenance of traditional wages and conditions of work.

When disputes arise, the contrast between new and old produces an interesting lopsidedness: new mobilizers demand the surrender of resources on general principle, as old groups resist on much more specific grounds. Thus in old-regime Europe bourgeois reformers argued that tax exemptions for nobles should be removed as a matter of justice and rationality, as the nobles asserted that tax exemption was their right through services long since rendered.

Current uncertainty that the claims a group is making on other groups will be honored is, I think, a powerful incentive to collective action. (That emphatically includes claims on governments.) Uncertainty can arise in a number of different ways. The stock of resources available to satisfy outstanding claims may diminish. Competing claims from other groups—including the current holders of the resources—may arise. The group's own ability to mount the requisite *form* of collective action (e.g., in an electoral system, to bring out enough votes) may atrophy, and new claims based on general principles may emerge from the group. All of these reduce certainty of payoff; in the short run, at least, all of them tend to spur mobilization and collective action.

To repeat, then, the extent of a group's collective action in any particular period and place is mainly a function of (1) the current extent of its mobilization; (2) its current power with respect to other groups; (3) the lightness of the repression ordinarily applied to its actions; and (4) the current uncertainty that the claims it is making on other groups will be honored.

Communities as Collective Actors

The general conditions ought to apply to communities just as to other groups. The level of a community's collective action is a positive function of its current mobilization and of the current uncertainty that the claims it is making on other groups will be honored. It is a negative function of the extent of repression ordinarily applied to its actions and (via the effect on mobilization) of its current power with respect to other groups. On these grounds we would not expect much collective action from a poor community with patronage in high places: the situation of an "urban village" as described by Herbert Gans. There, mobilization is likely to be low because there are few slack resources uncommitted to daily necessities, uncertainty is likely to be reduced by patronage, while power and repression remain moderate. We would, on the other hand, expect a good deal of collective action from a rich, homogeneous community whose claims to maintenance of its segregation pattern were being threatened by outsiders.

These points are obvious. The question is: under what conditions are communities more likely to be the actors than other sorts of groups? When:

1. Communities are homogeneous with respect to the main divisions of power at a regional or national level;

2. The cost of communication rises rapidly as a function of distance; and

3. Control over land (as compared with the other factors of production) is valuable but uncertain.

No doubt there are other conditions. These are the three which emerge most clearly from the Western experience on which I am building this discussion. Let me take up each in turn before trying to put them together.

Why should homogeneity with respect to power matter? There are two complementary reasons. First, a community which is homogeneous in regard to the main divisions of power at a regional or national level will generally mobilize at lower cost than one which is heterogeneous; the same procedure for drawing resources into the common pool can be used throughout the population. The analogy with tax collection, where the heterogeneity of the subject population and of its activities greatly increases the difficulties of enforcement, is strong and illuminating. Second, outside actions are more likely to challenge or invite claims which have simultaneous support throughout the community if the community is homogeneous: a threat to one is likely to be a threat to all, an opportunity for one is likely to be an opportunity for all. Segregation by power (which may, of course, be a by-product of segregation by occupation, race, religion or something else) will promote collective action, all other things being equal. The nineteenth-century segregation of European industrial cities into bourgeois and working-class quarters, after an earlier promiscuity of residence, generally facilitated collective action on both sides.

When the cost of communication rises rapidly as a function of distance —to take the second general condition for collective action by communities—a concentrated population has a great advantage. Lowering the cost of communication over distance reduces the advantages of proximity.

That much is a commonplace of urban analysis. It is the premise of Webber's arguments on the emergence of the "non-place urban realm" in times of communications efficiency. In their analysis of industrial location in the New York area, Hoover and Vernon made a similar observation: to oversimplify, such industries as garment manufacturing and advertising tend to locate at the center and resist urbanization, because so much of the success or failure of firms in those trades depends on their fast response to subtle shifts in opportunities and costs. To be away from Manhattan is to miss the coffee breaks, chance contacts and quick visits through which so much of the essential information passes.

If Richard Meier's analysis of the "civic bond" is correct, the advantage of the concentrated population should become even greater as the activity carried on is big and complex. Cities exist, according to Meier, largely because (1) such complicated activities as national government, the operation of specialized markets, and large-scale manufacturing couldn't happen at all unless numerous information gatherers, processors, and users were in close, cheap, and continuous contact with each other; and (2) the maintenance of links among such activities requires some minimum of interpersonal solidarity, which will not develop without some minimum of face-to-face contact.

In all these cases, the steeper the rise in the cost of communication as a function of distance, the more likely that people will organize their action —if they act at all—around a common territory. The reasoning applies easily to collective action. If the prevailing forms of social organization constrain the forms of mobilization and the forms and costs of mobilization shape the extent and character of collective action, then the same conditions which make communities the major contexts of social life will make them the prime vehicles for collective action.

In the modern West, the formation of national states reinforced the likelihood that communities would be major bases of collective action (see C. Tilly 1963c). Whatever else they do, states extract resources from the populations they control: money, men, food and supplies for their armies, land for their highroads, emoluments for their officials.

Even in the relatively prosperous conditions of sixteenth-century Europe, the rapid increase in the extractive efforts of growing states put a large strain on the capacities of the populations under their control. States were competing for resources which were not only scarce but also committed to other purposes, individual and collective. What is more, the costs of communication rose rapidly with distance.

For essentially the same reasons that ordinary citizens could hardly organize on any other basis than a territorial one, royal officials found it almost impossible to build their fiscal administrations except by making local units part of the structure. Recent innovations such as the income tax, although proposed from time to time before the nineteenth century, could not operate until (1) most people received most of their income in the form of regular cash wages, and (2) the government could build a system of registration, verification, and collection capable of operating with rough uniformity at a national scale. Until that time, governmental revenues took three main forms: (1) rents and fees from users of particular properties and services; (2) levies on flows and transfers of goods and persons— tolls, customs, excise taxes—collected at some fixed location; (3) locally administered assessments on land, movable property, and other assets controlled by individuals or groups. All three relied heavily on local structure, including villages themselves.

In the case of land taxes and similar imposts, the standard practice was to calculate the revenue needed from the country as a whole, inflate that figure by the estimated loss to collection costs (both legitimate and illegitimate), then break it into quotas for geographic subdivisions of the country based on their reputed ability to pay, as modified by their known ability to resist or escape. The subdivisions subdivided, until at last a quota arrived at the individual community; its authorities then had the obligation to apportion the burden among the local households, again weighing reputed ability to pay against known ability to resist or escape. By the end of such a process, obviously there were likely to be flagrant inequalities in the tax burden of similar communities in different regions, or even of adjacent farmsteads which fell into different jurisdictions. Taxation was the most prominent single issue in large-scale rebellions during the European state making of the sixteenth to nineteenth centuries. Inequity was one of the major reasons for its prominence. Similar localized, inequitable systems grew up in the conscription of men for military service; they aroused similar resentment.

The irony of these extractive arrangements is that they reinforced the administrative apparatus of local communities and thereby increased the capacity of communities for resistance. Placide Rambaud analyzes the experience of an Alpine village, la Maurienne, over the century or two during which the Piedmontese state was extending its control over the mountains:

> From a simple association of co-owners, the commune became a "political body organized to serve other interests than the immediate interests of those who comprised it." From a personal and spontaneous grouping, it became a territory with precise boundaries, and instrument of a government and a cell with definite functions, but functions defined from outside the community. (Rambaud 1962: 138)

The long-run result of this process was dependence and subordination. But in the short run, the community acquired the legal capacity to sue a neighboring community for infringement on its rights, and even to act against its own members for failure to meet their public obligations. Autonomy declined, but solidarity and the capacity for collective action both rose, in the short run. This meant the bulk of the community sometimes rose against their own officials, when the officials were simply doing their duty—as defined from outside—instead of bending to local needs. That was frequently, for example, the motif of food riots: the authorities should have assured and regulated the supply of food, so the citizens stepped in to coerce or supplant the delinquent officials (see L. Tilly 1971).

More to the point, when the local authorities aligned themselves with the villagers against outside claims, the same means which they employed routinely to extract local resources for external purposes served to hold those resources within the community, defend them from outsiders, and commit them to local ends. That is the motif of serious resistance to taxation and conscription: those outsiders have no *right* to demand this crop, that money, these men; we're not going to let them go. In effect, the administrative reinforcement of the community raised the cost of communication from one community to the next and increased the likelihood that the community itself would become the unit of collective action.

What of the value and uncertainty of control over land? The chief things members of all sorts of communities have in common is investment in the same territory—in land. The reasoning is simple: to the extent that land is worthless, people who share the same territory are less likely to have interests or claims in common. By the same token, others are less likely to make claims on them. To the extent that controls over the land are secure, spurs or opportunities for collective action with respect to those fundamental interests are infrequent. Uncertainty is low. Finally, if control over the land is stable, membership in the community tends to change slowly. A stable population has lower mobilization costs than an unstable one, despite the implications of numerous "collective behavior" theories that a shifting, mobile, and uprooted population is more inclined to mass action.

In summary, the general conditions for collective action are more likely to apply to communities when (1) communities are homogeneous with respect to the main divisions of power at a regional or national level, (2) the cost of communication rises rapidly as a function of distance, and (3) control over land (as compared with the other factors of production) is valuable but uncertain.

The Effects of Urbanization

In keeping with the elementary definition of community employed so far, let us use a stripped-down idea of urbanization. Cities are simply communities which exceed some arbitrary minimum size. Urbanization is the process whereby an increasing share of a given population comes to reside in cities. The process has three components: (1) net migration, (2) natural increase and (3) net reclassification of existing settlements from rural to urban and urban to rural. For urbanization to occur in the population over some segment of time, the rate of change of the sum of these three components for the urban sector of the population must be greater than the corresponding rate of change for the rural sector. When the rates of change are equal, there can be a great deal of urban growth without urbanization. If the rural rate is higher, the population *de*urbanizes.

Urbanization occurs in a number of different ways. All of them depend to an important degree on the increased involvement of the population in large, complex, coordinated activities which are widely dispersed in space. Trade, manufacturing, and political control are the three principal classes of urbanizing activities. To the extent that it is predominant, each produces a characteristically different type of city and pattern of urbanization. Many of the apparent effects of urbanization, then, are actually effects of the expansion of trade, manufacturing, and/or political control.

Nevertheless, urbanization has some regular accompaniments which are probably effects of urbanization as such. I proposed some generalizations earlier: urbanization raises and then lowers the power-homogeneity of communities, the value and the instability of control over land; it also lowers the distance-cost of communications more or less continuously; its short-run effects on community collective action will therefore vary with the relative pace of these different changes, but in the long run urbanization shifts the balance away from communities as collective actors. The general discussions of communities as actors has already touched on these transformations repeatedly. Our job now is to sort them out as briefly and neatly as possible.

Urbanization and the Power-Homogeneity of Communities

Remember the Alpine village, la Maurienne, analyzed by Placide Rambaud? The short-run effect of its incorporation into the expanding Piedmontese state was to homogenize the power positions of the village households; the distinctions among them made less and less difference in their efforts to get responses from the state, the state became an increasingly important repository of the crucial resources outside the community, and interactions with the state had for the most part to be mediated by the community's own elite. Most of these changes followed pretty directly from political centralization. Yet part of the effect was probably due to the fact that the sheer location of resources, as of people, was shifting to cities faster than the abilities of villagers to make claims on those resources were increasing. The resources that mattered accumulated disproportionately in Chambéry, then the Piedmontese capital. Moreover, in the short run the direct demand of cities for food, manpower, and other resources currently committed to local ends increased more rapidly than the ability of villages to supply them. Hence a squeeze on local resources and a homogenization of the power position of community members.

Over the long run, the general effect of urbanization was probably to differentiate the power positions of different segments of the community. In particular, the division between the mass of the local population and elites who were heavily involved in national politics, national markets, and national communications structures produced a fundamental heterogeneity of power, increased the likelihood that the elite would act in concert with similar elites from elsewhere, and decreased the possibility of collective action by the community as a whole.

The case of la Maurienne exemplifies a general process. The process probably flows from the logic of urbanization itself—at least of urbanization which begins in the midst of a peasant population. So long as cities constitute only a small part of the population, the resources necessary for the maintenance of urban activities and populations are likely to be committed to particular local ends, their supply inelastic, their production inefficient from a national point of view. When cities grow faster than the rural population under these conditions, the short-run effect is to create a serious struggle over resources already committed to rural uses: grain, manpower, land. Further urbanization does not occur unless the forces based in the city win out. The short-run consequence is therefore to deprive rural communities of some of the resources with which they would ordinarily carry on their collective life, but it also homogenizes the power positions of their members. Whether it stimulates greater collective action in the short-run therefore depends on whether the depletion of essential resources occurs more slowly than the homogenization of power.

In the longer run, however, rural communities respond to the pressure from outside by moving into the markets for labor, land, and commodities; productivity tends to increase, resources are freed, and specialization of producers occurs. An increasing proportion of the total population is in cities whose inhabitants are almost by definition heterogeneous with respect to power. At a more general level, the basic city-building activities— large, complex, coordinated activities which are widely dispersed in space —involve different segments of each community to different degrees. They cut across communities, leaving distinctions between cosmopolitans and locals, elites and masses, cash-crop farmers and true peasants, officials and citizens, owners and workers. Some of these crosscutting strata themselves become more likely bases for mobilization and collective action. So the long-run consequence of urbanization is to reduce the power-homogeneity of communities. Thus, if my argument is correct, it finally tends to reduce the prominence of communities as bases for collective action.

How Urbanization Affects the Value and Stability of Control Over Land

The situation of control over land looks quite similar to that of power-homogeneity. Consider the characteristic squeeze on scarce and already committed resources at the start of the urbanization of a predominantly rural population. The increase in the urban demand for the products of the land, for resources (e.g., labor, rents) committed to particular pieces of land, and for the land itself drives up the value of rural land, at least within the immediate hinterlands of the growing cities. The short-run struggle over access to those resources also tends to decrease the stability of control of the land; haciendas expand, enclosing landlords challenge communal grazing rights, a genuine impersonal market in land opens up. These are the conditions to which we find the European rural population responding by occupying fields, attacking landlords, and fighting off the bailiffs. In my analysis, the short-run increase in the value and instability of control over land spurs communal collective action.

Over the long run, however, the general effect of urbanization is no doubt to reduce the value of land relative to the other factors of production. The great city-building activities are, on the whole, labor- or capital-intensive. Over western Europe as a whole, the amount of land under cultivation and the agricultural population reached their maxima some time around 1900. Since then, people have drained out of the countryside, farmers have abandoned their farms, and the amount of agricultural land has dwindled. That same process has been occurring everywhere else in the West, depending on the pace and timing of urbanization, industrialization, and increases in agricultural productivity. It is the most obvious manifestation of the long-run shift away from land toward labor and capital. Urban land, of course, continues to increase in value, but not relative to the other factors of production.

Perhaps the same trend applies to the security of control over land: in the early stages of urbanization, an important rise in the insecurity of control over land; later, a long decline toward security. The trend of value itself suggests that conclusion, but the association of urbanization with the creation of an active market for land points in the other direction. What we would have to know is not how often titles changed hands at various points in the process of urbanization, but how often existing titles were subjected to challenges. Rapid rise and slow fall remain the more plausible summary. If my general argument about the conditions for collective action by communities is correct, this should have the effect, all other things being equal, of first stimulating and then dampening communal collective action.

Urbanization and the Distance-Cost of Communications

Over the long run, declining distance-cost of communications obviously goes with urbanization. H. A. Innis, his follower Marshall McLuhan, Richard Meier and Allan Pred have all argued, in their own ways, that where communications were both costly and crucial to the enterprises men were carrying on, men have agglomerated in towns and cities. The agglomeration is a response to high distance-cost. But, as these authors have usually pointed out, the relationship is reciprocal. The high premium placed on efficient communications stimulates urbanites to invent new media which will carry large volumes of information far and fast at low cost. Indeed McLuhan speculates—and here he rejoins Webber's notions of the nonspatial community—that the new inventions eventually make agglomeration unnecessary and place irrelevant. We arrive, in this account, at the Global Village.

That conclusion is not self-evident. The demand for information could continue to increase more rapidly than the supply, for several reasons: because people engage in ever more complex and information-hungry activities, because the maintenance of existing agglomerations itself absorbs a great deal of information, because the demand for information is a sort of self-perpetuating addiction—more, more, more! It isn't exactly clear how much of the increased communications flow is a consequence of urbanization as such, and how much a consequence of the big activities which generate urbanization. Nevertheless the correlations are there. Communications flows rise exponentially with urbanization. The cost per bit transmitted per distance goes down. More important, the curve between transmitting information one mile and a hundred flattens. At least some of that change results from the fact of agglomeration itself.

If this were the only effect of urbanization, the relative propensity of communities (as compared with other kinds of groups) for collective action would decline continuously as urbanization proceeded. By my argument, however, relative land values and the power-homogeneity of communities also affect collective action ... and they don't behave the same way. In the early phases of urbanization, according to the argument, they are changing in a direction which promotes community collective action, while the distance-cost of communications is changing relatively slowly in the other direction. Later all three factors move in the same direction. The argument predicts a short-term rise, then a long-term fall in community collective action. It leaves the extent of the rise and fall a function of the relative rates of change of the three factors. Figure 2 gives one hypothetical presentation of the change over a long span of urbanization.

Figure 2

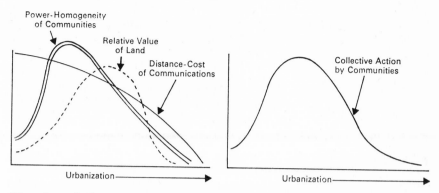

Hypothetical Changes in Community Collective Action and its Determinants in the Long Run of Urbanization

Implications for Peasant Collective Action

The fate of the agrarian classes under capitalism generally confirms this timetable, and the line of argument behind it. Recent work by Eric Wolf and others on the advance of capitalism into the peasant areas of the West has identified two very different points in the process which favor rural collective action. Assuming a preexisting peasant population (an agricultural population, settled in villages, with substantial control over the land it works), the first point comes early in the process. It is the collective resistance of still-organized peasants to encroachments on their rights to the local land: Zapata's bold reaction to the expansion of sugar-growing haciendas in southern Mexico stands as an archetype:

> When—at the beginning of the rainy season of 1910—the neighboring hacienda began to occupy community land already readied for corn planting, Zapata organized a group of eighty men to carry through the planting operation in defiance of the hacienda. Shortly after, Villa de Ayala and Noyotepec—two other communities—began to contribute to Zapata's defense fund. Thereupon Zapata proceeded to take over communal lands occupied by the haciendas, destroy the fences erected by them, and distribute land to the villagers. (Wolf 1969: 28; cf. Womack 1969)

The point in this case, and in all such cases, is *not* that peasants in general cling tenaciously to their land. Considering how general one version or another of capitalist consolidation of control over peasant land was in the West after 1500, instances of concerted resistance like that of Zapata were rare. The *hacendados* of southern Mexico, however, had cut into the land supply of established Indian villages without destroying their internal organization. Control over land became more valuable and less stable as Indian communities homogenized with respect to the main divisions of power at a regional level.

To sharpen the point: despite an incredibly widespread mythology to the contrary, peasants in the West were not extraordinarily attached to their soil *as such*; they were attached to the maintenance of conditions which supported the survival of themselves and their households as respected human beings. Those conditions generally included control of enough land to support a household under prevailing conditions of soil, technique, climate, and market. But peasants held land under a great variety of leases, traded plots fairly often, often exercised common rights, and sometimes even belonged to systems in which the land was entirely redistributed from time to time. Traditionalism, land hunger, and peasant individualism—to take three slogans which have commonly been used in accounting for the resistance of peasants to the introduction of "modern" agriculture—misstate the central features of such systems.

Joan Thirsk (1967) has made an acute distinction between the movements toward enclosure in highland and lowland England. The highlands had never supported extensive manors. Settlement was dispersed, communal controls and rights over land unimportant, farming divided between herding for cash and the raising of field crops for subsistence. There, peasants themselves played an important part in enclosure, little resistance occurred, and the fencing of land into private plots was well advanced by the sixteenth century. In the lowlands, broadly speaking, manors had been fundamental, extensive communal controls over the land existed, people tended to live in large villages, and an important part of the grain produced went to the market.

In the lowland situation, the landlords who could assemble a large contiguous tract of land for grazing stood to make handsome financial gains; to do so, however, required abridgement of communal rights in the land, expulsion of smallholders, and overlooking the furious resistance those two innovations frequently called up. The peasants who resisted were in no sense the most traditional, the most individualistic. They were the peasants whose survival as peasants depended on communally-enforced access to the land.

The second point in capitalist development which appears to favor rural collective action comes much later. To the extent that all the factors of production become responsive to national and international markets, the peasantry disappears. It has two main destinations, with many stopping-places in between: (1) the emergence of cash-crop farmers with considerable capital invested in their enterprises; and (2) the creation of an agricultural proletariat. Where the first becomes the dominant type, hired labor often plays a significant, if subordinate, role. Where the second prevails, a small class of landlords and managers inevitably accompanies it. The first was the French destination: a nation of peasants dissolving into cash-crop farmers; the second was English: a few landlords and yeomen surviving in the midst of a great mass of landless laborers.

At either of these destinations, associations of producers or of workers become significant bases of collective action. In North America we are mainly familiar with the producers' associations: the Grange, the National Farmers' Alliance, the Cooperative Commonwealth Federation, and so on. In Europe and Latin America, however, landless laborers have manned an important part of the agrarian collective action over the last century or so. Although their movements often look sudden and unfocused, they invariably rest on extensive, specialized local organization. In southern Spain, for example, the clandestine organization of agrarian workers on big estates—of *braceros*—began in the middle of the nineteenth century. (They may have drawn support, and even leadership, from rural artisans who were being squeezed by the de-industrialization of the Spanish countryside.) By the time of the revolution of 1868, braceros of Andalusia and elsewhere in the South had mounted numerous and effective labor organizations, were conducting frequent strikes, and had begun to take on the left-wing programs which characterized them up to the time of Franco.

As the nineteenth century rolled on, the day-to-day demands of landless workers shifted from control or redistribution of the land toward improvement of the conditions and returns of work. Nevertheless, the call for *reparto*—subdivision of the great estates—remained at the heart of rural revolutionary programs. As Diaz del Moral puts it:

> At that time socialism came to mean for the one and the other [the rich and the poor] the division of the property of the first among the second, which is to say a new land reform in which many individual landholders would substitute for the few who then owned the land. (Diaz del Moral 1967: 72)

During the Cantonalist rebellions of 1873 the Andalusian rebels commonly proclaimed *reparto*, and in some places actually began to redistribute the land. During the agrarian general strikes of 1918, the process began again. With a rapidly increasing population, the value of control over the land had only risen over the previous half-century.

What part did communities, as such, play in all this collective action? Only in the first phase were the actions based mainly on communities: Zapata si, Andalusia no. Where there was a still-organized peasantry defending existing claims on common land against capitalist encroachment, communities were the ordinary units of action. In the later phase, the action was larger in scale, based on associations with urban links and cutting across communities which were divided by power and interest.

How It Worked in Sicily

The transformation of rural collective action I have sketched occurred throughout the West. It probably occurs everywhere that capitalism spreads. The main variations are in its timing and in the degree to which the second phase—rural collective action based on associations transcending particular communities—occurs at all; many parts of the rural West drifted off into silent despair as their peasantries disappeared. We can see the full cycle, nevertheless, in numerous sections of Europe: the Po valley, the hinterland of Moscow, England's Midlands, and elsewhere. One of the more intriguing cases is Sicily.

Since early in the nineteenth century, and perhaps before, Sicily has acted like an analog computer—a computer designed to represent revolutionary processes. There were major insurrections in Palermo and its region in 1820, 1848, 1860, and 1866. Another large rebellion swept eastern Sicily in 1837. The revolutions of 1848 and 1860 directly involved much of the island. In 1893–1894 the movement of the Sicilian Fasci drew national attention and massive repression.

These were only the high points of collective action. With relatively small changes in basic social structure or day-to-day life, the same island has produced a stunning variety of political performances: rebellion, revolution, banditry, mafia, petty tyranny, and passivity in the face of gross injustice. To an important degree, the same people, areas, and social situations have produced these incompatible forms of action and inaction. They have even produced them in close succession. It is enough to make us doubt the evidence . . . or to shrug our shoulders and speak, with Salvatore Massimo Ganci (1954: 839) of "a peculiar cultural world in which elements of Christian mysticism and of fatalistic Mohammedanism coexist with residues of the pagan world."

Yet Sicily, for all the exotic nonsense that has been written about the place, is not a realm apart. Nor is it a mere leftover of a past, primitive world. In its time (which means before 1800), Sicily had been a center of civilization, one of the Mediterranean's prime granaries, a maritime emporium, a political prize. In the nineteenth century, it was one of the crucial arenas of popular action toward the unification of Italy. Garibaldi's largest contribution to that unification, after all, came with his 1860 landing in Sicily. The popular insurrection which coincided with the landing made possible Garibaldi's conquest of the South from the Bourbons.

Sicily, in short, was never a separate political world. Nor do Sicily's politics really follow separate rules. The processes which set man against man in modern Sicily have their counterparts in semirural areas through much of the modern world.

What elements go into this particular computer? First, there is a set of social classes, all dependent on the land in one way or another. At a minimum, we must distinguish (1) a large mass of landless or land-poor agricultural laborers, the residences of a peasantry, most of them working dispersed plots of land on short-term contracts or at a daily wage; (2) a small but crucial group of managers running from the *gabellotto* or estate manager to the paid thugs who kept the agricultural workers in line; and (3) the few *rentiers*, once well divided into nobles and bourgeois, but with the nineteenth century increasingly consolidated into a single land-owning class.

The second element is a simple set of power relationships among the classes. The managers extract an income for the *rentiers* from the agricultural workers, and receive several things from the rentiers in exchange: a share of the proceeds, a relatively free hand in controlling the local population, and protection from outsiders. In such a system the agricultural workers tend to be exploited and defenseless, the managers tend to expand their capital and their power by extending the range of their exactions, and the rentiers tend to remain economically inert and parasitic.

The third element is a simple but changeable relationship to outside centers of power, especially the state. Most of the time the relationship between the rentiers and the state remains parallel to that beween the managers and the rentiers: so long as the region remains docile, lends itself to exploitation, and yields its regular tribute, the state gives the rentiers a fairly free hand; it keeps its armed force available as a guarantee of the established order. But several agents can upset this relationship to the state: the managers and their henchmen may begin acting autonomously, and threaten the income of the *rentiers;* the guarantees of the state may weaken because of a diversion or paralysis of its armed force; potential allies of the agricultural workers may arrive on the scene and make a new coalition possible; agricultural workers may organize and move into collective action; or, more likely, several of these may happen at once.

The fourth and final element of our analog computer is a bit of a surprise. It is the expansion of capitalist property relations. The system I have described has such a 'feudal" tone, and has so often been treated as a "feudal" remnant, that its increasingly capitalistic character is hard to see. Under strong pressure from the British occupying forces, the Sicilians rid themselves of most of the juridical apparatus of feudalism between 1806 and 1812. More important, landlords and managers (and, from time to time, the state) collaborated thereafter in the consolidation of property rights: dismembering commons; restricting rights to glean, graze, and gather; seizing and selling church property; and so on. The net effect was to reduce the number of competing claims on the same piece of land, to build a market in land, and to accentuate the proletarian position—the sheer dependence on sale of their labor—of those who actually worked the land. It helped convert a population of peasants into a population of agricultural laborers. That process was well along by 1848.

The circumstances of nineteenth-century Sicily, then, broadly resembled those of Andalusia and Mexico. Sicily experienced the fundamental transition from reactive, local, peasant-based, community collective action to a larger-scale associational action during the nineteenth century. The class structure, the power relations, the unstable connection between inside and outside, and the general expansion of capitalist property relations interacted to produce both the short-term oscillations and the long-term transformations of rural collective action. Mafia, for example, is essentially an outgrowth of the private governments the landlords built, in collaboration with their managers, as they squeezed out the claims of peasants on the land (Blok 1973; Romano 1963). The enforcers acquired autonomy and retained protection. Whenever the ability of the landlords and managers to call up the armed force of the state declined, on the other hand, agricultural workers reasserted their claims to control of the land— most often by occupying usurped land directly and *en masse*. Likewise, when an important ally (e.g., the bourgeois in 1848, Garibaldi in 1860, labor organizers from the North in the early 1890s) became available, the agricultural workers began to act together against their exploiters.

The Sicilian revolution of 1848 epitomizes the interaction of the four factors. It was, as it happens, the first of the many European relations of 1848. On January 12th crowds of workers in Palermo demonstrated around the Italian tricolor, fought with the troops and police sent to disperse them, and set up barricades which gave them control of one of the city's poorer districts. An informal committee of bourgeois and liberal nobles allied themselves with the crowds, and provided them with some of their leadership.

Almost as soon as the insurrection began in Palermo, the countryside stirred. As Denis Mack Smith (1968: 416) describes it:

> The news from Palermo on 12 January was a signal for all who had a grievance to rise and remedy it, and this gave the revolt an immense and unexpected force. In the villages and towns there were bread riots and attacks on the 'clubs' where the *galantuomini* used to meet. Whole flocks of sheep were killed, crops and hay ricks burnt. Over the next weeks an enormous destruction took place in many of the surviving woodlands, as land was seized and cleared for cultivation. Often the Town Hall was attacked and there was a bonfire of the title deeds to property which symbolized centuries of social persecution. Government

ceased as officials fled for their lives. The tribal morality of a subject population was evidenced in a general assassination of policemen and suspected informers, sometimes with unbelievable cruelty.

He adds that men involved in the activities which would eventually be called Mafia took advantage of an open situation to consolidate their positions. Mack Smith's interpretation is essentially that in the weakening of public authority every violent impulse—noble or ignoble—had its chance.

There is something to that interpretation: the neutralization of royal control did permit ordinary Sicilians to undertake collective actions which would have been very risky when the police, troops, and Mafia were about their usual business. Yet their actions, for the most part, redressed specific and long-standing grievances. The deeds to property did not symbolize so much "centuries of persecution" as two or three decades in which the landlords and managers had been squeezing the agricultural workers out of their previously established common rights in the land. The woodlands were precisely the property over which landlords and managers had consolidated their control. The agricultural workers knew what they wanted; it was neither blind vengeance nor a liberal constitution, but reestablishment of their rights. In combination with the rather different actions of the other Sicilian classes, however, the net *effect* of the movement of agricultural workers was to reinforce the drive for an autonomous Sicily with a liberal constitution.

In Sicily, the revolutionary committees of Palermo rapidly became the revolutionary government of the entire island. At this point, the urban bourgeois were already close to their limited objectives: a liberal system of representation, autonomy for Sicily. They had allies who wanted much more—most importantly, a redistribution of the land. To some extent, they had to struggle with the radicals in their own midst. But the big problem was the workers of the city and countryside, who had organized and armed themselves during the opening moments of the revolution. The bourgeois succeeded both in checking the *squadre*, the armed bands of rural and urban workers, which had done an important part of the revolutionary work, and in eliminating workers and smallholders from the National Guard, the revolutionary regime's basic military force.

That accomplished, the new regime managed to enact an agrarian reform law of its own stamp: seizing the property of the Church, selling it off in large blocks, authorizing the purchasers to expel the tenants. As S. F. Romano (1952: 100) sums it up:

The law aimed in substance to give the bourgeoisie which had formed in the island through the accumulation of money the possibility of consolidating its position, becoming a landed bourgeoisie allied with the property holders of feudal origin at the expense of the weakest of the privileged classes of that time: the ecclesiastical class.

The law succeeded. The redistribution of church properties to the advantage of the island's bourgeoisie which had already occurred survived the end of the revolution in 1849; the dismemberment and sale began again with the revolution of 1860. That redistribution gave a great push to the proletarianization of the rural population.

Although their outcomes were different, the structures of the Sicilian insurrections of 1860 and 1866 had much in common with the revolution of 1848. The next great movement after them, by contrast, illustrates the powerful effect that organization of the working class could have on the entire configuration The movement of the Fasci attracted national attention in 1893 and 1894, and ended with the national government's use of massive military force to destroy the movement

The first Sicilian organization with the title Fascio ("bundle" or "grouping," with none of the word's later right-wing overtones) was that of Messina, founded in March, 1889. Its chairman was promptly arrested and convicted. He was only released in March, 1892, when the group resumed activity. In the meantime, a less exclusively working-class Fascio appeared in Catania; it had middle-class sponsors. The main impetus of the movement, which spread through the cities of the island in 1892, however, came from the Palermo Fascio; that group had connections with the Socialists of northern Italy.

The artisans of the cities quickly accepted the new organizations. In many cases, they were not enormously different from the old corporations and gilds; in other cases, they resembled the nascent unions and resistance leagues of the North. Native Sicilian bourgeois reformers and working-class activists carried the form of organization to rural areas at the end of 1892. The new form had the advantages of being technically legal and of having the support of political figures whose position was already established.

In January 1893, troops attacked some hundreds of agricultural workers who had begun to hoe the fields of formerly communal land which they had occupied at Caltavuturo. Eleven died on the spot. Although there was no Fascio in Caltavuturo, there was a group in the community which had announced the aim of establishing a consumer cooperative. The massacre gave a big impetus to urban socialists and Fascianti in their mission to the countryside. The Fascio looked like a form of organization well suited to carry the grievances of workers, peasants, and miners into the political arena. What is more, it appealed to the people themselves; the number of organized Fasci went from 35 in March 1893 to almost 200 in December

(Del Carria 1966: I, 221).

The immediate program of most Fasci was simple and concrete: reduction of consumption taxes, better wages, more favorable contracts for sharecroppers and tenant farmers. The idea of repossessing the lost land remained in the background. The program of taxes, wages, and contracts made a good deal of sense in Sicily of the 1890s. Local consumption taxes (collected both as tolls and as sales taxes) had been rising rapidly in the previous decade and cutting seriously into the income of a population which was increasingly dependent on wage-labor (hence on the purchase of goods in the market) for survival. An important part of the agricultural labor force consisted of landless men who got work by the day or the week at the morning shape-up in the local piazza. And Sicily was already famous for the unfavorable terms of its leases and sharecropping agreements. So each of the Fasci programs had a ready-made constituency.

Through the late spring and summer of 1893, strikes and demonstrations proliferated in the agricultural areas around Palermo, Corleone, and Caltanisetta. The landlords and managers frequently called in the police to break them up. From October 1893 through the beginning of 1894, communal and tax offices were attacked, records and buildings sacked, in dozens of Sicilian municipalities. Comandini's day-by-day history of nineteenth-century Italy mentions ten Sicilian tax rebellions in this period which involved at least fifty persons and some damage to persons or property. No one has yet sorted out the history of all these conflicts, but it appears they bore an ambivalent relationship to the Fasci: they were unlikely to occur unless a Fascio had begun to organize the local workers and focus their grievances; yet where the firmest political organization had emerged the Fascio was unlikely to foment, or even to tolerate, attacks on public property.

By the end of 1893, the vigilance and brutality of the authorities had increased significantly. Troops and police were quick to intervene. By the end of the year, ninety-two demonstrators had been killed and hundreds injured. In 1894, the new Crispi government crushed the movement. Crispi declared a state of siege, sent the fleet and 30,000 troops, and clapped numerous left-wing leaders in jail. The most prominent target of the repression was the Socialist deputy and mayor of Catania, de Felice. Although he was in no sense the general leader of the movement, his arrest underscores the nature of the revolutionary threat the government detected in Sicily: an alliance of the urban bourgeois with the workers of city and country against the landholding classes. As Romano analyses it:

> For the moment the spectre of the socialist revolution, or rather of the social, popular and Jacobin revolution, which was at bottom what the republicans feared, produced a closing of ranks among the previously

divided dominant political groups; they united to defend and conserve the established order against the threat of the political ascent of radicals and socialists on a mounting wave of popular action. (Romano 1959: 507–508)

In the course of the nineteenth century, communities lost their prominence as bases of collective action. In 1848, the Sicilian peasantry was already half-destroyed, but it was still making claims for the restoration of its rights. By 1893, the actors were not peasants, but rural proletarians who harbored few hopes of establishing durable individual control over the land. And they acted as members of associations, Fasci, which cut across —and sharply divided—community after community. Up to the revolutions of 1848 and 1860, the distance-cost of communications remained high, the uncertainty of control over land rose, the relative value of land (at least with respect to labor) moved up, and the power-homogeneity of communities probably didn't decline very much As the century wore on, land passed definitively into bourgeois hands, external communications proliferated, communities became increasingly divided with respect to power, and new forms of rural collective action took over. The contrast does not prove my general case. It is at least consistent with the argument.

Conclusion

Perhaps the old theories of urbanization and collective action are partly right, after all. If the arguments of this paper are sound, the urbanization of the world really *has* produced a decline in the relative importance of communities as bases of collective action. If the arguments are sound, it will continue to do so. Where the masters failed, I think, was in explaining how and why the decline occurred. Moral decay and decreasing solidarity are inappropriate explanations. They are nearly impossible to define and measure reliably. And where we come close to defining and measuring them, they don't work as they are supposed to.

Collective action depends to some degree on solidarity, to be sure. But the degree is small and the relationship contingent. It is not clear, in any case, that urbanization does sap the solidarity of communities, if we mean by "solidarity" the extent to which people have strong personal ties to others within the same localities. The decline in that regard is probably relative rather than absolute: local ties have diminished little or not at all, extralocal ties have increased. One can notice the rising proportion of extralocal contacts and regret it. One can compare present conditions of solidarity with an ideal integrated folk community and find the present wanting. But on the basis of present evidence one cannot claim that urbanization produced an absolute decline in community solidarity.

The *relative* decline in communities as bases of collective action, if I have analyzed it correctly, has resulted from changes in the structure of power inside and outside communities, from shifts in the relative efficiency of concentrated and dispersed groups in mobilizing resources, and from stabilization of the claims made by communities on other groups. Urbanization played a part in these transformations. So did other changes which have been generally associated with urbanization in the Western experience, but are by no means intrinsic to urbanization: the formation of national states, the growth of international markets, industrial concentration. Any serious effort to check my assertions against the historical record will have to include some means of separating the effects of urbanization as such from the effects of other massive changes. Anyone who wishes to generalize, however tentatively, from the Western experience to that of today's urbanizing world will have to make the same separation. Today state making, industrial concentration, and the extension of markets are all taking different courses from those they followed in the European heyday; their correlations with urbanization differ as well.

My analysis indicates that deliberate "community organization" as a tactic for engineering change is only likely to work under an unusual set of conditions. Community organization consists essentially of lowering mobilization costs by creating leadership, establishing communications lines and feeding in information. Generally speaking, the tactic should work better when the community in question is already partly mobilized, when it is relatively powerful, when it is relatively invulnerable to repression, and where claims which the group is already making are being challenged by other groups. In those circumstances a strategy which lends power, facilitates mobilization, and provides protection against repression through coalition with important outsiders looks like an effective complement to community organization tactics.

A territorial community should be a more favorable vehicle for collective action than other kinds of groups where the community is homogeneous with respect to power, where there are important barriers to long-distance communication, and control over land is valuable and unstable. In the contemporary North American urban scene, a wealthy, segregated ethnic group in an area of changing population and land use comes to mind as a prime candidate. But for the most part a legal association based not on proximity but on class, occupation, or other common interest seems a much more likely vehicle for collective action in the world's metropolises. Whether it is also a more *effective* vehicle for accomplishing common ends is, of course, a question this paper has not addressed at all.

REFERENCES

Ardant, Gabriel.
1971–1972 *Histoire de l'impôt.* Paris: Fayard; 2 vols.

Blok, Anton.
1973 *The Mafia of a Sicilian Village, 1860–1960.* New York: Harper and Row.

Boserup, Ester.
1965 *The Conditions of Agricultural Growth.* London: George Allen and Unwin.

Commons, John R.
1970 *The Economics of Collective Action.* Madison: University of Wisconsin Press; 2nd ed.

Del Carria, Renzo.
1966 *Proletari senza rivoluzione: Storia delle classe subalterne italiane dal 1860 al 1954.* Milan: Oriente; 2 vols.

Deutsch, Karl.
1966 *Nationalism and Social Communication.* Cambridge: M.I.T. Press; 2nd ed.

Díaz del Móral, Juan.
1967 *Historia de las agitaciones campesinas andaluzas—Cordoba.* Madrid: El Libro de Bolsillo; 2nd ed.

Gamson, William.
1968 *Power and Discontent.* Homewood, Illinois: Dorsey.

Ganci, Massimo.
1954 "Il movimento dei Fasci nella provincia di Palermo," *Movimento operaio,* new series, 6: 817–892.

Gans, Herbert.
1962 *The Urban Villagers.* New York: The Free Press of Glencoe.

Granovetter, Mark.
1972 "Alienation Reconsidered: The Strength of Weak Ties." Unpublished paper, Johns Hopkins University.

Hirschman, Albert.
1970 *Exit, Voice and Loyalty: Responses to Decline in Firms, Organizations, and States.* Cambridge: Harvard University Press.

Hoover, Edgar M., and Raymond Vernon.
1959 *Anatomy of a Metropolis.* Cambridge: Harvard University Press.

Innis, H. A.
1961 *The Bias of Communication.* Toronto: University of Toronto Press; 2nd ed.

Lees, Lynn, and Charles Tilly.
1973 "Le peuple de juin, 1848." *Annales: Economies, Sociétés, Civilisations,* forthcoming. Available in English as Working Paper Number 70, Center for Research on Social Organization, University of Michigan.

Levine, Bruce.
1970 "Economic Development and Social Mobilization: Spain, 1830–1923." Unpublished paper, University of Michigan.

Mack Smith, Denis.
1968 *A History of Sicily. Modern Sicily after 1713.* London: Chatto and Windus.

Macpherson, C. B.
1962 *The Political Theory of Possessive Individualism*. Oxford: Clarendon Press.

Malefakis, Edward W.
1970 *Agrarian Reform and Peasant Revolution in Spain*. New Haven: Yale University Press.

McLuhan, Marshall.
1962 *The Gutenberg Galaxy*. Toronto: University of Toronto Press.

Meier, Richard L.
1962 *A Communications Theory of Urban Growth*. Cambridge: M.I.T. Press.

Oberschall, Anthony.
1973 *Social Conflict and Social Movements*. Englewood Cliffs, N.J.: Prentice-Hall.

Olson, Mancur.
1965 *The Logic of Collective Action*. Cambridge: Harvard University Press.

Park, Robert Ezra.
1952 *Human Communities*. Glencoe, Ill.: The Free Press.

Pred, Allan.
1973 *Urban Growth and the Circulation of Information: The United States System of Cities, 1790–1840*. Cambridge: Harvard University Press, forthcoming.

Rambaud, Placide.
1962 *Economie et sociologie de la montagne*. Paris: Armand Colin.

Redfield, Robert.
1941 *The Folk Culture of Yucatan*. Chicago: University of Chicago Press.

Romano, Salvatore Francesco.
1952 *Momenti del Risorgimento in Sicilia*. Messina: D'Anna.
1958 *La Sicilia nell'ultimo ventennio del secolo XIX*. Palermo: Industria Grafica Nazionale. *Storia della Sicilia post-Unificazione*, part II.
1959 *Storia dei fasci siciliani*. Bari: Laterza.
1963 *Storia della Mafia*. Milan: Sugar.

Shorter, Edward, and Charles Tilly.
1973 *Strikes in France, 1830 to 1968*. New York: Cambridge University Press, forthcoming.

Snyder, David, and Charles Tilly.
1972 "Hardship and Collective Violence in France, 1830–1960." *American Sociological Review*, 37: 520–532.

Stein, Maurice.
1960 *The Eclipse of Community*. Princeton: Princeton University Press.

Stinchcombe, Arthur L.
1965 "Social Structure and Organizations," in James G. March (ed.), *Handbook of Organizations*. Chicago: Rand McNally, 142–193.

Suttles, Gerald D.
1972 *The Social Construction of Communities*. Chicago: University of Chicago Press.

Thirsk, Joan (ed.).
1967 *The Agrarian History of England and Wales, IV. 1500–1640*. Cambridge: The University Press.

Tilly, Charles.
1972a "Revolutions and Collective Violence," in Fred I. Greenstein and Nelson Polsby (eds.), *Handbook of Political Science*. Reading, Mass.: Addison–Wesley, forthcoming.
1972b "How Protest Modernized in France, 1845 to 1855," in William Aydelotte, Allan Bogue, and Robert Fogel (eds.), *The Dimensions of Quantitative Research in History*. Princeton: Princeton University Press.
1973a "Does Modernization Breed Revolution?" *Comparative Politics*, 5: 425–447.
1973b *An Urban World*. Boston: Little, Brown, forthcoming.
1973c "Reflections on the History of European Statemaking," in Charles Tilly (ed.), *The Formation of National States in Western Europe*. Princeton: Princeton University Press, forthcoming.

Tilly, Louise A.
1971 "The Grain Riot as a Form of Political Conflict in France," *Journal of Interdisciplinary History*, 2: 23–57.

Tönnies, Ferdinand.
1963 *Community and Society*. New York: Harper Torchbooks.

Webber, Melvin et al.
1964 *Explorations into Urban Structure*. Philadelphia: University of Pennsylvania Press.

Wellman, Barry, and Marilyn Whitaker.
1971 "Community—Network—Communication: An Annotated Bibliography." Toronto: Centre for Urban and Community Studies, University of Toronto; multilith.

Wirth, Louis (Albert J. Reiss, ed.).
1964 *On Cities and Social Life*. Chicago: University of Chicago Press.

Wolf, Eric.
1969 *Peasant Wars of the Twentieth Century*. New York: Harper and Row.

Womack, John Jr.
1969 *Zapata and the Mexican Revolution*. New York: Knopf.

Instrumentality and Community in the Process of Urbanization

R. E. PAHL

University of Kent at Canterbury, England

Comparative empirical evidence is presented to show the basic instrumentality of low-income urban dwellers to the existential circumstances they face. In Latin America, urban dwellers have seemingly internalised the urban/industrial values of capitalist society and, depending on the availability of jobs and other urban resources and facilities, choose the most rewarding strategy for obtaining benefits. Given the general lack of a well-established structure of secondary industry and the particularistic procedures presently most appropriate for getting jobs and other resources, the motives and basis for communal and collective action are lacking. This is seen most clearly in the example of squatting, where short-term collective action does not develop further, once the objectives of the squatters are achieved. Various forms of instrumental action are expressed in a typology based on subjective orientations and objective opportunities. In the light of the evidence cited, discussions of "marginality," "urban social movements" and "restructuring of community" are misplaced.

The notion of "community" or collective action in the process of urbanization has been discussed in many different forms and contexts. The discussion may range from accounts of the development of associations, based on locality of origin or ethnicity, of an expressive or recreational nature (Little 1965; Mangin 1959) to the development of solidaristic trade union activity (Epstein 1958) or urban tribalism (Bruner 1961; Cohen 1969). Communal consciousness has been seen at one extreme as a kind of emotional cushion based on kin and familiar faces which helps newly arrived migrants to cope with the tensions of a more complex urban situation; at the other extreme it may be seen as the beginning of radical action leading ultimately to revolution. Cities which are absorbing large numbers of migrants in a short time may be seen, therefore, either as seedbeds of revolution or collections of urban villages held together by crosscutting face-to-face ties. Logically both positions may be held simultaneously, since new urban dwellers may live and work in different sets of social relationships in different urban milieux, and they need not necessarily correlate (Mitchell 1966).

Some earlier accounts (Lewis 1964 and 1966; Pahl 1966) did indeed suggest that the common experience of urbanization on those at the bottom of the social hierarchy in many different cultures led to a common response. Thus insecurity of employment and a low collective bargaining position produced communities of common deprivation in urban villages in which ties with peers were complex and multistranded and the values of the encapsulating society were rejected or only partly assimilated. This position has come under very heavy attack in recent years: Mayer (1961) has shown that the same urban context can produce different responses among the "Red" and "School" Xhosa migrants into East London. In the case of the Red Xhosa the encapsulation effect was maintained, less because of the existential situation, than because of the pre-migration characteristics of the migrants themselves. On the other hand Balan (1969) and Epstein (1967) have pointed to the variety of different urban contexts that migrants can face: in particular, where there are abundant opportunities for individual advancement up the occupational hierarchy then *gemeinschaftlich* values will be less likely to develop.

Attempts to form some pattern from very disparate research findings from very different empirical situations have hitherto met with little success. Students of urbanization are faced with an increasing and embarrassing profusion of material, which ranges from detailed studies of the process in nineteenth-century Britain (e.g., Foster 1968; Anderson 1971) to contemporary empirical studies in the Third World. Recent attempts to generalize within and between continents such as those by Epstein (1967) or Morse (1971) have been of limited success, on their own admission, because of the enormous range of empirical material which they seek to encompass. As Epstein is at pains to emphasize, "African urbanism . . . is not characterized by uniformity" (1967: 284), and Morse echoes this with his assertion that "global comparisons of urbanization are treacherous" (1970: 19). It seems that we must be content with the careful analysis of specific sets of social relationships in specific contexts: the development of our understanding of urbanization is likely to come more from those immersed in specific sets of historical data or fieldwork material than from dubious attempts at comparative sociology at necessarily high levels of abstraction. It is at a processual level that useful comparative links may be made.[1]

If we mean by the *process* of urbanization a shift from one set of social, economic, and political circumstances to another, then the specific response that typical migrants have to make to a new set of circumstances might still provide the basis for a link between urbanization and the concept of community. Newly urbanized populations, faced with new problems simultaneously, may devise new social forms to handle the situation or may refurbish old forms in a new context (e.g., Bruner 1961 and Cohen 1969). In the case of new social forms, whether these are permanent class formations, sporadic urban social movements, or other forms of collective action will depend largely on the level of structural opposition engendered by the industrial-occupational structure of the local context (Banton 1965; Foster 1968; Roberts 1970). The problems which those taking part in rapid urbanization face can change as the process proceeds. Thus, as the "reception areas" of the inner city become overcrowded and their physical fabric deteriorates, or as migrants become more committed to and integrated in local labor markets, so a collective demand for new urban settlements at the edge of the city develops.[2]

Thus different social forms will be appropriate at different stages in the historical process of urbanization and as the local existential circumstances change. This raises more complications than I can reasonably address myself to in this present context. Rather, I hope to demonstrate that this model of a *collective* response to a *common* situation (even though that situation may vary historically and geographically) must be seriously questioned. I argue instead that there are a number of possible responses by migrants to the new urban context. These responses may vary according to the values and orientations they bring to the urban situation and the way they subjectively perceive that situation, as much as the objective circumstances within the city itself. It would be to prejudge the situation to assume that some form of collective or communal action is a *necessary* response to a common situation. Equally plausible is an individual response to a common situation. The "logic of collective action" has to be demonstrated.

In the analysis which follows I focus on two sets of constraining factors. The first set are the basic values and orientations of the newly urbanized populations. That is to say, the degree to which such populations have internalized the notions of "success," achievement, and individual social mobility—adopting universalistic criteria of merit such as educational credentials—and the degree to which they feel bound by particularistic and kin-based obligations. The second set of factors relates to what the city "offers" or allocates by way of jobs, housing facilities, access to medical and educational facilities, and so forth. This interaction between *orientations* and *opportunities* is the basis for the typology.

If instrumental individualism militates against the development of communal values so, too, does instrumental collectivism, which by no means implies the development of solidaristic or affective communal action. Indeed, this kind of collectivism is in many ways the antithesis of "community" (which I do not consider it would be useful attempting to define precisely).

I exemplify below different forms of instrumental action in different contexts. The Hausa of Nigeria illustrates the use of archaic forms for instrumental-collective ends; newly urbanized workers in nineteenth-century Lancashire illustrate the theme of individual instrumentalism and this, too, is shown from empirical data relating to contemporary Guatemala and the Argentine. Finally studies of squatter settlements, particularly in Peru, illustrate the short-term nature of what might be described as instrumental communal action. This is not meant to be an exhaustive analysis, rather by shifting the focus from a concern with "marginality" or "urban villages" I hope to open up a fruitful field for further analysis.

A TYPOLOGY OF MIGRANTS' COURSES OF ACTION

Taking into account the different job opportunities and differential access to urban resources and facilities on the one hand and the individual migrant's orientation to urban/industrial values on the other, it is possible

Figure 1

Quality of Job Opportunities and Access to Urban Resources and Facilities for Individual Migrant

		Poor	Good
Low Income Urban Dwellers' Orientation to Urban/Industrial Values	Acceptance	1. Collective Action (Squatting)	3. Individual Action (Occupational Mobility)
	Non-acceptance	2. Collective Accommodation or Withdrawal (Urban Villages)	4. Individual Dislocation or Tension (Nuclear Family Leaves Old Central City Base)

In situation (3) the opportunities for individual advancement inhibit the development of communal consciousness and action, as physical and social mobility scatter individuals through the urban social and spatial system. The so-called "urban villages" or communities of protection and retreat in situation (2) may be more or less short-lived depending on the way job opportunities change and develop. As migrants acquire or withdraw from the values of the dominant social order, or as the city's economic base changes or develops, so new opportunities or new blockages may occur at different levels in the hierarchy, promoting different forms of reaction. If collective action is provoked, this may be more or less long-term depending on the nature of the benefits accruing from such action. In situation (1) where the collective action is related to immediate objectives, such as the attainment of a firm position in the urban housing situation by organizing and taking part in a squatter movement, it may not continue in a broader, political context. The connection between sporadic, short-term and instrumental collective action and more long-term solidaristic communal action is complex and contentious (Collectif Chili 1972; Foster 1968; Tilly 1969). I elaborate this point below. Finally, in situation (4) there is likely to develop a tension between ascription and achievement, between individualistic and universalistic values, and one might expect young married couples to leave their families of origin and move physically, linking house and job career. (See Marris 1961 for an account of this in Lagos.)

Although this typology has a superficial attractiveness and certainly does something to accommodate the wide range of diverging field work material, it presents certain difficulties. It derives from the work of Balan (1969), Foster (1968), Epstein (1967), Touraine (1961) and others, and it suggests that collective action is a product of "marginal" nonuniversalistic values in a context where opportunities for individual advancement are low. It does not follow that solidaristic class action necessarily develops from such collective action. There are also situations where community solidarity of a non-class-based character can have great instrumental advantages for collective advancement.

Modifications of the Typology

This original typology must, however, be modified when we are dealing with a situation where the collective opportunities for success and advancement are good, with the conscious acceptance of nonurban industrial values by the collectivity.[3] Such a formulation simply does not fit a typology which implicity links individual advancement with commitment to urban industrial values—which are in fact the competitive, success-oriented values of Western capitalism. Not only must one avoid the assumption that there is evolutionary, unidirectional change from Gemeinschaft to Gesellschaft, but also one must avoid the error of assuming permanent placement in given typologies. That is to say, individual actors may engage in both collective communal action—such as being led by a poblador in the establishment of a new squatter settlement—and in individual mobility in the job market. In some circumstances gemeinschaftlich values may best serve his interests, whereas in others more gesellschaftlich values may be more appropriate. It is not a matter of community or association, of primary or secondary ties predominating, but rather of the most productive use of the one or the other in specific existential situations.

We may now, therefore, modify the first typology by subdividing cells (1) and (3) in Figure 1 according to whether the instrumental action is individual or collective and by maintaining the same variable for the horizontal axis—the quality of the access to jobs and urban resources and facilities. Hence, where urban opportunities are poor, urban migrants are likely to adopt strategies (1) and (2). Only when job conditions improve, the development of secondary industry advances, and workers become more concentrated in specific work places can the "luxury" of class conflict emerge. At present industrialization has lagged so far behind urbanization in Latin America that the basis for structured opposition has not developed. Where a clear opportunity for instrumental collective action does emerge then evidently action is taken: "The capacity for organization seems not to derive from any mystical ancestral communalism, but to be a creative response on the part of a highly selected, self-recruited set of people to an environment otherwise foreclosing opportunity" (Goldrich et al. 1967: 5).

Figure 2

Access to Urban Jobs, Resources, and Facilities

		Poor	Good
Type of Instrumentality of Low Income Urban Dweller with Orientation to Urban/Industrial Values	*Individual*	Particularistic Criteria (Kin, Patrons, Networks)	3. Universalistic Criteria (Credentials)
	Collective	Sporadic Short-term, Communal Action (e.g. Squatting)	4. Established Long-term Structured Communal Action (e.g., Solidaristic Class Action, Retribalization, etc.)

Note: This is an elaboration of Figure 1, cells (1) and (3). Here it is assumed that all individuals have internalized the goals of individual success and achievement in the urban industrial system. The *means* they use to achieve these ends will be individual or collective depending on the existential circumstances. Since this typology does not include categories which reject or have not assimilated the dominant value system, deviancy, illegitimate means, and noninstitutionalized conflict are not included.

I am indebted to my colleagues Richard Scase and Jack Winkler for discussion on this typology. The whole approach of this paper follows a line of analysis which is being developed independently by Winkler.

I now turn to a discussion of some recent empirical studies. The work by Cohen and Anderson on contemporary West Africa and nineteenth-century Britain serves as a necessary introduction to the more extensive review of work on Latin American urbanization.

THE CASE OF THE HAUSA

Cohen's study of the Sabo in the Yoruba town of Ibadan shows how a group of Hausa immigrants used ethnic exclusiveness to maintain their economic interests. This "closely knit Hausa community" (Cohen 1969: 15) is not simply the reflection of an attempt to maintain Hausa customs in an alien context since, as Cohen goes on to say: "There are tens of thousands of Hausa who migrate annually to Southern Nigeria to seek seasonal employment, who live in small, scattered, loosely-knit gangs of workers without forming or joining organized communities." Rather, the Sabo community is directly linked to the long-distance trade in cattle and kola nuts between the Savannah in the North and the forest in the South. Problems of fluctuations in demand and supply of the cattle are acute. Since they are likely to die from sleeping sickness if they are not slaughtered within one or two weeks of their arrival in the forest zone, the possibility of serious loss in a competitive situation is high. It is crucial for this and other reasons that traders have day-to-day information about changing conditions of supply and demand. They also must have immediate facilities for despatch, transport, and sale together with the necessary credit and trust for the organization of the trade. If men from the same tribe are able to control all the operations, these technical problems can be overcome.

> In the process, the monopolizing tribal community is forced to organize for political action in order to deal effectively with the increasing external pressure, to coordinate the co-operation of its members in the common cause, and to mobilize the support of communities from the same tribe in neighbouring towns. (Cohen, 1969: 20)

As a result of this control over the kola and cattle trade, Hausa communities were established throughout Yorubaland. It was important for the Hausa to emphasize their ethnic distinctiveness and in this way northern dealers were prepared to entrust their resources to their "brothers abroad" who live within a highly stable and organized community" (Cohen 1969: 22).

One does not have to accept the full detail of Cohen's analysis to take the main force of his argument. A strong trading monopoly could be maintained by emphasizing exclusiveness and community values. Cohen claims that the tension between private interest and common interests was overcome by the adoption of the Tijaniyya cult in the quarter, so that communal interests were cemented by a strong religious belief. This neat functional solution to a structural problem may be hard for some to take, and the emergence of "tribalism," religion, and community consciousness as a combined solution to an economic problem fits suspiciously nicely.

> The Hausa of Sabo are today more socially exclusive, or less assimilated into the host society, than at any time in the past. They thus seem to have completed a full cycle of "retribalization" . . . Hausa customs,

> norms, values, and beliefs are upheld by a web of multiplex social rela-
> tionships resulting from the intense interaction within the Quarter.
> (Cohen 1969: 186)

It might be claimed that this example is an exceptional case, a curious anachronism unearthed by a diligent anthropologist. Cohen would not accept this, since he argues that these ethnic groups are essentially *political* in character. Far from being a reversion to conservative and traditional ways, urban ethnicity may be simply a very effective way for a group to further its own interests in the struggle for power and resources: it is "a new social system in which men articulate their *new roles* in terms of tra-ditional ethnic idioms" (Cohen 1969: 194). Ethnic groups in a variety of situations "exploited some of their traditional values, myths and cere-monial in order to establish an elaborate political organization" (Cohen 1969: 192).

THE CASE OF NINETEENTH-CENTURY PRESTON

Another striking example of the point I am arguing is provided by Ander-son's scholarly study of the impact on urban-industrial life on working-class family structure in Preston, England, in the nineteenth century (An-derson 1971). Anderson convincingly demonstrates the importance of kinship ties amongst the new urban working class despite the fact that "when it became possible for actors to maximise satisfaction without re-course to kin, kinship obligations were, indeed, rejected" (Anderson 1971: 91). Far from kin ties being basically affective, Anderson suggests that their strength is directly proportionate to the amount of reward they can generate. Children adopted an attitude toward their nuclear families described by Anderson as "short-run calculative instrumental individual-ism" and in support of this he cites evidence on the relative incomes of young male offspring and their fathers to show that, other things being equal, offspring of badly paid fathers were the most likely to leave home.

> Children's highly individual wages allowed them to enter into relational
> bargains with their parents on terms of more or less precise equality, if,
> as was usually the case, a bargain could be struck which was imme-
> diately favourable to both parties, then all was well, and the relation-
> ship continued, though the degree of commitment to such a relationship
> must often have been low. If a better alternative was obtainable else-
> where the child could take it. (Anderson 1971: 131)

Such a choice was not available to children in rural areas because the father had complete control over his child's potential sources of income.

Nevertheless, in general, only kin could provide the necessary support for actors in situations such as sickness, bereavement, or unemployment and in dealing with problems such as old age, housing difficulties, and finding good employment, or of immigrants needing advice and shelter in a strange community. "Absence of self-reliance is therefore a necessary, but not a sufficient condition for kinship relationships to exist" (Anderson 1971: 172).

> Though neighbours did provide some help, and though there were certain bureaucratically organised assistance agencies, each had major drawbacks as a reliable and low cost source of aid. Neighbours lacked a firmly enough structured basis of reciprocation in a heterogenous and mobile society. Kinship, by contrast, could provide this structural link and could thus form a basis for reciprocation. Kin did, indeed, probably provide the main source of aid. However, because this was a poor (and also a rapidly changing) society, this aid, quite logically in terms of the perspective used here, was limited in cost, and family and kinship relationships tended to have strong short-run instrumental overtones of a calculative kind. (Anderson 1971: 171)

Both Cohen and Anderson, in their different ways, are stressing the basically instrumental and calculative use of custom and ethnicity (Cohen) or kinship (Anderson). Both, too, stress the existential situation: unless one has some knowledge of local labour markets, economic organization, and opportunities in the local context, the specific form of instrumental action remains problematic.

THE QUESTION OF "MARGINALITY" IN LATIN AMERICAN URBANIZATION[4]

The assumption in much sociological writing on urban studies that there is a single, unified and identifiable "urban system" to which given populations can relate or to which they can be "marginal" is questionable. The local economic organization in many Latin American cities would appear to lack the coherence and structure appropriate to the use of the word "system" and with a high level of "tertiarization,"[5] the "normal" economic situation may involve unstable employment and fluctuating earnings for a substantial section of the population.

MacEwen suggests that this postulated marginality may be characterized as encompassing combinations of the following conditions:

> First, regarding restricted formal or informal participation in the urban social system, we find unstable or restricted links with the urban

economy reflected in under- or unemployment which results in an impoverished style of life; isolation from the private housing market and consequent residence on inaccessible or undesirable sites with a lack of urban services and public utilities; irregularity of participation in the educational system (low levels of education and high rates of truancy and desertion), relative isolation from whatever welfare system exists, and a lack of sustained participation in the urban political and recreational systems. Second, regarding the assimilation of urban norms and values, marginality is indicated where there is a marked divergency from urban values and belief systems and the maintenance of certain cultural mores, usually derived from the place of origin such as language, dress, beliefs and superstitions (MacEwen 1972a: 43–44)

As MacEwen points out, much of the so-called marginality is a function simply of low class position. Hence there is a danger of assuming that "integration" and improved class position are one and the same thing. Furthermore, where the character of economic opportunities favours individual over collective advancement, group consciousness will be eroded by competitive desires for individual mobility. This would lead to an ego-oriented approach to integration, and the shanty towns might be seen as transit camps for individuals moving, as it were, into "the urban system." Individuals would be at different stages in the process of "integration" and their similar geographic position would be less the basis for collective action and more the result of a fortuitous combination of circumstances.

It did, indeed, seem to be the case that the socially fragmented nature of the squatters in an Argentinian town described by MacEwen was more the product of mobility than of urbanization. Patronage and apprenticeship limited occupational mobility. These, in turn, limited the possibilities of movement in the housing market.

> The overall result of this is the absence of any form of spontaneous community-based voluntary associations. Thus, although as a whole the squatters find themselves in a common situation of deprivation *vis à vis* the town, there is no form of collective organization based on their common identity as squatters. (MacEwen 1972a: 53)

INFORMALITY AND PARTICULARISTIC TIES IN GUATEMALA CITY AND AN ARGENTINIAN SHANTY TOWN

Roberts's study of low income families in Guatemala City provides further evidence for a similar argument. Again the local economic opportunity structure is the overwhelmingly important factor in determining the form of migrants' social organization. Roberts emphasizes the *discontinuity* which arises as the migrant shifts from one set of social experiences to another and the degree of *informality* in urban social organization, or the degree to which impersonal and standard rules of procedure do *not* apply in the allocation of and access to urban resources and facilities.

This latter factor is of particular interest for the current discussion— the instability of urban employment coupled with this informality factor means that an individual family must seek *individual* means of obtaining services and employment. Dealing with different sets of people outside the neighborhood means that

> Low-income families will be flexible in their interpretation of the possibilities offered by urban life and unstable in their commitments to any one urban situation. Furthermore, an individual's activity will not be confined by any one set of experiences or any one mode of coping with urban life. (Roberts 1970: 348)

Apparently relatively stable and cohesive urban neighborhoods or *barrios* had been typical of Guatemala City in the past, and strong, neighborhood-specific social networks had developed. Clearly this form of social organization could not be maintained with the rapid influx of population characteristic of recent years.

Non-locality-based associations have not taken the place of the *barrios* as the bases for communal activity. Labor unions include less than 5 percent of the working population and the development of recreational or mutual benefit associations is inhibited by the low incomes and the high geographical mobility of the population. Thus, these low-income families tend to be highly fragmented into discrete sets of social relationships. Links with rural areas still remain strong, adding a further fragmenting element.

Typically, low-income families respond to the exigencies of urban life individually and flexibly: they do not develop forms of collective action. The central city neighborhood of "San Lorenzo" did, in fact, show some incipient collective organization, prompted by the inadequate provision of services. Various local facilities have been developed by local initiative and the activities of "betterment committees." However this does not fundamentally affect Roberts's conclusion that "the social activity of families in the two neighbourhoods is spread throughout the city. Activity is not based either on the home or on ties formed with neighbours" (Roberts 1970: 370).

Chief earners tend to work in small enterprises throughout the city and there is little overlap between the sets of relationships based on home and work. Similarly relationships based on religious, political, and communal activities tend to be non-overlapping and discrete. "There is thus little social pressure for people to be consistent in their behaviour from one situation to another ... families in both neighbourhoods move between urban situations in which they deal with distinct sets of people and expectations" (Roberts 1970: 371–372). Like the empirical research reported by MacEwen, Roberts's material shows that low-income families improve their position within the urban system largely through *individual* and not through collective activity.

Further papers by MacEwen (1972b, 1972c) corroborate the general thesis of *differentiation* of newly urbanized low-income families. Indeed, she describes an "atmosphere of intense status competition" amongst squatters, who chose reference groups from the strata above them. This "strain towards individualization of the poor" and the consequent competition deprives them of a "basis for collective leadership and consciousness" (MacEwen 1972c: 17). Like Roberts, she finds that patronage in the labor market produces vertical and particularistic ties, and these are stronger than the lateral ties which could emerge from common occupational or housing insecurity.

Social interaction is almost totally confined to the kin group, and relations with neighbors are kept to the minimum. Localized "action sets" of kin provide the main basis for collective action to cope with specific needs. When individuals advance up the status hierarchy and establish themselves physically elsewhere they may also move away socially from their kin. Nonkin peers of a higher status take their place. With status parity as a new principle of association, interaction with status unequals may decline, and a form of privatization may emerge.

MacEwen provides an interesting account of the process of withdrawal and dissociation which has much in common with the process of privatization outlined by Goldthorpe and Lockwood (1963) for the British working class (see MacEwen 1972b: 19–26). Overwhelmingly it is the *instrumentality* of actors that is emphasized: as with the evidence cited by Anderson discussed above, MacEwen shows that when actors don't need kin as a means of getting access to scarce urban resources and facilities, but are able to maintain their own position by their own efforts (i.e., those who are socially mobile), then kin ties will decline. As she puts it:

> Any explanation of the relative strengths and weaknesses of the kinship system must lie in an examination of the uses to which it can be put by kinsmen, and therefore must refer to the availability (or non availability) of some resource which for that group is strategically important ... kinship is a credit bank for those who need to get something out of a social situation which can be provided by mutual alliance. ... However, a change in social situation may provide the need for new services which the kinship bank, through being restricted to a certain stratum, may not be able to provide. At this point it ceases to be of service, and flexible groupings have to be relied upon instead. (MacEwen 1970b: 27-28)

ORGANIZED SQUATTER SETTLEMENTS IN PERU

Quite evidently, not all urban resources and facilities are open even to those individuals who are occupationally mobile. There may be very severe blockages in access to housing, for example, which can only be overcome through collective action. A brief discussion of organized squatter settlements in Peru will indicate that the organizations developed there to get land and certain basic facilities for the new settlement are strictly instrumental, have few or no ties with more affectively oriented organizations, and may well cease to function when their basic mission is accomplished. Mangin (1967; 1968) has shown how certain goals may be realized through the formation of collective organizations, particularly in the establishment of squatter settlements:

> The organizing moves frequently were short-lived, eventuating in failure. Sometimes they left the communities more divided and alienated. But at other times they had the reverse effect. . . . most squatter settlements are constantly improving their environments and they represent a tremendous social and political investment in community organization as well as a multimillion dollar investment in house construction, the development of services, and the creation of small businesses. They are self-organizing communities that grow up outside of, and often in the face of open opposition from, national governments. . . . In hundreds of cases, thousands of people have . . . created their own communities in and around large urban centres. (Mangin 1968: 407-408)

Quite clearly much of the communal solidarity engendered within these *barriadas* is stimulated by government opposition. So long as collective solidarity was needed to maintain the position established from interference or "re-conquest" by public authorities, then some form of collective organization had to be maintained. There is a clear and necessary instrumental basis for its continuance. "As the *barriada* becomes more a part of the city and less under attack, and as local factionalism increases, the association loses power" (Mangin 1968: 416). The mobilization of the *barriada* is possible only for the defense of their homes: once these are well-established the sense of commitment or belongingness declines, Distinctions of class, status, and ethnicity become more important, personal social networks acquire greater salience and the process of differentiation typical of the other studies of low-income groups in Latin American cities emerges.

According to Mangin these *barriada* populations "are remarkably unaware of their accomplishments and their potential . . . most *barriada* residents are non-alienated, eternally hopeful yet properly cynical individuals" (Mangin, 1968: 419). This certainly rings true and fits in with the other evidence which refutes the notion that a new form of communal activity or urban social movement is arising based on these new squatter settlements. However, there are some indications that in Chile, Venezuela, and elsewhere the political importance of these groups may be greater (Collectif Chili 1972; Espaces et Sociétés 1971; Ray 1969; Vanderschueren 1972).

One might conclude that the certain way to stimulate collective communal action should contain the following ingredients:

1. Let the government provide very little public housing for low-income families, and let them make credit difficult or impossible to acquire.

2. Let the little housing that is available be in architect designed "projects" with zoning control and little opportunity for residents to keep animals or run little businesses.

3. Allocate what housing there is according to particularistic criteria with many complex bureaucratic rules and procedures as defenses.

4. Let there be confusion about the ownership and registration of "public" land.

5. Let the government not be in full control of planning, building, and land administration procedures.

6. Let there be harassment of the squatters on a sporadic and arbitrary basis by the police.

7. Let there be full opportunity for the press and T.V. to witness and report on such harassments.

The continuation of communal organization after the invasion and retention of land will depend on clear and specific tasks being available within the compass of squatter associations or the possibility of articulating such activity into national politics. (See Mangin 1967: 70; Ray 1969.) It is not possible at this stage to say whether squatter invasions are the only solid basis for communal organization among low-income families in the rapidly growing cities of Latin America. All one can be reasonably sure about is that there seem to be no other obvious candidates for such a basis.

However, it is hard to see such settlements as seedbeds of revolutionary activity, since one of the characteristics of these squatter settlements, noticed by observers in many different contexts, is the growth of small businesses associated with vigorous entrepreneurship and capitalist acumen. The processes of differentiation and privatization appear to be greater than processes making for solidaristic collectivism. The forces making for individual or collective instrumentalism are overwhelming, and individuals choose the better course pragmatically rather than ideologically. As Mangin remarks, people in squatter settlements "keep up with the news, become sophisticated about how to manipulate national and international bureaucracies, play off political parties and become real estate and legal specialists" (Mangin 1967: 79). The squatters are more likely to be conservative than radical: "For most Latin American squatters the *only* communal political action they perform is the original invasion and defence of the settlement" (Mangin 1967: 83). It is worth quoting Mangin's conclusions at length because they sum up very neatly an important theme of my paper.

> The dominant ideology of most of the active barriada people appeared to be very similar to the beliefs of the operator of a small business in 19th century England and the United States. These can be summed up in the familiar and accepted maxims: work hard, save your money, trust only family members (and them not too much), outwit the State, vote conservatively, if possible, but always in your own economic self-interest, educate your children for their future and as old age insurance for yourself. Aspirations are towards improvement of the local situation, with the hope that children will enter the professional class. All of the above statements pertain perfectly to favelas. (Mangin, 1967: 84–85)

Mangin does, however, go on to say that whilst migrants may be content at present with a steady income, a house of their own, and their children in school, their aspirations for their children are high, and if these are not satisfied then some change in the political situation may occur. As elsewhere, so much depends on the economic situation and the continuing opportunities for incorporation in local labor markets. It is one of the great merits of Turner's work (1969 & 1970; Brett 1972) that he is able to elaborate on the essential *practicality* of the squatters' motives and in particular how they take into account physical position and prospects in job markets: their housing strategies are ultimately geared to their goals for social and economic mobility. The extent to which low-income groups develop collective solidarity and political radicalism will depend, as Banton (1965), Foster (1968), and Roberts (1968) have pointed out, on the level of structural "class" opposition generated by the local labor-market.

Roberts shows that for Guatemala City, with a low proportion of employment in large-scale enterprises, a high incidence of informality in urban organizations, and a high degree of rural-urban continuity, the basis for common identity and purpose is considerably reduced. Rapid urbanization unaccompanied by rapid industrialization is likely to produce a similar situation. Like Mangin, Roberts also found a high degree of political awareness amongst the low-income urban residents he studied.

> However, when there are few opportunities for stable work in large scale enterprises and when procedures for obtaining work and necessary services are informed, each low income family develops a set of social relationships that is spatially extensive and socially heterogeneous, so as to take advantage of scarce urban opportunities. There are thus no structural situations in urban life to lead low-income strata to think and act politically as a group opposed to other social groups. (Roberts, 1968: 187)

It is on that note that I turn to my final conclusions.

CONCLUDING OBSERVATIONS

In the above account I have drawn material primarily from Anderson and Foster on nineteenth-century towns in England, from Cohen on contemporary West Africa, from MacEwen on Argentina, from Mangin on Peru, and from Roberts on Guatemala. I have been selective in what I have taken from their work, and not all of them were primarily interested in the instrumental and calculative aspects of social action, which I emphasized. Nevertheless, I think it is clear from the evidence I have chosen to present that an outstanding element in the existential circumstances of urbanization is the shrewd and self-interested calculation of the actors concerned. Solidaristic class action appears in only one context in the literature cited —that is in Oldham in nineteenth-century England (Foster 1968)—and solidaristic communal action once—amongst the Hausa in Yoruba land described by Cohen (1969)—although in the latter case it would be more accurate to say that the communal action was both solidaristic and instrumental. My point in general is that in the Latin American material there appears very little evidence for any kind of communal action which is not primarily of a short-term instrumental nature and that this, in turn, is a product of the economic situation.

I am very wary of making cross-cultural generalizations and even within the Latin American context there is barely enough material on which to make firm statements. Nevertheless, it does seem reasonable to conclude that where job opportunities are primarily physically scattered and lie mainly in the tertiary sector and where advancement is dependent on particularistic and informal vertical ties, individual mobility cannot be improved by collective action. This is really the nub of the matter: there is simply no payoff for communal action. Once the squatters have achieved their short-term objective of independent home ownership they return to a more privatized existence. Latin American peasants appear from the literature to be following the archetypal, Samuel Smiles syndrome of nineteenth-century Britain. They are at present between the period of instrumental collectivism of a non-class-based nature and the affective collectivism of community based upon job opportunities and a measure of economic security.

Many of the writers on Latin American urbanization are so concerned to refute the myths of marginality and rampant radicalism in the shanty towns that they have not always considered the implications of the opposite situation they describe. It is more rewarding for newly urbanized peasants to use their individual or collective resources pragmatically depending, in turn, on the context. The key to variations in the field work reports appears to be the nature of the job market and the way that this can be manipulated. Banton (1965) showed how this enabled differences between West and Central Africa to be understood, and similar arguments apply both in Latin America and elsewhere. Those who argue for some kind of affective community, providing solace and comfort to troubled and alienated peasants in an anomic urban situation, can find little support in the most widely respected field work. Clearly the evidence of Mangin, MacEwen, Roberts, and others could be wholly discounted and an alternative model postulated. It may indeed be the case that in Chile and Brazil the economic situation provokes more structural opposition and provides the stability necessary for affective communal ties to develop. Even if that is the case, the main thrust of my argument would still be unaffected.

This paper has attempted no more than to open up the subject of forms of collective and communal action under conditions of rapid urbanization and slow industrialization. When the job structure is experienced as stable, affective communal ties are most likely to develop. Otherwise, my argument is that where the individual orientation is necessarily calculative and self-seeking, in order to obtain maximum access to urban resources and facilities, than communal activity will be in the form of either a type of urban retribalization or of limited and instrumental collective action. The essence of urbanization and industrialization is change and development. As the process continues I would expect a more stable employment structure and more solidaristic class action to develop. That assumes a congruence of urbanization, industrialization, and capitalism. Where the conflicts and contradictions of capitalism do not apply the process of urbanization will take different forms, and one might expect the calculative, self-seeking and privatized orientation, seemingly typical of Latin American peasants, to be replaced by solidaristic and expressive communal action in order to maintain commitment rather than to exploit or generate conflict. Some evidence of this kind of "urban community" is appearing from studies of the People's Republic of China. Interesting material has been published by Luccioni (1972) and Salaff (1971). The evidence is not yet sufficiently plentiful to incorporate it into the general summary and analysis presented here. However, it is clear that until material from fundamentally different political systems is incorporated into our analyses of community, urbanization, and much else, they will suffer from the blinkered ethnocentrism of Western capitalism. There are signs that this point is becoming more generally understood (Castells 1972) but apart from acknowledging the point, it is difficult, in the absence of the necessary documentation, to make conceptual and analytic advances. The importance of the economic base and the political economy is crucial. Further evidence is needed on the values and ideologies of the second and third generation of urban migrants in different sociopolitical systems and on urban consciousness in noncapitalist cities.

NOTES

[1]See, for example, the interesting work by Roberts on Guatemala City (1968 and 1970) which is informed with the conceptual development of Mitchell (1966 and 1969) and others who are or have been at the University of Manchester, with its long tradition of research in the Central African Copperbelt. Thus Roberts emphasizes the: "discontinuity produced by urbanization in the life careers of low income families" (1970: 347), following Mitchell in his insistence on explaining urban behavior in terms of the urban social system in which the actors carry out their significant set of social relationships. I draw heavily on Roberts's work below.

[2]These "squatter settlements" in Latin America are more a reflection of urban commitment than marginality, as recent research demonstrates. (MacEwen 1972a, 1972b, 1972c; Mangin 1970 Turner 1969, 1970). It is of interest that in so far as these organized squatter settlements resemble urban social movements, they neither continue after the exercise nor, perhaps surprisingly, in Peru, do they build on existing Regional Association (Doughty 1970; Mangin 1970). I return to this below.

[3]Illustrated by the Hausa described by Cohen (1969) and discussed below.

[4]The remainder of this paper is devoted to a discussion of Latin American material. It is significant that whilst some of the most interesting material on urbanization has hitherto come from researchers doing their field work in Africa, now this no longer seems to be the case. During the last few years some very interesting field work has been reported by Leeds (1970, MacEwen (1972a, 1972b, 1972c), Mangin (1967, 1968, 1970), Morse (1971), Roberts (1968, 1970), and Turner (1969, 1970), the last-named of which has in turn been discussed by Brett (1972). I recognize this is a partial list, but it includes some of what I take to be the most relevant material and covers a broad enough spread for me to illustrate and discuss my theme.

[5]This cumbersome word is used by Morse (1971) and simply refers to the development of the service sector of the economy. Economists refer to the primary sector — mining, agriculture, fishing, and so forth; the secondary sector of manufacturing industry; and the tertiary sector of services such as insurance, banking, and a whole range of small-scale activities. In Latin America the urban economy has jumped to the service sector without passing through the phase of industrialization typical of the process of urbanization in Britain and North America. One important consequence is that the broad middle band of skilled workers is missing from Latin American cities.

REFERENCES

Anderson, M.
  1971 *Family Structure in Nineteenth Century Lancashire.* Cambridge, Eng.: Cambridge University Press.

Balan, J.
  1969 "Migrant-native Socio-economic Differences in Latin American Cities: A Structural Analysis," *Latin American Research Review* 4:1: 3–51.

Banton, M.
  1965 "Urbanisation and Role Theory." University of Bristol. Unpublished Ms.

Brett, S.
  1972 "Low-income Urban Settlements in Latin America: The Turner Model." University of York. Unpublished Ms.

Browning, Harley L., and Feindt Walfront.
  1971 "The Social and Economic Context of Migration to Monterrey, Mexico," *Latin American Urban Research* I: 45–70.

Bruner, E. S.
1961 "Urbanization and Ethnic Identity in North Sumatra," *American Anthropologist* 3: 508–521.

Castells, M.
1972 *La question urbaine.* Paris: François Maspero.

Cohen, A.
1969 *Custom and Politics in Urban Africa.* London: Routledge & Kegan Paul.

Collectif Chili.
1972 "Revendication urbaine, stratégie politique et mouvement social des 'pobladores' au Chili," *Espaces et Sociétés* 6–7: 35–57.

Doughty, P. L.
1970 "Behind the Back of the City: 'Provincial' life in Lima, Peru," in Mangin, *Peasants in Cities.* Boston: Houghton Mifflin.

Epstein, A. L.
1958 *Politics in an Urban African Community.* Manchester: Manchester University Press.
1967 "Urbanization and Social Change in Africa," *Current Anthropology* 8(4): 275–295.

Espaces et Sociétés.
1971 "Impérialisme et urbanisation en Amerique Latine," Special Issue No. 3.

Foster, J.
1968 "Nineteenth Century Towns—A Class Dimension," in H. J. Dyos (ed.), *The Study of Urban History.* London: Edward Arnold.

Goldrich, D. et al.
1967 "The Political Integration of Lower Class Urban Settlements in Chile and Peru," *Studies in Comparative International Development* 3:1.

Goldthorpe, J. H., and D. Lockwood.
1963 "Affluence and the British Class Structure," *Sociological Review* (N.S.) 11(2): 133–163.

Leeds, A.
1969 "The Significant variables determining the characteristics of Squatter settlements," *América Latina* 12(3): 44–86.
———, and L. Leeds.
1970 "Brazil and the Myth of Urban Rurality, Urban Experience, Work and Values in the 'Squatments' of Rio de Janeiro and Lima," in A. J. Field (ed.), *City and Country in the Third World.* Cambridge Mass.: Schenkman, 229–285.

Little, K.
1965 *West African Urbanization.* Cambridge, Eng.: Cambridge University Press.

MacEwen, A. M.
1972a "Stability and Change in a shanty town: a summary of some research findings," *Sociology* Vol. 6 No. 1: 41–57.
1972b "Kinship and Mobility on the Argentine Pampa." University of Essex, Department of Sociology. Unpublished Paper. April.
1972c "Differentiation amongst the Urban Poor: An Argentine Study." Unpublished Paper read to the British Sociological Association's Meeting in York, England. April.

Mangin, W. P.
1959 "The Role of Regional Associations in the Adaptation of Rural Population

in Peru," *Sociologus* 9(1): 23–35.

1967 "Latin American Squatter Settlements: A Problem and a Solution," *Latin American Research Review* 2(3): 65–98.

1968 "Poverty and Politics in Cities of Latin America," in Warner Bloomberg, Jr. and Henry J. Schmandt (eds.), *Power, Poverty and Urban Policy*. Beverly Hills: Sage Publications.

1970 (ed.) *Peasants in Cities*. Boston: Houghton Mifflin.

Marris, P.

1961 *Family and Social Change in an African City*. London: Routledge and Kegan Paul.

Mayer, P.

1961 *Townsmen or Tribesmen*. Oxford: Oxford University Press.

Mitchell, J. C.

1966 "Theoretical Orientations in African Urban Studies," in M. Banton (ed.), *The Social Anthropology of Complex Societies*. A.S.A. Monographs No. 4. London: Tavistock.

1969 (ed.) *Social Networks in Urban Situations*. Manchester: Manchester University Press.

Morse, R. M.

1971 "Trends and Issues in Latin American Urban Research 1965–1970," *Latin American Research Review* Vol. VI (1) 1971: 3–52 (Part I); Vol. VI (2) 1971: 19–75 (Part II).

Pahl, R. E.

1966 "The Rural-Urban Continuum," *Sociologia Ruralis* VI (3–4).

Ray, T.

1969 *The Politics of the Barrios*. Berkeley: University of California Press.

Roberts, B. R.

1968 "Politics in a neighbourhood of Guatemala City," *Sociology* 2(2): 185–203.

1970 "The Social Organization of low income families," in I. L. Horowitz (ed.), *Masses in Latin America*. New York: Oxford University Press, 345–382.

Salaff, Janet Weitzner.

1971 "Urban Residential Communities in the Wake of the Cultural Revolution," in J. W. Lewis (ed.), *The City in Communist China*. Stanford: Stanford University Press.

Tilly, C.

1969 "A travers le chaos des vivantes cités," in P. Meadows and E. Mizruchi (eds.), *Urbanism, Urbanization and Change*. Reading, Mass.: Addison-Wesley, 379–394.

Touraine, A.

1961 "Industrialisation et conscience ouvrière à Sao Paulo," *Sociologie du Travail* 3(4): 77–95.

Turner, J. F. C.

1969 "Uncontrolled Urban Settlement: Problems and Policies," in Gerald Breese (ed.), *The City in Newly Developing Countries*. Hemel Hempstead: Prentice-Hall.

1970 "Barriers and Channels for Housing Development in Modernising Countries," in Mangin, *Peasants in Cities*.

Vanderschueren, F.

1972 "Mobilisation politique et lutte pour le logement au Chili," *Espaces et Sociétés* 5: 21–29.

Planning
for
Community

Utopian Communities[*]

ROSABETH MOSS KANTER

Brandeis University
and
Harvard University

Utopian communities—an alternative community form—vary from large, comprehensive settlements in which most aspects of life are collectively organized to small informal households low on comprehensiveness and collectivization, like many contemporary communes. The initial stages, organizational problems, politics, and economic organization of both highly-structured large communes and minimally-structured small communes are discussed.

In the midst of present-day concern with the fate of cities and towns in modern nations and with the "loss of community" that is said to characterize advanced industrial societies, increasing numbers of people are turning to another community form. In this alternative they hope to regain closer, more fulfilling relationships and more control over their economic, political, and social life. This form of joint existence is the utopian community, formed by people who depart from conventional society and its established norms to establish their own territory on which they can create a unified social world based on utopian ideals and values and close, supportive relationships among members. Such settlements are *utopian* in that they are formed to create a more perfect, more fulfilling human existence in which people cooperate rather than compete, share goods and services rather than consume individually, have meaningful personal relationships, and attempt to bring all parts of life into harmony with each other. They are *communities* in that they involve, minimally, the sharing of living space, domestic life, an economy, and values, and maxi-

*Parts of this article have been adapted from *Communes: Creating and Managing the Collective Life*, New York: Harper and Row, 1973. Barry Stein and Bennett Berger provided helpful comments on this paper.

mally, occupy their own territories, run their own productive enterprises, comprise a political and a spiritual unit, and integrate family life with work life. Perhaps the best-known variety of utopian community is the contemporary commune, composed of a small number of people living collectively, sharing a house or a farm, in the midst of larger geographic communities. But communes and utopian communities of some kind have existed for centuries, and many of them were large enough to be towns or villages.

Writing about a subject as broad and barely researched as the "utopian community," in all of its forms and varieties, has inevitable limitations. First, some people might argue that present-day communes, particularly of the hip countercultural variety, are not utopian at all and should not, therefore, be discussed in the same breath with those alternative communities (such as Oneida, Twin Oaks, and the Israeli kibbutzim) that envision utopian world reform. Certainly, their primary thrust is elsewhere, perhaps back in the Garden of Eden rather than edging towards Utopia. But I think that there is value in viewing today's communal phenomena as manifestations of a recurrent urge to collectively create the perfect community; how contemporary hip communes differ from other collective communities can be made apparent by comparison. Second, the focus of this paper is on utopian communities as human organizations: how they come into being, how they manage their political and economic affairs. Such a focus ignores a wide range of important questions: the diversity of cultural flavors, ideas, and world views behind communal movements; the quality of interpersonal relationships; the meaning of communal phenomena in their historical and societal context. Concentrating on organization also means a bias toward examining the conditions for endurance or stability of various kinds of groups, even though it is entirely possible that some contemporary communes are intended from the outset to be temporary and disposable. With all of these limitations in mind, however, I argue that as a *community* form all variants of communal living have enough in common to warrant joint discussion: collective ownership or use of resources; interdependence of members through their joint work; deliberate, intentional formation in order to establish that kind of life-style members wish; and the valuing of fulfilling, spiritually sound human relationships above the accomplishment of any specific tasks. Some of these characteristics are captured in the words of a song from the Oneida community a nineteenth-century commune of over two hundred people that supported itself by light industry:

> We have built us a dome
> On our heavenly plantation
> And we all have one home
> And one family relation.

Utopian communities are distinguishable from one another, on the other hand, by their degrees of *collectivization* (how much of space, property, and relationships or family life are held or managed in common by all members) and *comprehensiveness* (how many parts of a person's life they contain within their own borders). At one extreme is a small urban commune which is low on both collectivization and comprehensiveness. Often without a name or stated purpose for the group, members live together in one house in the city but own little property in common, manage resources and relationships privately, work at outside jobs, and have separate political and spiritual affiliations and different sets of friends. These groups often have more in common with families than communities. At the other extreme is a fully collectivized, comprehensive communal village of several hundred such as the American Shakers or some Israeli kibbutzim: all property is owned jointly; resources are distributed by the collectivity; relationships are widely shared; close, intimate feelings throughout the group are expected; children are raised jointly; members have common religious and political affiliations, with the community itself a political entity; and practically all members work at community enterprises through which the whole group supports itself. Contemporary rural communes, such as the colorful "hippie" farms popularized by the mass media, fall somewhere in the middle on this continuum. Generally, the greater the degree of collectivization and comprehensiveness in the commune, the greater the group's purposefulness and intentionality, and the greater the accompanying need for order, organization, and joint planning. Smaller, less intentional groups, lower on these dimensions, have fewer areas necessitating collective decision making, and their joint life more often is characterized by spontaneity and informal rather than formally stated norms.

ORIGINS: VALUE-BASED SOCIAL MOVEMENTS

Utopian communities have grown out of radical social movements which combine rejection of the conventional society and its life-style with a vision of a better way to live and relate. One of the hallmarks of communes is an intense emphasis on developing and enhancing relationships within the group, often to the exclusion of any concern with the society around them— whether or not they are economically self-sufficient. If they wish to change or influence the surrounding society they hope to do it by example rather than by direct attack. By living a fulfilling and productive life themselves, they hope to demonstrate the satisfaction and viability of communal life to others, and eventually, more and more people will follow their lead and form utopian communities of their own—a revolutionary example. Thus, communes involve a certain measure of withdrawal, self-containment, and isolation. But such withdrawal is usually the final step. Generally, the groups forming communes have first come together in some direct radical action confronting and protesting a part of life in the established society. Many contemporary urban communes, for example, grew out of draft resistance movements or joint radical political action. Israeli kibbutzim developed from Zionist youth movements in Europe. A number of communes have grown out of radical religious sects. Synanon developed from a self-help group of drug addicts. Communes have grown out of many of the major social movements of their times, and so American communes have had roots and alliances with temperance, revivalism, spiritualism, abolitionism, anarchism, Pietism, money reform, socialism of the Owenite and Marxist varieties, feminism and women's rights, sexual experimentation, radical Catholicism, Zionism and liberal Judaism, the drug culture, the antidrug crusade, Eastern mysticsim, Christian homesteading, health fads (including a water cure in the nineteenth century and macrobiotics today) and new movements in psychotherapy. In the nineteenth century there were also radical attempts to create communes for black ex-slaves (Pease and Pease 1963).

Utopian communities develop at some times and places more than others. They arise out of the conjunction of two phenomena: a time of general social ferment, in which many people critically reassess the established order and strive to free themselves from its stresses; and the existence of utopian ideals, such as those carried by countercultures, which offer the possibility for new directions. Both factors (strain and idealism) are crucial in accounting for the historical development of communes and their appeal to educated, intellectual middle-class populations more than the poor and oppressed. B. F. Skinner published his utopian novel, *Walden Two*, in the late 1940s, but it was not until the social ferment of the 1960s that several groups tried to implement the Walden Two vision, and sales of the book dramatically increased. At the same time, to form radical communities as a response to social stress requires a measure of idealism and willingness to take risks; the benefits of such communities, in comparison to other social movements promising relief from strain, are relatively psychic, spiritual, and long-term.

David Plath (1969) contends that utopian communities develop when the stresses and strains of modernization or industrial expansion are most acute. The biggest wave of founding of communes in the nineteenth century in the United States began, according to Seymour Bassett, "... when the strains caused by American expansion were most acute. The shocks of this period were delivered by a new industrial system which was recognized but little understood and which operated in an unevenly but swiftly broadening market area ..." (Egbert and Persons 1952: 156). We may add, as another stressful situation, the costs of an unpopular or unsuccessful war such as the war in Vietnam or the German defeat in World War I.

Certain periods, then, contribute more than their share of utopian communities and communes: 1820–1860 in the United States, peaking around 1840; 1900–1930 in Japan; the 1920s in Germany. The response to such strains is often a movement of "revitalization," as Anthony Wallace termed it, from religious revivalism to movements promising a new relationship with God, with nature, or with other people (Wallace 1956). Such movements are deliberate, organized, conscious efforts to construct a more satisfying culture that promises a more immediate connection with God or with fellow human beings.

Many of the communes developing in these periods start first as part of another, more general movement. Both the Bruderhof and many kibbutzim had early connections with various German youth movements of the early twentieth century; in the case of the kibbutz, the outlook was mixed with Zionism, or the desire to establish a Jewish state. The German youth movement of the 1920s stressed themes similar to that of today's American communal counterculture: the regeneration of the individual and the society; the need to leave the city and return to nature; an asceticism connected with self-purification; and the collective joy of being together in an immediate emotional way and building a new life.

It is no accident that many communes develop from urban youth movements, and often middle-class youth. Young people are still available for mobilization; they have not yet made the life choices which may then serve to lock them into the established society. Middle-class urban youth, in particular, tend to be relatively well-educated and philosophically sophisticated; they are more likely to be motivated and mobilized by ideals and conceptions of the ideal community. A similar freedom to choose deviant alternatives is also experienced by the dispossessed and disinherited, the people on the fringes of society; yet without the idealism, they do not form communes. Jewish youth in Eastern Europe in the early twentieth century experienced both idealism and discrimination; the discrimination, the low status of Jewry, helped bring them together and make them available for migration to Palestine. Similar experiences of persecution undergone by religious groups in Europe and Japan led to migration and the establishment of communal orders; Harmony and Amana are among the nineteenth-century American communes founded by immigrant groups who came to the United States to escape prejudice. The combination of their deviance, pushing them out of the conventional established society where they had lived, and their religious idealism, giving them a vision of a better way of life, helped lead to the founding of several communes in America.

Neil Smelser's five-stage model for the development of collective behavior is applicable to the establishment of utopian communities (Smelser 1962). *Structural conduciveness* has already been discussed: at some times and in some societies, more than others, social conditions make it likely that instances of collective behavior will develop. The second factor is *structural strain*, or the experience of deprivation. This experience can be brought about by prejudice, discrimination, or the deprivation of freedom or by an incongruence between expectations and experience. (The latter phenomena are behind the frequently made statement that most revolutions occur when times are beginning to get better, because expectations rise faster than the possibilities for their fulfillment.) Attempts to account for the rise of American youth communes at the end of the 1960s call upon both of these factors: the Vietnam war threatened a deprivation of freedom; sanctions against drugs and long hair pushed many young people farther out; the permissiveness and love-orientation with which many of the postwar generation were raised led them to expect more love and warmth from adult life than impersonal institutions could provide.

Smelser's third factor is the existence of *generalized beliefs*. These are ideas, values, and emotional symbols that prepare people for action, that help them identify the sources of strain they experience and means for its solution. A set of beliefs is created which makes sense out of the weakness of the society and provides directions for its renewal. We have already discussed many of the beliefs behind communes and the frameworks of thought and even specific books which inspired them. Beliefs provide a general readiness for action; *precipitating events* often crystallize it. These are dramatic events which give the generalized beliefs concrete, immediate substance. Such events might include a pogrom (riot against the Jews) in Europe which finally moves a youth group to leave for Palestine and eventually start a kibbutz; or as in one Vermont commune, a conflict among members of the Liberation News Service in New York, crystallizing the desire of some to leave for a communal farm (Diamond 1971); or, in the case of the Shakers, the precipitating event could be the jailing of their founder, Ann Lee, and her visions in jail, bringing about the sect's movement to the United States; or, in the case of a Japanese commune, ostracism from the village (Plath 1966). Precipitating events are "radicalizing experiences" or, informally "the straws that break the camel's back."

Mobilization for action, Smelser's fifth factor, brings the movement together. Such mobilization most often occurs through the actions of leaders. Communes are often organized by one person who provides the initiative or becomes the symbolic representation of the group. Many communes are first brought together by charismatic leaders, persons whose dramatic presence and felt connection with larger ideals and transcendent sources of wisdom make other people willing to follow them. The history of communalism is dotted with such figures, both male and female. John Humphreys Noyes, a radical preacher, began a Bible class in his home in Putney, Vermont, that led to migration to Oneida, New York, in 1848. Eberhard Arnold provided the inspiration and the message for the Bruderhof (Zablocki 1971). And there are other well-known charismatic founders: Ann Lee of the Shakers, George Rapp of Harmony, and today, Charles Dederich of Synanon, Mel Lyman of Fort Hill, and Michael Metelica of The Brotherhood of the Spirit. Their messages have attracted followers and led to the creation of communities.

In other cases, one person may also aid mobilization, not by organizing and leading the movement but by providing facilities for it. The existence of one wealthy person with money, willing to offer money or land for the purposes of starting a commune, has also occurred in communal history. The most dramatic instance of this is Robert Owen's founding of New Harmony in 1825. This English industrialist bought an existing communal village from George Rapp's Harmony Society (which wished to move back to Pennsylvania) and then advertised for "the well-disposed of all nations" to join his community. The experiment was not successful, dissolving after two years, and the fact that Owen himself was generally absent from New Harmony has been considered one reason for its failure. Another example was Morningstar Ranch in California begun in 1966 and later closed by health authorities. Wealthy folksinger Lou Gottlieb bought the land, deeded it to God, and opened it to all comers. Flocks of hippies appeared, but the community was later closed by sanitation officials (Gustaitis 1969; Lamott 1968).

Mobilization can also occur through group interaction without the presence of a single, charismatic leader. Identifiable, historically known charismatic founders are conspicuously absent from kibbutz history, for example. The egalitarian ethic of much of the radical movement and commune culture today militates against any one person attaining pre-eminence and suggests that the impetus for establishing the commune should grow out of the interactions of the group members themselves. Discussion between members of a small group can not only reinforce members' beliefs in the rightness of their rejection of the established society and choice of alternatives, but also raise the stakes, impelling further action and making it harder for members to back out without losing face. Discussion groups or radical movement meetings have also prompted the founding of communes as diverse in times as Brook Farm, developed in the 1840s from a group of transcendentalist intellectuals and literary figures meeting in Boston, and many Boston communes, started over 120 years later in the same area, out of discussions by political organizers, intellectuals, and disaffected young professionals. Other communes start from conferences or meetings specifically designed to bring people interested in communes together.

EARLY STAGES OF ORGANIZATION

Most utopian communities do not start with a blueprint or a detailed plan for their life together. They begin, rather, with their discontent, some general ideals, and more-or-less vague notions about how to implement these ideals. As David Plath indicates:

> Few Utopian groups begin by drawing detailed plans for the new life. . . . None of the Japanese leaders did much programming, nor did many Western utopians other than Fourier and Cabet. Most of them set out with nothing more than a small fund of general principles—all things in common, or selfless service, or natural living—plus a great fund of discontent with the status quo, and a reservoir of determination to change it drastically. (Plath 1964: 4)

In case after case, this general principle is underscored: communes develop their arrangements gradually out of the critical issues they face as new social orders with general goals. The goals or ideals by themselves are not completely determinant of social organization. And those groups that do make detailed advance plans sometimes have to change them as they confront the realities of joint life. The Shakers, for example, did not adopt communalism until after Ann Lee's (the sect founder's) death; it was a response to their desire to retire to their own land where they could practice their religion in peace. Communal institutions developed one by one. Similarly, Harmony and other immigrant religious groups adopted economic communism first out of financial necessity; it was justified by religious principles and later became part of community ideology.

Even the most organized nineteenth-century communes did not spring into being full-blown from a blueprint. Instead, they went through periods of chaos, nondirection, high turnover, and open boundaries as they struggled to translate global ideals about community into specific behavior. The example of the Bruderhof illustrates this. The Bruderhof are now over fifty years old and well organized. But in their early years in Germany, the community struggled with issues of developing a group identity and defining the group's boundaries. In fact, during its first summer, the now traditional straightlaced, and organized religious group resembled many of today's new communes. It began with no financial resources, with an open-door policy to welcome all comers (and was consequently flooded with strange characters and curiosity seekers), and with no clear notion of how to translate ideology into practice. The numbers of people grew and declined (more in the summer, fewer in winter), living conditions were primitive, and the vast majority of members came from urban backgrounds and knew nothing of farming. They rented rather than owned their quarters. But group cohesion was prompted through song and celebration of all events, from picking up stones to hoeing beans. And out of the interaction of the diverse people who came together, group coherence gradually developed. The first crisis dealt with how the group would support itself, finding a task in which cooperation and shared fate would be embodied. Ideological and practical disagreements led to the definition of boundaries; who would become a member and who would not; which characteristics of members would be supported and which changed; what was the focus of the group (Arnold 1971; Zablocki 1971).

For other groups, practices also grew out of daily interactions and circumstances encountered after the initial decision to form a commune was made. The extent of a well-defined prior blueprint for community varied from group to group, but many practices were a result of communal values plus the practical requirements of building a group. Ideology both informed and justified choices. The contemporary Twin Oaks commune is an illuminating example, for it did have a clear blueprint in Skinner's *Walden Two*, the inspiration for its founding. Yet here, too, the first months were spent in an anarchistic system without structure or organization. Out of demands and limits of that situation systems for group order gradually emerged, and five years later, in 1972, they are still emerging. Many of the formal practices have been borrowed from *Walden Two* or guided by it, but many of the informal ones have grown out of members' interactions in a situation in which they are working out their relationships with one another and developing group coherence (Kanter 1972; Kincaid 1973).

The ideologies and social practices of communes, then, can be seen as more than an outgrowth of utopian values. They are the solutions arrived at in face-to-face interactions and daily life to the crucial issues all new and noninstitutionalized social groups face. Philip Selznick (1961) discusses several of the critical decisions all organizations must make early in their history, and we can see in the histories of communes a grappling with similar issues. The first decision he calls selection of a social base. That is, the group must decide on its stance with respect to the outside world— its mission, clientele, market, target, and allies—where its resources lie. For communes, this is often translated into questions about how the group will support itself, how dependent it will be on the outside. Stephen Diamond's rural commune, for example, faced questions of income and mortgage payments (Diamond 1971).

Selznick's second critical decision is the building of an "institutional core"—a homogeneous core who came to agree upon and reflect the basic ideals and politics of the organization. Communes struggle with variants of this issue in their early days; membership turnover is generally high, as people test their feelings about the group and each other. The ideology is specified and discussed, and ideological disagreements help pare the group down to believers. The group establishes its boundaries: who and what behavior it will tolerate. An "open-door" policy is characteristic of the early days of many communes, especially today's open-land hippie communes; doors begin to close soon after, however, as the group experiences the costs of too many visitors, too little responsibility, or too much turnover. Recruitment policies are set. Even among today's hippie communes, the doors have been reluctantly closed after too much openness created trouble for the group.

The final critical decision Selznick discusses is "formalization of procedure," the establishment of regularity and order. For some communes norms and procedures develop informally; in others, they require formal decisions and rules. There comes a point in the life of most communes where decisions must be made about the agreements and procedures of the group. The joyful period of spontaneity, freedom, and anarchism many communes experience in their early days may be beautiful, but it is also inherently unstable. According to Benjamin Zablocki,

> Most communes start out with no restrictions on behavior. Everyone is allowed to do his own thing at all times. It is expected that the gentleness, love, and compassion engendered by mystical drug experiences (or in other ways) will prove adequate substitutes for the moral and legal constraints which all other societies have found necessary. The initial experiences are often encouraging and exhilarating. . . . After a while, however, the strains inherent in such situations begin to reassert themselves. . . . Increased strain on one hand, and more complex tasks on the other, eventually lead most communes to abandon their absolute anarchism in favor of some more restricted alternative. (1971: 308–309)

At some point, members must decide how to divide the work, whether to pool all of their property, how to define interpersonal relationships, how to resolve interpersonal conflicts. Such issues are inherent in the process of life together. For example, a commune can exist for a time without deciding how to handle income and property by living on whatever members bring in. But what happens when the initial reserve is exhausted or when a new piece of equipment is needed? At such points the group begins to formalize its procedures and set its future course. These three general organizational issues are termed "critical decisions" because if they are not confronted, the likelihood of the group's dissolving in conflict is increased.

Even though the full flowering of communal social organization is slow to develop, a commune can weather early crises if it has a firm basis for cohesion. Strong shared beliefs and ritual experiences of togetherness provide such a basis for cohesion and perhaps are responsible for the strength and long life of such groups as the Bruderhof and the kibbutz. Melford Spiro's account of one kibbutz indicates that even before the members were actually on their own land, they found cohesion in their ideals and in Chasidism, an aspect of Judaism that helps promote ritual, joyousness, and intensely emotional religious experience (Spiro 1956). Similarly, the Bruderhof were very religious from the beginning and found much joy and solidarity in their collective celebrations, rituals, and shared Christian beliefs (Arnold 1971).

PROBLEMS OF ORGANIZATION

In general, communal groups desire a shared way of life that breaks down barriers between people, ensures feelings of participation, ends exclusive possession in favor of sharing, and bases life on values. Such aims involve difficult problems of social organization. In utopia, who takes out the garbage? The first issue with which a commune must cope is its human organization: how people come to do the work that the commune needs to survive as a group and how the group in turn manages to satisfy and involve its members. Communes grapple with the following organization problems:

1. How to get the work done, but without coercion;

2. How to ensure that decisions are made, but to everyone's satisfaction;

3. How to build close, fulfilling relationships, but without exclusiveness;

4. How to choose and socialize new members;

5. How much autonomy, individual uniqueness, and even deviance to tolerate;

6. How to ensure agreement and shared perception around community functioning and values.

Many of these issues can be summarized as ones of commitment: how members become committed to the commune's work, to its values, and to each other, and how much of their former independence they are willing to suspend in the interests of the group. Committed members are loyal and involved. They derive their rewards from participation, they have a sense of belonging, and they feel that the values of the group are an expression of their innermost selves. They work hard, participate actively, derive love and affection from the communal group, and believe strongly in what the group stands for.

Organizing in such a way as to build commitment is thus a crucial problem for communes. Research on nineteenth-century communes helps illuminate the kinds of commitment mechanisms, or commitment-producing social arrangements, that contribute to a group's success (Kanter 1968, 1972). This study compares nine long-lived communes ("successful") with twenty-one short-lived ones ("unsuccessful") in order to learn about those ways of organizing a commune that build commitment. Whether or not one agrees that longevity is a sufficient criterion of success, the groups with many commitment mechanisms at least had the strength to endure over time rather than dissolve at the first signs of trouble.

"Successful" nineteenth-century communes built strong commitment through the kinds of sacrifices and investments members made for and in the community; they gave up something and invested something in order to belong, thereby gaining a stake in the fate of the group. They built cohesiveness and group solidarity through discouraging extragroup ties and building strong family feeling within the community, by sharing property and work, and through rituals of communion. Finally, they enhanced the meaningfulness of their way of life through identity change processes which helped people cast away previous noncommunal habits and through elaborate ideologies, strong value systems and authority structures which provided order and direction for the community. Commitment-building arrangements include those aspects of communal life that many people value most: shared property, group symbols and rituals, and personal growth opportunities. *Commitment and Community* (Kanter 1972) describes such arrangements in detail.

Lessons from other enduring communes confirm the value of such commitment practices. In order to participate and believe fully in a new way of life, members must both shake off vestiges of the old way and gain a sense of the joys of the new—the two sides of commitment.

In particular, communes face the problem of resocialization: building community with people who often have no previous training in communal living and must learn to accept the rigors and stresses as well as the benefits. Benjamin Zablocki (1971) has observed that one of the lessons of the Bruderhof communes is that nothing less than total rebirth of the self will do to create people suitable to live together in community. Commitment mechanisms are a step toward this emergence of a new identity.

Long-lived communes of the past did not shy away from structuring and regulating their group life. But many contemporary communes start on entirely opposite premises: that the good community was one with no ways of ensuring that work get done, no fixed decision making procedures, and no clear limitations on individual behavior. Such communes as Morningstar Ranch in California tolerated a maximum of individual freedom and had no way of regulating behavior or resolving conflict (Lamott 1968). These characteristics make them extremely vulnerable both to outside pressures and to internal tensions and ultimately spell the end of the community. The comments of some members make it clear that they may have preferred more order and regulation; commitment mechanisms may make a more satisfying as well as a stronger group.

Commitment is made more possible where there are strong shared beliefs casting the community and its life in a spiritual framework. The Shakers provide a good illustration. Shaker spiritual principles informed practically every aspect of daily life in the community; their rituals provided communion and solidarity. The Shaker communes were strongly regulated and tightly controlled. Yet, the same spiritualism that led to the controls also provided outlets for tension among commune members.

Shaker spiritualism was full of rich imaginative fantasies. The dance and shaking ritual helped release tensions built up during the day; in many ways, these experiences resembled contemporary encounter groups. Often members had a chance to express love or interpersonal conflicts and to enjoy physical movement and fantasy in the Shaker spiritual exercises (Andrews 1962, 1963).

Another example of the kinds of commitment mechanisms growing out of shared beliefs is group confrontation, practiced by Oneida in the last century as "mutual criticism" and by contemporary groups as "encounter," or "feedback," or "sensitivity" sessions. Such sessions function simultaneously as an instrument of social control and group regulation and also a means for releasing and resolving tensions. Members receive feedback about their behavior oriented toward maintaining group norms as well as praise for their strong points. At the same time, feedback sessions permit the release and resolution of interpersonal tensions, the expression of grievances and strong positive feelings, that enable the group to develop warmth and solidarity.

Striking a balance between control and freedom, between order and spontaneity, is a difficult organizational problem for a commune. Too little order and organization may result in chaos, dissatisfaction, tension, and vulnerability to outside pressures. Too much order may result in an authoritarian system that requires rules and regulations, suppression, surveillance, and "brainwashing." Communes have been criticized for both sins. Hippie communes of the spontaneous, unorganized "openland" types (such as Morningstar) have been criticized for their primitive life, transience, chaos, and their lack of group feeling. Strong communes such as the Shakers, Oneida, and Synanon have been criticized for their suppression of the individual and, because of their large size, for hierarchical and authoritarian structures. How much commitment and social control is necessary to create a commune that is viable as well as satisfying is an important philosophic and moral issue for community builders (Kanter 1972, chapters 5 and 9).

TYPES OF GOVERNMENT

The politics of group life pervade practically every other aspect of a community's existence, for how a group distributes power and leadership functions and makes its collective decisions helps shape its character. Even the least collectivized and comprehensive communes must find a way to make and enforce the necessary joint decisions.

The first type of communal political system is a legal-rationalistic one characteristic of large groups of the past rather than the new, smaller hip communes. In such a system appointed or elected officeholders administer on the basis of stated and enacted "rules." The communal version of legal-rationalistic systems involves contracts or agreements whereby the group makes some specified decisions as an entity based on a stated principle (majority vote, consensus, etc.) and delegates other decisions and responsibilities to agents, individuals, or committees, elected by the group or appointed by current officeholders. Legal democratic authority generally involves formal procedures or routines and stated expectations, rules, or guidelines, as in a constitution. Legal-rationalistic systems in communes may include a definable structure of positions of authority and responsibility, as in a formal organization. Such forms of organized democracy tend to be found in groups of larger size whose philosophy or complexity does not permit participation by everyone in every decision. They involve delegation of fixed tasks and assigned areas of responsibility to committees, councils, or elected officials. In groups like the kibbutz with egalitarian ethics such officeholders rotate as frequently as possible, as many members as possible occupy leadership positions, and group forums retain control over major decisions.

The "direct democracy" of the Israeli kibbutzim has changed from the early days because of the kibbutzim's current stage of size and complexity. The foundations of kibbutz democracy are the general meeting, an organizational structure permitting rotation of members through functions, and a committee structure. In its early days of small size, homogeneous population, and agricultural base, a kibbutz could easily operate a direct democracy in which general meetings of the whole commune made all decisions. Specialization was limited, people could easily rotate jobs, and the general meetings were small enough to give people a voice in decisions. With increasing size, complexity, and heterogeneity, however, direct democracy does not work as well. The average member's awareness of commune affairs is decreasing, and impersonal rules and regulations are increasing. The need for specialization and formal education as the economic base of the kibbutz shifts from agriculture to industry limits job rotation. Some kibbutz members are undergoing formal training in managerial skills, and there is a danger that a managerial class will be created unless more members receive similar education. Research by Menachem Rosner (1970, 1973) also shows that as the size of a kibbutz increases there is a slight tendency for participation to decrease. The kibbutz experience indicates that direct democracy, then, may weaken with size and complexity of task, and a commune that grows too large or complex may become transformed into an impersonal bureaucracy. One challenge that the kibbutz faces in the future is to remain communal and egalitarian in the face of industrialization.

What John Bennett (1967) calls the Hutterites' "managed democracy" is slightly different. It is more authoritarian and less egalitarian than the

kibbutz system. It involves less participation by members and more control
by officials. As such, it has some similarities to communes directed by
charismatic leaders. There is another fundamental difference: whereas the
kibbutzim are secular communes interested in increasing affluence and
contact with the wider society, the Hutterian colonies are religious and
interested in maintaining austerity and withdrawal from the world. These
goals require more control by the community in order to combat "worldly
temptations" and maintain faith. Whereas kibbutzim often number their
populations in the thousands, the Hutterites deliberately maintain colonies
of 150. Each colony is governed by elders—religious leaders—and elected
managers, with policy made by councils. Once elected, managers have
great power. They patrol the boundaries of behavior, watching and setting
limits, approving expenditures, maintaining uniformity of consumption
so as to prevent feelings of deprivation, and shielding members from outside influences. Bennett indicates that this system works because members
are socialized to it from birth; because managers generally exercise their
power benignly, showing flexibility in enforcing rules; and because the
promise of responsibility is offered, through rotation giving everyone a
chance at managerial jobs.

The Hutterite submission to authority is even more characteristic of
communes centered around charismatic leaders, Weber's second type of
legitimate rule. Charisma as a basis for decision making involves guidance
of the group by one person invested with special, magical characteristics.
This leadership system is found frequently in the history of communes,
partly because they often coalesce around the spiritual teachings of the
charismatic person, and partly because investing authority in one person
provides a center for the group and avoids troublesome issues of group
decision making. According to Weber's classic definition, charismatic
authority is based on the personal devotion of the followers to the lord.
The charismatic's "gifts of grace" include magical abilities, revelations and
inspirations, and extraordinary powers of mind and speech. He or she is
capable of inspiring in followers a felt connection with a higher order,
nonroutine, system of meaning which moves them to exclusive obedience
to the leader. Other secondary authority figures gain their positions through
their special relationship to the charismatic.

Jemimah Wilkinson, the "universal friend," is a typical charismatic
leader of the nineteenth century. Her followers invested her with the power
of Jesus and established the community of Jerusalem. Similarly, the Shakers
felt that Ann Lee was the female half of the godhead. Oneidans believed
John Humphrey Noyes to be a permanent medium of Christ, and Oneida
women at one time signed a petition declaring that they belonged first to
God and second to John Humphrey Noyes. Today, followers of Michael
Metelica of Brotherhood of the Spirit (Warwick, Massachusetts) and
Allen Noonan of Messiah's World Crusade (San Francisco) make similar

claims to divinity. Members of Synanon often deny the divinity of their charismatic leader, Charles Dederich, but they attribute to him every other valuable quality and revere him in other ways.

Charismatic leaders often exercise their authority benignly and do not maintain total control even though their very existence may be seen as undemocratic. Oneida, for example, combined Noyes's spiritual guidance with participatory democracy. Daily evening meetings kept members informed and gave them a voice in decisions; a system of committees conducted the routine business of the community. The Harmony Society (1805–1905) had a dual leadership structure in its early years. George Rapp, the charismatic founder, handled spiritual matters while someone else managed other affairs. When the charismatic leader died, many communes of the past substituted either organized democracy or hierarchical systems like the Shakers' structure of elders.

Systems based on charisma also bring dangers, however, for it is sometimes difficult to tell what distinguishes them from totalitarian groups. The Synanon system has been called "brainwashing" by critics, for example, and Charles Dederich a "megalomaniac." Unquestioned devotion gives the charismatic leader immense power. "True belief" may obscure moral concerns and encourage followers to deny their own moral conscience and autonomy and to follow the leader blindly down paths which might otherwise inspire moral outrage. These dangers are certainly atypical of communes in general, even those centered around charismatic leaders, because most communes have at least minimal ethics which involve principles of equality and respect for human life and personal dignity. There are a few instances, however, which should be examined for their revelation of the negative potential in charismatic systems.

Fort Hill in Roxbury, Massachusetts, is one such instance. Mel Lyman's charisma is turned to ends that would not be applauded by everyone. Though described as insignificant and weak-looking, he has inspired famous jugband leader, Jim Kweskin, rock writer Paul Williams, and a former nun to join his following. (Fort Hill has a musical group, as does Brotherhood of the Spirit.) Like other charismatics, Mel is seen as a "whole different kind of person 'invested with divinity'." His followers take it as their mission to educate unbelievers, commenting "the whole world's going to be his community." (At least one member of Synanon has made the same remark about Synanon.) This devotion makes people willing to start again at the bottom regardless of former status, to live a life of austerity in the black ghetto of Roxbury, Massachusetts, to submit to the exercise of arbitrary authority in the guise of helping, and to be willing to engage in violence. David Felton's report (1971) that members of Fort Hill admire the Mafia and Hitler is indicative.

The third major communal political system involves no organized system of government at all. It is a kind of disorder in which it is assumed that decisions will be made spontaneously when needed, that individuals with good intentions will adjust their behavior so as to cooperate with one another, and that no formal rules, structures, or leaders are necessary. Such a system of disorder can be termed "naïve anarchism" to distinguish it from anarchism as a serious political philosophy, which believes in humanity's capacity to govern itself in the absence of authority through people's willingness to adjust their behavior to one another. Naïve anarchism, on the other hand, simply asserts the right of every person to "do his own thing" in the absence of any moral or social constraints. Says Zablocki,

> The anarchist strain [in communes] has little or nothing to do with the classical anarchism of the nineteenth century or the political and philosophical anarchist thinking of today. It is a naive anarchism, a *sui generis* response to specific conditions of post-industrial society. In part, it is a rebellion against the phony freedom of this society. . . . (1971: 306)

Disorder is especially characteristic of contemporary rural youth communes. Many of these begin with a desire to be free and open, to escape from the city and from what they experience as the oppressiveness of the larger society. They resist leadership and organization. "Doing your own thing" is a pervasive ethic in these communes, one which legitimates the right of each person to resist demands made by anyone else. In *Commitment and Community* (1972) I discuss disorder and its limits in rural retreat communes. Disorder in these groups is easier to define by what is absent rather than what is present. Members tend to come together out of friendship and shared rejection of the larger society, but they tend to lack an integrating philosophy, a set of affirmative principles which order and give meaning to group life and provide a basis for decision making. They are unwilling to erect boundaries which close the group or limit the freedom of members. In early stages they wish to be open to all comers and often are overrun with new members or visitors, making it difficult to build a sense of groupness. They tend to have few rules and little discernible order, so that a variety of needs and practices exist side-by-side uneasily, and there is no guarantee that the work gets done. People come and go as they choose, work or not as they choose. In short, such communes as an ideal type tend to be negative rather than affirmative, inclusive rather than exclusive, and permissive rather than strict.

These communes tend to dissolve easily; the average life of rural youth communes is only a year or two. Or, they revert to a less communal situation in which the group becomes a loose federation of separate individuals and families, as did Freedom Farm. Or, finally, they gradually institute a decision making and authority structure based on either charisma or democratic principles. The history of Twin Oaks illustrates this last progression. For a few months, the original eight members of the commune tried a kind of consensual anarchy with no assigned responsibilities. Gradually a loose kind of specialization evolved, with some people exercising control over a particular domain and making decisions without consulting the others. Dissatisfaction with such an ad hoc system led to the beginnings of organized democracy in the labor credit and manager-planner systems. Even with such a small group as eight, Twin Oaks experienced the limits of disorder. .

Zablocki (1971) describes both the joys and the problems of unstructured communes. He characterizes the hippie communes he studied as composed of a blend of naïve anarchism—a belief that authority itself is evil and that no information outside of one's own experience is valid—and antinomianism—a belief that intuition and immediate visceral reactions are a sufficient guide to behavior without the constraints of moral law. Such lack of restrictions, rules, controls, leadership, or organized decision making results, according to Zablocki, in a brief, exhilarating "golden age" in which the communes experience the joys of total individual freedom. What decisions need to be made are worked out in long, intense meetings. Conflicts eventually arise, however, involving jealousies and hatreds, the power of any one member to immobilize the group from action by refusing to contribute to consensus, exploitation of weaker members by stronger, and the group's inability to induce any member to work. Naïve anarchism is essentially a personal means of group regulation, relying on intimacy and mutual tolerance and bound together only by members' knowledge of one another's behavior, moods, and preferences. Understandings are tacit rather than formally stated. Whim or short-term preference dictate who does what job and how. Thus, new members are not easily integrated, and the group is subject to destruction by changes in individual desires or interpersonal tensions.

Zablocki also describes several modifications of disorder that communes adopt. Segmentation involves dividing into smaller units which essentially go their own way, requiring few areas of group agreement. But is this loose federation of individuals and families still a commune, or have they given in to the individualistic tendencies inherent in anarchism? Some people would argue that when Freedom Farm deserted the community center in favor of individual dwellings and minimal cooperative enterprises, it lost much of its communal flavor. The second modification involves contracts, stated agreements among members, worked out in meetings. Another involves group decisions based on consensus; some action is taken, again in meetings, but decisions must be satisfactory to everyone. The search for consensus has limitations of its own: such meetings are often time consuming and tedious, may generate compromise solutions satisfactory to no one, and may limit the group's action to areas where agreement is possible.

Impatient with disorder but unwilling to settle for a fixed distribution of authority, some groups adopt rotating leadership. A New Hampshire commune developed a system whereby each member, including children, was "guru" for a week. The guru assigned people to jobs and exercised unlimited authority. The commune felt there was little danger that anyone would abuse his power as guru, since in a week he would be out of office and subject to reprisals by the next guru.

Many modifications of the three major kinds of commune political systems exist. In small minimally organized communes in which decisions are supposed to be consensual, as in any society, informal relationships among members often dictate that some get their way more than others. The owner of the land, the person who put in the most money, the more verbal members, the people quickest to seize initative—these people often have more power over the course of the group despite stated norms that everyone has an equal voice. Seniority systems develop, too, in which the oldest members become the most influential (Gardner 1973). In all utopian communities, from the largest organized democracies to the smallest urban commune, informal power hierarchies may develop and group pressures become a form of social control, insuring that some people strongly influence others. (See Bennett 1967, Kanter 1972a and 1973b for a discussion of coercive processes in communes.)

A community's formal political system partly relates to its size and stage of development. Disorder tends to be characteristic of groups of small size and in early stages of development, as that form tends to be unstable over time. Organized democracies are found in older, larger groups, which cannot govern themselves by spontaneity, consensus, or participation of everyone in every decision. Charismatic leaders tend to be found in groups with a mission, often strongly spiritual in character. The type of political system developed is also a function of the work a commune has chosen for economic support, as we shall see in the next section.

TYPES OF ECONOMIC ARRANGEMENTS

One of the defining principles of communalism is the integration of economic and social life. Regardless of the specific type of economy and source of income a commune exhibits, economic decisions generally will be made in light of the social and egalitarian ideals of the group and in such a way as to enhance cooperation and brotherhood.

Communes adopt one of three primary economic stances. Some, particularly nineteenth-century American groups, sought to become comprehensive villages, economically self-sufficient, producing whatever they needed for their own use. Such groups develop their own internal supports. They may trade with the outside, but this trade is not primary. Others, like the Bruderhof and other contemporary communes, develop one or more specialized enterprises whose income through outside exchanges enables the group to acquire whatever else it needs for internal consumption. A third set of communes, particularly contemporary rural hip groups and urban communes, do not develop internal means of support and remain dependent on participation in external enterprises. The first group can be called economic *generalists*, the second economic *specialists*, and the third, *dependents*.

Oneida, the Shakers, and the North American Phalanx, are examples of generalists. Oneida was a small-scale but comprehensive village with internal workshops meeting the needs of the community, including a shoe shop, tailor shop, tin shop, laundry, and a dentist's office. The Amana Society (1843–1933), a group of seven communal villages in Iowa, provides another illustration. Amana's goal was to make products primarily for its own use and only secondarily to trade surplus. The communities tried to produce all the food they consumed, and each village has its own tailor, tinsmith, shoemaker, harnessmaker, blacksmith, and watchmaker; in the last part of the nineteenth century there were also three Society physicians.

The Society of Brothers (Bruderhof), Cedar Grove, and Tail of the Tiger, all contemporary communes, are examples of specialists: communities whose work consists of one or two primary income-producing enterprises, the profit from which is used to buy other goods and services needed by the group. The Bruderhof manufactures Community Playthings, a line of wooden toys, and runs a small publishing house. These enterprises support communities in New York, Connecticut, and Pennsylvania. Cedar Grove, a spiritual community in New Mexico, has a license to cut trees from a national forest and sell lumber. Tail of the Tiger runs a meditation center in Vermont and supports itself through its programs.

Many communes today, both urban and rural, are examples of dependents. The bulk of their income comes from outside employment or, in some cases, unearned sources such as welfare, government food stamps, scholarships, or special windfalls (Berger, Hackett, and Millar 1971).

For those groups that do try to create an alternative economic system, there are many more failures than successes. Yet some long-lived communes have often achieved dramatic economic and material successes. The kibbutzim continue to contribute much more than their proportional share to the Israeli economy. Christiana Knoedler of Harmony boasted of that community's achievements by 1830, six years after settling in the commune's third village, aptly named Economy (Knoedler 1954). The group had by then built dwellings, a church, a Great House for the leadership, a music hall, several factories, a heated washhouse run by steam, and a community store to which neighbors came from miles around. In the 1850s the commune began investing excess capital in railroad and canal bonds. Shaker enterprises were also notably successful, and the Bruderhof's current toy business is only held back by community concerns about the effects of too much prosperity.

Partly responsible for these successes and pervading communal existence in general, is the meaningfulness of work in communes. It is an explicit ideal of such groups that work be meaningful and infused with the communal spirit. Communal labor is meant to be unalienated labor. Thus, Berger, Hackett, and Millar (1971) report that contemporary hip communes are "anti-industry" unless the work is coupled with meaning and intrinsic value in line with commune beliefs, and, ideally, inseparable from play. Not surprisingly, group enterprises are more frequently found in those contemporary communes with some kind of religious or spiritual creed, for this creed gives meaning to the enterprise and promotes commitment to a relatively regularized "devotion to duty."

In communes work has a social as well as a spiritual meaning; it is part of an attempt to promote brotherhood and equality. For this reason many communes organize work in such a way as to make possible job rotation and group work efforts, both of which enhance a sense of participation in a meaningful, collective effort. Commune members do not specialize in the way that noncommune workers often do; "career" is not a communal concept, at least as it refers to occupation. Hutterites, for example, generally can perform at least two jobs requiring special skills along with a variety of more general tasks. Members of Synergia, a contemporary New Mexican group, all participated in at least three jobs: a private, money making venture, an ecological experiment in such areas as solar heat or hydrophonics, and acting in the commune's performing theater troupe. At Twin Oaks a positive value is placed on members learning to do as many jobs as possible. The commune code states that individuals are not to preserve their special skills as a private domain.

Job rotation is characteristic of many communes of the past and present. The Shakers rotated work assignments not only to maintain collective unity but also to recognize native ability, promote individual initiative, and enhance the satisfactions of variety in work. Men often had two or more specialties, as varied as weaver, editor, and preacher. Women also rotated through a variety of chores. Oneida jobs were assigned by committees and rotated after a period of months. Kibbutz jobs rotate where possible. Jobs requiring specialization may remain fixed for longer periods than more general work; every kibbutz member is still supposed to do his turn in the dining room, just as members of the North American Phalanx did a century ago. Some communes even assign work by the week, increasing the possibilities for rotation. The Twin Oaks labor credit manager does this weekly, as do the Hutterite elders and managers on Sunday evenings.

Communal work efforts, occasions on which large groups gather to collectively perform tasks, are also common. Agricultural work lends itself especially well to such efforts—harvest tasks such as corn picking and apple gathering—as does construction. When contemporary communes work outside as a group, they often work on building, barn raising, or house painting.

Communes also tend to consider both domestic and productive activities "work" and to organize them collectively and reward them equally. The closeness of home and work means that the commune children, whether raised collectively or in separate families, often become easily and naturally involved with adult work. The involvement of hip commune children in the commune's work is a striking feature of contemporary groups. Amana youth worked part-time in the factories. Kibbutz children may raise their own animals and till gardens. Children in Cedar Grove have their craft business. Hutterite children may participate in adult work.

Valuing work for its contribution to the quality of life or group cohesion means that communes often choose work that enables such contribution. The existence of "cottage industries" in many communes (home-based, small-scale handicraft industries) is not accidental. The predilection of contemporary communes for land and light organic farming also fits with this value, for both kinds of work involve physical labor, a minimum of differentiating skills, a more-or-less immediate product, low initial capital, an abundance of tasks that many people can do together, and, in the case of gardening, an attunement to the rhythms of nature. The products, in both cases, may be immediately useful to and usable by the commune. Much artistic effort in contemporary communes is channeled toward the production of useful crafts such as pottery mugs and dishes, just as Shaker artistry developed furniture for the community's own use. It is probably also not an accident that many contemporary communes do for a living what many suburban Americans do for a hobby: gardening and crafts.

Other forms of productive work chosen by communes also often have symbolic or social significance: for example, candle making, incense factories, and organic restaurants among today's urban communes. The Bruderhof manufacture toys of great safety, simple beauty, and educational value, in keeping with the community's interest in children. The kinds of chores to be done around Bruderhof woodshops can keep anyone busy regardless of skill level, from children to the elderly to visitors. Some have turned their rituals and music into enterprises: Synanon, Fort Hill, and the Brotherhood of the Spirit have all cut records. Other communes, like Tail of the Tiger and Lama, constitute themselves educational or personal growth centers, making community itself the enterprise. Social service is another area of communal work, as in Camp Hill Village's service to the mentally retarded. Several Japanese communes also offer educational experiences or social services. It should be noted that many of these enterprises require limited technology.

Property and finances are also handled according to communal values. Most long-lived American communes and most of the kibbutzim have been totally communistic, based on the principle "from each according to his ability, to each according to his needs." Just as everyone works, so is everyone's needs supplied from the common stock; just what is a "need," of course, is often a matter of considerable debate. Amana's communism is typical of this group. As members joined, they gave their real and personal property to the community. In return they were promised free board; a dwelling; support and care in sickness and old age, even when too infirm to work; and an annual maintenance allowance. (This allowance was fixed by the Trustee according to equity, and there was some jealousy when it was unequal.) The community sometimes even assumed the previous debts of new members.

Collective ownership and consumption sometimes included even clothing. Oneida communism extended to "best clothes"; Twin Oaks' members choose their wardrobe from the community clothes closet. Hutterite distribution policies are an example of an extremely formalized and routinized system; most communes distribute more casually. Food is eaten in two community dining rooms. Goods are distributed from central stocks, according to guidelines for each item and every possible case. For example, for the first baby, a couple would receive the following items of bedding, among others: a crib cover 1 by 1 yard; a mattress pad for a crib 41 by 24 inches; and a pillow 20 by 19 inches. Ten-year-old boys are allotted annually three-and-a-half yards of material for a jacket. Each family receives an annual allotment of beer and wine. All of these things are not owned by members, but given to them for their use. Very small items of personal property are allowed, such as may be purchased on the small adult allowances of about a dollar a month. This system is, of course, in line with the Hutterites' general policy of austerity and uniformity (Hostetler and Huntington 1967).

Other communes may interpret collective ownership to allow more latitude in individual consumption. Most contemporary American communes, particularly the disordered ones, do not own property in common. In general, however, collective ownership fosters commitment and strong group feeling, whereas private ownership and individual rewards foster a kind of self-interest detrimental to community.

IDEALS AND REALITIES

In the ideal community brotherhood, love, and harmony replace conflict and competition; purpose and meaning replace alienation; sharing and collective responsibility replace private hoarding of goods; and family warmth and intimacy replace isolation. Relationships are loving; work is meaningful; and behavior is self-fulfilling. The closeness with other people is mirrored in a closeness with both the natural and the supernatural.

But the ideal is attainable only with modifications. The majority of communes and utopian communities do not last more than a few years. They often have an uneasy relationship to the surrounding society, existing as a counter culture within an established order that is quite different and sometimes punishing.

Most communes that dissolve early in their history have failed to develop the sense of commitment and shared purpose, the closeness and family feeling that permit groups to struggle through early years of hardship, adjustment to a new life-style, and developing organization. Two example, Sunrise Hill and Oz, illustrate this. They both may be characterized as anarchistic "retreat communes," rejecting the established society and withdrawing to the land without developing an affirmative vision to help create a communal structure. Like Brook Farm in the nineteenth century, Sunrise Hill began with enthusiasm and a sense of promise but lasted less than a year. Yaswen (1970) describes the problems as stemming from anarchy and lack of organization. There were no effective decision making procedures or ways to legitimate demands for work and no clear vision or purpose. They lacked self-definition as well as transcendent ideals. Were the commune members a family strongly involved with one another and therefore legitimately entitled to expect much from each other, or were they a set of laissez-faire anarchists refraining from making demands on one another? They never developed a satisfactory definition. Beginning out of rejection of old societal norms, the commune attracted rebels who resisted any regimentation. Sunrise Hill developed from a conference on intentional communities; at this conference a group "high" occurred that was never to be recaptured, but which raised members' expectations for intense, ecstatic relationships. By the end of the group, members were not even speaking to one another (Kanter 1972). Oz had a similar brief existence. Some of its problems resemble those of Sunrise Hill; others came from its position as an open community overrun with visitors and vulnerable to persecution by the wider society (Houriet 1971).

Those communes that do last more than a few years, on the other hand, are not trouble free either. They change from revolutionary movements to ongoing organizations and face the danger of creating their own "establishment," institutionalizing and rigidifying a way of life that once was radical. Success itself has posed dilemmas for long-lived communes (Kanter 1972). Their original population ages, and if not replaced by birth and/or recruitment, the communes may die a natural death. If their leadership base is charisma, they may have trouble surviving the death of the charismatic figure unless succession is provided for; this too changes the commune. If children are produced and expected to continue the communal traditions, their commitment and interests are often very different from that of the first generation; parents chose the life, while children were born into it. As the commune continues to operate, the self-sacrifice and devotion of earlier years may produce a prosperity that undermines commitment. A commune cannot continue to be a revolutionary movement forever; newness wears off, and energy and attention may increasingly be devoted to practical matters. Increasing attention to everyday operation of the commune as an organization with production demands to be met may deflect attention from communal values, or even require forms of organization detrimental to community. The history of Oneida, from commune to industrial corporation in thirty-three years, shows such changes (Carden 1969).

Utopian communities do not last forever, and, like all human groups, they have their natural histories. They may dissolve in crisis in their first few years because their members feel they cannot "make it" any longer, or they may change gradually over time. The Israeli kibbutzim are now so prosperous that their federation is considering the establishment of a kibbutz university, but some members feel that with prosperity and increased size has come an increase of private consumption, reemerging emphasis on nuclear families rather than the communal group as a whole, and erosion of collective feeling. And numerous accounts of nineteenth-century American communes illustrate how these communities change over generations: Oneida into a business, Amana into a business and a church, Zoar into a township (Kanter 1972).

Communes and utopian communities are possible, then, but within limits. But regardless of the prospects for endurance of any one commune, their very existence serves as a challenge to the rest of society, holding up the vision of a meaningful, shared, cooperative, loving way of life that continues to be attractive in a materially rich society. The growth of some utopian communities and communal enterprises shows that different ways to live, work, and relate are possible. As John Humphrey Noyes wrote in the nineteeth century about his Oneida community:

> What if there is not another shining light in the
> world and this is but a small one? Turn your eyes
> toward it when you are tired of chaos, and you will
> catch a glimpse of a better world.

REFERENCES

Andrews, Edward Deming.
  1962 *The Gift To Be Simple*. New York: Dover.
  1963 *The People Called Shakers*. New York: Dover.
Arnold, Emmy.
  1971 *Torches Together: The Beginnings and Early Years of the Bruderhof*, 2nd ed. Rifton, N.Y.: Plough Publishing.
Bennett, John.
  1967 *Hutterian Brethren*. Stanford, Cal.: Stanford University Press.
Berger, Bennett, Bruce M. Hackett, and R. Mervyn Miller.
  1971 "Child-rearing practices of the communal family." Progress Report to NIMH, mimeo.
Bestor, Arthur.
  1950 *Backwoods Utopias*. Philadelphia: University of Pennsylvania Press.
Bishop, Claire Huchet.
  1950 *All Things Common*. New York: Harper and Brothers.
Conkin, Paul.
  1955 *Two Paths to Utopia: the Hutterites and the Llano Colony*. Lincoln, Neb.: University of Nebraska Press.
Diamond, Stephen.
  1971 *What the Trees Said*. New York: Delta.
Egbert, Donald Drew, and Stow Persons (ed.).
  1952 *Socialism and American Life*. Princeton, N.J.: Princeton University Press.
Felton, David.
  1971 "The Lyman family's holy siege of America," *Rolling Stone*, Number 98 (December 23).
Fried, Albert (ed.).
  1970 *Socialism in America: From the Shakers to the Third International*. Garden City, N.Y.: Doubleday-Anchor.
Gardner, Hugh.
  1973 "Crises and politics in rural communes," in Kanter (ed.), *Communes: Creating and Managing the Collective Life*. New York: Harper and Row.
Gustatis, Rasa.
  1969 *Turning On*. New York: Macmillan.
Hedgepeth, William, and Dennis Stock.
  1970 *The Alternative: Communal Life in New America*. New York: Macmillan.
Hostetler, John, and Gertrude Huntington.
  1967 *The Hutterites of North America*. New York: Holt, Rinehart and Winston, Chapter 3.
Houriet, Robert.
  1971 *Getting Back Together*. New York: Coward and McCann and Geogheoghan.
Infield, Henrik.
  1947 *Cooperative Communities at Work*. London: Kegan Paul, Trench, Trubner.
  1955 *Utopia and Experiment: Essays in the Sociology of Cooperation*. New York: Praeger.

Kanovsky, Eliyahu.
1966 *The Economy of the Israeli Kibbutz*. Cambridge, Mass.: Harvard Middle Easter Monographs, Harvard University Press.

Kanter, Rosabeth Moss.
1968 "Commitment and social organization: A study of commitment mechanisms in utopian communities," *American Sociological Review* 33 (August): 499–517.
1970 "Communes," *Psychology Today* 4 (July): 53–58.
1972 *Commitment and Community: Communes and Utopias in Sociological Perspective*. Cambridge, Mass.: Harvard University Press.
1973a (ed.) *Communes: Creating and Managing the Collective Life*. New York: Harper and Row.
1973b "The romance of community: Communes as intensive group-experiences," in M. Rosenbaum and A. Snadowsky (eds.), *The Intensive Group Experience*. New York: The Free Press (forthcoming).

Kincaid, Kathleen.
1973 *A Walden Two Experiment*. New York: Morrow.

Knoedler, Christiana F.
1954 *The Harmony Society*. New York: Vantage Press.

Lamott, Kenneth.
1968 "Doing their thing at Morningstar," *Horizon* 10 (Spring): 14–19.

Lofland, John, and Rodney Stark.
1965 "Becoming a world-saver: A theory of conversion to a deviant perspective," *American Sociological Review* 30 (December): 862–875.

Mosher, Craig.
1973 "One: An urban community," *Journal of Applied Behavioral Science* 10 (March).

Newman, Barry.
1971 "Distasteful as it is, many communes turn to business techniques," *The Wall Street Journal* December 22.

Noyes, John Humphrey.
1961 *History of American Socialisms*. New York: Hillary House.

Pease, William H., and Jane Pease.
1963 *Black Utopia: Negro Communal Experiments in America*. Madison: State Historical Society of Wisconsin.

Plath, David.
1969 "Modernization and its discontents: Japan's little utopias," *Journal of Asian and African Studies* 4 (January): 1–17.
1968 "A case of ostracism—and its unusual aftermath," *Transaction* 5 (January–February): 31–36.

Rosenfeld, Eva.
1951 "Stratification in a 'classless' society," *American Sociological Review* 16 (December): 766–774.

Rosner, Menachem.
1973 "Direct democracy in the Kibbutz," in Rosabeth M. Kanter (ed.), *Communes: Creating and Managing Collective Life*. New York: Harper and Row, 178–191.
1970 "Communitarian experiment, self-management experience, and the Kibbutz," *Group Process* 3 (Summer): 79–100.

Selznick, Philip.
   1961 "Critical decisions in organizational development," in Amitai Etzioni (ed.), *Complex Organizations*. New York: Holt, Rinehart and Winston, 355–361.
Shambaugh, Bertha Maud.
   1932 *Amana That Was and Amana That Is*. Iowa City, Iowa: The State Historical Society of Iowa.
Smelser, Neil J.
   1962 *Theory of Collective Behavior*. New York: The Free Press.
Spiro, Melford E.
   1956 *Kibbutz: Venture in Utopia*. Cambridge, Mass.: Harvard University Press.
   1958 *Children of the Kibbutz*. Cambridge, Mass.: Harvard University Press.
Turner, Ralph, and Lewis Killian.
   1957 *Collective Behavior*. Englewood Cliffs, N.J.: Prentice-Hall.
Tyler, Alice Felt.
   1962 *Freedom's Ferment: Phases of American Social History from the Colonial Period to the Outbreak of the Civil War*. New York: Harper Torchbooks.
Wallace, Anthony F. C.
   1958 "Revitalization movements," *American Anthropologist* 58: 264–281.
Yaswen, Gordon.
   1969 "Sunrise Hill post-mortem, Edition 2." Reprinted in Rosabeth Moss Kanter (ed.), *Communes: Social Organization of the Collective Life*. New York: Harper and Row, 1973.
Zablocki, Benjamin.
   1971 *The Joyful Community*. Baltimore, Maryland: Penguin.

Planning for New Towns: The Gap Between Theory and Practice*

LAWRENCE SUSSKIND

Massachusetts Institute of Technology

Influential members of the urban planning profession have developed certain ideas about new town design, including notions such as self-containment, social balance, and the neighborhood unit. These parallel, to some extent, concepts that have emerged from the field of community sociology. Efforts to put these ideas into practice have fallen far short of the mark. Without more sophisticated implementation mechanisms, better theories of social interaction at the neighborhood level, and new approaches to citizen participation, efforts to build new towns are likely to remain severely crippled. The aim of this paper is to summarize past efforts to translate implicit theories of social organization into actual new town designs. The possibilities of closing the gap between theory and practice through the use of more explicit forms of social experimentation are discussed in the context of the fledgling new towns program in the United States.

New Towns have been built for many reasons: to relieve congestion and overcrowding in large urban centers (Britain), to develop frontier regions (the Soviet Union), to exploit concentrated resources (Venezuela), to defend captured territories (Israel), to provide a showcase for technological innovations (United States), to symbolize a new political or economic orientation (Turkey), and to absorb and acculturate

*I am indebted to Professor Lloyd Rodwin for his advice and encouragement; although we disagree on some of the points presented in this paper, his thinking on the subject has strongly influenced my own.

migrants (Australia).[1] However, many of the ideas upon which planners
have based their designs have not been subjected to rigorous analysis.
This is particularly true in so far as the social organization of planned communities is concerned. This paper identifies several concepts of social
organization that new town planners have deployed for their purposes—
largely unsuccessfully. There are some interesting parallels between the
ideas of the new town planners and the work of community sociologists, although there appear to be few if any direct linkages.

SELF-CONTAINMENT, SOCIAL BALANCE, AND
THE NEIGHBORHOOD UNIT

In their study of Springdale (an upstate New York town) Vidich and
Bensman identified a number of institutional mechanisms by which small
communities sustain the illusion that the pressures of urbanization, industrialization, and bureaucratization are subordinate to local demands.[2]
Although the reverse is more likely to be true, the extent to which local
activity patterns can reinforce certain life-styles points to the highly sophisticated process of socialization that takes place at a community level.

Vidich and Bensman did not publish their study of *Small Town in Mass
Society* until the late 1950s, but earlier versions of the same idea are not
difficult to spot. Their diagnosis is reminiscent, for example, of the ideas
advanced by one of the earliest community sociologists—Ferdinand
Tönnies. In his major work, *Gemeinshaft und Gesellschaft*, Tönnies argued
that "members of a community are relatively immobile in a physical and
a social way: individuals neither travel far from their locality of birth nor
do they rise up the social hierarchy."[3] Hillary's exhaustive review of the
literature suggests that most community studies assume that a person's
fate depends more on local patterns of local interaction than on broader
societal forces.[4]

What Vidich and Bensman labeled the myth of local autonomy recalls
Ebenezer Howard's original proposal for self-contained garden cities.
Howard's proposal, aimed originally at decanting London's large and
growing population, called for the development of new self-contained
communities of approximately 30,000 people. Each community was to be
surrounded by a permanent greenbelt and equipped to meet a full range
of social, economic, and cultural needs. Unified land ownership and clearly
articulated neighborhood units were intended to capture the most desirable aspects of city and country living. Howard assumed that each new
town would be able to meet all the social needs of its residents and to re-
capture the simpler life of pre-industrial England.[5]

To the extent that planned communities have lured families away from overcrowded metropolitan areas, they have done so by creating and sustaining the illusion that it is possible to escape the pervasive influences of mass society. This has been accomplished by suggesting that everyone can find better housing and higher-paying jobs merely by moving to a new town; assurances have been offered that a planned community can control its destiny through the manipulation of land uses and careful adherence to a master plan. In a very real sense, the success of a new town depends on the developer's ability to market the illusion of local autonomy. From the planners' standpoint, social networks and supporting institutions must be established that will engender a common sense of purpose and a shared image of how the community should look in the distant future.

A second new town planning concept is the notion of social balance. Socially balanced communities are those which provide a mix of places to work and to live as well as a population that is heterogeneous with respect to age, occupation, income, ethnicity, and class. J. S. Buckingham's plan for New Victoria (1849), for example, called for

> An entirely new town . . . peopled by an adequate number of inhabitants with such due proportions between the agricultural and manufacturing classes and between possessors of capital, skill, and labour as to provide . . . the highest degree of health, contentment, morality, and enjoyment yet seen in any existing community.[6]

Howard's garden city proposal suggested the desirability of including "all true workers of whatever grade."

The Reith Committee, set up in 1945 to plan the development of the British new towns program, suggested that the main problem was "one of class distinctions . . . if the community is to be truly balanced, so long as social classes exist, all must be represented in it. A contribution is needed from every type and class of person, the community will be poorer if all are not there."[7] The Committee seemed to accept the need for social balance without any reservation.

The balanced community explicitly recognizes the existence of class distinctions but attempts to induce social mixing through physical proximity and the sharing of facilities. It has been suggested by many new town planners that there are good reasons for seeking such balance: the upper and middle classes provide models for emulation, models of enterprise, and to a lesser extent, models of behavior. Balance also implies social harmony. Moreover, the economic life of a new town might be seriously jeopardized without a diversity of skill groups in the local population. Still other interpretations have been ventured. Ruth Glass argues that a balanced community provides for social control (under the guise of leadership) that would otherwise be lacking in the working class, which, if brought together without the restraints of the old established community, might constitute a threat to the established order.[8] Similar arguments, implicitly supporting the *embourgeoisement* of the working class, have found their way into planning strategies designed to promote social balance in American new towns.[9]

Implicit theories of community stratification provide a scaffolding upon which the concept of social balance rests. The presumption that various social groups have different childrearing practices and social service needs is basic to the programming of new town facilities. Warner, Hollingshead, Lenski, Landecker, and others have argued that in every community an unambiguous class structure exists based on differentials in social position, family status, and relative influence in local affairs; this sustains the planners' presuppositions.[10] Although stratification studies have come under increasing fire within the sociological profession in recent years, the news has yet to penetrate the planning literature. Indeed, the possibility that planners may be reinforcing some aspects of stratification by freezing class differentials into rigid physical designs is rarely discussed in planning circles.

To planners involved in the creation of new towns, social balance implies reproducing some standard or average demographic profile.

> In the development of Crawley New Town the aim was to achieve a similar balance to that of England and Wales in the local (new town) population. In social class terms, a balanced community is thus one which conforms to the class characteristics of England and Wales . . . .[11]

Social balance can refer to the population mix in the town as a whole (what Gans calls macro-integration) or to the mix of social groups within residential or neighborhood clusters (micro-integration).

> Micro-integration carries with it the possibility of actual integration; it means that people of different classes and races will be sharing those physical spaces in which potential integration could become actual integration. Micro-integration does not automatically require actual integration, however, for even next door neighbors can avoid social intercourse. Nevertheless, such avoidance is not easy, and more important, it is not pleasant, for most people want to be friendly with their neighbors if at all possible. Macra-integration puts less pressure on people to engage in actual integration, without, however, precluding it. Instead they have the opportunity to engage in social relations with heterogeneous community members on a voluntary basis.[12]

The principles of micro-integration were given their classic formulation by Clarence Perry in what he defined as the neighborhood unit:

a residential area which provides housing for the population for which one elementary school is ordinarily required, its actual area depending on its population density ... bounded on all sides by arterial streets sufficiently wide to facilitate its bypassing instead of penetration by through traffic.... Sites for the school and other institutions having service spheres coinciding with the limits of the unit should be suitably grouped around a central point.[13]

Most new town plans call for little more than a collection of neighborhood units organized around a central business district. For example, the British new town of Harlow is divided into four neighborhood clusters of 20,000 people each. The clusters are made up of two, three, or four small neighborhoods of 5,000 to 6,000 based on the size of catchment areas for primary education.

In the smaller neighborhoods, which remain the basic planning units, the primary school is brought within safe walking distance for children, and the housewife is never more than one-half kilometer from a small group of shops. At the same time the neighborhood center placed at the principal focus within the cluster can support a very considerable range of community services.[14]

Each neighborhood is intended to facilitate close social interaction among families presumed to share the same set of values and life expectations. There have been serious disagreements on the appropriate size of neighborhoods. Proposals range from 5,000 or even less up to 20,000. Those favoring smaller neighborhoods argue that they are more cohesive and offer more intimate contact. Others argue that 15,000 to 20,000 people are required to support an effective and varied neighborhood center.[15] Population arrangements are enforced through the design and pricing of residential units. The key assumption in neighborhood planning is that most people will value convenience, that is, a shorter distance from home to services and amenities, more than they will value extremely low densities.[16]

The neighborhood concept was not invented by sociologists, but various interpretations of the neighborhood principle (ranging from the notion of a service area designed to reduce unnecessary expenditures of time and energy to an effort to recreate a rural way of life with its closely compacted primary groups) find indirect support in classic studies of social stratification.[17] This is true not only in terms of what sociologists have identified as the need for separate settings for different groups in the same community but also in terms of the conflicts that sociologists have warned are likely to arise if incompatible groups are forced to live at close quarters.

The neighborhood unit was discarded in plans for the new town of Corby (England), for Cumbernauld (Scotland), and, more recently, in the new town of Skelmersdale (England). The planning consultants involved pointed out that increasing car ownership has created a more mobile population better able to satisfy its interests over a wider field. This seems to make sense. Nevertheless, the neighborhood unit has reappeared in almost all recent master plans for American new towns.[18] Perhaps its reappearance suggests a hidden agenda. The neighborhood unit may be the only acceptable means of achieving social balance without opening up the floodgates of indiscriminate mixing of social classes.

To understand why and how key concepts have found their way into the planning field, Gans suggests that it is important to ask who the planners are, what means they have at their disposal, and what interest groups they feel they are serving.[19] Most planners bring a middle-class view of city life to their professional careers and are beholden to government agencies and private developers for their jobs. Gans suggests that the neighborhood boundaries typically drawn by professional planners tend to ignore class divisions in the population, except those manifested by differences in housing type.

> Favoring low density and small-town living, the planners seek to achieve the cessation of residential mobility and the control and minimization of future growth. The only land uses programmed for future growth [are] those favored by affluent residents, high-status industrial and commercial establishments, and real estate interests catering to these and the tax collector.[20]

His caricature is probably overdrawn, but it does raise some important questions. If the British experience is any indication, new town planners in the United States are likely to have considerable difficulty trying to make their new town plans work. The next section of this paper examines some of the problems involved and possibilities of implementing the concepts mentioned above.

THE GAP BETWEEN THEORY AND PRACTICE

As a means of promoting economic development in lagging regions and of organizing additional growth in metropolitan areas, new towns have worked reasonably well.[21] The first generation of British new towns, for example, proved that public development was a decidedly feasible strategy.[22] As examples of physical design, new towns have not been extraordinarily exciting, but there have been instances of highly competent and imaginative architecture.

To get a sense of what new towns have been able to do, it is necessary to look at their overall impact on national growth patterns, or at the very least, their influence on development trends within key metropolitan areas.[23] In Britain the initial function of the new towns effort was to service the overspill population of London and to tidy up the excesses of speculative development. The most significant possibility—that of guiding, perhaps even dominating, critical interragional and intraregional relationships—did not come into play until the initiation of a second generation of new towns in the mid-1960s.[24]

One element of the success of the British new towns program was the government's willingness to provide incentives for industrial relocation. When a system of depreciation allowances (permitting write-offs of new investments against taxes) proved inadequate, the government offered more powerful grants-in-aid and tax incentives to help with the initial costs of capital construction. The British experience supports the planners' assertion that new towns can be used to implement national development poliices as long as the public sector plays a leading role. This is not to say that private interests need not be involved. However, if public policy had not informed decisions regarding the number, scale, and location of planned new towns, the relative advantages of this form of development would never have been realized.

The new city of Ciudad Guayana in Venezuela attests to the fact that it may be possible to realize a "social profit" via public land ownership and intelligent tax policy.[25] Late in 1960 the Venezuelan government set up the Corporacion Venezolana de Guayana (CVG) to develop the Guayana region, one of the country's greatest natural resource areas. The CVG was given the job of planning and building a major new city. Since the government owned the land, CVG was able to preserve the essence of its plan through public land ownership. The Corporation kept the land it needed for community purposes. Above all, public ownership offered CVG an opportunity to capture a reasonable share of the income and concentration of values it helped to create. Since commercial land and some of the better quality residential and industrial sites were likely to be the most profitable, CVG retained this land and sold the remainder (subject to restrictions on its use).

Although the opportunity to build a new city from the ground up seemed at the outset to be the answer to a planner's dream, there were serious stumbling blocks. The absence of trained technicians and workers, established community relations and loyalties, basic consumer and business services, and adequate community facilities created certain strains. Attracted by the prospect of jobs, poor migrants invaded the area, putting up makeshift shelters and complicating the task of organizing land uses and public services. Because of the great distance to an established city center, the initial cost of development was enormously inflated. Nevertheless, by the early 1970s, the city was well on its way to achieving its projected population of 250,000. The natural riches of the area were successfully drawn into the mainstream of the Venezuelan economy.

Offset against these partial successes have been a series of difficult problems. The experience to date confirms the early predictions of the new town critics who claimed that (1) small size and low density would not be essential to the design of desirable living environments; (2) investments in new towns would shortchange inner city redevelopment efforts; (3) serious problems of adjustment would plague new residents during the first stages of development; and (4) difficult social issues would arise which had been overlooked entirely.

Sufficient evidence has now accumulated to support many of these predictions. First, limitations on size and density have indeed created problems. For one thing, the cost of living in new towns has been somewhat higher than in big cities. Although individual neighborhoods were organized around compact service centers, overall densities have been relatively low and have resulted in higher prices not only for housing, but also for many public services spread out over larger areas.[26] Higher costs, in turn, have narrowed the range of residents, lopping off any chance of relocation for the lowest income groups. Lower densities have also minimized the attractiveness of certain industrial sites. Industries looking for densely settled areas to provide outlets for their products, proximity to smaller supporting firms, and highly specialized labor have not been attracted to new towns.

Restrictions on horizontal or slightly upward mobility from one job to another have handicapped new town residents expecting to live near their place of work. Increased mobility, in fact, has been a key factor in shattering the self-containment concept in Britain. A recent study shows that in the eight original new towns built around London "there are 76 persons who live in a new town and work outside it or commute to a new town for work, for every 100 who both live and work in the same new town."[27] The relatively small size of most new towns has also minimized the chances of providing diversified services and amenities. Specialty shops and cultural activities have been difficult to sustain outside high density urban centers. As it turns out, small size and relatively low density, even in a totally planned environment, only make sense when one assumes that the residents will settle into a job, a house, and a neighborhood for all time to come.

The second prediction that came true was that new towns would undercut efforts to rebuild central cities. Not only have new town planning programs siphoned off money that might have been used to rehabilitate deteriorating core areas, but they also have skimmed off upwardly mobile workers who otherwise might have stayed behind and tried to improve matters. Certain industries intent on expanding were lured to new towns on the outskirts of metropolitan areas and subsidized by the government while the fiscal capacities of central cities continued to erode. In what may have been the most unexpected blow, new towns riveted public attention on the suburbs and promoted the fantasy of garden city living, thus drawing a curtain over the difficulties plaguing big cities.

A number of studies have reported a phenomenon known as the "new town blues" or "transitional neurosis."[28] Early new town residents have had great difficulty making friends. They feel cut off from long-standing social ties. Wives in particular are lonely. Lives in general are more strained. Shops and public houses, close at hand in old inner city neighborhoods, are nonexistent or more distant in new towns and thus unable to serve as social centers.[29] To a great extent these problems are transitory, but in a larger sense the migration to new towns has ripped apart the close-knit fabric of kin and neighbors in many cities. While some degree of disorientation has always accompanied a move, families in difficulty in new towns are not likely to find helping institutions to fall back on.

Other social issues have also arisen for which the planners were not prepared. In his study of two British new towns, Willmott identifies a number of problems, including imbalance in the population structure and the difficulty of integrating social groups via the neighborhood unit.[30] People moving to new towns have been predominantly young couples with small children. This age bias has created an early demand for extensive social services and facilities that quickly become outmoded as the population matures.[31] It has also generated a lack of diversity in social activities.[32]

Few of the assumptions regarding the importance of the neighborhood unit as a socializing device have been borne out.[33] As a way of structuring community life around the provision of schools, shops, and other services, the concept has not worked particularly well. Perhaps it has been applied too inflexibly. In England, the emphasis on the distinctiveness of neighborhood populations did not fit with the patterns of social interaction that developed.[34] Perhaps, too, the neighborhood unit was too large a locality (5,000 to 10,000 residents) for most people. The residents did not identify with the neighborhoods laid out by the planners.[35] Part of the problem stemmed from the surprising degree of cross-commuting into and out of many new towns.[36] In any event, the neighborhood unit is not the locus of informal social relations it was supposed to be.

The problems of achieving social balance and of organizing a community into manageable parts have taken their toll of new town planning theory. The search for fresh paradigms of social and economic organization goes on. In the meantime, preliminary results of privately financed efforts to build new towns in the United States suggest two other difficulties. The first is race relations. The second is the problem of maintaining the myth of local autonomy in the face of encroaching social disorganization.

Too little is known about attitudes toward racial integration and about behavior in integrated situations to permit firm conclusions about whether or not racial integration is possible in new towns.[37] However,

> Racial micro-integration is rare, except temporarily when communities are in racial transition and until the "tipping point" is reached, and it is rare in most new towns because it has not often been tried, except on a token basis. Still, it exists in new towns such as Columbia, Reston, and the Levitt-built Willingboro, but partly because the blacks who moved into these towns were of high status.[38]

What seems to be emerging is general agreement on at least one point: racial integration among neighborhoods or residential clusters will be most feasible when there are no significant class differences between the races, or when minority racial groups are of higher status than the whites.[39] Gans suggests that racial integration will probably be most feasible in upper-middle-class areas. This is not very promising, however, because the new towns program in the United States is supposed to provide housing for low- and moderate-income groups and particularly for minority groups trapped in the central city. The task of weaving low-income minority families into the social fabric of a new town is beyond anything planners can handle at the present time.

The notion of the new town as a sanctuary from overcrowding and urban blight is already breaking down in the United States. In Columbia, Maryland, one of the few American new towns to reach a preliminary population threshold of 10,000, the problems of crime, vandalism, and racial tension have already surfaced.[40] Future efforts to market planned communities as morally cohesive minisocieties immune to larger social problems will become increasingly difficult. Developers must find new ways of sustaining the myth of local autonomy, otherwise they will lose their drawing power.

One last problem also deserves attention. Private developers in the United States and public development corporations in other countries have all had great difficulty finding ways to involve new town residents in community governance. Unless community residents are involved at least to some extent in development decisions and ongoing management operations they can impede the pace of development.[41] The negative aura of community dissent can also sabotage a new town's marketability, to say nothing of the corrosive effects such confrontation can have on the fragile bonds of trust and friendship that new residents must try to build.

In summary, there appear to be at least three major obstacles to implementing the concepts of social organization implicit in most new town plans. The first is the lack of sufficiently powerful implementation mechanisms. Techniques for attracting and maintaining a heterogeneous population have no more than a hit-or-miss quality about them. There are neither incentives nor controls strong enough (except in a totalitarian regime) to induce balanced migration or social interaction among groups that prefer not to mix. Efforts to organize local patterns of family life around neighborhood service centers have faltered: first, because they have failed to take account of sharp discontinuities in the age structure; and second, because the trade-off between density and convenience has not been as important as the planners originally suspected. Finally, the problem of maintaining the illusion of economic opportunity and self-sufficiency in the face of preliminary signs of social deterioration has become more difficult than ever. Greater mobility, the increasing impact of mass communications, and the footloose character of a highly urbanized population make it extremely difficult to pretend that new towns can somehow be shielded from social problems typically found in central cities.

A second obstacle is the lack of a grounded theory of social interaction at the neighborhood level. We have yet to discover how to organize supporting institutions to help ease the process of entry. Moreover, there does not seem to be any general agreement about the best way of arranging social services and community facilities. Most new towns are organized around the neighborhood unit (which in turn assumes that elementary education is the key to social organization). In addition, it is impossible to disregard the often violent reactions of suburban dwellers to the in-migration of blacks, the poor, and other minority groups. In the United States, civil rights groups have spearheaded efforts for many years to pierce the exclusivity of the suburbs. Racial equality, fair housing, and integration have been their bywords. Today, however, the passion for ethnic autonomy has confused the issue. With political control of several major cities practically within their grasp, many black leaders are extraordinarily wary of new town proposals which they view as part of a dispersal or integrationist strategy. Anything that threatens to dilute their emerging political majority is subject to careful scrutiny and, more often than not, severe criticism. It is not clear whether one segment or the other of the black community will dominate, or whether an alliance will be forged that can somehow reinforce their separate objectives. Nor is it clear how other groups will react to this situation. It may be, however, that various minority groups will prefer to build new towns that they can control and in which they can remain relatively separate.[42]

A third obstacle is the problem of responding to resident demands for participation in local affairs. The financial feasibility of a new town as well as its hope for a more efficiently organized land use pattern, hinge on adherence to a master plan. This seems to preclude any significant role for new community residents in the decision making process. Moreover, in light of the fact that the first wave of residents may want to "pull up the drawbridge," this is a particularly knotty problem. These are indeed serious problems, and they threaten the success of the fledgling new towns program in the United States. There may be a number of ways, however, of overcoming these obstacles and of narrowing the gap between theory and practice.

THE TRANSFORMATIONAL POSSIBILITIES

The concept of planning has broadened over time, escalating from an early preoccupation with town and county problems, to a regional and even a national concern for the formulation of overall growth strategies. While efforts to build small, self-contained new communities were supported originally as a way of decentralizing big cities, recent generations of planners have argued for larger new towns which they hope will act as magnets pulling growth to lagging regions. The problems of planning for social aspects of community life, however, are still as intractable as ever.

The British new towns program was launched on the assumption that the long-term problems caused by the industrial revolution could be solved by restoring people to the land and by financing continuing city improvements out of the increment in land values collected via rents (public ownership). Social problems, to the extent that they were considered at all, were correlated with unlimited city size, high neighborhood density, and the great distance between job opportunities and residential areas. While big cities implied unlimited size and high densities, new towns would be programmed to achieve an optimal size and density. The problematic journey to work would be eliminated because people would live where they worked. The neighborhood unit was selected as the basic building block in the planners' design, representing a coherent clustering of social groups with relatively similar needs and expectations. It all seemed to make such good sense, yet the outcome has been surprisingly unsuccessful. In what ways were the new town planners misdirected? Might it be possible to adjust the new towns policy recently adopted in the United States in order to avoid many of the same disappointments?

New town development in the United States began in earnest with the passage of the Urban Growth and New Community Development Act of 1970. This act provides attractive incentives to public and private entrepreneurs and investors interested in the planned development of "socially and economically sound new communities." The U.S. Department of Housing and Urban Development is empowered to provide loans, grants, and interest subsidies for the development of new-towns-in-town (the clearance and redevelopment of "functionally obsolete properties" in the central cities), planned suburban communities, and new towns or growth centers in rural areas. As of June, 1973, the federal government had committed upwards of $250 million to fourteen new towns scattered throughout the United States (Table 1). Unfortunately, no justification for the selection of sites or the approval of plans has been forthcoming.[43]

The new towns program in the United States will be judged in several ways. First, by the extent to which it serves the poor and the disadvantaged.

Table 1 Summary of New Towns Approved and Subsidized by the U.S. Department of Housing and Urban Development

Community	Projected Population	Projected Jobs	Dwelling Units	Per Cent of Housing for Low and Moderate Income Families	Location	Date and Amount HUD Guarantee Commitment (in thousands)
Jonathan, Minn.	49,996	18,152	5,500 in 10 years	25	20 mi. SW of Minneapolis	21,000 2/70
St. Charles Communities, Md.	79,145	14,890	25,000 in 20 years	20	25 mi. SE of Wash., D.C.	24,000 6/70
Park Forest South, Ill.	110,000	N.A.	35,000 in 15 years	16	30 mi. S of Chicago	30,000 6/70
Flower Mound, Tex.	64,141	16,454	18,000 in 20 years	20	20 mi. NW of Dallas	18,000 12/70
Maumelle, Ark.	45,000	N.A.	14,000 in 20 years	23	12 mi. NW of Little Rock	7,500 12/70
Cedar-Riverside, Minn.	31,250	14,609	12,500 in 20 years	44	downtown Minneapolis	24,000 6/71
Riverton, N.Y.	25,632	11,180	8,000 in 16 years	40	10 mi. S of Rochester	12,000 12/71
San Antonio Ranch, Tex.	87,972	17,990	28,000 in 30 years	35	20 mi. NW of San Antonio	18,000 2/72
Woodlands, Tex.	150,000	40,000	49,160 in 20 years	27	30 mi. NW of Houston	50,000 4/72
Gananda, N.Y.	55,808	12,890	17,200 in 20 years	21	12 mi. N of Rochester	22,000 4/72
Soul City, N.C.	44,000	18,000	12,096 in 30 years	37	45 mi. NW of Raleigh-Durham	14,000 6/72
Lysander, N.Y.	18,355	N.A.	5,000 in 20 years	50	12 mi. NW of Syracuse	*
Harbinson, S.C.	21,343	6,100	6,500 in 20 years	35	8 mi. NW of Columbia	13,000 10/72
Welfare Is., N.Y.	17,000	7,500	5,000	55	East River between Manhattan and Queens, N.Y.C.	†

Source: Office of New Communities Development, U.S. Department of Housing and Urban Development, as of January, 1973.

* Funded by the New York State Urban Development Corp., approved by HUD June, 1972.

† Funded by the New York State Urban Development Corp., approved by HUD December, 1972.

The fourteen new towns approved thus far (with a population of 800,000 projected over the next thirty years) are scheduled to provide roughly 65,000 units of housing for families with low and moderate incomes. Of the 200,000 new jobs likely to be created, it is not clear what proportion will be accessible to those who are currently unemployed or unskilled. Another measure of success will be the extent to which the new towns can link to recuperative efforts in the central city. Few new towns approved to date have been designed to revitalize decaying central city areas. A third, and probably the most important test of the new towns program, will be whether or not the planners are able to discover appropriate techniques for re-creating social networks and stimulating positive social interaction at something approximating a neighborhood level. Will it be possible to develop more sophisticated theories grounded in a better understanding of social dynamics at the community level? Although lip service has been given to the notion of technological innovation, almost no attention has been paid to the problems and prospects of serious social experimentation.

New communities provide special opportunities for social learning.[44] Although discussions have centered around the possibility of testing new technological hardware, new waste control systems, industrialized housing and other building systems, and new modes of transportation, the potential for deploying sophisticated technology is not the central issue. Important as such innovations may seem, it is the process of managing social and economic development that requires special attention. New towns can provide an opportunity to study the process of working back and forth between what is desirable and what is feasible. It is at this nexus that planners and sociologists can collaborate in interesting and important ways.

Two decisions usually made early in the planning process have an almost irreversible impact upon the ultimate character of a community: the selection of a site and the amount and nature of the financing commitment. Experiments might be aimed at opening up these decisions to the ultimate users who, quite literally, have to live with the consequences. It might be possible, for instance, to identify the potential users of a new town so that they could help design the community before a final decision on site selection was made. The planners of Soul City have considered ways of identifying prospective residents so that they can be involved in the initial planning stages.[45] If this is too difficult, consultants and advisors might be selected whose interests are similar to those likely to live in the new town. (One word of warning here: involvement of surrogate users must go beyond the traditional market survey; they must have a part in generating the range of options as well as evaluating specific alternatives.) Either strategy should yield much needed information on social service preferences and the extent to which different groups will cluster when given the opportunity.

Another useful strategy would be to defer as many decisions as possible which affect the form of development until residents are on the scene. Indeed, the initial development might include temporary quarters for residents (short-term rentals) while they become directly involved in planning activities. Designs might be sought which break down what are presently large capital investments such as sewer and road systems into smaller components which may (or may not) be added incrementally, thereby avoiding long-term commitments to an overall physical form.

Still another possible approach might be to build several smaller neighborhoods simultaneously, so that each could offer very different combinations of site and cash flow characteristics. Neighborhoods which are deliberately planned to grow slowly (temporary users might be allowed to pay for the carrying costs of the land) might be paired with others which are planned to grow as rapidly as possible. Financing commitments might vary accordingly. These suggestions imply great flexibility in holding open site and cash flow arrangements—flexibility which only government backing can help to ensure. In each case it should be possible to adjust physical designs to respond to emerging activity patterns and to learn more about the processes by which neighborhood groups sort themselves out.

The development of more permanent institutions in a new community provides another opportunity for experimentation. Preventive health care on a community scale (as in Columbia, Maryland) and prepaid group practice arrangements might become a major part of a plan for the delivery of health services. Various ownership formats—condominiums, cooperatives, etc.—and other mechanisms for local control could be tested along with institutional innovations such as:

Small quasigovernmental units. Can control over services traditionally provided by city-wide governments be dispersed to small groups of residents or to neighborhood associations? What are the effects of disaggregation?

Special service districts or corporations. Can local development corporations be designed to control the delivery of services? Can debt repayment be transferred from the developer to the community or service districts in small increments?

Crisis management. Can better ways be found of raising issues of community concern, disseminating information, and resolving conflict through neighborhood forums, ombudsmen, or new forms of media, particularly cable television?

From experiments such as these it should be possible to discover which forms of community organization provide adequate support for newcomers and which contribute most to the satisfaction of various resident groups.

Most, if not all of these experiments presume that social researchers will be able and willing to evaluate the process of new town development. New towns are obviously more conducive to this kind of research than established neighborhoods. Reactions to continuous probing are likely to be less severe in a new town than in an established inner city area. Moreover, developers often make it clear from the outset that part of the price of living in a new town will be a continuous bombardment of surveys and questionnaires. Participant observers can move into a new town somewhat less obtrusively. The most important difference, however, is that the evolution of social arrangements in a new town is relatively transparent whereas in older neighborhoods, successive waves of immigration, the interplay of impinging pressures from nearby communities, and the time-bound hierarchy of residency make it difficult to study the *process* of social transformation.

Experiments in new town design are different from experiments in the physical sciences in at least three ways: the large number of variables involved in any situation makes it virtually impossible to undertake classical matched-pair experiments; "scaling up" may change the nature of the problem and invalidate the results of a pilot experiment, and since humans are involved, successes and failures are always relative and subjective concepts.[46] Nevertheless, experiments in institutional design and the study of their subsequent impact on social organization are an absolutely necessary step in building more sophisticated theories of new town planning.

A rigorous monitoring system is also a prerequisite for learning from new town experiments. Monitoring should indicate the performance of the community at the local level, where feedback will allow for frequent adjustments, and at the national level where alternative new town development strategies can be evaluated. Since communities take years to develop, long-term recording of events, perceptions, and changes will be required. The process of research should begin with each initial participant in the development process recording his or her expectations: designers ought to spell out the various opportunities they envision for each new town, and investors ought to be specific about profit expectations. Monitoring should include the periodic collection of photographic, visual, and verbal records of the community, and an archivist should be designated to collect and hold impressions and records in every new town.

What has been missing is a sense that we know what community life should be like—for one or for all segments of the population. Unfortunately, we do not. To the extent that new towns start out representing different models of social and economic activity, they provide an opportunity to gauge the probable reactions of various population groups. Most attempts to construct social experiments have failed; partly because the risks involved are great and partly because planners and social scientists have been too timid to suggest such large-scale ventures. New towns can change all that, first, because no one need be an unwitting captive of a new town experiment and second, because the climate is obviously ripe for such bold adventures. We need to advance our understanding about possible ways of improving the quality of community life. The burden is now on the shoulders of those who have hidden behind the protective covering of descriptive research. Much as they despise the thought, there is no way to avoid the need for policy-oriented or prescriptive experimental research.

New town planners may well be guilty of replacing one illusion with another. A fresh start will not necessarily produce better results, especially if no one is clear about what he is striving for. The only way to reduce the chance of failure is to develop a better process of social learning. In so far as new town development is concerned, experimentation might help to generate a clearer perception of the real value of alternative new town designs. This is an effort, though, that will require an input from planners whose implicit social theories are rarely grounded in systematic research and from community sociologists who have often failed to focus on the process of social change. If the two professions are unable to work in tandem the gap between theory and practice is likely to become even wider.

NOTES

[1] William Alonso, "What Are New Towns For?" *Urban Studies*, Vol. II, No. 1, January, 1970, pp. 37–55; William Alonso, "Needed and Spontaneous New Towns," in Harvey Perloff and Neil Sandberg (eds.), *New Towns—Why and For Whom* (New York: Praeger), 1973, pp. 237–241. For a brief description of the international new towns movement see Pierre Merlin, *New Towns* (London: Methuen), 1971. For more detailed materials on the British new towns see Lloyd Rodwin, *The British New Towns Policy* (Cambridge: Harvard University Press), 1966 and Frederic J. Osborn and Arnold Whittick, *The New Towns: The Answer to Megalopolis* (London: Leonard Hill, 1963; Harold Orlans, *Stevenage: A Sociological Study of a New Town* (London: Routledge), 1962. Useful case studies of new town development in other countries includes Erika Speigel, *New Towns in Israel* (New York: Praeger), 1967; U.N. Department of Social Affairs, *Planning of Metropolitan Areas and New Towns* (New York: United Nations), 1967; Lloyd Rodwin and Associates, *Planning Urban Growth and Regional Development* (Cambridge: M.I.T. Press), 1969. The American new town experience is described in Edward Eichler and Marshall Kaplan, *The Community Builders* (Berkeley: University of California Press), 1967; Clarence Stein, *Toward New Towns for America*, 2nd edition (Cambridge: M.I.T. Press), 1966; and James Clapp, *New Towns and Urban Policy* (New York: Dunellen), 1971.

[2] Arthur J. Vidich and Joseph Bensman, *Small Town in Mass Society* (Garden City: Doubleday), 1960. Originally published by Princeton University Press in 1958.

[3]J. C. McKinney and C. P. Loomis, "The Application of Gemeinschaft and Gesellschaft as Related to Other Typologies," in the introduction to the American Edition of Ferdinand Tönnies, *Community and Society* (New York: Harper Torchbook), 1963, pp. 12–29. Originally published by Michigan State University Press, East Lansing, 1957.

[4]George A. Hillery, *Communal Organizations: A Study of Local Societies* (Chicago: University of Chicago Press), 1968.

[5]Ebenezer Howard, *Garden Cities of Tomorrow* (London: Faber), 1945; 3rd edition (Cambridge: MIT Press), 1965.

[6]J. S. Buckingham, "National Evils and Practical Remedies," London, 1849, p. 141, quoted in Harold Orlans, *op. cit.*

[7]Committee on the New Towns, Final Report, Comd. 6876, p. 10.

[8]Ruth Glass, "Urban Sociology," *Current Sociology*, Vol. 4, No. 4, 1955, pp. 14–19.

[9]Herbert Gans, "The Balanced Community: Homogeneity or Heterogeneity in Residential Areas," in *People and Plans* (New York: Basic Books), 1968, pp. 166–182.

[10]W. Lloyd Warner and Paul S. Lunt, *The Social Life of a Modern Community* (New Haven: Yale University Press), 1941; W. Lloyd Warner and Paul S. Lunt, *The Status System of a Modern Community* (New Haven: Yale University Press), 1942; A. B. Hollingshead, *Elmtown's Youth* (New York: John Wiley), 1949: Gerhard E. Lenski, "American Social Classes: Statistical Strata or Social Groups," *American Journal of Sociology*, LVIII, Nov. 1, 1952, pp. 139–144; Warner S. Landecker, "Types of Integration and Their Measurement," in Roland Warren (ed.), *Perspectives on the American Community* (Chicago: Rand McNally and Co.), 1966, pp. 227–238.

[11]B. J. Heraud, "Social Class and the New Towns," in *Urban Studies*, Vol. 5, No. 1, February 1968, pp. 33–58.

[12]Herbert Gans, "The Possibilities of Class and Racial Integration in American New Towns: A Policy-Oriented Analysis," in Perloff and Sandberg (eds.), *op. cit.*, pp. 137–157.

[13]Richard Dewey, "The Neighborhood, Urban Ecology, and City Planning," in Paul K. Hatt and Albert J. Reiss, *Cities and Society* (New York: The Free Press), 1951, p. 786.

[14]Lesley E. White, "The Social Factors Involved in the Planning and Development of New Towns," in U.N. Department of Social Affairs, *op. cit.*, pp. 194–200.

[15]*Ibid.*

[16]Margaret Willis, "Sociological Aspects of Urban Structure," *The Town Planning Review*, Vol. 39, No. 4, January 1969, pp. 296–306.

[17]James Dahir, *The Neighborhood Unit Plan, Its Spread and Acceptance* (New York: Russell Sage Foundation), 1947. Also see Reginald Isaacs' well-known critique of the neighborhood unit in "The Neighborhood Theory," *Journal of the American Institute of Planners*, XIV, Spring 1948, pp. 15–23.

[18]Willis, *op. cit.*, p. 296.

[19]Herbert Gans, "City Planning in America: A Sociological Analysis," in *People and Plans, op. cit.*, pp. 57–77.

[20]*Ibid.*, p. 62.

[21]Lloyd Rodwin, *Nations and Cities* (Boston: Houghton-Mifflin), 1970.

[22]Lloyd Rodwin, *The British New Towns Policy, op. cit.*

[23]Arie Shachar, "The Role of New Towns in National and Regional Development: A Comparative Study," in Perloff and Sandberg (eds.), *op. cit.*, pp. 30–47.

[24]Rodwin, *Nations and Cities, op. cit.*

[25]Rodwin, *Planning Urban Growth and Regional Development, op. cit.*, Chapter 1.

[26]Nathaniel Litchfield, "Economic Opportunity in New Towns" in Perloff and Sandberg (eds.), *op. cit.*, pp. 48–67.

[27]Ira M. Robinson, "Small, Independent, Self-contained and Balanced New Towns: Myth or Reality?" in Perloff and Sandberg (eds.), *op. cit.*, pp. 2–27.

[28]Peter Willmott, "Social Research and New Communities," in the *Journal of the American Institute of Planners*, Vol. 33, 1967, Nov., pp. 387–398.

[29]Herbert Gans, *The Levittowners* (New York: Pantheon), 1967.

[30]Peter Willmott, "Housing Density and Town Design in a New Town," *Town Planning Review*, Vol. XXXIII, July 1962, pp. 115–127.

[31]Norman Pritchard, "Planned Social Provision in New Towns," *Town Planning Review*, Vol. XXXVIII, No. 1, April 1967, pp. 25–34.

[32]Jennifer Moss, "New and Expanded Towns: A Survey of the Demographic Characteristics of Newcomers," *Town Planning Review*, Vol. XXXIX, No. 2, July 1968, pp. 117–139.

[33]Willis, *op. cit.*

[34]Heraud, *op. cit.*

[35]Willmott, "Housing Density and Town Design in a New Town," *op. cit.*

[36]A. A. Ogilvy, "The Self-Contained New Towns" in *Town Planning Review*, Vol. XXXIX, No. 1, April 1968, pp. 38–54.

[37]Herbert Gans, "The Possibilities of Class and Racial Integration," *op. cit.*

[38]*Ibid.*

[39]Study prepared by the Metropolitan Applied Research Center for the U.S. Department of Housing and Urban Development cited in Jack Underhill, "The New Community Development Process" in an unpublished volume of essays edited by Gideon Golany, Penn State University.

[40]Jay Rosenthal, "A Tale of One City," *New York Times Magazine*, December 26, 1971.

[41]David Godschalk, "Participation, Planning, and Exchange in Old and New Communities: A Collaborative Paradigm," unpublished Ph.D. dissertation, Department of City and Regional Planning, University of North Carolina, 1972.

[42]One suggestion along these lines was made by Ervin Golantay, "Black New Towns," *Progressive Architecture*, August, 1968, pp. 126–131.

[43]Lloyd Rodwin and Lawrence Susskind, "The Next Generation of New Towns" in James Bailey (ed.), *New Towns in America* (New York: John Wiley), 1973.

[44]The possibilities of experimentation in new towns were first discussed by this author in Lawrence Susskind and Gary Hack, "New Towns in a National Urban Growth Strategy," *Technology Review*, February, 1972, pp. 30–42.

[46]David Godschalk, *The Planning Process for New Town Development: Soul City*, Department of City and Regional Planning, University of North Carolina, Chapel Hill, 1969.

[48]Donald Schon, "On Bringing Technology to Social Problems," *Technology Review*, February, 1971, pp. 46–51.

REFERENCES

Dahl, Robert A., and Charles E. Lindblom.
1963 *Politics, Economics, and Welfare: Planning and Politico-Economic Systems Resolved into Basic Social Processes.* New York: Harper.
Litwak, Eugene, and Henry J. Meyer.
1966 "A balanced theory of coordination between bureaucratic organizations and community primary groups," *Administrative Science Quarterly* 11 (June, 1966–March, 1967): 31–58.
Litwak, Eugene et al.
1970 "Community participation in bureacratic organizations: principles and strategies," *Interchange* 1: 44–60.
Riesman, David.
1950 *The Lonely Crowd.* New Haven: Yale University.
Stoloff, David.
1970 "Model cities: model for failure," *The Architectural Forum* 132 (January–February): 101–115.
Tönnies, F.
1940 *Fundamental Concepts of Sociology.* New York: American Book Company.
Truman, David B.
1953 *The Governmental Process.* New York: Knopf.
Weber, Max.
1947 *The Theory of Social and Economic Organization,* 2nd ed., translated by A. M. Henderson and Talcott Parsons. New York: Wiley.

Bureaucracies and
Community Planning

PAUL E. MOTT

Since much of what is said below is based on the writer's personal obser-
vations of bureaucracies in the United States, a few comments on that
experience are necessary. For the last eight years he has studied or worked
in several Washington agencies. The first six years were devoted to studies
of the Executive Office of the President, the Department of Housing and
Urban Development, the Office of Economic Opportunity, the National
Aeronautics and Space Administration, and the Department of Health,
Education and Welfare. For the next two years (1971–73) he worked for
the Administrator of the Social and Rehabilitation Service (SRS) which
is located in DHEW. SRS had the third largest agency budget in the fed-
eral government ($15 billion) and contained at that time programs for the
aged, youth, handicapped, and for the provision of medical and sub-
sistence payments to dependent children and their families. This sojourn
into the bureaucracy provided an unusual opportunity to compare some
sociological concepts and theories about bureaucracies with the realities
of bureaucratic life.

The purpose of this article is to discuss four propositions
about public bureaucracies and their effects on the efforts of communities
to mobilize themselves for community action.

1. Public bureaucracies, which are often portrayed as monolithic in-
truders in a pluralist American society, are in fact usually pluralis-
tically organized themselves.

2. Vested with the diffusion of power that accompanies pluralist organization, bureaucracies have greater difficulty initiating collective
action and bringing it to a successful conclusion than they do preventing such action.

3. Given these difficulties in achieving collective action, public bureaucracies are almost incapable institutionally of solving the problems of communities, which intrinsically require holistic solutions.

4. If comprehensive solutions to community problems are to be implemented, then major modifications must be made in the ways the American public bureaucracies function.

BUREAUCRACY AND SOCIAL PLURALISM

Whenever the subject of bureaucracy comes up in courses in sociology, it is begun, almost inevitably, with a discussion of Weber's (1947: 329–341) definition of that concept. Except that it was not a definition: it was what Weber called an ideal type. Ideal types are logical constructs which, like the Ideal Gas Law, do not necessarily exist in the real world. They are analytical tools, and Weber constructed his ideal type as a model against which to compare existing bureaucracies. It was in the comparison that insights could be gained about the social forces that molded bureaucracies into the various structures actually found in societies. But, nonetheless, Weber's ideal type is often confused with a definition which, in the case of worldly objects, is an attempt to denote as accurately as possible something that actually exists. Perhaps people equated this ideal type with a definition of bureaucracies because it seemed so similar to the German beaucracies of his time or because the current, popular conception of bureaucracies shares so much with Weber's construct. At any rate, the important point is that the equation, where it occurs, is unfortunate, because public bureaucracies in the United States seldom bear more than a superficial resemblance to the ideal type. Perhaps these differences can best be summarized by the following table:

Weber's Ideal Type	Bureaucracies in the United States
The higher the role is in the hierarchy, the greater the authority it contains.	The authority vested in roles may be little more than a paper statement. People lower in the hierarchy may have greater power than those higher up.
The units or offices in the hierarchy are welded into an integrated structure by rules, procedures, and discipline.	The units or offices are very commonly autonomous with few close ties with each other.
The major forms of influence are giving advice up the hierarchy and giving orders down.	Bargaining and coalition formation are the most common methods of exercising influence.
Rationality governs the selection of efficient means to achieve ends.	Inefficient means are frequently preferred to achieve ends.

It is not difficult to support with abundant examples the statements on the right-hand side of the table. For example, while the Secretary of a federal department has greater authority on paper than his agency heads, the latter can very often nullify his policies and even get him removed from office. The well-known autonomy of the FBI under J. Edgar Hoover was so great that that agency could defy the Attorney General even when he was the brother of the President of the United States. What is less well known is that this autonomy of the agencies in departments is more the rule than the exception. Examples abound. It is very difficult for a Secretary of HUD to give orders to the Federal Housing Administration even though it reports to him on paper, because the FHA has powerful allies in Congress and in the banking community. The ability of each of the Armed Services to control Secretaries of the Department of Defense is well known. In DHEW the health and education components have considerable ability to pursue their own courses of action because of the strength of their constituencies and their relationships with Congress. But even within the health and education agencies there are subunits (bureaus) that have the power to control their own actions at the expense of agency heads and Secretaries, again largely because of personal ties with the President, powerful constituencies, or members of Congress.

This autonomy also has a horizontal dimension in that cooperative efforts between bureaus is the exception rather than the rule, even though they may be dealing with common clients and common problems. For example, there are over a dozen programs for child health in government agencies. Some are in the health section of DHEW, but others are in the Office of Education, Social Security Administration, the Social and Rehabilitation Service (SRS), or outside of DHEW altogether in such agencies as the Office of Economic Opportunity. Despite enormous overlaps in these programs, there has been little effort to coordinate them or to engage in joint projects. The Administration on Aging, which has a legal mandate to coordinate the efforts of departments and agencies to help senior citizens, has experienced great difficulty in obtaining the cooperation it needs from other agencies to assure that they give adequate expression to the needs of the aged in their programs.

The problem exists at all levels of government, not just at the national level. Stoloff (1970: 101, 114) reports the difficulties that the East New York Model Cities planning group experienced getting the cooperation of established agencies in planning for services in the selected model city area. The Board of Education said that it could not guarantee the number of schools the planners wanted for the area and also that it would not support any innovative curricular programs unless they were the ones with which the Board itself was experimenting. The Department of Social Services refused to engage in joint planning for day care facilities in the model area, noting that it was developing its own plan.

Dahl and Lindblom (1963: 302–6) once defined a pluralist organization as one in which there is a diversity of groups or organizations that have a large measure of autonomy over which no unified body of leaders exerts control. This definition applies very nicely to public bureaucracies in the United States. Each is best described as a collection of relatively autonomous groups whose relationships with each other are more nearly bargaining than they are hierarchical. Some of the groups in the bureaucracies have strong permanent relationships with each other while others have none at all, and a great many of them form only temporary coalitions with each other around specific issues. But the strongest relationships are likely to exist with groups outside of the bureaucracy: with the committees of Congress that control their appropriations and with associations in the private sector for whom their program has relevance.

It is this intimate relationship with Congress and groups in the private sector that causes the pluralism of the bureaucracy. Congress was conceived and still functions as an area in which pluralist forces can vie with each other (Truman, 1953). Members of Congress very often prefer categoric legislation—legislation that is directed to specific groups in the population—because they hope to attract the votes of those groups. Consequently, they would rather write legislation for the aged, the construction of highways, or the handicapped than to include these interests in more general legislation like revenue sharing under which the States or localities are simply given money for very generally stated purposes. Interest groups usually share this penchant, because it is a lot less chancy to have their own categoric legislation and appropriations that they can lobby for periodically with their own categoric, but probably friendly, committees—a lot less chancy than competing with other pressure groups for money made available through revenue sharing.

By designating a new agency to implement a categoric law, pluralism is transmitted to the Executive Branch. Attempting to find its place in the power system of administrative agencies, mindful of its prerogatives, and necessarily jealous of its territory, the new agency quickly learns that it is easier to build its own program than it is to weave together the resources of other mindful, jealous agencies. Besides, the pragmatic agency head knows that his career hinges on his success at satisfying the special interests represented in the legislation he administers. Joint program action with other agencies consumes energies better devoted to his own program, and it is less likely to make him politically visible than is solo action. Consequently, the federal government is really a congeries of agencies, each of which is devoted to carrying out a rather narrowly defined legislative mission.

This diffusion of power has another dimension that extends beyond the federal government that makes it difficult for even a categoric agency to fulfill its narrow mission, much less cooperate with other agencies to achieve broader ones. I am referring to the pluralist nature of federal, state, local, and private sector relationships. In addition to being categoric, federal programs usually allocate funds to States or communities on a formula basis, which means that the federal agency is expected to provide each State or city with the proportion of appropriated funds that the formula in the law provides. By this means Congress assures that the agencies will have very little to say about whether or not a State receives money or how it actually uses it. Sometimes this formula money has few, if any, strings attached to it: the agencies refer to it as "stump and run" money. ("We just leave it on a stump and run.") In this case the agency is little more than a check writing office. Other times some constraints are written into the law which give the agency some control over how the States use the money. But federal efforts to enforce these laws usually lead to the countermobilization of political power by irate mayors and governors who seek to neutralize the agency's actions. For instance, in 1971, when SRS sought to make California comply with the welfare regulations, it was eventually forced to back down when the State appealed successfully to President Nixon. The very powerful States like New York and California and powerful mayors like Richard Daley of Chicago routinely circumvent the bureaucracy and make their cases directly with the political leadership.

But the State bureaucracies are not monolithic either, because the same forces are at work in them to assure that they will exhibit the virtues of social pluralism. And county and city organizations are similarly molded (or riven) by our pluralist culture.

We add only one more complicating dimension—the existence of hundreds of private agencies and foundations, often with missions identical to those of public bureaucracies and each other, and often separated by strong associational and professional jealousies—to complete our Gordian picture. Whatever service or problem one cares to look at, whether it is health care for the poor or police protection, the picture of federal, State, local, and voluntary bureaucracies is uncomprehendingly complex both internally to each bureaucracy and externally in their relationships to each other. Internally or externally they are usually the epitomes of the concept of social pluralism.

It would be a mistake to label the resulting picture "fragmented" or "segmented" rather than pluralistic. Fragmentation or segmentation exists, but that is only a part of the picture. Strong alliances and coalitions also exist. In the vocational rehabilitation field, for example, strong ties bind some friendly members of Congress with the federal, State, local, and private sector rehabilitation agencies. They are easily coalesced against outsiders like governors or State welfare directors who might intrude on their prerogatives, and yet they are very sensitive to the locations of drift fences among their own prerogatives. Occasional expediency might even dictate temporary alliances with the American Medical Association, the Manpower Administration of the Department of Labor, or some other momentarily convenient political bedfellow. It is this middle ground between the monolithic and the anarchic models that offers the most accurate picture of American bureaucracies.

A natural reaction to such complexity of pluralist bureaucratic systems would be to throw up one's hands and wish a pox on their unintegrated houses, but it is our purpose here, rather, to describe the consequences of bureaucratic pluralism for collective social action, particularly community problem solving. Our point is essentially that the pluralist nature of public bureaucracies seriously undercuts the willingness and ability of their managers to help solve the problems of communities, which, by their multifaceted and comprehensive nature, require holistic, collective solutions.

COMMUNITY NEEDS AND BUREAUCRATIC STRUCTURE

The antithetical character of bureaucracies and communities has been discussed many times in the literature in sociology, but most recently by Litwak and his colleagues (1966, 1970). They start with the same premise used by earlier theorists (Tönnies 1940: 18–28; Weber 1947: 354–358), that the structures and cultures of bureaucracies and communities are so different from each other that they have great difficulty developing mutually beneficial interfaces. Litwak et al. went on to identify the seemingly incompatible characteristics of each of these types of groups. Bureaucratic emphasis on expertise, pragmatic, highly focused relationships, impersonality, and rules is opposite to a community's emphasis on open, diffuse, affective relationships, and informality. Where the community wants the bureaucrat to be concerned about the plight of human beings like those suffering from black lung disease or living in inadequate housing, the bureaucrat is concerned about whether the people are eligible for the services that they are seeking. Where the community would like prompt action based on a minimum of formalized procedures, the bureaucrat prefers deliberation and adherence to established procedures. The conflict was succinctly illustrated for this writer during a training session that OEO sponsored to equip community leaders to do community planning and write grant applications. The instructor was discussing the meaning and importance of cost/benefit analyses to an increasingly restive group when one community leader who had become particularly angry stood up and shouted, "To hell with the costs, we just want the benefits!"

The cultural and structural differences between communities and bureaucracies are very real, and they do make it extremely difficult for them
to work together. But pointing to the classic characteristics of bureaucracies as the sources of the problem is only partially accurate for two
reasons. First, we have already suggested that the characteristics in
Weber's ideal type often bear little resemblance to the realities of American
bureaucracies. Sometimes bureaucracies make their decisions based on
impersonal criteria, but at other times they are extremely concerned about
who made the request or who the decision will affect and are quite willing
to find a way to bend the rules to assure that favored or feared people
receive what they want. A research proposal coming from the congres-
sional district of the chairman of their appropriations committee usually
will receive favored treatment; at the very least it will not be set aside
lightly without a few inquiries being made. In some areas the expertise
of the bureaucracy, as in the cases of disease control or criminal detection,
is obvious. In others it is not. For example, an agency may require that
proposals be based on social planning yet not have any people in it who
really know what social planning is or how to do it.

Second, very often bureaucrats invoke the letter of the rules or adhere
to impersonal standards as a defense against much deeper problems.
For example, if a community's proposal required the agency to deliver resources in new, unaccustomed ways, the evaluators are likely to couch
their rejection in terms of the ineligibility of the applicants, errors in the
proposal, or some similar reason. It other words, bureaucrats often assume
the appearance of the Weberian ideal-type bureaucracy when it is convenient for them to do so in order to avoid some more serious problem, and
it is those more serious problems that concern us here.

Therefore, while we accept the notion that bureaucracies and communities have many antithetical elements and that many of them have to
do with the formal characteristics of bureaucracies, we propose that a
more fundamental reason communities and bureaucracies have difficulties
engaging in joint action has to do with the pluralist character of most
bureaucracies and the inappropriateness of that form of organization for
dealing with many community problems.

Problems are invariably embedded intimately into the fabric of a community, which means that they cannot be treated in isolation from other
aspects of community life. Arresting drug abusers will not solve a community drug problem, because the practice may be the result of many
other factors—unemployment, poor housing, discrimination, psychological
depression, or alienation—which are likely to generate new drug users.
Unless the attack on the problem is fairly broad, it is unlikely to be solved.
Given their categoric bases, bureaucracies are not geared to make sufficiently comprehensive attacks on community problems. Consider, for in-

stance, the problem of providing adequate health care in a poor inner-city neighborhood. Health facilities have to be developed, people enrolled in programs for which they are eligible, and information about services and transportation to them must be provided. Yet because of their categoric character, no single agency can provide for all of these needs. The Medicaid agency can accept for enrollment all of the people in the neighborhood who are eligible for that program, but it does not build health facilities or provide transportation. Facilities can be obtained via a project grant under Title V of the Social Security Act which is administered by a different agency. And transportation to the health facility can be arranged by social service caseworkers. Outreach workers who would go out into the neighborhood and get eligible people into the program are unlikely to be available in any of these agencies, but the OEO program might have them. In other words, the problems are integrated, but the resources to deal with them are not. Furthermore, we have already suggested that attempts to aggregate resources and bring them to bear on problems must struggle against the pluralist characteristics of bureaucracies. Even among the best intentioned managers it is very difficult to put together a joint project. Eligibility standards in the different programs do not match; rules and standards block action; distrust and suspicion are easily aroused. And since they are so seldom practised, the techniques of managing projects that cut across agencies often are little understood and poorly used by program managers.

But more commonly, and for reasons developed earlier, agency personnel are not inclined to work on joint projects with people from other agencies. They get their rewards for performance within their own programs and not for their contributions to other programs, and resources devoted to joint projects must be taken from other program areas that may be more highly valued by the agency or its client groups. In the earlier example of the East New York model city area, the Board of Education's reluctance to meet the demand of the model city planning group was based on real concerns. Meeting the requests of the planning group would mean diverting resources from other areas of the city and other potentially powerful and vocal interest groups.

Categoric bureaucracies can have a second, subtler impact on communities, one that erodes the ability of the latter to organize themselves for social action. By sticking to their categoric programs and delivering their services or money to clients on an individual basis, bureaucracies can be an individuating influence in communities. A veteran confined to a wheelchair may receive job training and income support but be unable to visit others in his neighborhood because architectural barriers have not been removed. The economic well-being of the aged may be improved through Social Security payments, but their social well-being may inadvertently be lessened because they live alone, isolated from the community. Since the government takes care of the aged, there is no apparent need for community action; neighbors don't stop by to see if the person is well—that is the job of the public health nurse. Marriages are often precluded by the potential loss of welfare payments or Social Security checks. Ironically, the more effective bureaucracies are at delivering their categoric services, the more they are likely to sap the community's will to organize itself and, without community organization, the more organic problems of community life are likely to go unsolved.

BUREAUCRATIC RESPONSES TO COMMUNITY ACTION

Usually aware that the pluralist design of their organizations is not very appropriate for dealing effectively with community problems, agency leaders have responded to community action in a variety of ways, not all of them constructive.

Traditional bureaucratic responses have been commonplace. Community grant applicants were required to use the usual procedures to obtain a grant: an almost hopeless task unless aid could be obtained from knowledgeable people or institutions. Or when community groups attempted direct action with political or bureaucratic leaders, they found it easier to get their attention than to get some follow-up action on their demands. In one scenario, the top agency leaders would appear at the petitioners' rallies or meetings and suggest strategies for helping them that involved meetings between representatives of the agencies and the community. In those meetings and under the guise of cooperation, the agency representatives would gradually lead the community people into the game of bureaucratic procedures. Solving the community's problems was posed as a series of hurdles to be jumped, but jumping those hurdles would prove to be such a long and complicated process that little was ever likely to occur. Nonetheless, it was important for the community people to think that success was just around the corner.

Another almost opposite approach was to give the community a planning grant. Very often these grants were little more than bribes to the community leaders, since many of them would receive salaries from them. These grants might actually be followed by other grants to demonstrate one service or another in the community, but rarely did they touch the mainstream of money that the agencies administered. By placating the community somewhat, the agencies protected themselves from the grim prospect of diverting money from the traditional channels or increasing the demand for the programs that they administered.

Especially galling to local political leaders were the programs of OEO. These programs struck at the very core of the political apparatus of the city, if there was such a core. In some areas the activist efforts at community organization competed with the traditional ward organization of the city. Where the ward organizations were used to maintain the status quo while gathering votes, the new organizations proposed radical change that undercut the power of the ward organization. In many areas the new organizations supplanted or captured the older ward organizations. Communities also learned to use the courts to force city leaders to act, and they did it via lawyers supported on grants from OEO. It took a while, but eventually the countermobilization of the city leadership proved effective, and the OEO programs were brought under greater control by the city leaders. This is the situation today.

Other responses have been more constructive. They center around increased consumer involvement in planning either by informal or legislated mechanisms. Some agencies have begun involving consumer groups systematically in their planning. Since 1970, the Social and Rehabilitation Service, for example, has gotten the advice of the National Welfare Rights Organization and many other organizations on new regulations governing its programs. That same agency also consulted with a wide variety of client groups in its planning for future programs. But these efforts are few in number, seldom institutionalized, and do not exist at all levels of government. If community involvement in bureaucratic planning and operations is to become more prevalent and institutionalized, legislative action is required.

This line of reasoning led to the insertion of consumer or client participation articles in various laws. Usually these insertions took the form of simple statements that consumers must be involved in the planning for a program. Because of the genuine difficulties involved, specific criteria rarely were established for the types of consumer groups that should be included or what constituted adequate participation. Therefore, actual practice usually varied greatly from the intent of these laws. The planners would involve representatives from the establishment client groups rather than the more militant, unpredictable ones. Or they would brief client groups on the finished proposals rather than involve them in the construction of those proposals. Legislative draftsmen have been aware of these potential abuses but reluctant to write stronger, more concise language into their laws. There are several reasons for this reluctance. First, many lawmakers believe that specific criteria should appear in administrative regulations and not in laws. Second, there is a valid opinion that it is impossible to write such criteria because of the complexity of the problems and the ultimate ability of anyone who really wishes to circumvent the intention of the law to do just that. Third, there is the more typically bureaucratic reason that having stated there should be consumer participation, responsibility for what occurs is shifted elsewhere—the bureaucracy has done what it could.

Perhaps the most comprehensive and imaginative effort to deal with the problems that have been discussed above has been the Allied Services Act, which was drafted by the Department of Health Education, and Welfare and submitted to the 92nd Congress and again to the 93rd. This bill would put greater power in the hands of governors or any agent designated by the State to focus aggregated services on particular problems. It also would give the governor or other State designee the power to transfer significant sums of money from one program to another. At the local level the bill required that local planning groups include client representatives in the planning process and that every planning effort begin with a careful study of actual community needs. While the bill would restore the power of governors and mayors and increase the role of community groups in community planning, it would also force categoric agencies and professional groups to foresake some of their territorial imperatives to achieve some collective objectives. For example, a community planning group could determine that one of its major priorities was providing adequate health care for the poor. It would then design a service plan that pulled together the services of several local agencies. If a particular service were in inadequate supply, the plan might recommend that funds be transferred from another, less valued program to strengthen the valued one. The Allied Services Act would not eliminate the categoric character of bureaucracies, but it would remove some of the barriers to collective action. However, because it is limited to DHEW programs, this proposal is not the ultimate answer to the problems raised in this paper.

Currently, revenue sharing is being posed by the Administration as the ultimate answer. Under revenue sharing the States or localities are given formula grant money to achieve a variety of generally stated purposes. The difference from the usual formula grant money is the generality of the objectives listed in the legislation; they can range from no stated objectives to lists of relatively generic categories like family planning, interurban transportation systems, or secondary education. The theory is that by being given such unfettered money local governments can determine what their major problems are and solve them directly without the intervention of several federal agencies.

However, in this case theory and practice are little likely to be related. While the encroachments of the federal bureaucracy are eliminated, pluralism still exists and State and local agencies and pressure groups still exist. These social forces and groups can be expected to operate when revenue-shared funds are allocated, and, therefore, it is quite likely that the money will be divided among existing agencies. In other words, the categoric programs and agencies would probably still exist at the local level, doing business in the same way as prior to revenue sharing, and still no more capable of serving comprehensive community needs.

Revenue sharing will not be a strategy readily accepted by many groups, because it undercuts their roles in the pluralist system. Many members of Congress are concerned that revenue sharing might undercut their prerogatives to specify the uses of funds: to develop priorities of their own. And they recognize that a vote for revenue sharing is not as politically useful as a vote for a veterans' bill or a senior citizens' project. Many federal agency managers see revenue sharing as a further erosion of their control over their programs. They argue for a larger federal role to prevent the States from misusing the funds.

The greatest potential advantage to revenue sharing is that the States and localities can use the pooled money to attack problems more comprehensively. If a State already has a good interurban transportation system, it can put more of its money in some other area where the need is greater. This is precisely what worries the representatives of various pressure groups: that they will have to compete with each other for rather limited noncategoric money. More of them are realizing the security of their older categoric programs. Whether revenue-sharing will become increasingly popular is problematic. Whether such funds will be used for comprehensive attacks on community problems is even more problematic.

CONCLUSIONS

Overcoming the pluralism of American bureaucracies in order to deal comprehensively with the problem of communities will not be easily or readily accomplished. But more people are recognizing the problem, and articles are being included in legislation that require studies of community needs and the development of plans that are responsive to those needs. The Allied Services Act is one example, but the Older Americans Act and the Developmental Disabilities Act are others. Unfortunately, these laws are relatively narrowly focused in terms of the clients they serve and the problems they deal with.

As we saw, revenue sharing is unlikely to solve the problem, because although it eliminates one source of categoric activity—the federal bureaucracy—it does not eliminate the others. Once the money reaches the States and moves from there to the local level, it is most likely to travel well-worn paths through existing agencies.

Perhaps one useful long-term solution would be to combine the philosophy built into the Allied Services Act with revenue sharing. Allied Services proposes a balanced power relationship among governments at the federal, State and local level. Much of the debate over how to allocate power in the American system has focused on centralization versus decentralization, as if these were the only options. The Allied Services Act vests power in general purpose governments, rather than trying to avoid them, and says that each level of government has an important and different set of functions to perform in solving human problems. Unlike revenue sharing,

Allied Services says that the Congress has a major role in the establishment of societal priorities. If it states these priorities very generally—family planning, crime control—it does not fulfill its function, because the money would then be stump and run money. If, on the other hand, it is too specific in its priorities—provide maternity care for 750,000 poor, pregnant women by the following means—it has moved beyond priority setting to doing the job for the States and local governments. Allied Services recognizes that every State and every community is in some ways unique, each possessing its own particular combination of problems. Therefore, the task of determining how much emphasis to give each federal priority or how to implement it is best managed at those levels. Power is balanced then in the sense that all levels are involved in social policy formulation and implementation, with each level having different functions in that process. At the local level a representative planning group would be able to develop a comprehensive plan to deal with community problems. In its plan it would have to show the contributions of the different agencies to the implementation of the plan and how the revenue-shared money would be allocated among them. The planning group could also make proposals to integrate the agencies or some agency functions, like developing a common intake function for all of them.

This proposal is not new or untested. Other countries have recognized the conflict and the needs of communities and have been more successful than we in dealing with them. Yugoslavia has used the system of nationally set priorities around which communities develop their plans. That system also allocates some funds for nonpriority items, thus recognizing that communities are bound to have some unique problems that they want very much to have solved. Great Britain has used the local features of this model in its planning for services to children. Local councils composed of public and private sector agencies and citizens plan for the services needed in the community. Then each of the representatives on the planning group indicates its contribution toward the achievement of the plan. For example, if the plan involves the development of a dozen day care centers, the national government may contribute teachers and psychologists, a charitable organization may volunteer transportation services for the children, and so on. Rather than having several different agencies working in unconcerted fashion on the same or overlapping problems, a single plan is created to which they all contribute systematically.

It would not be necessary, therefore, to start from scratch to reshape American bureaucracies. Most of the elements of necessary law exist. There is ample experience in other countries and in some American programs to suggest which practices work and which do not. What seems to be required is broader recognition and acceptance of the problem among decision makers at the national level and a willingness among them to solve it.